T0205772

Lecture Notes in Artificial Intelligence 12873

Subseries of Lecture Notes in Computer Science

Series Editors

Randy Goebel
University of Alberta, Edmonton, Canada
Yuzuru Tanaka
Hokkaido University, Sapporo, Japan
Wolfgang Wahlster
DFKI and Saarland University, Saarbrücken, Germany

Founding Editor

Jörg Siekmann
DFKI and Saarland University, Saarbrücken, Germany

More information about this subseries at http://www.springer.com/series/1244

Stefan Edelkamp · Ralf Möller ·
Elmar Rueckert (Eds.)

KI 2021: Advances in Artificial Intelligence

44th German Conference on AI
Virtual Event, September 27 – October 1, 2021
Proceedings

 Springer

Editors
Stefan Edelkamp 🆔
Czech Technical University in Prague
Prague, Czech Republic

Ralf Möller 🆔
University of Lübeck
Lübeck, Germany

Elmar Rueckert 🆔
University of Leoben
Leoben, Austria

ISSN 0302-9743   ISSN 1611-3349   (electronic)
Lecture Notes in Artificial Intelligence
ISBN 978-3-030-87625-8   ISBN 978-3-030-87626-5   (eBook)
https://doi.org/10.1007/978-3-030-87626-5

LNCS Sublibrary: SL7 – Artificial Intelligence

This Springer imprint is published by the registered company Springer Nature Switzerland AG
The registered company address is: Gewerbestrasse 11, 6330 Cham, Switzerland

Preface

KI 2021 was the 44th German Conference on Artificial Intelligence organized in cooperation with the Fachbereich Künstliche Intelligenz der Gesellschaft für Informatik (GI). The conference took place in an online fashion during September 27 to October 1, 2021. The German AI Conference basically started 45 years ago with the first GI-Fachgruppe KI meeting on October 7, 1975. KI is one of the major European AI conferences and traditionally brings together academic and industrial researchers from all areas of AI, providing an ideal place for exchanging news and research results on theory and applications. KI 2021 was organized in combination with INFORMATIK 2021, and we would like to thank Daniel Krupka and Alexander Scheibe from GI for their collaboration.

The technical program of KI 2021 comprised paper and poster presentations as well as tutorials and workshops. Overall KI 2021 received about 60 submissions of which 21 were selected as technical communications and papers, together with 6 poster presentations. We were honored that very prominent researchers kindly agreed to give very interesting keynote talks (alphabetical order, see also the abstracts below):

- Tristan Cazenave (Université Paris-Dauphine, France) Monte Carlo Search
- Giuseppe De Giacomo (Sapienza University of Rome, Italy) Autonomy in AI: Reactive Synthesis, Planning and Reinforcement Learning in Linear Temporal Logic on Finite Traces
- Birte Glimm (University of Ulm, Germany) Ontologies for Providing Map Knowledge to Autonomous Vehicles
- Kristian Kersting (TU Darmstadt, Germany) The Third Wave of AI [Joint Keynote with INFOMATIK2021]
- Katja Mombaur (University of Waterloo, Canada) Motion Intelligence for Human-Centred Robots
- Stuart Russell (University of California, Berkeley, USA) Human-Compatible Artificial Intelligence

An extensive range of special meetings, a tutorial, and several workshops rounded off the program:

Special Events

- CLAIRE National Meeting
- Early Career Research Consortium
- Meeting of the FBKI task force "AI in Education" (Arbeitskreis KiS)

Tutorial

- Christoph Stockhammer and Mihaela Jarema: Deep Learning Workflows for Biomedical Signal Data – A Practical Example

Workshops

- Christoph Beierle, Marco Ragni, Frieder Stolzenburg, and Matthias Thimm: 7th Workshop on Formal and Cognitive Reasoning FCR 2021
- Barbara Hammer, Malte Schilling, and Laurenz Wiskott: Trustworthy AI in the Wild
- Ulrich John, Petra Hostedt, and Mario Wenzel: 35th Workshop on (Constraint) Logic Programming (WLP 21)
- Sylvia Melzer, Stefan Thiemann, and Jost Gippert: Humanities-Centred AI (CHAI)
- Jürgen Sauer and Stefan Edelkamp: Planen und Konfigurieren (PuK)
- Andreas Hein, Mark Schweda, Silke Schicktanz, Stefan Teipel, and Thomas Kirste: Artificial Intelligence and Ethics

As Program Committee (PC) chairs, we would like to thank our speakers for their interesting and inspirational talks. Our thanks also go out to the organizers of INFORMATIK 2021 who provided support in terms of registration and setting up a virtual conference. We would like to thank the Program Committee members and additional reviewers for their efforts. Without their substantial voluntary work, this conference would not have been possible. We would also like to thank EasyChair for their support in handling submissions and Springer for their support in making these proceedings possible. Our institutions, the Czech Technical University in Prague (Czech Republic), the University of Lübeck (Germany), and the University of Leoben (Austria), also provided support for our participation, for which we are grateful. Many thanks go to Tanya Braun and Marcel Gehrke for helping with web pages and proceedings. We also thank the Fachbereich Künstliche Intelligenz der Gesellschaft für Informatik, in particular Matthias Klusch and Ingo Timm, for their ongoing support and dedication to KI 2021. Last but not least, we would like to thank our sponsors:

- Springer Verlag (https://www.springer.com)
- DFKI (https://www.dfki.de/)
- team neusta the digital family (https://www.team-neusta.de)
- singularIT (https://www.singular-it.de)
- PRC (https://www.pattern-recognition-company.com)

August 2021   Stefan Edelkamp
                                                                            Ralf Möller
                                                                            Elmar Rueckert

Organization

Program Committee

Martin Aleksandrov	TU Berlin, Germany
Klaus-Dieter Althoff	DFKI/University of Hildesheim, Germany
Martin Atzmüller	Osnabrueck University, Germany
Franz Baader	TU Dresden, Germany
Christoph Beierle	University of Hagen, Germany
Christoph Benzmüller	Freie Universität Berlin, Germany
Ralph Bergmann	University of Trier, Germany
Tarek Besold	DEKRA DIGITAL, Germany
Ulf Brefeld	Leuphana Universität Lüneburg, Germany
Gerhard Brewka	Leipzig University, Germany
Stefan Edelkamp (Chair)	Czech Technical University in Prague, Czech Republic
Manfred Eppe	University of Hamburg, Germany
Simone Frintrop	University of Hamburg, Germany
Johannes Fürnkranz	Johannes Kepler University Linz, Austria
Barbara Hammer	Bielefeld University, Germany
Malte Helmert	University of Basel, Switzerland
Andreas Hotho	University of Wuerzburg, Germany
Steffen Hölldobler	TU Dresden, Germany
Eyke Hüllermeier	LMU Munich, Germany
Gabriele Kern-Isberner	Technische Universitaet Dortmund, Germany
Kristian Kersting	TU Darmstadt, Germany
Angelika Kimmig	Cardiff University, UK
Matthias Klusch	DFKI, Germany
Stefan Kopp	Bielefeld University, Germany
Ralf Krestel	Hasso Plattner Institute, University of Potsdam, Germany
Bernd Ludwig	University Regensburg, Germany
Thomas Lukasiewicz	University of Oxford, UK
Till Mossakowski	University of Magdeburg, Germany
Ralf Möller (Chair)	University of Luebeck, Germany
Jörg Müller	TU Clausthal, Germany
Bernhard Nebel	Albert-Ludwigs-Universitaet Freiburg, Germany
Heiko Paulheim	University of Mannheim, Germany
Nils Rottmann	University of Luebeck, Germany
Elmar Rueckert (Chair)	Montanuniversität Leoben, Austria
Jürgen Sauer	University of Oldenburg, Germany
Ute Schmid	University of Bamberg, Germany
Lars Schmidt-Thieme	University of Hildesheim, Germany

Claudia Schon	Universität Koblenz-Landau, Germany
Lutz Schröder	Friedrich-Alexander-Universität Erlangen-Nürnberg, Germany
Daniel Sonntag	DFKI, Germany
Myra Spiliopouloumyra	Otto-von-Guericke-University Magdeburg, Germany
Heiner Stuckenschmidt	University of Mannheim, Germany
Matthias Thimm	Universität Koblenz-Landau, Germany
Paul Thorn	HHU Düsseldorf, Germany
Sabine Timpf	University of Augsburg, Germany
Marc Toussaint	University of Stuttgart, Germany
Anni-Yasmin Turhan	TU Dresden, Germany
Diedrich Wolter	University of Bamberg, Germany
Stefan Woltran	Vienna University of Technology, Austria
Britta Wrede	Bielefeld University, Germany
Stefan Wrobel	Fraunhofer IAIS and University of Bonn, Germany
Honghu Xue	University of Luebeck, Germany
Özgür Özçep	University of Lübeck, Germany

Additional Reviewers

Abdelnaby, Modeus
Ahmed, Nourhan
Booshehri, Meisam
Caus, Danu
Cohen, Liat
Dittmar, Christian
Eberts, Markus
Eisenstadt, Viktor
Elsayed, Shereen
Fryen, Thilo
Göttlinger, Merlin
Hecher, Markus
Hoffmann, Maximilian
Jain, Nitisha
Keller, Thomas
Kobs, Konstantin
Kolpaczki, Patrick
Lauri, Mikko
Leemhuis, Mena
Lenz, Mirko
Lienen, Julian
Lüers, Bengt
Mahon, Louis

Malburg, Lukas
Mischek, Florian
Morak, Michael
Profitlich, Hans-Jürgen
Rego Drumond, Rafael
Repke, Tim
Rolff, Tim
Sallinger, Emanuel
Sarhan, Noha
Schoenborn, Jakob Michael
Schurr, Hans-Jörg
Schwalbe, Gesina
Seitz, Sarem
Sierra-Múnera, Alejandro
Sifa, Rafet
Solopova, Veronika
Stolzenburg, Frieder
Tornede, Alexander
Tritscher, Julian
Van Daele, Dries
Wilms, Christian
Zeyen, Christian

Abstracts of Invited Talks

Monte Carlo Search

Tristan Cazenave

Université Paris-Dauphine, France

Monte Carlo Search is a family of general search algorithms that have many applications in different domains. It is the state of the art in perfect and imperfect information games. Other applications include the RNA inverse folding problem, Logistics, Multiple Sequence Alignment, General Game Playing, Puzzles, 3D Packing with Object Orientation, Cooperative Pathfinding, Software testing and heuristic Model-Checking. In recent years, many researchers have explored different variants of the algorithms, their relations to Deep Reinforcement Learning and their different applications. The talk will give a broad overview of Monte Carlo Search and of its applications

Autonomy in AI: Reactive Synthesis, Planning and Reinforcement Learning in Linear Temporal Logic on Finite Traces

Giuseppe De Giacomo

Sapienza University of Rome, Italy

A central topic in AI is building autonomous agents that act intelligently. Reactive Synthesis, Planning in Nondeterministic Domains and Reinforcement Learning are all about automatically synthesizing an agent behavior/strategy/policy to accomplish a task in a partially controllable (nondeterministic) world. In this context, it is important to sharply distinguish between the world model (the domain) and the task specification (the goal), to take into account the fact that model of world seldom change, while the tasks that the agent has to accomplish in it change unceasingly as the agent operates. As a result, the agent will work for a task only for finite amount of time (before switching to the next), while the world continues to exist when the task is over. In this talk we discuss these issues, and consider various forms of synthesis, where the world and the agent tasks are expressed in Liner Temporal Logic, LTL, the formalism most commonly used in Formal Methods for specifying dynamic properties, as well as in its finite-trace variant, LTLf, which is particularly useful for specifying intelligent agent tasks.

Ontologies for Providing Map Knowledge to Autonomous Vehicles

Birte Glimm

University of Ulm, Germany

In order to understand its surroundings, an autonomous vehicle needs a detailed, high-definition map, which acts as a powerful virtual sensor. The current map ecosystem experiences, however, a range of challenges: First, despite ongoing standardization efforts, maps come in several proprietary formats. Second, current high-definition maps are so detailed that it is largely impossible to simply store a complete map within a navigation system. Instead, map data is sent dynamically to the vehicles based on the current position. Last but not the least, maps are highly dynamic and errors may easily be introduced. In order to address the challenges of scalability, velocity, and map data quality, we propose an ontology-based architecture with an embedded quality assurance mechanism. The dedicated low-level ontologies. The knowledge required for autonomous driving functions is then transferred into a more light-weight unified high-level ontology, which is queried by application functions, e.g., to determine whether a lane change is indicated. Our empirical evaluations provide evidence that this approach enables effective map data integration while providing efficient map updates with ensured map data quality.

The Third Wave of AI

Kristian Kersting

TU Darmstadt, Germany

Most of AI in use today falls under the categories of the first two waves of AI research. First wave AI systems follow clear rules, written by programmer, aiming to cover every eventuality. Second wave AI systems are the kind that use statistical learning to arrive at an answer for a certain type of problem. Think of image classification system. The third wave of AI envisions a future in which AI systems are more than just tools that execute human programmed rules or generalize from human-curated data sets. The systems will function as partners rather than as tools. They can acquire human-like communication and reasoning capabilities, with the ability to recognize new situations and to adapt to them. For example, a third wave AI system might note that a speed limit of 120 km/h does not make sense when entering a small village by car. In this talk I shall argue that it is time to usher in the third way of AI. We have deep models, even deep models that know when they do not know. We have the first models that combine learning and reasoning. We have machines that capture our moral compasses. We have machines that engage with us in order to be right for the right reasons.

Motion Intelligence for Human-Centred Robots

Katja Mombaur

University of Waterloo, Canada

Human-centred robots have the potential to support and facilitate people's lives, ranging from improved well-being and increased independence to reduced risk or harm, a removal of boring jobs. They can take the form of humanoid robots, wearable robots or other types of mobility assistance robots and have to enter in in close physical interactions with humans or support them physically. For this, human-centred robots require motion intelligence or embodied intelligence that makes the robot aware of how it moves in and interacts with its dynamic environment and with humans. In this talk, I will give an overview of our research on endowing human-centred robots with motion intelligence, covering examples from humanoid robotic co-workers to exoskeletons and external assistive devices in medical applications. An important ingredient of this research is to gain a fundamental understanding of the biomechanics of human movement and human-human and human-robot interaction and to translate this understanding into predictive mathematical models. Another core component of our research is the development of efficient algorithms for motion generation, control and learning, combining advanced model-based optimization with model-free approaches.

Human-Compatible Artificial Intelligence

Stuart Russell

University of California, Berkeley, USA

It is reasonable to expect that AI capabilities will eventually exceed those of humans across a range of real-world-decision making scenarios. Should we "expect the machines to take control," as Alan Turing and others have suggested? Or will AI complement and augment human intelligence in beneficial ways? It turns out that both views are correct, but they are talking about completely different forms of AI. To achieve the positive outcome, a fundamental reorientation of the field is required. Instead of building systems that optimize arbitrary objectives, we need to learn how to build systems that will, in fact, be beneficial for us. I will argue that this is possible as well as necessary. The new approach to AI opens up many avenues for research, including several that connect to core questions in philosophy and the social sciences.

Contents

Poster Papers

Technical Programme

RP-DQN: An Application of Q-Learning to Vehicle Routing Problems

Ahmad Bdeir, Simon Boeder, Tim Dernedde[(✉)], Kirill Tkachuk,
Jonas K. Falkner, and Lars Schmidt-Thieme

University of Hildesheim, 31141 Hildesheim, Germany
{bdeir,boeders,dernedde,tkachuk}@uni-hildesheim.de
{falkner,schmidt-thieme}@ismll.uni-hildesheim.de

Abstract. In this paper we present a new approach to tackle complex routing problems with an improved state representation that utilizes the model complexity better than previous methods. We enable this by training from temporal differences. Specifically Q-Learning is employed. We show that our approach achieves state-of-the-art performance for autoregressive policies that sequentially insert nodes to construct solutions on the Capacitated Vehicle Routing Problem (CVRP). Additionally, we are the first to tackle the Multiple Depot Vehicle Routing Problem (MDVRP) with Reinforcement Learning (RL) and demonstrate that this problem type greatly benefits from our approach over other Machine Learning (ML) methods.

Keywords: Reinforcement learning · Deep Q-learning · Combinatorial optimization · Vehicle routing problem · CVRP · MDVRP

1 Introduction

Routing problems are very important in business and industry applications. Finding the best routes for delivery vehicles, finding the best pick up order of trading goods in a warehouse or the optimal machine paths in a manufacturing factory are just a few examples for such problems. Due to their importance, many of these problems have been thoroughly studied and the traditional operations research community has identified a wide variety of problem types including various constraints and developed many heuristics for solving these [24]. Recently, the Machine Learning (ML) community has proposed to learn heuristics with models instead of handcrafting them. The main advantage of ML methods is that once initially trained, they can solve new problem instances very quickly, while traditional heuristics solve every problem individually which in the general case takes up significantly more time.

As optimal labeled solutions are expensive or intractable to compute, usually RL is employed to optimize these models. Specifically, various forms of the

---

A. Bdeir, S. Boeder, T. Dernedde and K. Tkachuk—Equal contribution.

© Springer Nature Switzerland AG 2021
S. Edelkamp et al. (Eds.): KI 2021, LNAI 12873, pp. 3–16, 2021.
https://doi.org/10.1007/978-3-030-87626-5_1

REINFORCE [28] algorithm were applied [1,5,15,18]. A recent method by Kool et al. [15] has proven to find good solutions on a variety of problem types including the CVRP. Their architecture consists of an encoder and decoder setup that constructs the tour sequentially. The encoder computes a representation of the graph and its nodes and is run once in the beginning of the tour construction. Then the decoder is applied on the embeddings repeatedly to add nodes to the solution until the tour is finished. This method is limited to static node features, since the encoder is applied only once. Using dynamic features, and hence a more rich representation, would require the encoder to be run at every step. This quickly becomes memory-expensive when using REINFORCE, as all intermediate representations have to be stored over the whole episode in order to execute backpropagation.

Motivated by this limitation, we propose a model that enables the use of dynamic features in the encoder. Encoder and decoder are then applied in every step. To make this memory-feasible, we optimize our model with a temporal-difference algorithm. When learning only on single transitions, the intermediate representations do not have to be stored for the whole episode. Specifically, we will use Q-Learning [17].

We show that the improved state representation leads to performance improvements on the CVRP. Additionally, we show that our approach is more sample efficient which can be an important factor when environments become more complex and expensive to compute. Finally, we show, when extending to more complicated problems like the MDVRP, the improved state representation is of even greater importance. As to our knowledge we are the first to explore the MDVRP with RL-methods, thus we extended the model by Kool et al. [15] to solve the MDVRP and compare to our approach and several established OR-methods.

2   Related Work

The operations research community has studied a plenitude of different routing problems over the last 70 years. Various different soft and hard constraints, objective functions and other problem properties like stochasticity have been considered and many optimal and heuristic solution approaches with and without formal guarantees were proposed. As a comprehensive overview in this context is not possible the following related work will focus on the ML literature. We refer the reader to a survey by Toth and Vigo [24].

Machine Learning has largely considered two approaches for solving routing problems. The first one autoregressively inserts one node at a time from a partial tour until a solution is complete. Vinyals et al. [26] proposed the Pointer-Network and used this approach to tackle the TSP. Their model was learnt from optimal examples. As these are expensive, Bello et al. [1], Nazari et al. [18] proposed approaches that used RL for optimization. Specifically, variants of REINFORCE [28] were employed and the problem catalogue was extended to the CVRP. Kool et al. [15] then proposed an encoder-decoder model based on the Transformer architecture and showed that good solutions can be learnt for various related problem types for instances with up to 100 nodes. Falkner and Schmidt-Thieme [5] proposed an extension to incorporate time windows. While both also use variants of REINFORCE, Khalil et al. [13] built a graph model based on S2V [3] optimized with Q-Learning. Instead of directly inserting the predicted next node, they choose its position with a best insertion heuristic. However their results on the TSP were only comparable with simpler constructive heuristics like farthest insertion [20]. The autoregressive approaches have considered different search algorithms to use during inference, like Sampling, Beam Search and Active Search.

The second paradigm that was considered with ML approaches is the use of improvement heuristics. They operate on initial solutions and improve these repeatedly. Usually local search is applied. Traditionally, meta-heuristics like Large-Neighbourhood Search (LNS) [22] or Guided-Local Search (GLS) [27] are used in conjunction with local search operators like 2-opt [16] to avoid local minima. Various meta-heuristics and local operators are implemented in Perron and Furnon [19]. ML approaches here range from only learning the initial solution and then applying a traditional method [30] to learning to perform local search [2,29].

Other approaches that do not fit these two categories include constructing a tour non-autoregressively by predicting a heatmap of promising edges with a graph convolutional neural network [12], augmenting traditional dynamic programming approaches for Routing with deep learning [14] and changing the action space from nodes to full tours and solving the sub-problem of the best route to insert [4].

3   Problem Definition

We consider two problem variants in this paper: the CVRP and the MDVRP.

CVRP. The problem can be described by a graph $G(N, E)$, where $N = C \cup D$ is the set of nodes consisting of customers $C = \{1, ..., n\}$ and one depot $D = \{n+1\}$. Each customer $c \in C$ has a positive demand d. We assume a complete graph, thus the set of edges E contains an edge $e_{i,j}$ representing the distance for every pair of nodes $(i, j) \in N$. We also assume a fleet of homogeneous vehicles K having the same maximum capacity Q with no restriction on the fleet size. For a valid solution all customers have to be visited exactly once. All routes must start and end at the depot. For all routes the total sum of demands must satisfy the maximum vehicle capacity. As an objective we want to minimize the total sum of distances. This formulation is also used by other works like [1,15]. Note however that other formulations with limited, heterogeneous vehicles or other objective functions are possible.

MDVRP. The MDVRP generalizes this problem by allowing for multiple depots $D = \{n + 1, ..., n + m\}$. We require that every tour of the vehicle ends at the same depot that it has started but the model is allowed to decide at which depot a vehicle should start. Again note that other problem formulations are possible. For instance, vehicles could be fixed and set to certain depots or allowed to return to any depot.

4 Method

We base our architecture on the model by Kool et al. [15]. First we present the original model and then show which adaptions our new approach makes as well as how solutions are constructed for the CVRP and MDVRP and how the model is optimized.

4.1 Original Attention-Model

The attention model [15] solves routing problems using an encoder-decoder architecture and learns a policy model π that autoregressively inserts one node at a time until a solution is complete.

Encoder. The encoder takes the set of nodes N consisting of the customer nodes and the depot node and creates an embedding of each node. The node features consist of the coordinates and the demand. These features are considered static, meaning they don't change during decoding. Thus the node embeddings are calculated once at the beginning of the episode and are reused at each step.

The encoder creates initial node embeddings h_i by applying a node-wise linear projection, scaling up every node to the embedding dimension $h_{dim} = 128$. h_i represents the i-th node embedding. To differentiate between the depot node and the customer nodes, weights are not shared and two projections are learned.

$$h_i^{(0)} = W^{\text{node}} n_i + b^{\text{node}} \tag{1}$$

$$h_0^{(0)} = W^{\text{depot}} n_0 + b^{\text{depot}} \tag{2}$$

These embeddings are then updated through L attention blocks (AB):

$$H^{(L)} = \text{AB}_L(\ldots(\text{AB}_1(H^{(0)}))) \tag{3}$$

where H is a concatenation of the initial embeddings, and $L = 3$ for VRPs. Every block AB consists of a multi-head self-attention layer (MHA) [25], a node-wise feed-forward layer (FF), along with batch normalization (BN) [11] and skip connections (skip).

$$\text{AB}(H^{(l)}) = \text{BN}\left(\text{FF}^{\text{skip}}\left(\text{BN}\left(\text{MHA}^{\text{skip}}\left(H^{(l-1)}\right)\right)\right)\right) \tag{4}$$

where the MHA layer uses 8 heads. The FF^{skip} layer has one sublayer with ReLU activation and an intermediate dimension of size 512.

$$\text{FF}^{\text{skip}}(h_i) = W_2 \max(0, W_1 h_i + b_1) + b_2 + h_i \tag{5}$$

Decoder. The decoder is run at every timestep t and parametrizes a probability distribution over all the nodes. It takes a context $C^{(t)} = [h^{\text{graph}}; c^{(t)}; h^{\text{last}}]$ as input, where h^{graph} is the mean of the node embeddings, $c^{(t)}$ is the current vehicle capacity and h^{last} refers to the node embedding of the last position. This context is transformed with another MHA layer, where the context only attends to nodes that are feasible in this timestep. This is done with a mask M. Note that the context is the query and the node embeddings are the keys of this layer. In contrast the encoder computes the self attention between all pairs of nodes. The decoder instead only computes attention between context and node embeddings to arrive at a transformed context $\hat{C}^{(t)}$. This avoids the memory quadratic complexity of the MHA-layer.

$$\hat{C}^{(t)} = \text{MHA}\left(C^{(t)}, H, M\right) \tag{6}$$

Now, compatibility scores u_i between the transformed context and the nodes are calculated as in a Single-Head Attention (SHA) mechanism where the context is again the query:

$$u_i = \frac{W^q \hat{C}^{(t)} W^k h_i}{\sqrt{d_k}} \tag{7}$$

This gives a single value for each node and infeasible nodes are masked with $-\infty$. To arrive at the final probabilities, a softmax is applied. For more details, we refer the reader to the original paper by Kool et al. [15].

4.2 RP-DQN

Most of the models complexity is in the encoder, however it only considers the static components of the problem. The dynamic information that can be used in the context is quite constrained. The original model has very limited access to information about which nodes have already been visited or are infeasible due to other constraints. The only time this information is passed is in Eq. 6 with an inner masking that prevents attention from infeasible nodes to the context.

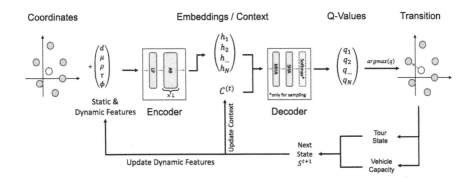

Fig. 1. Architecture overview

We feel that using dynamic node features in the encoder makes the model more expressive and utilizes its complexity better. However, in that case the encoder has to be executed in every step. As discussed already, to make this memory feasible, our model is optimized with Q-Learning. Thus, our model also has to output Q-values instead of probabilities and therefore we do not use the softmax. The inner masking is also not needed anymore and we omit it completely.

Now, the four dynamic features $\mu_i^{(t)}, \rho_i^{(t)}, \tau_i^{(t)}, \phi_i^{(t)}$ represent boolean variables that indicate whether at time step t the node i has already been inserted in the tour, cannot currently be inserted due to capacity constraints, represents the current position of the vehicle or in the multi-depot case represents the current depot.

$$\mu_i^{(t)} = \begin{cases} 1 & \text{if } i \in \mathcal{R}^{(t)} \\ 0 & \text{otherwise} \end{cases} \quad (8) \qquad \rho_i^{(t)} = \begin{cases} 1 & \text{if } d_i^{(t)} > c^{(t)} \\ 0 & \text{otherwise} \end{cases} \quad (10)$$

$$\tau_i^{(t)} = \begin{cases} 1 & \text{if } i \in \mathcal{R}^{(t)} \wedge i \notin \mathcal{R}^{(t-1)} \\ 0 & \text{otherwise} \end{cases} \quad (9) \qquad \phi_i^{(t)} = \begin{cases} 1 & \text{if } i \text{ is active depot} \\ 0 & \text{otherwise} \end{cases} \quad (11)$$

$\mathcal{R}^{(t)}$ is the set of customer nodes that have been visited at time t. Then the set of node features for the CVRP includes $[x_i, y_i, d_i^{(t)}, \mu_i^{(t)}, \rho_i^{(t)}, \tau_i^{(t)}]$, where x_i and y_i are the coordinates of node i and $d_i^{(t)}$ is the demand. $d_i^{(t)} = 0$ for nodes that have been served at time step t. In the MDVRP case, $\phi_i^{(t)}$ is also added to the set of node features. The rest of the architecture stays the same. Although it potentially could be simplified, we opted to stay close to the original architecture. We show that performance improvements come mainly through our better state representation. Our model is called Routing Problem Deep Q-Network (RP-DQN). An architecture overview can be seen in Fig. 1.

MDVRP Decoding. For the MDVRP we expand the context by the current depot embedding. This is done for our model as well as for our extension of the model by Kool et al. [15] to the MDVRP. Next we describe the decoding procedure. In the first step the model has not selected any node yet. We mask all customers and force it to select a depot. This depot becomes the current depot and the model selects nodes until it chooses to come back to the current depot. We don't allow for back to back depot selection and the model cannot come back to a different depot than it started from. After a route is completed the model can start another route by choosing the next depot and the procedure is repeated until all customers are inserted. The Q-values of infeasible actions are masked with $-\infty$.

Q-Learning. To optimize our model we implemented Double DQN [8,17] with a prioritized replay buffer [21]. For exploration, we experimented with Boltzman exploration [23] with decaying softmax temperature and ϵ-Greedy with decaying ϵ. In the end we used ϵ-Greedy and linearly decayed the rate over half of the total training episodes. Although Boltzman exploration initially speeds up the convergence, the model also plateaus at slightly higher costs than with ϵ-Greedy. Choosing Double DQN was mainly due to its proven success but in principle any temporal difference algorithm is suited. Thus, future work could include to study the effect on performance and model behavior of various more advanced algorithms like for instance [7, 10].

5   Experiments

5.1   Baselines

For the CVRP we differentiate baselines from four different categories. The first category includes specialized solvers. Gurobi [6] was used in Kool et al. [15] as an optimal solver for the CVRP. This becomes intractable for instances with more than 20 customers, thus the highly optimized LKH3 [9] was employed by Kool et al. [15] alternatively. It transforms constrained problems into TSPs via penalty functions and other means and then solves those heuristically. The second category consist of ML approaches that construct solutions sequentially and use greedy inference. We compare our model with the approaches by Kool et al. [15], Nazari et al. [18], Falkner and Schmidt-Thieme [5]. The third category also includes ML based approaches with sequential construction, but this time using sampling or beam search inference. We compare with the same models as in the previous category. Our model, Kool et al. [15] and Falkner and Schmidt-Thieme [5] use sampling while Nazari et al. [18] uses beam search. The last category encompasses improvement heuristics that use local search. We include it for completeness sake. They operate on an initial solution and improve it iteratively by selecting solutions in the neighborhood. OR-Tools [19] is a classical approach using meta-heuristics while Wu et al. [29] is a machine learning approach. For the MDVRP, no ML baselines are available. Thus, we adapt the model by Kool et al. [15] to support MDVRP and train it ourselves. We set up the decoding procedure and context as for our model. For a traditional baseline we stick to Google OR-Tools as it provides a flexible modeling framework. However OR-Tool does not provide an out of the box MDVRP solver, thus we use the CVRP framework and simulate the MDVRP by setting different starting and finishing points to the vehicles.

5.2   Data

For the training of the model synthetic data was used. We created data with $|C| = 20, 50, 100$ and train a model for each of these. In the main experiments, the problem size stays the same for training and testing. Additionally, we conducted a generalization study that shows how the models perform on different problem sizes, which can be seen in Sect. 5.7. Since an unlimited amount of samples can be generated, we will use every problem instance only once and generate new data after every episode. Note that the data can be generated with various different properties. For instance, the customers can have a special alignment in grids or star-like structures, be sampled uniformly or according to some other distribution. In order to compare, our data generation follows Nazari et al. [18]. Their dataset is used by most of the ML literature. For testing we have used the exact test set that was provided by Nazari et al. [18] for each problem size. It consists of 10,000 instances that were generated with the same properties as the training data. It uses the euclidean distance. Demands $d \in [1, 9]$ are sampled uniformly. Coordinates are sampled uniformly from the unit square. Vehicles have capacity 30, 40 and 50 depending on the problem size. For the MDVRP we generate the data in the same fashion and create our own test set.

5.3   CVRP Results

Table 1 shows that our approach outperforms all other models that construct the solution by sequentially selecting nodes. This applies for both greedy and sampling inference. Only the improvement method by Wu et al. [29] achieves better results. However, improvement heuristics operate on an initial solution and will try to improve this repeatedly. It has been shown that these approaches

Table 1. CVRP Results: The columns show the average distance and relative percentage gap to the best known solution on the three fixed test datasets. The greedy results are deterministic. While the sampling is not deterministic in principle, the variability in the results when repeating the experiments is so low that it lies in the realm of floating point precision and is thus not worth reporting.

Method		Problem size					
		20		50		100	
		Mean	Gap %	Mean	Gap %	Mean	Gap %
Specialized solver	Gurobi	6.1	0.00	–	–	–	–
	LKH3	6.14	0.66	10.38	0.00	15.65	0.00
Sequential policy (Greedy)	RP-DQN	**6.36**	4.26	**10.92**	5.20	**16.59**	6.01
	Kool	6.4	4.92	10.98	5.78	16.8	7.35
	Falkner	6.47	6.07	11.44	10.21	–	–
	Nazari	6.59	8.03	11.39	9.73	17.23	10.10
Sequential policy (Sampling/Beam search)	RP-DQN 1024 s)	**6.24**	2.30	**10.59**	2.02	**16.11**	2.94
	Kool 1280 s)	6.25	2.46	10.62	2.31	16.23	3.71
	Falkner 1280 s)	6.26	2.62	10.84	4.43	–	–
	Nazari (10bs)	6.4	5.41	11.31	8.96	17.16	9.65
Local search	Wu (5000 steps)	**6.12**	0.33	**10.45**	0.67	**16.03**	2.43
	OR-Tools	6.43	5.41	11.31	8.96	17.16	9.65

scale to better final performance when given a better initial starting solution [30]. Thus better approaches to find initial solutions like ours can be used to kick-start improvement methods like OR-Tools or the machine learning approach by Wu et al. [29]. We also notice that our percentage gain increases with the problem size, stressing the importance of dynamic features for larger, real world problems. Section 5.6 gives a more detailed comparison including the timings of some of the methods.

5.4   MDVRP Results

In Table 2 an even greater lift as for the CVRP can be seen. The model by Kool et al. [15] reaches only subpar performance when the problem size increases. We attribute the results to the more powerful state representation of our model. We assume that this has more impact on the MDVRP as it is a more complicated problem than the CVRP. We also want to highlight that training our model is much more memory efficient compared to the standard model by Kool et al. [15].

Table 2. DVRP Results: The columns show the average distance and relative percentage gap to the best known solution on the three test datasets.

Method	Problem size					
	20		50		100	
	Mean	Gap %	Mean	Gap %	Mean	Gap %
RP-DQN - Greedy	5.48	2.62	8.04	4.15	11.99	4.08
Kool - Greedy	5.68	6.37	8.84	14.51	13.17	14.32
RP-DQN - Sampling 1024	**5.34**	0.00	**7.72**	0.00	**11.52**	0.00
Kool - Sampling 1024	5.42	1.50	8.11	5.05	12.15	5.47
OR-Tools	6.74	26.23	9.02	16.84	12.92	12.15

5.5   Learning Curves

In Fig. 2 we exemplify the learning behavior of both models on the MDVRP with 50 customers run on the same hardware. Due to the use of a buffer, the sample efficiency is improved greatly. While this is less important for simple environments, it has significant impact for problems that are more expensive to compute. For routing, this can include environments with more hard and soft constraints, stochastic components and objective functions that trade-off multiple goals. Figure 2 shows that the learning of our model starts off slower, however we converge significantly faster.

5.6   Runtime Comparison

Reporting the runtime is difficult as it can differ in order of magnitudes due to implementation differences (C++ vs Python) and hardware. Kool et al. [15]

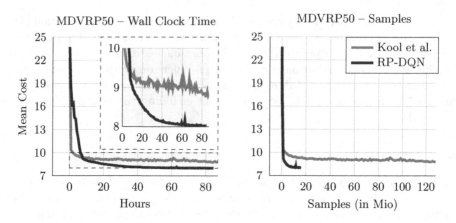

Fig. 2. Learning Curves for the MDVRP with 50 customers comparing the wall clock time and sample efficiency.

thus decided to report the runtime over the complete test set of 10,000 instances. Other literature like Wu et al. [29] has followed them. We feel that this adds another layer of obscurity over the runtime comparison as they then decided to parallelize over multiple instances. ML approaches were parallelized via batch computation. Most traditional methods are single threaded CPU applications. They were parallelized over instances by launching more threads if the CPU has them available. We feel that for practical applications if enough instances have to be solved for instance parallelization to be useful, the corresponding hardware can be bought. More important is the time it takes to solve a single instance or alternatively the time it takes to solve the 10,000 instances when not parallelizing over instances. In Table 3 we collect some timings reported by the

Table 3. CVRP Results and Timings to solve all 10,000 instances

Method	Problem size					
	20		50		100	
	Mean	Time	Mean	Time	Mean	Time
Gurobi	6.1	–	–	–	–	–
LKH3	6.14	(2 h*)	10.38	(7 h*)	15.65	(13 h*)
RP-DQN – Greedy	6.36	(3 s†/10 min††)	10.92	(14 s†/30 min††)	16.59	(50 s†/78 min††)
Kool – Greedy	6.4	(1 s†)	10.98	(3 s†)	16.8	(8 s†)
RP-DQN –1024 s	6.24	(52 min**)	10.59	(5 h**)	16.11	(15 h**)
Kool –1280 s	6.25	(6 min**)	10.62	(28 min**)	16.23	(2 h**)
Wu (5000 steps)	6.12	(2 h†)	10.45	(4 h†)	16.03	(5 h†)
OR-Tools	6.43	(2 min‡)	11.31	(13 min‡)	17.16	(46 min‡)

*32 instances were solved in parallel on two CPUs [15].
†Time for solving many instances in parallel through GPU batch computation.
‡Time reported by Wu et al. [29]. Only one Thread.
**Time for solving one instance at a time.
††Time for solving one instance at a time on CPU

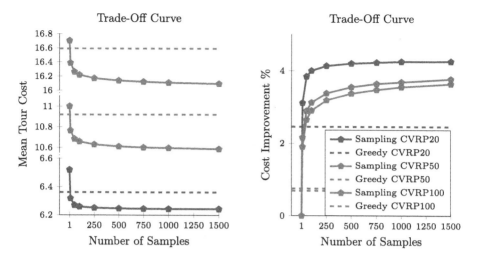

Fig. 3. This figure shows how much additional samples improve the solution quality.

literature and our own. Note that the timings are not directly comparable due to the discussed reasons. Also note that most methods have some way of trading performance and time off. Beam Searches can have bigger width, more solutions can be sampled and improvement methods can make more steps. Additionally, none of the methods will improve indefinitely but hit diminishing returns instead. Thus there are more and less reasonable spots to trade-off. Ultimately however, this is also application dependent. Reporting full trade-off curves for all of the methods is not possible. Our method is extremely quick in greedy and then takes more time the more samples are used. This behaviour is respectively the same for the Kool model although our model expectedly takes more time as the encoder is run at every step. 15 h for the size 100 model with sampling seems high, however consider that one instance was solved at a time, thus a single instance still only takes less than 6 s. The only two methods that have better results are LKH3 and Wu et al. [29]'s improvement approach. For both the time was only reported with a high degree of instance parallelization, thus it should be expected that our model takes less time than them on a fair single instance comparison.

Additionally, 1024 samples is already at a point on the trade-off curves where there are negligible performance improvements as can be seen in Fig. 3.

5.7 Generalization Study

This study tests the ability to generalize. All models were trained on one size and tested on instances between 20 and 200 nodes. Figure 4 shows the percentage gap to the best model from both inference settings. The brittleness of ML models in this scenario was already observed in [15] and is an open shortcoming compared to traditional methods.

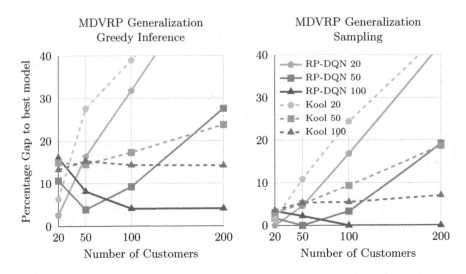

Fig. 4. This figure shows the generalization to different problem sizes.

6   Conclusion

In this paper we present a new approach to tackle complex routing problems based on learning from temporal differences, specifically through Q-Learning, when optimizing autoregressive policies that sequentially construct solutions by inserting one node at a time for solving routing problems. We showed that this learning procedure allows the incorporation of dynamic node features, enabling more powerful models which lead to state-of-the-art performance on the CVRP for autoregressive policies. Additionally, the sample efficiency is greatly improved. Although our model still falls short of specialized solvers like LKH3 and improvement methods, it is useful to find very good initial solutions. Future work could include combining powerful initial solution finders like RP-DQN with improvement heuristics. We also demonstrated that the dynamic components become more important for the MDVRP, a problem type that was not explored with RL before. We assume that this holds for other more complicated problem types like CVRP with time windows. Future work could include extending our model to these problem types. Further, more work is needed to improve generalizability. This could include training on broader distributions and building automatic data generators from real life datasets.

Acknowledgement. This work is co-funded via the research project L2O (https:// www.ismll.uni-hildesheim.de/projekte/l2o_en.html) funded by the German Federal Ministry of Education and Research (BMBF) under the grant agreement no. 01IS20013A and the European Regional Development Fund project TrAmP (https:// www.ismll.uni-hildesheim.de/projekte/tramp.html) under the grant agreement no. 85023841.

References

1. Bello, I., Pham, H., Le, Q.V., Norouzi, M., Bengio, S.: Neural combinatorial optimization with reinforcement learning. CoRR (2016). http://arxiv.org/abs/1611.09940
2. Chen, X., Tian, Y.: Learning to perform local rewriting for combinatorial optimization. In: Advances in Neural Information Processing Systems, vol. 32. Curran Associates, Inc. (2019)
3. Dai, H., Dai, B., Song, L.: Discriminative embeddings of latent variable models for structured data. In: Proceedings of the 33rd International Conference on International Conference on Machine Learning, ICML 2016, vol. 48, pp. 2702–2711 (2016)
4. Delarue, A., Anderson, R., Tjandraatmadja, C.: Reinforcement learning with combinatorial actions: an application to vehicle routing. In: Advances in Neural Information Processing Systems, vol. 33, pp. 609–620. Curran Associates, Inc. (2020)
5. Falkner, J.K., Schmidt-Thieme, L.: Learning to solve vehicle routing problems with time windows through joint attention (2020). http://arxiv.org/abs/2006.09100
6. Gurobi Optimization, LLC: Gurobi optimizer reference manual (2021)
7. Haarnoja, T., Zhou, A., Abbeel, P., Levine, S.: Soft actor-critic: off-policy maximum entropy deep reinforcement learning with a stochastic actor. In: ICML (2018)
8. van Hasselt, H., Guez, A., Silver, D.: Deep reinforcement learning with double q-learning. In: Proceedings of the Thirtieth AAAI Conference on Artificial Intelligence, AAAI 2016, pp. 2094–2100. AAAI Press (2016)
9. Helsgaun, K.: An extension of the Lin-Kernighan-Helsgaun TSP solver for constrained traveling salesman and vehicle routing problems (2017). https://doi.org/10.13140/RG.2.2.25569.40807
10. Hessel, M., et al.: Rainbow: combining improvements in deep reinforcement learning. In: AAAI (2018)
11. Ioffe, S., Szegedy, C.: Batch normalization: accelerating deep network training by reducing internal covariate shift. In: Proceedings of the 32nd International Conference on Machine Learning, Proceedings of Machine Learning Research, Lille, France, vol. 37, pp. 448–456. PMLR (2015)
12. Joshi, C.K., Laurent, T., Bresson, X.: An efficient graph convolutional network technique for the travelling salesman problem. CoRR (2019). http://arxiv.org/abs/1906.01227
13. Khalil, E., Dai, H., Zhang, Y., Dilkina, B., Song, L.: Learning combinatorial optimization algorithms over graphs. In: Advances in Neural Information Processing Systems, vol. 30. Curran Associates, Inc. (2017)
14. Kool, W., van Hoof, H., Gromicho, J., Welling, M.: Deep policy dynamic programming for vehicle routing problems (2021). http://arxiv.org/abs/2102.11756
15. Kool, W., van Hoof, H., Welling, M.: Attention, learn to solve routing problems! In: International Conference on Learning Representations (2019)
16. Lin, S., Kernighan, B.W.: An effective heuristic algorithm for the Traveling-Salesman problem. Oper. Res. **21**(2), 498–516 (1973). https://doi.org/10.1287/opre.21.2.498
17. Mnih, V., et al.: Human-level control through deep reinforcement learning. Nature **518**(7540), 529–533 (2015). https://doi.org/10.1038/nature14236. ISSN 00280836
18. Nazari, M.R., Oroojlooy, A., Snyder, L., Takac, M.: Reinforcement learning for solving the vehicle routing problem. In: Advances in Neural Information Processing Systems, vol. 31. Curran Associates, Inc. (2018)
19. Perron, L., Furnon, V.: OR-Tools 7.2 (2019)

20. Rosenkrantz, D.J., Stearns, R.E., Lewis, P.M.: An analysis of several heuristics for the Traveling Salesman problem. In: Ravi, S.S., Shukla, S.K. (eds.) Fundamental Problems in Computing, pp. 45–69. Springer, Dordrecht (2009). https://doi.org/10.1007/978-1-4020-9688-4_3
21. Schaul, T., Quan, J., Antonoglou, I., Silver, D.: Prioritized experience replay (2015). http://arxiv.org/abs/1511.05952
22. Shaw, P.: Using constraint programming and local search methods to solve vehicle routing problems. In: Maher, M., Puget, J.-F. (eds.) CP 1998. LNCS, vol. 1520, pp. 417–431. Springer, Heidelberg (1998). https://doi.org/10.1007/3-540-49481-2_30
23. Sutton, R.S., Barto, A.G.: Reinforcement Learning: An Introduction, 2nd edn. The MIT Press (2018)
24. Toth, P., Vigo, D.: Vehicle Routing: Problems, Methods, and Applications, 2nd edn. No. 18 in MOS-SIAM Series on Optimization, SIAM (2014). ISBN 9781611973587
25. Vaswani, A., et al.: Attention is all you need. In: Advances in Neural Information Processing Systems, vol. 30, Curran Associates, Inc. (2017)
26. Vinyals, O., Fortunato, M., Jaitly, N.: Pointer networks. In: Advances in Neural Information Processing Systems, vol. 28, Curran Associates, Inc. (2015)
27. Voudouris, C., Tsang, E.: Guided local search and its application to the Traveling Salesman problem. Eur. J. Oper. Res. **113**(2), 469–499 (1999). https://doi.org/10.1016/S0377-2217(98)00099-X
28. Williams, R.J.: Simple statistical gradient-following algorithms for connectionist reinforcement learning. Mach. Learn. **8**(3–4), 229–256 (1992)
29. Wu, Y., Song, W., Cao, Z., Zhang, J., Lim, A.: Learning improvement heuristics for solving routing problems (2020). http://arxiv.org/abs/1912.05784
30. Zhao, J., Mao, M., Zhao, X., Zou, J.: A hybrid of deep reinforcement learning and local search for the vehicle routing problems. IEEE Trans. Intell. Trans. Syst. 1–11 (2020). https://doi.org/10.1109/TITS.2020.3003163

κ-Circulant Maximum Variance Bases

Christopher Bonenberger[1,2(✉)], Wolfgang Ertel[1], and Markus Schneider[1]

[1] Ravensburg-Weingarten University of Applied Sciences
(Institut für Künstliche Intelligenz), Weingarten, Germany
bonenbch@rwu.de
[2] Universität Ulm (Institut für Neuroinformatik),
James-Franck-Ring, 89081 Ulm, Germany

Abstract. Principal component analysis (PCA), a well-known technique in machine learning and statistics, is typically applied to time-independent data, as it is based on point-wise correlations. Dynamic PCA (DPCA) handles this issue by augmenting the data set with lagged versions of itself. In this paper, we show that both, PCA and DPCA, are a special case of κ-circulant maximum variance bases. We formulate the constrained linear optimization problem of finding such κ-circulant bases and present a closed-form solution that allows further interpretation and significant speed-up for DPCA. Furthermore, the relation of the proposed bases to the discrete Fourier transform, finite impulse response filters as well as spectral density estimation is pointed out.

Keywords: PCA · Circulant matrices · Toeplitz matrices · Linear filtering · Discrete fourier transform · Dynamic PCA · Representation learning

1 Introduction

The quest for an effective data representation is a driving force in machine learning. Often the data at hand has intrinsic regularities that are concealed in the original space. An appropriately chosen transform from the input space $\mathcal{I}$ to some feature space $\mathcal{F}$ can significantly improve the performance of machine learning algorithms. This is why feature engineering and feature learning are important tasks in machine learning [3].

Yet, a proper feature map is even more important, when there are regularities in the given data that are independent of time (or position) as it is the case for time series or image data [2]. In this context, feature engineering and feature learning are closely connected to signal processing and many of the well-known integral transforms (and their discrete counterparts [19]) are still used for feature engineering [8]. These integral transforms, as for example Fourier, Gabor

This work is supported by a grant from the German Ministry of Education and Research (BMBF; KMU-innovativ: Medizintechnik, 13GW0173E). We would like to express our gratitude to the reviewers for their efforts towards improving this work.

S. Edelkamp et al. (Eds.): KI 2021, LNAI 12873, pp. 17–29, 2021.
https://doi.org/10.1007/978-3-030-87626-5_2

and Wavelet transforms, rely on a fixed basis (or frame), whereas another well-established technique – principal component analysis [12] – can be used to learn an orthogonal basis based on available data by finding the direction of maximum variance. As it is desirable to have data-adaptive representations, principal component analysis and similar techniques for dimensionality reduction are frequently used in machine learning and pattern recognition [22,24].

State-of-the-art machine learning techniques, as for example convolutional neural networks (CNNs) [1] and sparse dictionary learning (SDL) [20] build on these ideas, i.e., signal representations are learned based on available data, while enforcing certain properties (e.g. discriminative or sparse representations). However, the convolutional layers in CNNs are intrinsically offering shift-invariance [7]. In contrast, in dictionary learning algorithms specific structures are imposed to the dictionary, in order to find a shift-invariant basis (or frame, e.g. [17]). Typically, these structures are introduced by means of Toeplitz or circulant matrices [9]. These matrices establish the link to CNNs, as both can be interpreted as a finite impulse response (FIR) filter, just like the filters in CNNs [15]. In both techniques (CNNs and SDL) the filter coefficients are learned adaptively.

The contribution of this work is a mathematical framework, that generalizes classical principal component analysis as a problem of matched[1] FIR filtering, by requiring the principal component to be shift-invariant. In particular, we present a constrained linear optimization problem, that formulates the classical optimization problem of PCA as a shift-invariant problem. This means, instead of finding the direction (a vector) of maximal variance in the input space $\mathcal{I}$, we seek a κ-circulant basis $\mathbf{G}_\kappa$ that maximizes variance (total dispersion [18]) in the feature space $\mathcal{F}$, where $\mathbf{G}_\kappa : \mathcal{I} \to \mathcal{F}$. The mathematical formulation of this optimization problem, which allows a closed-form solution and hence a better understanding of the results, is based on the decomposition of circulant matrices into a matrix polynomial of a simple circular permutation matrix.

As a result, we obtain a class of data-adaptive bases, that constitute classical PCA as well as discrete Fourier analysis (depending on the choice of parameters) and allows a data-adaptive time-frequency decomposition as known from wavelet analysis.

2   Preliminaries

Before we turn to the optimization problem of variance maximizing circulant bases, we recapture related methods. In this paper we focus on two specific orthogonal transforms, namely the discrete Fourier transform and principal component analysis.[2] Beneath classical PCA we also introduce dynamic PCA,

---

[1] Matched filters are learned in a supervised setting, while here we restrict ourselves to the unsupervised case. Hence, the "matching" of the filter coefficients is according to a variance criterion (similar to PCA).

[2] Principal component analysis is almost equivalent to the Karhunen-Loève transform (KLT) [14]. Further information regarding the relationship between PCA and KLT is given in [10].

because it is closely related to κ-circulant bases. Finally, in Sect. 2.3 κ-circulant matrices are introduced along with FIR filters.

2.1 Principal Component Analysis

Let $\mathbf{X} \in \mathbb{R}^{D \times N}$ be a data set consisting of N observations $\mathbf{x} \in \mathbb{R}^{D}$ with zero-mean. In order to find the principal component w.r.t. $\mathbf{X}$, the optimization problem

$$\max_{\mathbf{u} \in \mathbb{R}^{D}} \left\{ \|\mathbf{u}^{T} \mathbf{X}\|_{2}^{2} \right\} \text{ s.t. } \|\mathbf{u}\|_{2}^{2} = 1. \tag{1}$$

has to be solved. In a geometric meaning, we seek the vector $\mathbf{u}^{*}$ (the principal component) being most similar to the observations $\mathbf{x}$ in the data set.[3] The corresponding Lagrangian

$$\mathbf{L}(\mathbf{u}, \lambda) = \mathbf{u}^{T} \mathbf{X} \mathbf{X}^{T} \mathbf{u} - \lambda(\mathbf{u}^{T} \mathbf{u} - 1) \tag{2}$$

leads to the eigenvalue problem

$$\mathbf{X} \mathbf{X}^{T} \mathbf{u} = \lambda \mathbf{u}, \tag{3}$$

where $\mathbf{X} \mathbf{X}^{T}$ is proportional to the sample covariance matrix $\mathbf{S} \in \mathbb{R}^{D \times D}$ of the data at hand ($\mathbf{X}^{T}$ denotes the transpose of $\mathbf{X}$). The symmetric covariance matrix $\mathbf{S}$ can be diagonalized as $\mathbf{\Lambda} = \mathbf{U}^{T} \mathbf{S} \mathbf{U}$, i.e.,

$$\frac{1}{N-1} \mathbf{X} \mathbf{X}^{T} \mathbf{U} = \mathbf{S} \mathbf{U} = \mathbf{U} \mathbf{\Lambda}. \tag{4}$$

The column vectors of $\mathbf{U}$ are the eigenvectors (eigenbasis) of $\mathbf{S}$ and form an orthogonal basis for $\mathbb{R}^{D}$. The eigenvector corresponding to the largest eigenvalue is the principal component and points in the direction of maximum variance.

The representation $\mathbf{x}'$ of some signal $\mathbf{x} \in \mathcal{X}$ in a subspace $\mathcal{S}$ can be found as $\mathbf{U}_{k}^{T} \mathbf{x}$, where $\mathbf{U}_{k}^{T} : \mathcal{X} \rightarrow \mathcal{S}$ contains only the eigenvectors belonging to the k largest eigenvalues. The reconstruction $\mathbf{x}'$ of the signal $\mathbf{x}$ is then found as $\mathbf{U}_{k} \mathbf{U}_{k}^{T} \mathbf{x}$, i.e., $\mathbf{U}_{k} : \mathcal{S} \rightarrow \mathcal{X}$.

In the context of this work it is especially of interest, that depending on the underlying stochastic process, the covariance matrix may have a Toeplitz-like structure (cf. Sect. 4.1) and the corresponding eigenbasis approximates a Fourier basis [21].

2.2 Dynamic Principal Component Analysis

In [13] Ku et al. proposed dynamic PCA for statistical process monitoring, where the original data set is augmented by lagged versions of itself. Hereby the number of lags L is a free parameter. This method of data augmentation is used in order to achieve circular permutation invariance and to overcome the static behavior

---

[3] The dot product $\mathbf{u}^{T} \mathbf{x}$ serves as measure of similarity.

of classical PCA. In fact, a classical PCA is performed, yet instead of the original data set $\mathbf{X}$ the augmented data set $\mathbf{X}_A$ is used. This can be formalized as

$$\mathbf{X}_A = \begin{bmatrix} \mathbf{P}^0\mathbf{X} & \mathbf{P}^1\mathbf{X} & \cdots & \mathbf{P}^{L-1}\mathbf{X} \end{bmatrix}, \tag{5}$$

where $\mathbf{P}$ is the permutation matrix

$$\mathbf{P} = \begin{bmatrix} 0 & 1 & 0 & \cdots & 0 \\ 0 & 0 & 1 & & 0 \\ \vdots & & & \ddots & \vdots \\ 0 & & & & 1 \\ 1 & 0 & 0 & \cdots & 0 \end{bmatrix} \in \mathbb{R}^{D\times D}. \tag{6}$$

Hence, for DPCA the principal component is the eigenvector $\mathbf{u}^*$ of $\mathbf{X}_A\mathbf{X}_A^T$ with the largest corresponding eigenvalue, which can also be found as a solution to the optimization problem

$$\max_{\mathbf{u}\in\mathbb{R}^D} \left\{ \left\| \mathbf{u}^T\mathbf{P}^0\mathbf{X} \right\|_2^2 + \cdots + \left\| \mathbf{u}^T\mathbf{P}^{L-1}\mathbf{X} \right\|_2^2 \right\} \text{ s.t. } \|\mathbf{u}\|_2^2 = 1. \tag{7}$$

2.3 κ-Circulant Matrices

A circulant matrix $\mathbf{C} \in \mathbb{R}^{D\times D}$ is formed by a vector $\mathbf{c} \in \mathbb{R}^W$ and its lagged versions, e.g. when $W = D$ it is a matrix of the form

$$\mathbf{C} = \begin{bmatrix} c_0 & c_1 & \cdots & c_{W-1} \\ c_{W-1} & c_0 & \cdots & c_{W-2} \\ \vdots & & \ddots & \vdots \\ c_1 & c_2 & \cdots & c_0 \end{bmatrix} = \begin{bmatrix} - & \mathbf{c}^T & - \\ - & \mathbf{c}^T\mathbf{P} & - \\ & \vdots & \\ - & \mathbf{c}^T\mathbf{P}^{D-1} & - \end{bmatrix} = \sum_{w=0}^{W-1} c_w\mathbf{P}^w, \tag{8}$$

where $\mathbf{P}$ corresponds to a circular permutation as defined in Eq. 6. An example of a simple circulant is shown in the top left graph of Fig. 1.

A circulant matrix can be diagonalized as

$$\mathbf{C} = \mathbf{F}\mathbf{\Lambda}\mathbf{F}^{-1}, \tag{9}$$

where $\mathbf{F} \in \mathbb{R}^{D\times D}$ is the discrete Fourier matrix with components $f_{j,k}$ that are given as $f_{j,k} = \exp(-2\pi ijk/D)/\sqrt{D}$ for all $0 \le j,k < D$ with $i^2 = -1$ [11]. The eigenvalue matrix $\mathbf{\Lambda} = \sqrt{D} \operatorname{diag}(\mathbf{F}\mathbf{c})$ is a diagonal matrix with the discrete Fourier transform of $\mathbf{c}$ on its diagonal. Hence, the eigenvectors of a circulant matrix are the Fourier modes and the eigenvalues can be computed from the DFT $\hat{\mathbf{c}} = \sqrt{D} \, \mathbf{F}\mathbf{c}$ of the vector $\mathbf{c}$, i.e., $\lambda_j = \hat{c}_j$.

This can also be understood by means of the convolution theorem: multiplying a circulant matrix $\mathbf{C} \in \mathbb{R}^{D\times D}$ (that is based on the vector $\mathbf{c} \in \mathbb{R}^D$) with some vector $\mathbf{x} \in \mathbb{R}^D$ realizes a discrete circular convolution[4], i.e., $\mathbf{C}\mathbf{x} = \mathbf{x} \circledast \mathbf{c} = \mathbf{F}^{-1}\mathbf{\Lambda}^H\mathbf{F}\mathbf{x}$ with $\mathbf{\Lambda}^H$ being the conjugate transpose of $\mathbf{\Lambda}$.

---

[4] The discrete circular convolution of two sequences $\mathbf{x}, \mathbf{y} \in \mathbb{R}^D$ is written as $\mathbf{x} \circledast \mathbf{y}$, while the linear convolution is written as $\mathbf{x} * \mathbf{y}$.

A linear convolution can be expressed as a circular convolution, when zero-padding is used. Hence, $\mathbf{C}$ can describe a simple FIR filter [23]. For a filter-kernel $\mathbf{c} \in \mathbb{R}^W$ and data $\mathbf{x} \in \mathbb{R}^D$ the linear convolution $\mathbf{c} * \mathbf{x}$ can be written as

$$\mathbf{C}\mathbf{x} = \mathbf{c} * \mathbf{x} = \left(\sum_{w=0}^{W-1} c_w \mathbf{P}^w \right) \mathbf{x} \quad \text{where} \quad \mathbf{x}, \mathbf{P} \in \mathbb{R}^{W+D-1}. \tag{10}$$

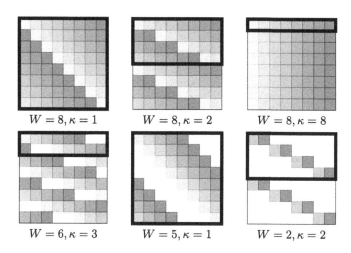

Fig. 1. Examples of κ-circulant matrices $\mathbf{C}_\kappa$ according to Eq. 11 for $D = 8$ and the equivalent (sub)matrices $\mathbf{G}_\kappa$ according to Eq. 20 (framed black). Equation 19 formulates the problem of finding the optimal kernel $\mathbf{g}$ given a fixed structure of $\mathbf{G}_\kappa$. For ease of visualization these exemplary matrices are based on a kernel $\mathbf{c} \in \mathbb{R}^W$ that is a simple ramp (e.g. $\mathbf{c}^T = [0.125 \ 0.25 \ 0.375 \ \cdots \ 1]$ is the first row in the top left matrix). Note that the bottom right matrix is a wavelet-like structure.

A κ-circulant matrix $\mathbf{C}_\kappa \in \mathbb{R}^{D \times D}$ is the generalization of a standard circulant and has the form [4]

$$\mathbf{C}_\kappa = \begin{bmatrix} c_0 & c_1 & \cdots & c_{D-1} \\ c_{D-\kappa} & c_{D-\kappa+1} & \cdots & c_{D-\kappa-1} \\ \vdots & & \ddots & \vdots \\ c_\kappa & c_{\kappa+1} & \cdots & c_{\kappa-1} \end{bmatrix} = \begin{bmatrix} - & \mathbf{c}^T & - \\ - & \mathbf{c}^T \mathbf{P}^\kappa & - \\ & \vdots & \\ - & \mathbf{c}^T \mathbf{P}^{\kappa(D-1)} & - \end{bmatrix}, \tag{11}$$

where the subscripts are modulo D. Some examples are shown in Fig. 1.

3   Maximum Variance Bases

In this section, we present a novel optimization problem, that generalizes PCA and DPCA. This more general optimization problem is based on the idea of searching a basis, that is inherently translation-invariant. This is enforced, by choosing circulant structures, that are based on circular permutations. We refer to those as "matched" κ-circulant matrices.

3.1   Simple Matched Circulants

For the sake of simplicity, before treating the general case of κ-circulant bases, in this section we restrict ourselves to the case of standard circulant matrices ($\kappa = 1$). In order to find a basis that maximizes variance we formulate a constrained linear optimization problem analogously to PCA (cf. Eq. 1). However, instead of a single vector we seek a circulant matrix $\mathbf{G}$ (a filter, cf. Sect. 2.3) that solves

$$\max_{\mathbf{g} \in \mathbb{R}^W} \left\{ \|\mathbf{G}\mathbf{X}\|_F^2 \right\} \text{ s.t. } \|\mathbf{g}\|_2^2 = 1, \tag{12}$$

where $\| \cdot \|_F$ denotes the Frobenius norm and

$$\mathbf{G} = \sum_{w=0}^{W-1} g_w \mathbf{P}^w. \tag{13}$$

According to Eq. 10 $\mathbf{G}$ is a FIR filter with coefficients $\mathbf{g}$. Hence Eq. 12 may also be understood as the problem of designing a FIR filter such that the transmitted energy is maximized.[5] Hence, Eq. 12 poses power spectral density estimation as a constrained linear optimization problem. The corresponding Lagrangian is

$$\mathbf{L}(\mathbf{g}, \lambda) = \sum_{\nu=1}^{N} \langle \sum_w g_w \mathbf{P}^w \mathbf{x}_\nu, \sum_w g_w \mathbf{P}^w \mathbf{x}_\nu \rangle - \lambda \left(\mathbf{g}^T \mathbf{g} - 1 \right)$$

$$= \sum_{\nu=1}^{N} \mathbf{x}_\nu^T \left(\sum_w g_w \mathbf{P}^{-w} \right) \left(\sum_w g_w \mathbf{P}^w \right) \mathbf{x}_\nu - \lambda \left(\mathbf{g}^T \mathbf{g} - 1 \right),$$

where the product $\mathbf{G}^T\mathbf{G} = \left(\sum_w g_w \mathbf{P}^{-w} \right) \left(\sum_w g_w \mathbf{P}^w \right)$ is

$$\mathbf{G}^T\mathbf{G} = g_0^2 \mathbf{P}^0 + \cdots + g_0 g_{W-1} \mathbf{P}^{W-1} + \cdots + g_{W-1} g_0 \mathbf{P}^{1-W} + \cdots + g_{W-1}^2 \mathbf{P}^0.$$

Thus the derivative of $\mathbf{L}(\mathbf{g}, \lambda)$ w.r.t. g_k can be given as

$$\frac{\partial \mathbf{L}}{\partial g_k} = -\sum_{\nu=1}^{N} \langle \mathbf{x}_\nu, \left(\sum_w g_w \left(\mathbf{P}^{w-k} + \mathbf{P}^{k-w} \right) \right) \mathbf{x}_\nu \rangle + 2\lambda g_k. \tag{14}$$

Due to $\langle \mathbf{P}\mathbf{x}, \mathbf{x} \rangle = \langle \mathbf{x}, \mathbf{P}^T \mathbf{x} \rangle$ and because the transpose $\mathbf{P}^T$ of a circulant matrix equals its inverse (i.e., $\mathbf{P}^T = \mathbf{P}^{-1}$) we can write $\langle \mathbf{x}, \mathbf{P}^{k-w}\mathbf{x} \rangle + \langle \mathbf{x}, \mathbf{P}^{w-k}\mathbf{x} \rangle = \langle \mathbf{x}, \mathbf{P}^{k-w}\mathbf{x} \rangle + \langle \mathbf{P}^{k-w}\mathbf{x}, \mathbf{x} \rangle$ and hence using the symmetry of the scalar product we find

$$\frac{\partial \mathbf{L}}{\partial g_k} = -2 \sum_\nu \langle \mathbf{x}_\nu, \sum_w g_w \mathbf{P}^{w-k} \mathbf{x}_\nu \rangle + 2\lambda g_k. \tag{15}$$

With the abbreviation $z_{k,w} = \sum_\nu \langle \mathbf{x}_\nu, \mathbf{P}^{k-w}\mathbf{x}_\nu \rangle$ for the components of the matrix $\mathbf{Z} \in \mathbb{R}^{W \times W}$ this leads to

$$\begin{bmatrix} z_{0,0} & \cdots & z_{0,W-1} \\ \vdots & \ddots & \vdots \\ z_{W-1,0} & \cdots & z_{W-1,W-1} \end{bmatrix} \mathbf{g} = \mathbf{Z}\mathbf{g} = \lambda \mathbf{g}. \tag{16}$$

---

[5] Due to the constraint $\|\mathbf{g}\|_2^2 = 1$ this is not trivial.

Note that $\mathbf{Z}$ is a symmetric Toeplitz matrix that is fully determined by its first column vector $\mathbf{z}$, because the value of $z_{k,w}$ only depends on the difference of the indeces $k - w$ but not on the absolute value of k and w. The components $z_{k,w}$ of the matrix $\mathbf{Z}$ are given as (cf. Eq. 15)

$$z_{k,w} = \sum_\nu \langle \mathbf{x}_\nu, \mathbf{P}^{k-w}\mathbf{x}_\nu \rangle \tag{17}$$

This means the value of $z_{k,w}$ depends on the similarity of $\mathbf{x}_\nu$ and the lagged versions $\mathbf{P}^{k-w}\mathbf{x}_\nu$. In case of zero-mean data, this corresponds to the circular sample autocorrelation[6] $\mathbf{r} \in \mathbb{R}^D$, which can be estimated by

$$\mathbf{r} \propto \sum_{\nu=1}^{N} \left[\mathbf{F}^{-1} \left(\mathbf{FX} \odot \overline{\mathbf{FX}} \right) \right]_{w,\nu}, \tag{18}$$

where $\odot$ denotes the Hadamard product (pointwise matrix multiplication). Due to $\mathbf{z} \propto \mathbf{r}$ the sample autocorrelation matrix $\mathbf{Z}$ can be computed in $\mathcal{O}(D \log D)$ by means of the fast Fourier transform (FFT).

3.2 Matched κ-Circulant Matrices

The generalization of Eq. 12 for κ-circulant matrices is

$$\max_{\mathbf{g} \in \mathbb{R}^W} \left\{ \|\mathbf{G}_\kappa \mathbf{X}\|_F^2 \right\} \text{ s.t. } \|\mathbf{g}\|_2^2 = 1. \tag{19}$$

The matrix $\mathbf{G}_\kappa$ is defined as

$$\mathbf{G}_\kappa = \mathbf{M}_\kappa \sum_{w=0}^{W-1} g_w \mathbf{P}^w, \tag{20}$$

where the "masking" matrix $\mathbf{M}_\kappa$ has components

$$m_{j,k} = \begin{cases} 1 & \text{if } j = k \in [0, \kappa, 2\kappa, \cdots, \lfloor D/\kappa - 1 \rfloor \kappa] \\ 0 & \text{else.} \end{cases} \tag{21}$$

Left multiplication of this masking matrix to a circulant matrix $\mathbf{G}$ essentially preserves only every κ-th rows of $\mathbf{G}$ (cf. [17]). The effect of $\mathbf{M}_\kappa$ and the resulting structure of the matrix $\mathbf{G}_\kappa$ is shown in Fig. 1.

The derivative of the Lagrangian resulting from Eq. 19 is

$$\frac{\partial \mathbf{L}}{\partial g_k} = \sum_{\nu=1}^{N} \langle \mathbf{x}_\nu, \left(\sum_w g_w \left(\mathbf{P}^{-w}\mathbf{M}_\kappa^T \mathbf{M}_\kappa \mathbf{P}^k + \mathbf{P}^{-k}\mathbf{M}_\kappa^T \mathbf{M}_\kappa \mathbf{P}^w \right) \right) \mathbf{x}_\nu \rangle - 2\lambda g_k. \tag{22}$$

---

[6] This interpretation is only valid under the assumptions mentioned in Sect. 3.3. Furthermore, the normalization of the autocorrelation (autocovariance) is to be performed as $\mathbf{r}' = \frac{\mathbf{r}}{r_0}$, with the first component r_0 of $\mathbf{r}$ being the variance [16].

Analogously to Eq. 16 we find an eigenvalue problem

$$\mathbf{Z}_\kappa \mathbf{g} = \lambda \mathbf{g}, \tag{23}$$

where the symmetric matrix $\mathbf{Z}_\kappa \in \mathbb{R}^{W \times W}$ has components

$$z_{k,w} = \sum_{\nu=1}^{N} \langle \mathbf{x}_\nu, \mathbf{P}^{-w} \mathbf{M}_\kappa \mathbf{P}^k \mathbf{x}_\nu \rangle. \tag{24}$$

Note that the resulting matrix $\mathbf{Z}_\kappa$ is a consequence of the structure of $\mathbf{G}_\kappa$, in other words, fixing the parameters κ and W means to hypothesize a certain model. Assume – as an example – a circulant data matrix: in this case the sample covariance matrix $\mathbf{S}$ becomes a symmetric circulant matrix and is equal to the sample autocorrelation matrix. Hence, the parameters κ and W imply a certain model.

3.3   Relation to PCA, DPCA and DFT

The closed-form solution for a κ-circulant variance maximizing bases presented in the previous section has many implications. In the following the relation of the presented solution to PCA, DPCA and DFT is described.

PCA. When $\kappa = W = D$ the optimization problem formulated in Eq. 19 is equivalent to the problem of finding principal components as described in Eq. 1. In this case the only non-zero component of $\mathbf{M}_\kappa$ is $m_{0,0} = 1$, such that $\mathbf{Z}_\kappa = \mathbf{Z}_D \propto \mathbf{S}$, i.e., the matrix $\mathbf{Z}$ is proportional to the sample covariance matrix (as for usual PCA this only holds when the underlying data set has zero-mean data). This can also be understood from Fig. 1, where this case is depicted by example ($W = D = \kappa = 8$).

DPCA. When choosing $\kappa = 1$ and $W = D$ we can identify the number of lags L for DPCA with the kernel width W. This can be seen, when comparing Eq. 7 with the equivalent problem

$$\max_{\mathbf{g} \in \mathbb{R}^D} \left\{ \left\| (\mathbf{P}^0 \mathbf{g})^T \mathbf{X} \right\|_2^2 + \cdots + \left\| (\mathbf{P}^{W-1} \mathbf{g})^T \mathbf{X} \right\|_2^2 \right\} \text{ s.t. } \|\mathbf{g}\|_2^2 = 1, \tag{25}$$

which in turn is equivalent to Eq. 12. However, computing $\mathbf{Z}_1$ as $\mathbf{Z}_1 = \mathbf{X}_A \mathbf{X}_A^T$ in $\mathcal{O}(D^3)$ is less efficient than using Eq. 18 with $\mathcal{O}(D \log D)$. This case is shown by example in Fig. 1 in the top left matrix ($W = D = 8, \kappa = 1$).

Introducing another masking matrix $\mathbf{M}_\gamma$ similar to $\mathbf{M}_\kappa$ it is possible to augment Eq. 12, such that DPCA with a smaller number of lags ($L < D$) can be modeled. This matrix $\mathbf{M}_\gamma$ has to be a diagonal matrix with the first $L - 1$ diagonal entries being one and the rest being zero. The solution of this problem is analogously to Eq. 23 with $\mathbf{M}_\kappa$ in Eq. 24 being replaced by $\mathbf{M}_\gamma$. Yet, when narrow range dependencies are expected, it is more efficient to choose $\kappa = 1$ and $W < D$.

DFT. Assuming equidistantly sampled zero-mean data that stems from a wide-sense stationary stochastic process, in the case $D = W$ and $\kappa = 1$, the matrix $\mathbf{Z}_1$ is proportional to the circular sample autocorrelation matrix [6]. The circular autocorrelation is symmetric and hence the resulting matrix $\mathbf{Z}_1$ is a symmetric circulant, i.e., according to Eq. 9 we have $\mathbf{Z}_1 = \mathbf{F}\mathbf{\Lambda}\mathbf{F}^{-1}$ with $\mathbf{\Lambda} = \sqrt{D}\,\mathrm{diag}\,(\mathbf{Fr})$. This means that the optimal D-dimensional shift-invariant basis (maximizing the total dispersion[7]) is the discrete Fourier basis $\mathbf{F}$, because this is the eigenbasis of the matrix $\mathbf{Z}_1$. Furthermore, under the assumptions stated above, the vector $\mathbf{p} = \sqrt{D}\,\mathbf{Fr}$ is an estimate of the power spectral density, which is by definition the discrete time Fourier transform of the sample autocorrelation [16].

4   Numerical Results

In the following the presented theory is demonstrated using the example of a stationary random process, i.e., data points $\mathbf{x} \in \mathbb{R}^{128}$ are sampled from a moving-average (MA) process (cf. [16]). This moving average process is based on a modulated and truncated Gaussian $f(t) = \sin(2\pi t)\exp(-t^2)$ (cf. Fig. 2) that is sampled on the interval $[-2, 2]$ (with sampling frequency 16 Hz such that $\mathbf{f} \in \mathbb{R}^{64}$). Additionally we visualize the results based on a stationary process that realizes random shifts of a fixed signal. Although these settings are rather specific, they serve the purpose of demonstrating the proposed framework and visualize the main results.

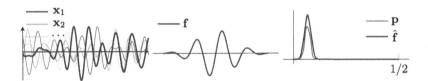

Fig. 2. Observations of the data (left graph) taken from a moving average process with the kernel $\mathbf{f}$ shown in the middle graph. The right graph shows the absolute value of the discrete Fourier transform $\hat{\mathbf{f}}$ of $\mathbf{f}$ and its estimate $\mathbf{p}$, i.e., the (single-sided) spectral density of the corresponding random process (the x-axis is the frequency axis showing halfcycles/sample).

In the examples presented here, the parameters W and κ are always chosen appropriately although such a clear setup does not always naturally arise. Yet, in most cases this is a minor problem. If W, D and κ are inconsistent, zero-padding can be used to overcome this issue (as it is done for discrete Fourier transform). However, as shown in Fig. 1 in the bottom left graph, the effect of $\mathbf{M}_\kappa$ is not always as desired. In fact κ and W should be chosen such that $\mathrm{mod}(D, \kappa) =$

---

[7] Let $\mathbf{Y} = \mathbf{G}_\kappa\mathbf{X}$. Maximizing $\|\mathbf{Y}\|_F^2$ (cf. Eq. 19) means maximizing the trace of the covariance matrix $\mathbf{S} \propto \mathbf{YY}^T$, which in turn is a measure for the total dispersion [18].

$\mathrm{mod}(D, W) = 0$. This is not a strong restriction, when zero-padding (or another kind of padding, e.g. symmetric) is used.

4.1 MA Process

In Fig. 2 an overview about the data and the generating process is given. In the right graph of Fig. 2 the power spectral density and its estimate from the sample autocorrelation is shown. Figure 3 shows four different configurations of the matrix $\mathbf{Z}$. As the underlying process is a MA process, the covariance matrix $\mathbf{S}$ (which stems from Eq. 24 with $\kappa = D$) is almost Toeplitz-structured. Yet, estimating the process characteristic incorporating shift-invariance ($\kappa = 1$) to the model leads to a better approximation. This can also be seen from Fig. 4, where the "principal component" is depicted as a function of W. In Fig. 5 the first 5 eigenvectors are depicted for $W = D/2$ and $W = D/4$. Finally it is interesting to note that the basic optimization problem stated in Eq. 12 is strongly related to a MA model.

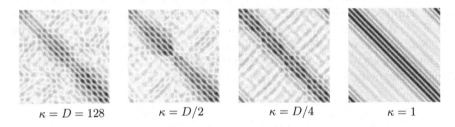

$\kappa = D = 128$ $\kappa = D/2$ $\kappa = D/4$ $\kappa = 1$

Fig. 3. The matrix $\mathbf{Z}_\kappa$ for different values of κ (with $W = D$). The left matrix corresponds to the covariance matrix (PCA) and the right matrix is equivalent to the autocovariance matrix. The matrices in between show two "intermediate" steps.

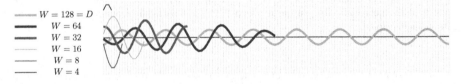

$W = 128 = D$
$W = 64$
$W = 32$
$W = 16$
$W = 8$
$W = 4$

Fig. 4. The eigenvector $\mathbf{g}^* \in \mathbb{R}^W$ belonging to the largest eigenvalue for varying W.

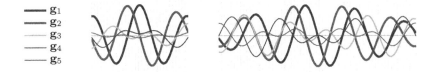

Fig. 5. The first 5 eigenvectors $\mathbf{g}_1, \ldots, \mathbf{g}_5$ corresponding to the 5 largest eigenvalues for $W = 32 = D/4$ (left graph) and $W = 64 = D/2$.

4.2 Circular Process

The characteristic of the process and example data is shown in Fig. 6, whereas the generating function is chosen as in the previous section, i.e., we observe random shifts of a noisy modulated gaussian. The corresponding matrices $\mathbf{Z}_\kappa$ are shown in Fig. 8 for a variety of parameters. In Fig. 7 the reconstruction of a sample signal is shown for different parameter settings. The example shown in Fig. 7 is restricted to the case $W = \kappa$, which means PCA is performed on various scales. The result is less trivial when $\kappa < W$, as then a frame (cf. [5]) is resulting instead of an orthogonal basis.

Fig. 6. Examples of the data (left graph) generated by random shifts of the kernel **g** shown in the middle graph with additive noise. The right graph shows the power spectral density $\hat{\mathbf{g}}$ of **g** and its estimate **p**.

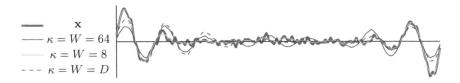

Fig. 7. Example of the reconstruction of a signal (from the two first principal components) drawn from the process described with four different settings. As expected the reconstruction improves with decreasing W (increasing resolution).

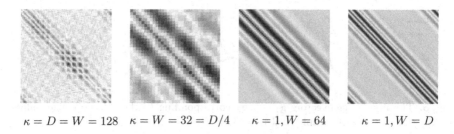

$\kappa = D = W = 128$ $\kappa = W = 32 = D/4$ $\kappa = 1, W = 64$ $\kappa = 1, W = D$

Fig. 8. The matrix $\mathbf{Z}_\kappa$ for different values of κ estimated from $N = 32$ samples of a circular random process generated from random shifts of the vector $\mathbf{g}$ depicted in Fig. 6 (middle graph). The left matrix corresponds to PCA ($\mathbf{Z}_1 = \mathbf{S}$ when $W = D = \kappa$), the right matrix is an estimate of the autocovariance matrix and the two graphs in the middle show matrices $\mathbf{Z}_\kappa \in \mathbb{R}^{W \times W}$ of reduced dimension $W < D$.

5   Conclusion

PCA and linear filtering (FIR filters) are both relevant topics with many applications in machine learning. Our work presents a mathematical framework that establishes a link between those techniques and hence allows a better understanding. Beyond that, our formulation allows to estimate models that may incorporate time-frequency trade-offs in data-adaptive representations. Inherent to the presented theory is a mathematical formulation, that generalizes PCA in terms of shift-invariance. This way the relation between PCA and FIR filters, DFT and DPCA is made explicit and an FFT-based implementation of DPCA can be proposed. A signal processing point-of-view is provided along with examples on stationary stochastic processes.

References

1. Albawi, S., Mohammed, T.A., Al-Zawi, S.: Understanding of a convolutional neural network. In: 2017 International Conference on Engineering and Technology (ICET), pp. 1–6. IEEE (2017)
2. Bagnall, A., Lines, J., Bostrom, A., Large, J., Keogh, E.: The great time series classification bake off: a review and experimental evaluation of recent algorithmic advances. Data Min. Knowl. Disc. **31**(3), 606–660 (2016). https://doi.org/10.1007/s10618-016-0483-9
3. Bengio, Y., Courville, A., Vincent, P.: Representation learning: a review and new perspectives. IEEE Trans. Pattern Anal. Mach. Intell. **35**(8), 1798–1828 (2013)
4. Bose, A., Saha, K.: Random Circulant Matrices. CRC Press (2018)
5. Casazza, P.G., Kutyniok, G., Philipp, F.: Introduction to finite frame theory. Finite Frames, pp. 1–53 (2013)
6. Chatfield, C.: The Analysis of Time Series: An Introduction. Chapman and Hall/CRC (2003)
7. Ismail Fawaz, H., Forestier, G., Weber, J., Idoumghar, L., Muller, P.-A.: Deep learning for time series classification: a review. Data Min. Knowl. Disc. **33**(4), 917–963 (2019). https://doi.org/10.1007/s10618-019-00619-1

8. Fulcher, B.D.: Feature-based time-series analysis. In: Feature Engineering for Machine Learning and Data Analytics, pp. 87–116. CRC Press (2018)

9. Garcia-Cardona, C., Wohlberg, B.: Convolutional dictionary learning: a comparative review and new algorithms. IEEE Trans. Comput. Imaging **4**(3), 366–381 (2018)

10. Gerbrands, J.J.: On the relationships between SVD, KLT and PCA. Pattern Recogn. **14**(1–6), 375–381 (1981)

11. Gray, R.M.: Toeplitz and Circulant Matrices: A Review (2006)

12. Jolliffe, I.T.: Principal components in regression analysis. In: Jolliffe, I.T. (ed.) Principal Component Analysis. SSS, pp. 129–155. Springer, New York (1986). https://doi.org/10.1007/978-1-4757-1904-8_8

13. Ku, W., Storer, R.H., Georgakis, C.: Disturbance detection and isolation by dynamic principal component analysis. Chemom. Intell. Lab. Syst. **30**(1), 179–196 (1995)

14. Orfanidis, S.: SVD, PCA, KLT, CCA, and all that. Optimum Signal Processing, pp. 332–525 (2007)

15. Papyan, V., Romano, Y., Elad, M.: Convolutional neural networks analyzed via convolutional sparse coding. J. Mach. Learn. Res. **18**(1), 2887–2938 (2017)

16. Pollock, D.S.G., Green, R.C., Nguyen, T.: Handbook of Time Series Analysis, Signal Processing, and Dynamics. Elsevier (1999)

17. Rusu, C.: On learning with shift-invariant structures. Digit. Signal Process. **99**, 102654 (2020)

18. Seber, G.A.: Multivariate Observations, vol. 252. Wiley, Hoboken (2009)

19. Strang, G., Nguyen, T.: Wavelets and Filter Banks. SIAM (1996)

20. Tošić, I., Frossard, P.: Dictionary learning. IEEE Signal Process. Mag. **28**(2), 27–38 (2011)

21. Unser, M.: On the approximation of the discrete Karhunen-Loeve transform for stationary processes. Signal Process. **7**(3), 231–249 (1984)

22. Vaswani, N., Narayanamurthy, P.: Static and dynamic robust PCA and matrix completion: a review. Proc. IEEE **106**(8), 1359–1379 (2018)

23. Vetterli, M., Kovačević, J., Goyal, V.K.: Foundations of Signal Processing. Cambridge University Press (2014)

24. Zhao, D., Lin, Z., Tang, X.: Laplacian PCA and its applications. In: 2007 IEEE 11th International Conference on Computer Vision, pp. 1–8. IEEE (2007)

Quantified Boolean Solving
for Achievement Games

Steve Boucher and Roger Villemaire[(✉)]

Department of Computer Science, UQAM, Montreal, Canada
steve.boucher@live.ca, villemaire.roger@uqam.ca

Abstract. Recent developments in the propositional representation of achievement games have renewed interest in applying the latest advances in Quantified Boolean Formula technologies to solving these games. However, the number of quantifier alternations necessary to explore the solution space still impairs and limits the applicability of these methods. In this paper, we show that one can encode blocking strategies for the second player and express the last moves of the play with a single string of existential quantifiers, instead of the usual alternations of universal and existential quantifiers. We experimentally show that our method improves the performance of state-of-the-art Quantified Boolean Formula solvers on Harary's Tic-Tac-Toe, a well-known achievement game.

Keywords: Achievement game · Quantified Boolean formula · Winning strategy · Harary's Tic-Tac-Toe

1 Introduction

In an achievement game, also known as a positional game, two players take turns at adding a stone of their color on some board. The first player whose stones form a target *shape* wins the game. If no player achieves a target shape, the game is a *draw*. Tic-Tac-Toe, Gomoku, and Hex are the most well-known examples.

Typically, these games (in fact their generalizations to arbitrary board sizes) are PSPACE-complete. This is for instance the case for Gomoku [21] and Hex [20]. QBF, which ask whether a Quantified Boolean Formula is satisfied, or not, is the emblematic example of a PSPACE-complete problem [23]. It is therefore natural to apply QBF methods, developed in the wake of impressive advances in Propositional Satisfiability Testing (SAT) [1], to achievement games.

Games have also attracted the attention of theoreticians that have produced many involved combinatorial results [4]. In a way similar to the application of SAT solving to combinatorial problems, such as [14], it is hence also quite natural to apply QBF algorithms to the study of combinatorial games.

However, from a QBF perspective, the search for a winning strategy in a game gives rise to QBFs with many quantifier alternations, in stark contrast to most other application fields [22]. This is clearly a bottleneck, even if QBF game encodings have greatly improved recently [6,18].

S. Edelkamp et al. (Eds.): KI 2021, LNAI 12873, pp. 30–43, 2021.
https://doi.org/10.1007/978-3-030-87626-5_3

We present in this paper a QBF encoding for achievement games. We divert from the standard practice of encoding the existence of a winning strategy for the first player and rather search for a strategy for the second player that allows her to either win or get a draw. These two approaches are equivalent since the first player will win the game, if and only if, the second cannot win or get a draw. Moreover, we restrict the second player to follow, in the last steps of the game, a so-called pair paving strategy, which offers the benefit of being expressible with a string of existential quantifiers, instead of the usual alternation of universal and existential quantifiers.

With state-of-the-art QBF solvers, we evaluate our approach on Harary's Tic-Tac-Toe (HTTT), a game that has been extensively studied [3,12,13] and has also already been used to evaluate QBF game encodings [6,18]. We show that our encoding leads to efficient QBF solving for HTTT, and furthermore that it can be combined with conventional winning strategy encodings to further improve solving time by iterative deepening.

This paper is structured as follows. Section 2 recalls basic notions on QBF, Sect. 3 presents Harary's Tic-Tac-Toe, and Sect. 4 recalls related work on QBF encodings of games. Section 5 presents our encoding and Sect. 6 our experimental evaluation. Finally, Sect. 7 concludes the paper.

2   Quantified Boolean Formulas

We consider *Boolean variables*, i.e., variables that can take value 1 (*true*) or 0 (*false*). A *literal* is either a variable or its negation. A *clause* is a disjunction (OR) of literals and a formula in *Conjunctive Normal Form* (CNF) is a conjunction (AND) of clauses. A CNF is furthermore *satisfiable* if there is an assignment of values to its variables that makes the formula true under the usual Boolean operators' semantics.

A *Quantified Boolean Formula (in prenex CNF form)* (QBF), is a CNF (the QBF's *matrix*) preceded by universal ($\forall$) and existential ($\exists$) quantifiers on the Boolean variables. QBF semantics can be recursively defined on the number of quantifiers. However, there is an alternative approach that is more relevant to this paper. Namely, one can consider a QBF to be a game between two players, *existential* and *universal*. The play follows the quantifiers from left to right; the existential player choosing a value for existentially quantified variables and the universal player choosing a value for universal quantified variables. The play ends when all quantifiers have been processed. The existential player then *wins* the game if the chosen assignment satisfies the QBF's matrix, otherwise the universal player *wins* the game. A QBF is then *satisfied* if the existential player has a winning strategy, namely if the existential player can make choices (that depend on the universal player's previous moves) assuring him to win the game.

3   Harary's Tic-Tac-Toe

F. Harary [7,11] established the combinatorial analysis of achievement games by considering two players, usually called Black (first) and White (second), playing on an $N \times N$ square (regular) board with target shapes formed of the rotations and reflections of a *polyomino* (or *square animal*), which is an edge-connected set of cells. An animal for which the first player (Black) has a winning strategy is said to be a *winner*, otherwise it is a *loser*. A classic *strategy stealing* argument shows that there is in fact no winning strategy for White, since Black could play according to this strategy, by pretending that there is already some white stone on the board. So, when there is no winning strategy for Black, there is a *blocking* strategy for White that ensures a draw.

Fig. 1. Snaky   **Fig. 2.** Symmetry breaking

Harary has also established that 11 animals are winning when the board size is large enough and that all other animals, with a single exception, are losers. For these losers, he determined that White has a domino paving strategy, i.e., there is a partition of the board into 2-cells animals (dominoes), such that any target animal on the board contains at least one of these dominoes. White's blocking strategy is then simply to play on the second cell of the domino containing Black's previous move in order to block Black from winning the game.

For the unsettled case, that of *Snaky* (Fig. 1), Harary [7] conjectured that it is a winner, and furthermore that this should be the case for boards of size 15×15 and more, at least. This question, however, is still open.

As the last remaining case, it is not surprising that Snaky has attracted quite a lot of attention. For instance, Snaky has been shown to be a loser on 7×7 and 8×8 boards [10] by giving an explicit winning strategy for White that was found by a branch-and-cut algorithm that supplements a search for a blocking strategy for White, with a search for a paving of the board by pairs.

4   Related Work

Encodings of games have received some attention by the QBF research community. For instance, [9] gives a representation of the Connect-4 game in QBF. This encoding represents, with Boolean variables, the game configuration and move, in each turn, up to a maximum of k turns. Since there is a maximum number of possible turns (for a fixed board size), k is set to this value. A *gameover* variable, one in each turn, is also used to determine the first player that wins the game. Finally, existential (universal) quantifiers represent moves of the first (second) player and the QBF expresses the existence of a winning strategy for the first player. However, this paper establishes that there are some concerns as to how to encode the rules of the game.

Indeed, adding game rules as conjuncts to the QBF's matrix would allow the second player to break a rule, falsifying the formula, and win the game. Similarly, adding game rules to the matrix as hypothesis in an implication would allow the first player to break a rule, satisfying the formula, and win the game.

The paper's solution is to introduce so-called *cheat variables*. These are existentially quantified variables for which conjuncts assuring their equivalence with a specific *cheat* (breaking of a rule) by a specific player are added to the matrix. Conjuncts are then added to the matrix so that a cheat by some player makes the other player win.

Following [9], a QBF encoding for HTTT and GTTT(p, q), a generalization of HTTT allowing multiple stones to be laid in one move [5], is proposed in [6]. Experiments on 84 instances on a 3×3 board both normal and torus, and 96 instances on a 4×4 board, shows that all 3×3 instances can be solved in 10 s but that no combination of presented solvers and preprocessors allows to solve all 4×4 instances in 1000 s.

In [18] a general *corrective* encoding for achievement games is presented. The successive turns of the game are encoded, and a variable is used to determine when the game is over. However, contrary to [9] and [6], as soon as the game is over the board does not change anymore. This allows to check the winning condition solely in the last turn, strongly reducing the number of Boolean variables.

Another innovative aspect of this encoding is that universal variables represent White's (second player) choices in a binary encoding. Such a choice determines White's move at his turn, except if the game is already over, or if this choice is illegal (for instance if the position is already occupied). This allows a White's choice at every turn. The ladder encoding of [8] is furthermore used to ensure a single move of a player at her turn. This enforces a single move of White, even if his choice was illegal. All this prevents White from falsifying the formula, while keeping the total number of Boolean variables low.

The encoding is evaluated on 20 Hex hand-crafted puzzles and 96 instances of HTTT on a 4×4 board. It is shown that in terms of number of variables and clauses this encoding of HTTT is much more compact than that of [6] and solving time is much shorter. Furthermore, all 96 HTTT instances are solved within a timeout of 1000 s. The paper finally proposes five game challenges for the QBF community including achieving Snaky on a 9×9 board.

5   The Pairing Encoding

For an achievement game, we consider blocking strategies for the second player, i.e., ensuring either a win by this second player or a draw. There is a winning strategy for the first player exactly when there is no blocking strategy for the second player. Our QBF instances are hence satisfiable (SAT) exactly when the corresponding instance in one of the previous encodings is unsatisfiable (UNSAT). We furthermore restrict ourselves to the following pair paving blocking strategies.

A paving of the board by pairs, i.e., a partition of the board in pairs of distinct cells, such that any target shape contains at least one of those pairs, yields a so-called *pair paving blocking strategy* (for short a pair paving strategy) in the following way. The second player simply chooses the cell paired with the previous move of the first player. Since any target shape contains a pair, and hence a second player's stone, the first player does not win the game. Note that the existence of a pair paving simply necessitates a string of existential quantifiers, compared to an alternation of universal and existential quantifiers for a general strategy and should have a positive impact on QBF solving time.

While the existence of a pair paving strategy is enough to settle the game, its non-existence still leaves open the possibility that there could be some more involved blocking strategy for the second player. However, similarly to [10], it is possible to rather look for a pair paving strategy at *some* point of the game.

Our pairing encoding hence represents a play of the game where, at any point, the second player can stop the game and search for a pair paving of the remaining cells. Formally, the pairing encoding represents a game of length k, where the winning condition checks for a paving of the non-occupied cells by pairs of cells, such that any target shape, at any position, is *canceled*, i.e., contains either a second player's stone or a pair of the paving.

When k is the maximal play length, our winning condition reduces to checking that any target shape, at any position contains a second player's cell, i.e., that the first player has lost the game. So, with maximal play length k, our instances will be UNSAT if and only if the first player has a winning strategy. It hence solves the status of the game but in a complementary way to the usual encodings.

For HTTT this approach should work well with the losers for which Harary has shown the existence of a domino (hence pair) paving strategy. However, Harary's winners could be losers on the board sizes of our experimental section, and there is no known pair paving strategy in these cases. Finally, Harary's considered only regular boards, while we also experiment on torus boards that "wraps around" on board edges.

To simplify the presentation, we will present the encoding in HTTT's setting. The Pairing encoding follows the corrective encoding of [18] but for the fact that Black/White are universal/existential players, since we are encoding a blocking strategy, and the winning condition is the existence of a paving.

The encoding is parameterized by W, H, the width and height of the board, and k the number of turns. Time lapses $0, 1, \ldots, k$, the board being initialized at time 0 to contain no stones and moves occur at time points (turns) $1, \ldots, k$. A stone is added to the board at the same time point as the move occurs. Black hence plays at turns $1, 3, \ldots$, and White at turns $2, 4, \ldots$. There are WH cells on the board, and we index pairs of cells by $id = 1, \ldots, WH(WH-1)/2$. Similarly, we index target shapes $i = 1, 2, \ldots$.

The variables representing the game, and their intended meaning, are defined as follows.

$$time_t; \text{ the game is running at time point } t \tag{1}$$

$$moveL_{t,j}; \ j-\text{th digit of the binary encoding of Black's move choices} \tag{2}$$

$$move_{t,x,y}; \text{ a stone is laid on cell } (x,y) \text{ at time point } t \tag{3}$$

$$ladder_{t,m}; \text{ ladder encoding for Black's moves (explained below)} \tag{4}$$

$$black_{t,x,y}; \text{ there is a black stone on cell } (x,y) \text{ at time point } t \tag{5}$$

$$white_{t,x,y}; \text{ there is a white stone on cell } (x,y) \text{ at time point } t \tag{6}$$

$$occupied_{t,x,y}; \text{ cell } (x,y) \text{ is occupied at time point } t \tag{7}$$

$$pair_{id}; \text{ the pair } id \text{ is in the paving} \tag{8}$$

$$canceled_{i,x,y}; \text{ shape } i \text{ at position } (x,y) \text{ is canceled} \tag{9}$$

Quantifier blocks appear in turn order as follows. In turn $t = 0$,

$$\exists time_0 \tag{10}$$

for $t = 1, \ldots, k$,

$$\exists time_t \tag{11}$$

$$\forall moveL_{t,j}; \text{ in Black's turns } t = 1, 3, \ldots, \tag{12}$$

$$\exists move_{t,x,y} \exists ladder_{t,m} \exists black_{t,x,y} \exists white_{t,x,y} \exists occupied_{t,x,y} \tag{13}$$

and as last quantifier block

$$\exists pair_{id} \exists canceled_{i,x,y} \tag{14}$$

The constraints are as follows, where $t = 1, \ldots, k$, $x = 1, \ldots, W$, and $y = 1, \ldots, H$.

If the game is still running at time t, it was running at time $t - 1$.

$$time_{t-1} \vee \neg time_t \tag{15}$$

There is no stone on the board at time $t = 0$.

$$\neg black_{0,x,y} \wedge \neg white_{0,x,y} \wedge \neg occupied_{0,x,y} \tag{16}$$

Both players cannot own the same cell.

$$\neg black_{t,x,y} \vee \neg white_{t,x,y} \tag{17}$$

A stone on a cell remains there at the next turn.

$$(\neg black_{t-1,x,y} \vee black_{t,x,y}) \wedge (\neg white_{t-1,x,y} \vee white_{t,x,y}) \tag{18}$$

When the game is over, no new stones appear on the board.

$$(time_t \vee black_{t-1,x,y} \vee \neg black_{t,x,y}) \wedge (time_t \vee white_{t-1,x,y} \vee \neg white_{t,x,y}) \tag{19}$$

If a cell is played, then it is occupied.

$$(\neg black_{t,x,y} \lor occupied_{t,x,y}) \land (\neg white_{t,x,y} \lor occupied_{t,x,y}) \tag{20}$$

If a cell is occupied, then it is black or white.

$$\neg occupied_{t,x,y} \lor black_{t,x,y} \lor white_{t,x,y} \tag{21}$$

When the game is over, no more moves are allowed.

$$time_t \lor \neg move_{t,x,y} \tag{22}$$

The move is not allowed if the cell is already occupied.

$$\neg occupied_{t-1,x,y} \lor \neg move_{t,x,y} \tag{23}$$

A move sets a stone. Here *player* is either *black* when the turn t is odd or *white* if it is even ($t > 0$).

$$\neg move_{t,x,y} \lor player_{t,x,y} \tag{24}$$

The universal player, Black, makes a move choice, specified by the $moveL_{t,j}$ bits assignation and the $move_{t,x,y}$ variables are set accordingly. More precisely, each cell choice (x, y) is encoded by a string of bits $[x, y]$ of length $\lceil \log_2(WH) \rceil$. We will denote by $[(x, y)]_0$ the set of i's for which the i-th bit in this string is 0 and by $[(x, y)]_1$ the set of i's for which it is 1.

We therefore have, for Black's turns, $t = 1, 3, \ldots$, that if the game is not over and the cell (x, y) not occupied at the previous turn, a choice of (x, y) (by the $moveL$ variables) performs a move on (x, y) (*move* variables).

$$\neg time_t \lor occupied_{t-1,x,y} \lor$$
$$\bigvee_{j \in [x,y]_0} moveL_{t,j} \lor \bigvee_{j \in [x,y]_1} \neg moveL_{t,j} \lor move_{t,x,y} \tag{25}$$

By symmetry under rotations, it is sufficient to consider the case where the first player (Black) plays on the lower left quarter in her first turn, and by reflection (on the diagonal, see Fig. 2) this can be further reduced to the lower left triangle of the square board. When generating clauses (25), for the first move of the first player, only choices of moves in this triangle is hence considered.

For $player, other \in \{white, black\}$, $player$ being the color of turn t's player and $other$ the color of the other player, we have that a player's stone that was not placed at this turn, was already there at the previous turn. Similarly, the other player's stones were already there at the previous turn.

$$(move_{t,x,y} \lor player_{t-1,x,y} \lor \neg player_{t,x,y}) \land (other_{t-1,x,y} \lor \neg other_{t,x,y}) \tag{26}$$

In order to ensure that, at each turn where the game is still running, a single move is done, the corrective encoding [18] uses the ladder encoding of [8]. There are hence $ladder_{t,m}$ variables, one for each possible move m. To ensure that a single move is done, the move m is determined from the position of the "shift", from 0 to 1, in the ladder variables. Here, to ease the presentation, the moves (or equivalently the ladder variables for a turn) are considered ordered, in some arbitrary way. The key point is that to ensure a unique shift, the last ladder variable is set to true, and the ladder variables are constrained to be increasing.

More precisely, we have the following constraints.

Ladder variables are increasing and when the game is running, the last ladder variable is true.

$$(\neg ladder_{t,m} \vee ladder_{t,m+1}) \wedge (\neg time_t \vee ladder_{t,last}) \tag{27}$$

When the "shift" in the ladder variables occurs, this determines the move. Therefore, for the first move $m = first$ in the ladder encoding order, if the variable $ladder_{t,first} = 1$, then move m is done. For a move m different from the first, if $ladder_{t,m-1} = 0$ and $ladder_{t,m} = 1$, then move m is done. Here (x, y) is the destination of move m.

$$(\neg ladder_{t,first} \vee move_{t,x,y}) \wedge (ladder_{t,m-1} \vee \neg ladder_{t,m} \vee move_{t,x,y}) \tag{28}$$

Conversely, if a move is done, the "shift" in the ladder encoding occurs at that move. Therefore, if the move m to (x, y) is done, then $ladder_{t,m} = 1$ and, but for the first move, $ladder_{t,m-1} = 0$.

$$(\neg move_{t,x,y} \vee ladder_{t,m}) \wedge (\neg move_{t,x,y} \vee \neg ladder_{t,m-1}) \tag{29}$$

We finally add our winning pair paving condition.

We first have to ensure that if a pair of cells is in the paving, then no cell of this pair is occupied. Hence, for a pair of cells id and (x, y) one of its cells, we have the following constraint.

$$\neg pair_{id} \vee \neg occupied_{k,x,y} \tag{30}$$

Furthermore, no two pairs of the paving have a common cell. Therefore, for distinct pairs $id1, id2$ with a common cell we have the following clause.

$$\neg pair_{id1} \vee \neg pair_{id2} \tag{31}$$

Also, if a pair is in the paving, it cancels any shape containing it. We therefore have, for all pairs id contained in shape i at position (x, y), the following clause.

$$\neg pair_{id} \vee canceled_{i,x,y} \tag{32}$$

Furthermore, if the cell contains a white stone, then a target shape at some position that contains this cell is canceled. We hence have, for all cells (x', y') contained in shape i at position (x, y), the following clause.

$$\neg white_{k,x',y'} \vee canceled_{i,x,y} \tag{33}$$

Conversely, if a target shape at some position is canceled, then either one of its cells contains a white stone or it contains some pair. We therefore have, for target shape i at position (x, y), $\mathcal{C}$ its set of cells and $\mathcal{P}$ the set of pairs contained in this shape at this position, the following clause.

$$\neg canceled_{i,x,y} \vee \bigvee_{(x',y') \in \mathcal{C}} white_{k,x',y'} \vee \bigvee_{id \in \mathcal{P}} pair_{id} \tag{34}$$

Finally, any shape i at any position (x, y), is canceled.

$$canceled_{i,x,y} \tag{35}$$

6   Experimental Results

All experiments are run on a 2 CPU X5570 Xeon Processor, 2.93 GHz, 64 GB Memory, with a timeout of 1000 s. We consider HTTT instances for polyominoes formed by at most 6 cells that fit on the board, and this both for normal and torus boards. We hence have 48 instances on 3×3, 98 instances on 4×4, and 110 instances on 5×5 boards. We also show some results about the Snaky polyomino. We used the following QBF solvers versions: DepQBF v6.03 [16], CAQE v4.0.1 [24], Qute v1.1 [19], QESTO v1.0 [15], and four preprocessors (including none): QRATPre+ v2.0 [17], HQSPre v1.4 [26], and bloqqer v37 [2]. Every system is used with default command line parameters.

Table 1. 3×3 solving time in seconds with and without preprocessor

Solver	Preprocessor	DYS	COR	Pairing
DepQBF	None	**12.85**	**1.12**	**0.77**
QESTO	None	3171.66	9.21	3.00
DepQBF	QRATPre+	7.97	**0.85**	**0.32**
QESTO	bloqqer	**3.47**	1.65	1.69

On 3×3 boards we compare the DYS encoding of [6], the corrective encoding COR [18] and our own Pairing encoding. We show in Table 1 the best solver, with no processor, and the best pair (solver/preprocessor) on 3×3 boards. There was no timeout in this case and there are exactly 8 winners and 40 losers. In all cases, both with and without preprocessor, the Pairing encoding allows the shortest solving time. Furthermore, confirming the results of [18], the DYS encoding is largely less efficient. For boards of size 4×4 and more, we hence concentrate on the COR and Pairing encodings.

On a 4×4 board (Table 2), a striking observation is that, in all cases, the Pairing encoding is more than two orders of magnitude faster than the COR encoding, with no timeouts. Preprocessing time (Table 3) is also much shorter for bloqqer and QRATPre+ than for HQSPre, but still, it is, for these two preprocessors, comparable to solving time for the Pairing encoding.

Table 2. 4×4 solving time in seconds, numbers of Unknowns, Winners, Losers

Solver	Preprocessor	COR				Pairing			
		Time	U	W	L	Time	U	W	L
DepQBF	None	**17159.72**	**7**	14	77	**114.63**	**0**	14	84
DepQBF	bloqqer	**12949.31**	5	14	79	93.35	0	14	84
DepQBF	QRATPre+	14176.01	5	14	79	**61.31**	**0**	14	84

It is also interesting to compare COR and Pairing in terms of instances size. We show in Table 4 total number of literals, clauses, and quantifiers over all shapes for normal and torus boards. While numbers of quantifiers are similar for both encodings, Pairing generates more literals and clauses, in particular for torus boards.

Table 3. 4×4 preprocessing time in seconds

	COR			Pairing		
	Bloqqer	HQSPre	QRATPre+	Bloqqer	HQSPre	QRATPre+
Avg.	1.78	27.98	0.10	1.87	8.99	0.38
Max.	2.11	65.39	0.20	2.25	40.95	0.71
Total	174.03	2742.51	9.65	183.30	881.19	37.31

On 5×5 boards we tested only the solver and solver/preprocessors pairs that gave the best performance on 4×4 boards (as shown in Table 2). We see, in Table 5, that COR solves only 7 out of 110 instances, while Pairing solves 72 (70 with no preprocessor). As for run time, Pairing needs less than half the time required by COR. Pairing hence again clearly outperforms COR.

Table 4. Total number of literals, clauses, and quantifiers on 4×4 boards

	COR				Pairing			
	Lits.	Clauses	Univ.	Exist.	Lits.	Clauses	Univ.	Exist.
Normal	554629	227944	1568	66850	675390	285428	1568	70682
Torus	637683	253794	1568	70241	950037	388083	1568	75329

Run time increases rapidly with play length k and solving the game necessitates a $k = 25$ on a 5×5 board, while $k = 9$ and $k = 16$ suffice for 3×3 and 4×4

boards, respectively. It could hence be appropriate to apply iterative deepening that could establish a winning strategy for a smaller value of k. However, we go a step further and combine the corrective encoding of [18] that searches for a winning strategy for Black and our encoding that search for a blocking strategy for White. This allows to establish, as soon as either return a SAT instance, the status (winner/loser) of the polyomino.

Table 6 shows the cumulative time of solving instances for increasing values $k = 0, 1, 2, \ldots, 25$ using the Pairing encoding for even k and the COR encoding for odd k, stopping at the first SAT instance.

Table 5. 5×5 solving time in seconds, numbers of Unknowns, Winners, Losers

Solver	Preprocessor	COR				Pairing			
		Time	U	W	L	Time	U	W	L
DepQBF	None	**103083.14**	**103**	7	0	41365.22	40	10	60
DepQBF	bloqqer	103213.42	103	7	0	**38901.20**	**38**	10	62
DepQBF	QRATPre+	103114.56	103	7	0	39393.55	38	10	62

Comparing Tables 5 and 6, one sees that iterative deepening combining COR and Pairing is indeed effective. It, in fact, reduces the total number of timeouts and solving time almost by one half, compared to Pairing that gives the best results in Table 5.

Table 6. 5×5 iterative deepening solving time in seconds, numbers of Unknowns, Winners, Losers

Solver	Preprocessor	Normal				Torus			
		Cum. time	U	W	L	Cum. time	U	W	L
DepQBF	None	1023.71	1	7	47	21376.28	21	7	27
DepQBF	bloqqer	1016.29	1	7	47	21012.67	20	7	28
DepQBF	QRATPre+	1015.34	1	7	47	21310.61	20	7	28

Table 6 further shows that there is a stark difference between normal and torus boards. Another surprising fact on 5×5 instances is that preprocessors yield very small performance gain, both in terms of solving time than in terms of number of solved shapes. This is in stark contrast to 4×4 and 3×3 boards.

It is instructive to look at the distribution of the last considered k with this iterative deepening method on 5×5 boards. Figure 3 shows, for each $k = 0, \ldots, 11$, the number of polyominoes for which the first SAT instance (or timeout) is reached for this value of k. Note that there are polyominoes settled at each intermediate value of k, both even and odd. It follows that neither even nor

Table 7. Snaky pairing

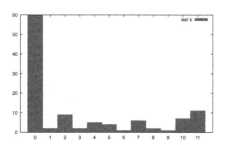

Fig. 3. Last k, DepQBF

Board	k	Result	Time
6 × 6	0	UNSAT	1.53
	2	SAT	17.53
7 × 7	0	UNSAT	0.81
	2	UNSAT	345.64
	4	SAT	2277.39
8 × 8	0	UNSAT	0.79
	2	UNSAT	1857.64
	4	UNSAT	10596.75
	6	UNSAT	120004.47

odd k's can be avoided and both COR and Pairing are instrumental in making this method effective.

Obviously, the big open question around HTTT is the status of Snaky on a 9×9 board, and as stated by [18] this is a challenge to the QBF community. It is hence interesting to see how the Pairing encoding fares with this polyomino. However, as shown in Table 7 that shows solving time in seconds for DepQBF on normal boards, the loser status of Snaky on an 8×8 board [10] is already out of reach of our Pairing encoding. Solving Snaky on a 9×9 board will hence need further advances in QBF solving and encoding.

7   Conclusion

We showed that the QBF Pairing encoding leads to very effective QBF solving for HTTT on 3×3 and 4×4 boards. Furthermore, iterative deepening combining the COR and Pairing encodings can solve HTTT on 5×5 boards for most target shapes. However, determining shapes on a 5×5 torus board often necessitates higher values of k, and would require further development in QBF game solving.

On a methodological level our contribution is to draw attention to the effectiveness, in the QBF solving setting of achievement games, of considering "dual" encodings with blocking strategies, and furthermore restricting the kind of blocking strategy sought.

Indeed, while describing in QBF the existence of a winning strategy for the first player is the natural approach, one can equivalently encode the existence of a blocking strategy by the second player. This is reminiscent of the use of primal and dual encodings [25] that have been shown to both have their advantages in the QBF analysis of synchronous system.

Furthermore, in order to show the existence of a winning strategy, one can as well show the existence of some specific kind of strategy, as this could lead to further performance gain, as is the case with the Pairing encoding for HTTT.

While our results advance the QBF solving of achievement games, it still come short of solving Snaky's status on a 9×9 board. This will need further advances in QBF solving, where "dual" encodings and restricting the kind of sought strategy could play a role.

References

1. Biere, A., Heule, M., van Maaren, H., Walsh, T. (eds.): Handbook of Satisfiability, Frontiers in Artificial Intelligence and Applications, vol. 185. IOS Press (2009)
2. Biere, A., Lonsing, F., Seidl, M.: Blocked clause elimination for QBF. In: Bjørner, N., Sofronie-Stokkermans, V. (eds.) CADE 2011. LNCS (LNAI), vol. 6803, pp. 101–115. Springer, Heidelberg (2011). https://doi.org/10.1007/978-3-642-22438-6_10
3. Csernenszky, A., Martin, R.R., Pluhár, A.: On the complexity of chooser-picker positional games. INTEGERS: Electron. J. Comb. Number Theory **11**(G2) (2011)
4. Demaine, E.D., Hearn, R.A.: Playing games with algorithms: algorithmic combinatorial game theory, pp. 3–56. Mathematical Sciences Research Institute Publications, Cambridge University Press (2009)
5. Diptarama, Narisawa, K., Shinohara, A.: Drawing strategies for generalized Tic-Tac-Toe (p, q). In: AIP Conference Proceedings, vol. 1705, no. 1, 020021 (2016)
6. Diptarama, Yoshinaka, R., Shinohara, A.: QBF encoding of generalized Tic-Tac-Toe. In: Quantified Boolean Formulas, QBF 2016. CEUR Workshop Proceedings, vol. 1719, pp. 14–26 (2016)
7. Gardner, M.: Mathematical games. Sci. Am. **240**(4), 18–28 (1979)
8. Gent, I., Nightingale, P.: A new encoding of all different into SAT. In: Modelling and Reformulating Constraint Satisfaction Problems, pp. 95–110 (2004)
9. Gent, I., Rowley, A.R.: Encoding Connect-4 using quantified Boolean formulae. In: Modelling and Reformulating Constraint Satisfaction Problems, pp. 78–93 (2003)
10. Halupczok, I., Schlage-Puchta, J.C.: Achieving snaky. INTEGERS: Electron. J. Comb. Number Theory **7**(G02) (2007)
11. Harary, F.: Achieving the Skinny animal. Eureka **42**, 8–14 (1982)
12. Harborth, H., Seemann, M.: Snaky is an edge-to-edge loser. Geombinatorics **V**(4), 132–136 (1996)
13. Harborth, H., Seemann, M.: Snaky is a paving winner. Bull. Inst. Combin. Appl. **19**, 71–78 (1997)
14. Heule, M.J.H., Szeider, S.: A SAT approach to clique-width. ACM Trans. Comput. Log. **16**(3), 24 (2015)
15. Janota, M., Marques-Silva, J.: Solving QBF by clause selection. In: International Joint Conference on Artificial Intelligence, IJCAI, pp. 325–331. AAAI Press (2015)
16. Lonsing, F., Egly, U.: DepQBF 6.0: a search-based QBF solver beyond traditional QCDCL. In: de Moura, L. (ed.) CADE 2017. LNCS (LNAI), vol. 10395, pp. 371–384. Springer, Cham (2017). https://doi.org/10.1007/978-3-319-63046-5_23
17. Lonsing, F., Egly, U.: QRATPre+: effective QBF preprocessing via strong redundancy properties. In: Janota, M., Lynce, I. (eds.) SAT 2019. LNCS, vol. 11628, pp. 203–210. Springer, Cham (2019). https://doi.org/10.1007/978-3-030-24258-9_14
18. Mayer-Eichberger, V., Saffidine, A.: Positional games and QBF: the *Corrective* encoding. In: Pulina, L., Seidl, M. (eds.) SAT 2020. LNCS, vol. 12178, pp. 447–463. Springer, Cham (2020). https://doi.org/10.1007/978-3-030-51825-7_31
19. Peitl, T., Slivovsky, F., Szeider, S.: Qute in the QBF evaluation 2018. J. Satisfiability Boolean Model. Comput. **11**(1), 261–272 (2019)

20. Reisch, S.: Hex ist PSPACE-vollständig (Hex is PSPACE-complete). Acta Informatica **15**, 167–191 (1981)
21. Reisch, S.: Gobang ist PSPACE-vollständig (Gomoku is PSPACE-complete). Acta Informatica **13**, 59–66 (1980)
22. Shukla, A., Biere, A., Pulina, L., Seidl, M.: A survey on applications of Quantified Boolean Formulas. In: International Conference on Tools with Artificial Intelligence, ICTAI 2019, pp. 78–84. IEEE (2019)
23. Stockmeyer, L.J., Meyer, A.R.: Word problems requiring exponential time: preliminary report. In: ACM Symposium on Theory of Computing (STOC), pp. 1–9. ACM (1973)
24. Tentrup, L.: CAQE and QuAbS: abstraction based QBF solvers. J. Satisfiability Boolean Model. Comput. **11**(1), 155–210 (2019)
25. Gelder, A.: Primal and dual encoding from applications into quantified Boolean formulas. In: Schulte, C. (ed.) CP 2013. LNCS, vol. 8124, pp. 694–707. Springer, Heidelberg (2013). https://doi.org/10.1007/978-3-642-40627-0_51
26. Wimmer, R., Reimer, S., Marin, P., Becker, B.: HQSpre – an effective preprocessor for QBF and DQBF. In: Legay, A., Margaria, T. (eds.) TACAS 2017. LNCS, vol. 10205, pp. 373–390. Springer, Heidelberg (2017). https://doi.org/10.1007/978-3-662-54577-5_21

Knowledge Graph Based Question Answering System for Financial Securities

Marius Bulla[1]([⊠])(iD), Lars Hillebrand[1,2]([⊠])(iD), Max Lübbering[1,2]([⊠])(iD), and Rafet Sifa[2]([⊠])

[1] Department of Computer Science, University of Bonn, 53113 Bonn, Germany
mbulla@uni-bonn.de
[2] Fraunhofer IAIS, 53757 Sankt Augustin, Germany
{lars.patrick.hillebrand,max.luebbering,rafet.sifa}@iais.fraunhofer.de

Abstract. Knowledge graphs offer a powerful framework to structure and represent financial information in a flexible way by describing real world entities, such as financial securities, and their interrelations in the form of a graph. Semantic question answering systems allow to retrieve information from a knowledge graph using natural language questions and thus eliminate the need to be proficient in a formal query language. In this work, we present a proof-of-concept design for a financial knowledge graph and with it a semantic question answering framework specifically targeted for the finance domain. Our implemented approach uses a span-based joint entity and relation extraction model with BERT embeddings to translate a single-fact natural language question into its corresponding formal query representation. By employing a joint extraction model, we alleviate the concern of error propagation present in standard pipelined approaches for classification-based question answering. The presented framework is tested on a synthetic dataset derived from the instances of the implemented financial knowledge graph. Our empirical findings indicate very promising results with a F1-score of 84.60% for relation classification and 97.18% for entity detection.

Keywords: Question answering · Knowledge graphs · Finance

1 Introduction

Information plays a crucial role in the pricing of financial securities. The linkage between financial securities and information is one of the fundamental concepts in finance postulated in the efficient-market hypothesis [7]. Leveraging informational insights is thus highly significant for investment decisions and can potentially translate into financial gains. Data about securities are usually plentiful and available to all market participants. Hence, the main problem is not to obtain data but rather to filter and extract relevant information from a vast heterogeneous pool of unstructured data. Knowledge graphs provide a flexible and intuitive architecture to structure this data. Information is modeled in the

© Springer Nature Switzerland AG 2021
S. Edelkamp et al. (Eds.): KI 2021, LNAI 12873, pp. 44–50, 2021.
https://doi.org/10.1007/978-3-030-87626-5_4

form of triple statements where two resources, i.e. things or concepts, are linked with a predicate describing their relationship, forming a directed graph. Allowing each resource to be linked to any other resource results in a graph-like network which gives this database its name. Semantic schemes comprised of logic based taxonomies and vocabularies as well as other types of metadata allow to enrich these statements with extensive information. Retrieving information stored in a knowledge graph requires proficiency in a formal query language with a well-defined syntax. Semantic question answering systems eliminate this technical barrier by allowing users to retrieve information asking questions in natural language. Single-fact based questions are the most common type of questions for knowledge graph based question answering. These type of questions comprise exactly one triple statement and thus exhibit a fixed logical form structure. Followingly, question-answering can be modeled as a classification problem where the objective is to predict the missing triple element given the subject entity and predicate extracted from the input question.

Neural network based approaches for single-fact based question answering [5,10–12] typically follow a pipelined process. First, an entity detection model filters all candidate entities from the input question. The relation extraction task then tries to identify relations between these entities. Systems following this procedure already achieve state-of-the-art performance [4]. Recently models have emerged that simultaneously process both the entity recognition and the relation classification task [1,2,8,9]. Although these models are not specifically designed for question answering, they are able to overcome the concern of error propagation present in the decomposed approach for question answering. That is, an erroneous entity classification may also lead to a misclassification of the relation. Joint extraction models are thus potentially useful for semantic question answering. In addition to that, there has been a transition from a sequence-based entity tagging approach to a span-based approach [6,14] which allows to identify overlapping entities by carrying out exhaustive searches over all spans in the input token sequence.

In this paper, we introduce a proof-of-concept design for a financial knowledge graph where single-fact based questions can be queried using natural language. The question-answering framework presents a novel approach for tackling the semantic parsing problem, i.e. the translation of a natural language utterance into a formal query representation, using a span-based joint entity and relation extraction model with BERT embeddings.

2   Framework

The internal work flow of the application including an example is demonstrated in Fig. 1. The following Sect. 2.1 first describes the design of the implemented financial knowledge graph before Sect. 2.2 outlines the semantic question answering system.

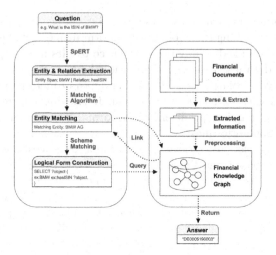

Fig. 1. Illustration of the internal flow of the semantic question answering system.

2.1   Knowledge Graph Construction

The primary data basis for the financial knowledge graph is comprised of disclosure documents for financial securities - also known under the term security prospectuses. These documents offer substantial insights into a security including basic information about the security as well as detailed information about the issuing entity such as projected earnings, investments, liabilities and risks. The knowledge base of the graph is comprised of 56 financial prospectuses. Each of these documents contain manually annotated information including up to 52 predicates and corresponding object properties. In order to extract the information from the financial documents and store it in a semantic graph database, each financial document needs to be processed with the subtasks outlined in the following paragraphs. The aggregation of the processed financial prospectuses then constitutes the financial knowledge graph.

Preprocessing. Firstly, the input PDF files are parsed using an off-the-shelf optical character recognition model. All annotations including predicate type and the corresponding object value are then extracted from each parsed document. The data is first preprocessed before represented in the triple format to improve overall data quality and to enrich it with valuable metadata. Moreover, it enhances the answer representation and enables the use of boolean and mathematical operators in queries. The preprocessing procedure includes the mapping and potential standardization of each object value to its corresponding data type for string, boolean, date, period or decimal values. Categorization is applied to object properties with a finite set of possible properties, e.g. accounting standard of a company. A matching algorithm is applied to find a potential match of the processed information with one of the instances of the pre-defined finite candidate space. In addition to that, a sequence matcher is used for annotations with certain patterns, e.g. for the International Securities Identification Number (ISIN) to further increase data quality.

Linking. One of the key features of knowledge graphs is the interoperability with other knowledge sources. Whenever the same resource is present in more than one knowledge graph, information about the resource can be interlinked. This allows to enrich a knowledge graph with further information about a resource using already existing well-structured information from a different knowledge graph. For this application, resources were linked to the Wikidata Knowledge Graph [13], which constitutes the largest freely available accumulation of structured information on the web. In order to match a resource with its potential counterpart in the Wikidata Knowledge Graph, all Wikidata entries corresponding to the statement first need to be queried using a Wikidata SPARQL endpoint. The query output needs to include the identifier, official name, and optimally, alternative names for the resource to improve matching chances. The returned list constitutes the candidate space of potential matches for the resources in the processed documents. A matching algorithm based on the Levenshtein distance is implemented. In a first attempt, the algorithm tries to find an identical match between the object value of the statement and the Wikidata query result. In the case that no perfect match has been found, an approximate fuzzy string matching algorithm in combination with a lower bound threshold is implemented. This is iterated over the entire candidate space. Given the threshold is exceeded, the best candidate is then linked to the Wikidata resource.

Serializing. Lastly, the preprocessed and linked information must be parsed into statements corresponding to the previously outlined triple structure. The N-Triples format is used as serialization format due to its high performance with large datasets. Before the statements can be serialized, all entities and predicates first need to be mapped into their uniform resource identifier representation. This procedure follows a simple dictionary approach. The ontology mainly used for this knowledge graph is the Financial Industry Business Ontology (FIBO) outlined in [3].

2.2   Semantic Question Answering System

The semantic question answering framework illustrated on the left-hand side of Fig. 1 can be structured into three modules: (i) joint entity and relation extraction using SpERT, (ii) entity linking with a matching algorithm based on string similarity, and (iii) logical form construction followed by query execution and answer representation.

(i) Entity and Relation Extraction. The distinctive feature of the SpERT model outlined in [6] is its capability to extract entities and relations simultaneously. Initially it was designed to capture entities and relations within statements rather than questions. The underlying premise of the model is that a relation occurs within a span between two entities. However, defining question-, command- or

request words as entity types makes it possible to apply this model in the context of question answering. The workflow of this model can be divided into three steps. Firstly, the input question is tokenized and passed through a pre-trained BERT model. In the second step, each span s among the set of all possible token subsequences $\mathcal{S}$ is classified into an entity type including none to detect all entities within the question. The entity space $\mathcal{E}$ encompasses the types *company*, *interrogative word* (including question words, commands and requests), as well as a *count*, *aggregate* and *arg min/max* operator. A softmax function is applied to represent the output as a probability distribution over the set of pre-defined entity types $\mathcal{E}$ yielding

$$\hat{\boldsymbol{y}}^s = \text{softmax}(\boldsymbol{W}^s \cdot \boldsymbol{x}^s + \boldsymbol{b}^s) \tag{1}$$

where $\boldsymbol{x}^s$ denotes the concatenation of a max-pooling fusion function over s with a prior over the span length $\boldsymbol{w}$ as well as a context token obtained through the BERT embeddings. All spans that do not contain an entity are removed resulting in a set of spans $\mathcal{S}$ presumably only containing entities. Lastly, after all entity candidates are detected, the corresponding relation within the question can be determined. A relation classifier aims to predict the correct relation r from the set of all pre-defined relations $\mathcal{R}$ for each candidate span pair $(s_1, s_2) \in \mathcal{S}$. The relation candidate space is comprised of the 52 predicates present in the financial knowledge graph. In general, relations are not symmetric. Followingly, it is necessary to classify both (s_1, s_2) and (s_2, s_1). The softmax function

$$\hat{\boldsymbol{y}}^{1/2} := \sigma(\boldsymbol{W}^r \cdot \boldsymbol{x}^r_{1/2} + \boldsymbol{b}^r) \tag{2}$$

is applied where σ represents a sigmoid function of size $\mathcal{R}$. Here, $\boldsymbol{x}^r_{1/2}$ denote the concatenation of any two candidate entity span embeddings with a context token $\boldsymbol{c}(\boldsymbol{s_1}, \boldsymbol{s_2})$ which only considers the span of tokens between the two candidate entities. A relation is assumed to hold whenever the sigmoid passes a pre-defined threshold α. The learnable parameters of the model for the entity and relation classification task are represented by $\boldsymbol{W}^s, \boldsymbol{b}^s, \boldsymbol{w}$ and $\boldsymbol{W}^r, \boldsymbol{b}^r$. In order to find the optimal parameter values for the SpERT model, a joint loss function is used where a cross-entropy loss criterion for entity classification and a binary cross-entropy criterion for relation classification are averaged over the samples of each batch. The span classifier uses all labeled entities from an example sentence as positive examples. In addition to that, it uses a fixed number of randomly chosen spans not containing an entity as negative examples. Similarly, the relation classifier takes all relations mentioned in a sentence as positive examples but also generates negative examples between any two entity pairs without a relation.

(ii) Entity Matching. After the model predicts the entity span, it is necessary to match the extracted entity to its counterpart in the knowledge graph. The matching criteria is based on the Levenshtein distance. The candidate space consists of all entity names and alternative labels present in the financial knowledge graph and queried from the Wikidata Knowledge Graph. The string sequence in

the detected entity span is compared to all these entries. Given that a predefined threshold is exceeded, the algorithm returns the best match.

(iii) Logical Form Construction. The last step of the KGQA system requires to arrange the extracted and linked entities, relations and operators in the proper order so that the resulting query returns the correct answer. This becomes straightforward for single-fact based questions as this type of question always exhibits a fixed structure. Hence, the previously extracted relation and subject entity only need to be filled into this fixed structure.

3   Experiments

Dataset. In the absence of a suitable training dataset for the model outlined in Sect. 2.2, artificial questions were generated. These questions contain annotated relations and entities extracted from the financial knowledge graph. The entity space consists of two types: (1) companies and (2) interrogative words which include so-called "wh" question words (*what, when, where, which, who, why, whom, whose*), indirect requests and commands. Generally, questions follow a certain syntactical pattern. That is, a question word, request or command is followed by a relation and the corresponding entity. The questions in the dataset are thus created combining both entity types with one instance of the relation entity space and fill-words such as "the", "is" or "of" to make the questions appear more natural. In order to force the model to learn more difficult representations, these parts are also permutated. That is, the order of both entity types and the relation is randomized. This results in a dataset consisting of 213,840 questions.

Evaluation. The framework performs particularly well with classifying the correct entity spans including the corresponding entity type within the question context. It shows a F1-score of 97.18% for macro-averaged and 98.22% for micro-averaged values. This is expected and can potentially be attributed to the fixed structure of questions, their relatively short length and the occurrence of certain patterns within company names. Moreover, the system also performs relatively well for the relation classification task in the question setting even though the size of the relation candidate space is significantly larger than in [6]. The macro-averaged F1-score exhibits a value of 84.60% while the micro-averaged score is slightly smaller with 83.40%.

4   Conclusion

For the lack of a suitable training dataset, a synthetic dataset comprising questions and commands was generated and specifically adjusted for the implemented financial knowledge graph. Due to the design of the joint entity and relation extraction module, the evaluation of common benchmark question and answer datasets is prohibitively costly. Even though this limits comparability with other approaches to semantic question answering, the model performs considerably well for its designated purpose, i.e. the introduced financial knowledge graph.

In future work, the investigation of alternative approaches to string based matching such as graph neural network based embeddings should be explored to further improve the system.

References

1. Bekoulis, G., Deleu, J., Demeester, T., Develder, C.: Adversarial training for multi-context joint entity and relation extraction. arXiv preprint arXiv:1808.06876 (2018)
2. Bekoulis, G., Deleu, J., Demeester, T., Develder, C.: Joint entity recognition and relation extraction as a multi-head selection problem. Expert Syst. Appl. **114**, 34–45 (2018)
3. Bennett, M.: The financial industry business ontology: best practice for big data. J. Bank. Regul. **14**(3), 255–268 (2013)
4. Chakraborty, N., Lukovnikov, D., Maheshwari, G., Trivedi, P., Lehmann, J., Fischer, A.: Introduction to neural network based approaches for question answering over knowledge graphs. arXiv preprint arXiv:1907.09361 (2019)
5. Chen, D., Manning, C.D.: A fast and accurate dependency parser using neural networks. In: Proceedings of the 2014 Conference on Empirical Methods in Natural Language Processing (EMNLP), pp. 740–750 (2014)
6. Eberts, M., Ulges, A.: Span-based joint entity and relation extraction with transformer pre-training. In: 24th European Conference on Artificial Intelligence (2020)
7. Fama, E.F.: Efficient market hypothesis. Dissertation, Ph.D. thesis, Ph.D. dissertation (1960)
8. Gupta, P., Schütze, H., Andrassy, B.: Table filling multi-task recurrent neural network for joint entity and relation extraction. In: Proceedings of COLING 2016, the 26th International Conference on Computational Linguistics: Technical Papers, pp. 2537–2547 (2016)
9. Li, F., Zhang, M., Fu, G., Ji, D.: A neural joint model for entity and relation extraction from biomedical text. BMC Bioinform. **18**(1), 1–11 (2017)
10. Lin, Y., Shen, S., Liu, Z., Luan, H., Sun, M.: Neural relation extraction with selective attention over instances. In: Proceedings of the 54th Annual Meeting of the Association for Computational Linguistics (Volume 1: Long Papers), Berlin, Germany, pp. 2124–2133. Association for Computational Linguistics, August 2016. https://doi.org/10.18653/v1/P16-1200. https://www.aclweb.org/anthology/P16-1200
11. Mohammed, S., Shi, P., Lin, J.: Strong baselines for simple question answering over knowledge graphs with and without neural networks. arXiv preprint arXiv:1712.01969 (2017)
12. Petrochuk, M., Zettlemoyer, L.: Simple questions nearly solved: a new upperbound and baseline approach. arXiv preprint arXiv:1804.08798 (2018)
13. Vrandečić, D., Krötzsch, M.: Wikidata: a free collaborative knowledgebase. Commun. ACM **57**(10), 78–85 (2014)
14. Wadden, D., Wennberg, U., Luan, Y., Hajishirzi, H.: Entity, relation, and event extraction with contextualized span representations. arXiv preprint arXiv:1909.03546 (2019)

Semi-unsupervised Learning: An In-depth Parameter Analysis

Padraig Davidson$^{(\boxtimes)}$, Florian Buckermann, Michael Steininger, Anna Krause, and Andreas Hotho

Chair of Computer Science X, University of Würzburg, Würzburg, Germany
{davidson,buckermann,steininger,anna.krause,
hotho}@informatik.uni-wuerzburg.de

Abstract. Creating datasets for supervised learning is a very challenging and expensive task, in which each input example has to be annotated with its expected output (e.g. object class). By combining unsupervised and semi-supervised learning, semi-unsupervised learning proposes a new paradigm for partially labeled datasets with additional unknown classes. In this paper we focus on a better understanding of this new learning paradigm and analyze the impact of the amount of labeled data, the number of augmented classes and the selection of hidden classes on the quality of prediction. Especially the number of augmented classes highly influences classification accuracy, which needs tuning for each dataset, since too few and too many augmented classes are detrimental to classifier performance. We also show that we can improve results on a large variety of datasets when using convolutional networks as feature extractors while applying output driven entropy regularization instead of a simple weight based $L2$ norm.

Keywords: Semi-unsupervised learning · Deep generative models · Classification

1 Introduction

Labeling datasets is very expensive in terms of manpower and time, often requires expert knowledge, and the amount of available data is usually limited. A recently proposed learning paradigm, which aims to overcome these issues, is semi-unsupervised learning (SuSL) [29,30]. It allows to specify tasks where only a subset of classes have sparsely labeled examples while other classes may have no labels at all. Willets et al. [29] proposed to use a Deep Generative Model (DGM) architecture to solve such tasks. While it has been shown that the proposed method is able to solve a semi-unsupervised learning task, several aspects have not been analyzed in this case. For example, it has not been evaluated how the amount of labeled data and the number of classes without labeled samples influences the training result. It has been shown that these aspects highly impact the performance of the trained classifiers in the case of semi-supervised

© Springer Nature Switzerland AG 2021
S. Edelkamp et al. (Eds.): KI 2021, LNAI 12873, pp. 51–66, 2021.
https://doi.org/10.1007/978-3-030-87626-5_5

learning [17]. Furthermore, [29] only evaluated DGMs based on Multi-Layer Perceptrons (MLPs). It is not clear to which extent more advanced architectures like Convolutional Neural Networks (CNNs) can be trained with SuSL. This lack of in-depth analysis makes it difficult to grasp under which circumstances it is feasible to apply this paradigm to a specific problem.

In this work, we aim to alleviate these issues by broadening the analysis of the semi-unsupervised learning paradigm. Additionally, we propose modifications to the exiting DGM approach for SuSL tasks which can improve model performance further. Our contributions are fourfold: **(1)** we asses the performance of several drop-in replacements of the MNIST dataset, with larger and more complex class distributions, **(2)** we analyze the impact of each parameter (amount of labeled data, the number of augmented classes and the properties of hidden classes) on the quality of prediction, **(3)** we introduce a weight-invariant regularization to adapt the basic network for convolutional DGMs, which enables us to use pre-trained models, too **(4)** we improve the reported classification accuracy on all datasets, including the larger and imbalanced variants.

The remainder of this paper is structured as follows: In Sect. 2 we describe related work that influenced our work or follows a similar direction. Section 3 focuses heavily on the foundations for our work, comprising a description and formal definition of the different learning paradigms. It contains theoretical background for learning methods in semi-unsupervised settings, including our extensions. All datasets used in our experiments are listed in Sect. 4 with details to their size and distribution. In Sect. 5 we outline the experimental settings for all datasets. This two part section first describes and discusses the results for the classification task itself, including the larger datasets. Second it analyzes the effect of the key variables defining semi-unsupervised learning. We conclude with Sect. 6, including an outlook describing future work.

2   Related Work

The term semi-unsupervised learning was first coined by [29,30]. They used multilayer perceptrons to realize DGMs [21]. In their experiments they compared their approach to the semi-supervised variational autoencoder (VAE) [11] and found their approach to perform better in the unsupervised and semi-unsupervised setting.

DGMs have been used in several cases to solve semi-supervised learning tasks. [14] added auxiliary variables to the latent space of a VAE for a semi-supervised classification task. Another common method for deep generative models are generative adversarial networks (GAN). [16] adapted a GAN for a semi-supervised learning task to increase the performance of a classifier that has only access to a small set of labeled data samples. [22] proposed a categorical GAN in which the discriminator has to additionally learn a consistent categorization (e.g. unsupervised classes) of the generated samples.

Beside semi-supervised or unsupervised learning, there is another extreme case of dealing with unlabeled data: zero-shot-learning (ZSL) [2,31,32]. While in a semi-unsupervised setting unlabeled observations with unknown classes are available during training, no observations of unknown classes are available for zero-shot-learning. Thus, a trained model has to map unseen observations to unknown classes during testing. To achieve a sufficient classification performance, available auxiliary information (e.g. image captions) are used to increase the expressiveness of observations [27].

Multi-positive and unlabeled [34] (MPU) learning is another related learning paradigm, in which $k - 1$ classes are partially labeled (positive data) and one unknown class (negative data) is completely unlabeled. The task is to classify unlabeled data into k classes. SuSL generalizes MPU. Therefore we do not include MPU into our indepth analysis of SuSL.

An earlier, but related approach to ZSL is transfer learning [18,28]. With transfer learning a model is pre-trained on an available (labeled) dataset and afterwards tuned for the target task. This approach realizes a knowledge transfer that increases the extraction of generalizing features for the tuned model. It is especially useful for deep learning where models usually need large datasets to achieve a sufficient performance for unseen samples [5,24].

3   Methodology

3.1   Learning Paradigms

A labeled dataset $D_l = \{(x_1, y_1), \ldots, (x_n, y_n)\}$ consists of pairs of observations x_i and labels y_i. An unlabeled dataset $D_u = \{x_{n+1}, \ldots, x_{n+m}\}$ only contains observations without corresponding labels. We denote the sizes of the labeled and unlabeled datasets with n and m respectively. The observations represent the input data (e.g. an image) for a machine learning model. For the labeled dataset, y_i represents the class for the corresponding observation x_i. The possible class set is $C_l := \{c_1, \ldots, c_k\}$, where $y_i \in C_l$.

For our experiments, we are considering some extreme cases of the well-known learning paradigms supervised (SL), semi-supervised (SSL) and unsupervised (UL) learning. We deal with UL if only an unlabeled dataset D_u is available. In contrast, for fully SL we are only considering examples of a labeled dataset D_l. For SSL, the observations are only partially labeled. Therefore, we have two datasets D_l and D_u from the same data source. While the observations in both sets correspond to the same set of target classes C_l, the actual class mappings are only known for the labeled dataset D_l. In this case, a machine learning model has to learn the relationship between the observations and labels but also infer the labels for the unlabeled dataset.

Semi-unsupervised learning is a mixture of SSL and UL, in which we augment the class set by unknown classes $C_a := \{\hat{c}_1, \ldots, \hat{c}_u\}$ to arrive at the full class set of $C := C_l \cup C_a$, with $C_l \cap C_a = \emptyset$. Again, the task of a machine learning model is to infer the classes for the unlabeled samples. In addition, the model has to identify unknown classes that are not present in the set of known classes C_l [29].

3.2   Semi-unsupervised Learning with Deep Generative Models

We can solve SSL tasks by using the semi-supervised variational autoencoder (SSVAE) [11]. This model is a gaussian mixture extension of the variational

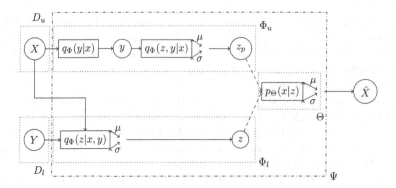

Fig. 1. Basic network structure. The full network Ψ encapsulates two encoders: Φ_u, Φ_l and a decoder Θ. The left part displays the unlabeled encoder Φ_u which maps the unlabeled dataset D_u into the latent space, with an additional meta-mapping to latently encode the class. The right part shows Φ_l which is responsible for encoding the labeled dataset D_l into the latent space z. The decoder Θ reconstructs the latent vector back into the input space, either with only mean, or mean and variance.

autoencoder [12]. By making small changes in the joint probability distribution p_Θ, [30] derived a Gaussian Mixture Deep Generative Model (GM-DGM):

$$p_\Theta(x, y, z) = p_\Theta(x|z)p_\Theta(z|y)p(y)$$
$$p_\Theta(z|y) = \mathcal{N}(z|\mu_\Theta(y), \sigma_\Theta(y))$$
$$p_\Theta(x|z) = \mathcal{N}(\mu_\Theta(z), \sigma_\Theta(z))$$

To overcome classification bias towards labeled classes, the authors specify a prior by partitioning probability mass between known and augmented classes [30]:

$$p(y) = \frac{1}{2} \cdot \begin{cases} \frac{1}{|C_l|} & \text{if } y \in C_l \\ \frac{1}{|C_a|} & \text{else} \end{cases}$$

This implies uniform distribution within both partitions, i.e. the class count is expected to be equal. GM-DGMs satisfy the inductive bias requirement, since the assigned clusters (the found classes for D_u) correspond well with the actual classes [30]. The variational posteriors remain the same as in the case of the SSVAE [30] [Eq. 7–10]. The basic structure of the complete network with all posteriors can be seen in Fig. 1. The loss function for the labeled data D_l can then be formulated as [11]:

$$\mathcal{L}_l = \mathbb{E}_{z \sim q_\Phi(z|x,y)} \log \frac{p_\Theta(x, y, z)}{q_\Phi(z|x, y)}$$

Additionally the loss function for unlabeled data is adapted to account for unseen classes [29]:

$$\mathcal{L}_u = \mathbb{E}_{z,y \sim q_\Phi(z,y|x)} \log \frac{p_\Theta(x, y, z)}{q_\Phi(z, y|x) \cdot q_\Phi(y|x)}$$

[30] proposed to use a gaussian normal ($\mu = 0, \sigma^2 = 1$) log-density based $L2$ regularization:

$$\mathcal{L}_r(\Psi, \mu, \sigma) = -\tfrac{1}{2} \cdot \sum_{\psi \in \Psi} \left[\psi^2 + \log 2\pi \right]$$

where Ψ is the overall network and ψ is a weight factor in Ψ. The overall loss function is now given by [11,30]:

$$\mathcal{L} = \mathop{\mathbb{E}}_{x,y \in D_l} \left[\mathcal{L}_l(x, y) - \alpha \cdot \log q_\Phi(y|x)) \right] + \mathop{\mathbb{E}}_{x \in D_u} \left[\mathcal{L}_u(x) \right] + \gamma \cdot \mathcal{L}_r(\Psi)$$

We can use $q_\Phi(y|x)$ as a classifier, but it only appears in the evidence lower bound (ELBO) of the unlabeled data, thus it had to be added to the labeled loss explicitly.

Our Modifications. In contrast to [30], we propose to use the entropy regularization, which regularizes the prediction surface rather than the weights of the network [7]:

$$\mathcal{L}_r(\lambda; D_l, D_u) := \sum_{x,y \in D_l} \log q_\Phi(y|x) + \lambda \cdot \sum_{x \in D_u} \sum_{c \in C} q_\Phi(c|x) \cdot \log q_\Phi(c|x)$$

This regularization already contains the cross entropy for the labeled data. Furthermore this enables us to use arbitrary pre-trained models, since we do not change weights. The overall loss function is now given by:

$$\mathcal{L} := \mathop{\mathbb{E}}_{x,y \in D_l} \left[\mathcal{L}_l(x, y) - \alpha \cdot \log q_\Phi(y|x) \right]$$

$$+ \mathop{\mathbb{E}}_{x \in D_u} \left[\mathcal{L}_u(x) - \gamma \cdot \lambda \cdot \sum_{c \in C} q_\Phi(c|x) \cdot \log q_\Phi(c|x) \right]$$

with γ controlling the impact of the unlabeled cross-entropy.

In our work we focus on using convolutional neural networks (CNNs) for the specific forms of the posteriors, as opposed to multilayer perceptrons (MLPs) presented in [30]. Especially when extracting spatial features, CNNs have shown great success over fully connected neural networks [13].

4   Datasets

For our experiments, we use several MNIST-like datasets, varying in difficulty of objects and size of the dataset, as well as distribution and availability of labels.

MNIST [13]. The MNIST dataset consists of 28×28 centered, greyscale images of handwritten digits. It contains 60.000 training samples, whereas the test set comprises of 10.000 images, nearly equally distributed for all numbers from 0–9.

Fashion-MNIST [33]. The Fashion-MNIST (FMNIST) is a drop-in replacement for the MNIST dataset. Instead of handwritten numbers, it displays ten classes of clothing apparel, ranging from shoes to shirts. Training and test set have the same size and distribution as mentioned above and contain 28×28 greyscale images, not strictly centered.

Kuzushiji-MNIST [3]. The Kuzushiji-MNIST (KMNIST) is another drop-in replacement for the MNIST dataset. Images depicted in this dataset represent ten symbols of the Hiragana alphabet to mimic the ten-class system of MNIST. Training and test set remain the same size and distribution as MNIST, again depicting 28×28 greyscale images of the handwritten symbols.

Kuzushiji-49 [3]. The Kuzushiji-49 (K49MNIST) is an extension of the KMNIST dataset. It consists of 49 classes, representing 48 Hiragana symbols, as well as one iteration mark. The examples are 28×28 greyscale images, but this version is much larger containing 232.365 training images, as well as 38.547 test images. Furthermore it is highly imbalanced in contrast to all other MNIST versions. Details for the class distributions and symbols can be found in [3] [Fig. 5,8].

Extended MNIST [4]. The extended MNIST (EMNIST) is a variant of the original NIST-19 dataset, containing not only numbers, but also upper- and lowercase Latin letters. Instances are 28×28 greyscale images. The authors introduce several variants of EMNIST following the same creation procedure as the MNIST dataset. In our experiments, we opted for the *ByMerge* variant, containing 47 classes (ten digits [0–9], 26 uppercase [A–Z] and 11 lowercase letters). This version has 731.668 training samples and 82.587 testing images, unequally distributed within the classes [4] [Fig. 2].

5 Experiments

5.1 Semi-unsupervised Classification

Experimental Setting. In the first set of experiments, we are comparing our approach (GM-DGM+) to the one presented in [30] (GM-DGM): in the ten-class datasets, we use classes 0–4 in the labeled set C_l, and used 20 % of those labeled instances. The least often occurring class determines the number of labeled instances, since we want equally distributed classes in D_l. This results in around 1000 labeled examples per class. The unlabeled dataset D_u contains all images corresponding to the classes 5–9, as well as the remaining images excluded from the labeled set. In EMNIST we hid classes with indices 5–9 ([5–9]), 26–30 ([Q–U]) and 38–40 ([d–f]). Without loss of generality, we used the same hiding scheme for K49MNIST.

Implementation Details. All networks were implemented in pyTorch [19] and trained using the Adam optimizer [10]. We re-implemented the approach presented in [30] to produce the results on the other datasets. We performed a random search [1] for the parameters shown in Table 1. Predictions on the test set were done using the model yielding the best accuracy on a validation set, which was created by a train-validation split of 80/20 on the training dataset. We used batch sizes of 512 for training, where each batch contained the same

Table 1. Parameters and their corresponding search space for the random search. *randint* stands for a uniform integer distribution in the given interval. *loguniform* represents a log uniform (reciprocal) distribution with the shown borders. *expon* encodes a exponential distribution, where the first parameter denotes the center, and the second one the scale. z was used for the size of the latent space. Distributions are taken from scipy [26] and sampled via sklearn [20].

Parameter	Search space	Parameter	Search space
$|C_a|$	$[5, 10, 20, \ldots, 50]$	ss	$[.01, .1]$
lr	$\mathrm{loguniform}(10^{-5}, 10^{-1})$	sd	$[1, 3]$
z	$\mathrm{randint}(10, 100)$	γ	$\mathrm{expon}(0, 0.5)$

amount of labeled and unlabeled examples (256). In the common case, that $|D_l| \neq |D_u|$, we randomly sampled instances of the smaller dataset to pad the batch. All images were pre-processed via 0/1 normalization, and the class labels were one-hot encoded with respect to the size of C.

Our approach is implemented mainly using convolutional neural networks. The labeled encoder Φ_l consists of two convolutional blocks, where each block entails a 2d-convolutional layer, a ReLU [6] activation function and a max-pooling layer. The extracted features are then flattened and enriched (concatenate) by the one-hot encoded vector y. Using two multilayer perceptrons (MLPs), we directly transform those features to mean and variance of dimension z. For Φ_u, where y is latent, we use the same convolutional blocks, flatten the extracted features and use a MLP to transform the input to the desired size of $|C|$. $q_\Phi(z, y|x)$ is realized by two MLPs to transform the input to mean and variance of dimension z. We also tried to use a further MLP meta-layer with dropout for feature space reduction before z, but found no noticeable improvement using this.

The decoder Θ at first re-transforms the latent space z via a MLP and a ReLU function, which is then reshaped for the convolutional decoding. This decoding consists of two blocks, where each block entails an upsampling (nearest neighbor) and convolutional layer and a ReLU activation function. The final activation a sigmoid function. We used the mean squared error as the reconstruction loss function, since we found it to perform better in combination with sigmoid than the Bernoulli log density. More details can be seen in Table 2. As mentioned in [7], when using gradient based methods for optimization, it is useful to successively increase the regularization factor λ from zero to one, which we did after every *step distance* (*sd*) fully completed epoch. We also tested different sizes of the increase with the parameter *step size* (*ss*). Further we set the classifier importance $\alpha = 1$.

Evaluation. Evaluation is done by cluster-and-label, the same manner as proposed in [9]:

$$\mathrm{ACC} = \max_{f \in \mathcal{F}} \frac{\sum_{i=1}^{|D|} \mathbb{I}[t(y_i) = f(y_i)]}{|D|}$$

Table 2. Network details for the used posteriors. *Conv2d(out channels, kernel size, padding size)* represents a 2d-convolutional layer. *MaxPool(kernel size, stride)* denotes a max-pooling layer with specified kernel size and stride. *Upsample(factor)* describes an upsampling layer by the given factor. *MLP(out features)* defines a fully connected layer with specified output size.

Layer	Elements
Encoder Φ_u	Conv2d(32,3,1) + ReLU + MaxPool(2,2)
	Conv2d(64,3,1) + ReLU + MaxPool(2,2)
	Flatten + MLP(y) + 2 * MLP(μ, σ)
Encoder Φ_l	Conv2d(32,3,1) + ReLU + MaxPool(2,2)
	Conv2d(64,3,1) + ReLU + MaxPool(2,2)
	Flatten + Concat(y) + 2 * MLP(μ, σ)
Decoder Θ	MLP(64*7*7) + ReLU + Reshape(64,7,7)
	Upsample(2) + Conv2d(32,3,1) + ReLU
	Upsample(2) + Conv2d(1,3,1) + Sigmoid

where $\mathcal{F}$ is the set of possible one-to-one mappings from assignment $f(y_i)$ to ground-truth label $t(y_i)$. For the unbalanced versions of the datasets, we used a balanced accuracy version of this approach: we first calculate the accuracy for each class and then average those accuracies over the number of ground truth classes.

Results and Discussion. Table 3 displays the classification accuracy on the test sets of each dataset. We listed all mentioned learning schemes: UL, SuSL, SSL and SL. In all settings with labels available, GM-DGM+ outperforms GM-DGM. Within UL, GM-DGM performs consistently better, except for MNIST.

Classification reports and confusion matrix for MNIST (Fig. 7), FMNIST (Fig. 5) and KMNIST (Fig. 6) in the SuSL setting are available in the appendix. All figures display the confusion matrices for the ten class datasets using GM-DGM+ in the SuSL paradigm, with hidden classes 5–9 and 20 % labels. The confusion matrices are normalized by prediction, i.e. by column. In FMNIST the classes *Shirt, Coat, Pullover* and *Top* show the lowest prediction quality. Conceptually these classes can be grouped into *top clothing*, sharing similar visual characteristics. This implies a more challenging separation of (unlabeled) classes that likely decrease performance. Especially the class *Shirt* is often clustered with labeled, but similar classes. This means, if in doubt the classifier clusters hidden classes with labeled clusters, but unlabeled instances of known classes with the expected cluster. If two hidden classes are similar, they are equally likely misclustered. In KMNIST only the symbol す highly deviates from the average accuracy (0.81 versus 0.91) with three main ambiguities (つ,は,ま).

Misclusterings are directly visible when visually observing the latent space. For that we plotted the t-SNE [15] projections of the latent space vector z

Table 3. Classification results for the different datasets. The left hand side of the table describes the evaluated models with GM-DGM+ being our approach. The remaining columns denote the achieved test set accuracy with standard deviation over four runs. Rows marked with * indicate that balanced accuracy was used. Scores marked with † are taken from [30]. Standard deviation is shown with two significant places.

Dataset	Model	% Labeled data (Accuracy ± SD)%			
		0 (UL)	20 (SuSL)	20 (SSL)	100 (SL)
MNIST	GM-DGM	$90.0 \pm 1.5^{\dagger}$	$92.5 \pm 0.3^{\dagger}$	$97.7 \pm 0.1^{\dagger}$	98.7 ± 0.1
	GM-DGM+	$\mathbf{96.1 \pm 0.3}$	$\mathbf{99.0 \pm 0.1}$	$\mathbf{99.4 \pm 0.0}$	$\mathbf{99.5 \pm 0.0}$
FMNIST	GM-DGM	$\mathbf{75.8 \pm 0.3^{\dagger}}$	$78.2 \pm 1.1^{\dagger}$	$86.9 \pm 0.1^{\dagger}$	90.0 ± 0.1
	GM-DGM+	74.3 ± 0.3	$\mathbf{81.7 \pm 0.4}$	$\mathbf{89.4 \pm 0.3}$	$\mathbf{92.0 \pm 0.3}$
KMNIST	GM-DGM	$\mathbf{78.1 \pm 0.5}$	88.5 ± 0.5	89.4 ± 0.3	94.5 ± 0.2
	GM-DGM+	76.7 ± 0.5	$\mathbf{91.3 \pm 0.5}$	$\mathbf{96.0 \pm 0.3}$	$\mathbf{97.6 \pm 0.1}$
K49MNIST*	GM-DGM	$\mathbf{49.9 \pm 1.1}$	69.0 ± 0.7	67.4 ± 0.7	89.5 ± 0.2
	GM-DGM+	46.2 ± 0.9	$\mathbf{77.0 \pm 0.6}$	$\mathbf{82.7 \pm 0.5}$	$\mathbf{91.7 \pm 0.1}$
EMNIST*	GM-DGM	$\mathbf{64.3 \pm 1.2}$	80.8 ± 0.8	83.3 ± 0.3	85.2 ± 0.3
	GM-DGM+	57.6 ± 1.1	$\mathbf{82.7 \pm 0.7}$	$\mathbf{83.4 \pm 0.4}$	$\mathbf{88.4 \pm 0.2}$

in Fig. 2. Clusters for labeled classes are very clear in any dataset. With larger sizes of C_a we allow for further distinctions, which can be seen in the number of distinct clusters. The more coherent (Fig. 2a > Fig. 2c > Fig. 2b) these clusters are, the higher the prediction quality.

5.2 Parameter Analysis

We mentioned in Sect. 3 that we have three key variables defining the learning environment of SuSL: the number of augmented classes, the amount of available labels and the combination of classes we hide or label. These variables potentially gravely impact the prediction quality, but often are predominated by the real world dataset. In this superficial setting of SuSL, we can quantify the effect of these, showing pitfalls in real world applications. For that, we maintain the experimental setup described in Sect. 5.1, except we keep certain variables at constant values in the accompanying random search. The ranges for the variables remain the same as in Table 1. Results are always obtained from the best performing model given the specific search. Due to training time constraints, we are performing these experiments only on the ten-class versions of the MNIST dataset.

Does the Size of C_a Matter? As mentioned in Sect. 3, we are extending the set of possible classes in SSL by C_a. [30] named this parameter n_{aug} and kept it constant for all experiments with $n_{aug} = 40$. In these experiments, we are interested in which role the size of the additional class set factors into the classi-

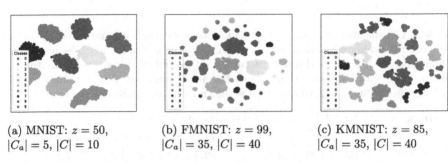

(a) MNIST: $z = 50$, $|C_a| = 5$, $|C| = 10$

(b) FMNIST: $z = 99$, $|C_a| = 35$, $|C| = 40$

(c) KMNIST: $z = 85$, $|C_a| = 35$, $|C| = 40$

Fig. 2. Clustering Visualization. t-SNE visualization of the latent space on various test sets in the SuSL setting using the best performing setting of GM-DGM+. z is the dimension of the latent space vector, $|C_a|$ the amount of hidden classes added and $|C|$ the size of the classification layer.

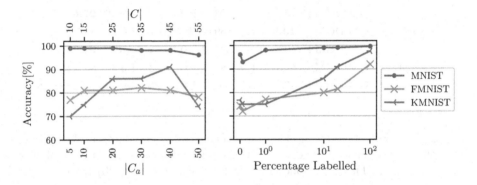

Fig. 3. Parameter analysis. (left) Does the size of C matter? Accuracy over augmented classes. All datasets have ten classes ($|C_a| = 5, |C| = 10$). (right) How many labels do we need? Accuracy over percentage of labeled data (log-scale).

fication accuracy, or the cluster purity. We are testing with $|C_a| \in \{5, 15, \ldots, 45\}$. This means the size of the full class set is $|C| \in \{10, 20, \ldots, 50\}$.

Results and Discussion. Figure 3 (left) displays the number of invisible classes added versus the prediction accuracy. Within MNIST, accuracy ranges from 96 % to 99 %, with accuracy decreasing with the number of available classes. In FMNIST, predictions show a plateau, limited by 77 %, 82 % and 78 %. Accuracy in KMNIST increases with $|C_a|$, but with a very clear peak at 91 % ($|C_a| = 40$), quickly dropping afterwards.

We can observe that the number of added classes gravely impacts prediction quality. A too small class space limits available clusters and results in lower accuracy, whereas a too large space allows for too many sub-classes of the expected classification task. If the classes are highly separable, we can limit the search space of classes available (e.g. MNIST), but with more complicated patterns, we should add more classes. The number of classes added seems to produce best results within 20–40 (e.g. FMNIST, KMNIST).

How Many Labels Do We Need? As mentioned in Sect. 5.1, we are only labeling 20 % of the available data in the labeled set D_l. In these experiments we want to analyze the effect of the size of the labeled dataset, i.e. is there a point of available labels with no noticeable improvement in accuracy. To do so, we are testing with 20 %, 10 %, 1 % and 0.1 % (~1000, 500, 50 and 5 examples per class) of the available labels.

Results and Discussion. In Fig. 3 (right) we plotted the percentage of available labels over the test set accuracy. In MNIST the accuracy quickly saturates, reaching supervised classification starting at 10 % labeled instances. Within KMNIST, the prediction quality ranges from 75 % to 98 %, but convergence is not as quickly reached as in MNIST. Lastly FMNIST is bound between 72 % and 92 %, with a nearly linear trend in accuracy gain.

In the case of hardly any labels available (0.1 % ~ 5 labels per class), predictions tend to be worse than in the unsupervised setting. Thus the classifier is very dependent on the labeled examples and we must take care which instances are labeled. Recall that we kept $\alpha = 1$ constant over all experiments. This probably forces the network to overly rely on those labeled examples, in contrast to the unsupervised setting, where $\alpha = 0$. [11] suggested to use $\alpha = 0.1 \cdot n$. Further analysis to set α via formula or by search must be done.

Which Classes Can We Hide? In Sect. 3 we outlined, how we can mimic SuSL with a supervised dataset. By intentionally hiding the latter half of labeled classes, we can organically create other variations of labeled and unlabeled classes. We are interested, if there are certain splits of hidden versus shown classes, that show higher accuracy than others. Alongside the split 0–4/5–9 (labeled/hidden), we are testing 5–9/0–4 (inverted), odd/even and even/odd.

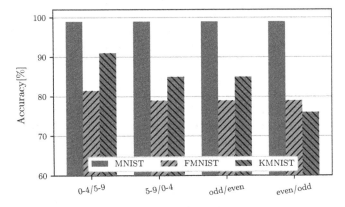

Fig. 4. Which Classes can we hide? Different split versions of labeled and unlabeled classes plotted over the accuracy of the prediction. The splits are encoded *labeled/unlabeled* classes. That is, 0–4/5–9 is the default SuSL setting.

The second split variation is inspired by FMNIST, since it contains classes inherently easy to be confused: top clothing and footwear.

Results and Discussion. Figure 4 shows different splits of the datasets against the achieved accuracy on the test set. For the MNIST dataset there is no difference in classification accuracy (99 %) when training on different splits. In FMNIST there are small changes in the overall accuracy, ranging from 82 % to 79 %. KMNIST shows the biggest gap between the default split (91 %) and other splits (76 %, even/odd).

Except for MNIST, we can see that the combination of labeled and hidden classes largely impacts the prediction accuracy. Even in settings where two symbols occur partially labeled, but in combination with different hidden classes, contrasting results can be observed.

6   Summary and Outlook

In this work, we provide in-depth analysis of the SuSL core hyper-parameters: number of classes added, number of available labels, and the definition of the labeled dataset, as well as further understanding of their influence on prediction quality. Additionally, we extended [29,30] by replacing the MLPs with CNNs as feature extractors and switching from a weight based ($L2$) regularization to a class based (entropy regularization) one, finding improved performance with this approach.

Our parameter study found that the number of added classes requires careful tuning as too few and too many augmented classes degrade classification performance. Classification performance increases strictly with the amount of available labels, whereas with too few labeled examples SuSL is outperformed by UL. By testing different permutations of labeled and hidden classes, we showed that performance depends on which classes are hidden and which are known. However, in real world SuSL datasets we have no control over these combinations, since we do not know how many and which classes are hidden.

Besides these findings, there are many ways to further investigate this relatively new learning paradigm. We propose the following three directions: **(1)** With the presented weight invariant regularization, we opened directions for further research, since we can now use any architecture as VAE, e.g. fully convolutional VAEs [23], ResNets [8] or transformer-based networks [25]. **(2)** By including K49MNIST and EMNIST we showed that SuSL is applicable to imbalanced datasets. However, the labeled dataset was balanced in all our experiments. It is worth analyzing how this approach would handle unequally distributed versions of the labeled dataset D_l. **(3)** As mentioned in Sect. 3, we divide the probability mass between supervised and unsupervised classes in half and uniformly weight each unseen class in the prior. Other weighting schemes could improve prediction quality and help with modeling skewed label distributions in the labeled dataset.

Appendix

Classification Reports in SuSL

(See Tables 4, 5 and 6).

Table 4. Classification report for the FMNIST dataset in SuSL.

	P	R	F1
T-shirt/top	0.70	0.90	0.79
Trouser	0.99	0.96	0.98
Pullover	0.72	0.81	0.76
Dress	0.86	0.91	0.88
Coat	0.72	0.84	0.77
Sandal	0.91	0.79	0.84
Shirt	0.62	0.20	0.31
Sneaker	0.83	0.84	0.83
Bag	0.92	0.97	0.95
Ankle boot	0.84	0.94	0.88
Accuracy			0.82
Macro	0.81	0.82	0.80
Weighted	0.81	0.82	0.80

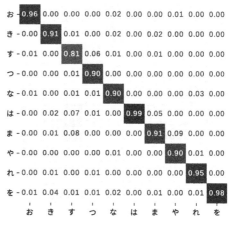

Fig. 5. Confusion matrix for the FMNIST dataset in SuSL.

Table 5. Classification report for the KMNIST dataset in SuSL.

	P	R	F1
お	0.94	0.97	0.95
き	0.92	0.93	0.92
す	0.78	0.89	0.83
つ	0.92	0.99	0.95
な	0.89	0.93	0.91
は	0.96	0.88	0.92
ま	0.94	0.78	0.85
や	0.91	0.94	0.92
れ	0.95	0.96	0.96
を	0.98	0.87	0.92
accuracy			0.91
macro	0.92	0.91	0.91
weighted	0.92	0.91	0.91

Fig. 6. Confusion matrix for the KMNIST dataset in SuSL.

Table 6. Classification report for the MNIST dataset in SuSL.

	P	R	F1
0	1.00	1.00	1.00
1	1.00	0.99	1.00
2	0.99	1.00	0.99
3	0.98	0.99	0.99
4	0.99	0.99	0.99
5	0.97	0.99	0.98
6	1.00	0.99	0.99
7	0.99	0.99	0.99
8	0.99	0.99	0.99
9	0.99	0.95	0.97
Accuracy			0.99
Macro	0.99	0.99	0.99
Weighted	0.99	0.99	0.99

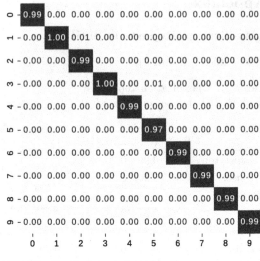

Fig. 7. Confusion matrix for the MNIST dataset in SuSL.

References

1. Bergstra, J., Bengio, Y.: Random search for hyper-parameter optimization. J. Mach. Learn. Res. **13**(1), 281–305 (2012)
2. Changpinyo, S., Chao, W.L., Gong, B., Sha, F.: Synthesized classifiers for zero-shot learning. In: Proceedings of the IEEE Conference on Computer Vision and Pattern Recognition (CVPR), June 2016
3. Clanuwat, T., Bober-Irizar, M., Kitamoto, A., Lamb, A., Yamamoto, K., Ha, D.: Deep learning for classical Japanese literature. arXiv preprint arXiv:1812.01718 (2018)
4. Cohen, G., Afshar, S., Tapson, J., van Schaik, A.: EMNIST: an extension of MNIST to handwritten letters (2017)
5. Erhan, D., Courville, A., Bengio, Y., Vincent, P.: Why does unsupervised pre-training help deep learning? In: Proceedings of the 13th International Conference on Artificial Intelligence and Statistics. Proceedings of Machine Learning Research, vol. 9, pp. 201–208. JMLR Workshop and Conference Proceedings (2010)
6. Glorot, X., Bordes, A., Bengio, Y.: Deep sparse rectifier neural networks. In: Proceedings of the Fourteenth International Conference on Artificial Intelligence and Statistics, pp. 315–323. JMLR Workshop and Conference Proceedings (2011)
7. Grandvalet, Y., Bengio, Y.: Semi-supervised learning by entropy minimization. In: Advances in Neural Information Processing Systems, pp. 529–536 (2005)
8. He, K., Zhang, X., Ren, S., Sun, J.: Deep residual learning for image recognition (2015)
9. Kilinc, O., Uysal, I.: Learning latent representations in neural networks for clustering through pseudo supervision and graph-based activity regularization. arXiv preprint arXiv:1802.03063 (2018)
10. Kingma, D.P., Ba, J.: Adam: a method for stochastic optimization (2017)

11. Kingma, D.P., Mohamed, S., Jimenez Rezende, D., Welling, M.: Semi-supervised learning with deep generative models. In: Advances in Neural Information Processing, vol. 27, pp. 3581–3589 (2014)
12. Kingma, D.P., Welling, M.: Auto-encoding variational bayes. arXiv preprint arXiv:1312.6114 (2013)
13. LeCun, Y., Bottou, L., Bengio, Y., Haffner, P.: Gradient-based learning applied to document recognition. Proc. IEEE **86**(11), 2278–2324 (1998)
14. Maaløe, L., Sønderby, C.K., Sønderby, S.K., Winther, O.: Auxiliary deep generative models. In: Proceedings of The 33rd International Conference on ML. Proceedings of ML Research, vol. 48, pp. 1445–1453. PMLR, 20–22 June 2016
15. Van der Maaten, L., Hinton, G.: Visualizing data using t-SNE. J. Mach. Learn. Res. **9**(11) (2008)
16. Madani, A., Moradi, M., Karargyris, A., Syeda-Mahmood, T.: Semi-supervised learning with generative adversarial networks for chest X-ray classification with ability of data domain adaptation. In: 2018 IEEE 15th International Symposium on Biomedical Imaging (ISBI 2018), pp. 1038–1042 (2018)
17. Oliver, A., Odena, A., Raffel, C.A., Cubuk, E.D., Goodfellow, I.: Realistic evaluation of deep semi-supervised learning algorithms. In: Bengio, S., Wallach, H., Larochelle, H., Grauman, K., Cesa-Bianchi, N., Garnett, R. (eds.) Advances in Neural Information Processing Systems, vol. 31. Curran Associates, Inc. (2018). https://proceedings.neurips.cc/paper/2018/file/c1fea270c48e8079d8ddf7d06d26ab52-Paper.pdf
18. Pan, S.J., Yang, Q.: A survey on transfer learning. IEEE Trans. Knowl. Data Eng. **22**(10), 1345–1359 (2010)
19. Paszke, A., et al.: Pytorch: an imperative style, high-performance deep learning library. In: Advances in Neural Information Processing Systems, pp. 8026–8037 (2019)
20. Pedregosa, F., et al.: Scikit-learn: machine learning in Python. J. Mach. Learn. Res. **12**, 2825–2830 (2011)
21. Rezende, D.J., Mohamed, S., Wierstra, D.: Stochastic backpropagation and approximate inference in deep generative models. In: Proceedings of the 31st International Conference on Machine Learning. Proceedings of Machine Learning Research, vol. 32, pp. 1278–1286. PMLR (2014)
22. Springenberg, J.T.: Unsupervised and semi-supervised learning with categorical generative adversarial networks. In: International Conference on Learning Representations (2016)
23. Springenberg, J.T., Dosovitskiy, A., Brox, T., Riedmiller, M.: Striving for simplicity: the all convolutional net. arXiv preprint arXiv:1412.6806 (2014)
24. Tan, C., Sun, F., Kong, T., Zhang, W., Yang, C., Liu, C.: A survey on deep transfer learning. In: Kůrková, V., Manolopoulos, Y., Hammer, B., Iliadis, L., Maglogiannis, I. (eds.) ICANN 2018. LNCS, vol. 11141, pp. 270–279. Springer, Cham (2018). https://doi.org/10.1007/978-3-030-01424-7_27
25. Vaswani, A., et al.: Attention is all you need. arXiv preprint arXiv:1706.03762 (2017)
26. Virtanen, P., et al.: SciPy 1.0 contributors: SciPy 1.0: fundamental algorithms for scientific computing in python. Nat. Methods **17**, 261–272 (2020). https://doi.org/10.1038/s41592-019-0686-2
27. Wang, W., Zheng, V.W., Yu, H., Miao, C.: A survey of zero-shot learning: settings, methods, and applications. ACM Trans. Intell. Syst. Technol. **10**(2) (2019)
28. Weiss, K., Khoshgoftaar, T.M., Wang, D.D.: A survey of transfer learning. J. Big Data **3**(1), 1–40 (2016). https://doi.org/10.1186/s40537-016-0043-6

29. Willetts, M., Doherty, A., Roberts, S., Holmes, C.: Semi-unsupervised learning using deep generative models. In: NeurIPS (2018)
30. Willetts, M., Roberts, S.J., Holmes, C.C.: Semi-unsupervised learning: clustering and classifying using ultra-sparse labels. In: IEEE International Conference on Big Data 2020: ML on Big Data (2021)
31. Xian, Y., Lorenz, T., Schiele, B., Akata, Z.: Feature generating networks for zero-shot learning. In: Proceedings of the IEEE Conference on Computer Vision and Pattern Recognition (CVPR), June 2018
32. Xian, Y., Schiele, B., Akata, Z.: Zero-shot learning - the good, the bad and the ugly. In: Proceedings of the IEEE Conference on Computer Vision and Pattern Recognition (CVPR), July 2017
33. Xiao, H., Rasul, K., Vollgraf, R.: Fashion-MNIST: a novel image dataset for benchmarking machine learning algorithms. arXiv preprint arXiv:1708.07747 (2017)
34. Xu, Y., Xu, C., Xu, C., Tao, D.: Multi-positive and unlabeled learning. In: Proceedings of the Twenty-Sixth International Joint Conference on Artificial Intelligence, IJCAI 2017, pp. 3182–3188 (2017). https://doi.org/10.24963/ijcai.2017/444

Combining Transformer Generators with Convolutional Discriminators

Ricard Durall[1,2,3(✉)], Stanislav Frolov[4,5(✉)], Jörn Hees[5], Federico Raue[5],
Franz-Josef Pfreundt[1], Andreas Dengel[4,5], and Janis Keuper[1,6]

[1] Fraunhofer ITWM, Kaiserslautern, Germany
`ricard.durall.lopez@itwm.fraunhofer.de`
[2] IWR, University of Heidelberg, Heidelberg, Germany
[3] Fraunhofer Center Machine Learning, Sankt Augustin, Germany
[4] Technical University of Kaiserslautern, Kaiserslautern, Germany
`stanislav.frolov@dfki.de`
[5] German Research Center for Artificial Intelligence (DFKI),
Kaiserslautern, Germany
[6] Institute for Machine Learning and Analytics, Offenburg University,
Offenburg, Germany

Abstract. Transformer models have recently attracted much interest from computer vision researchers and have since been successfully employed for several problems traditionally addressed with convolutional neural networks. At the same time, image synthesis using generative adversarial networks (GANs) has drastically improved over the last few years. The recently proposed TransGAN is the first GAN using only transformer-based architectures and achieves competitive results when compared to convolutional GANs. However, since transformers are data-hungry architectures, TransGAN requires data augmentation, an auxiliary super-resolution task during training, and a masking prior to guide the self-attention mechanism. In this paper, we study the combination of a transformer-based generator and convolutional discriminator and successfully remove the need of the aforementioned required design choices. We evaluate our approach by conducting a benchmark of well-known CNN discriminators, ablate the size of the transformer-based generator, and show that combining both architectural elements into a hybrid model leads to better results. Furthermore, we investigate the frequency spectrum properties of generated images and observe that our model retains the benefits of an attention based generator.

Keywords: Image synthesis · Generative adversarial networks · Transformers · Hybrid models

1 Introduction

Generative adversarial networks (GANs) [15], a framework consisting of two neural networks that play a minimax game, made it possible to train generative

---

R. Durall and S. Frolov—Equal contribution.

© Springer Nature Switzerland AG 2021
S. Edelkamp et al. (Eds.): KI 2021, LNAI 12873, pp. 67–79, 2021.
https://doi.org/10.1007/978-3-030-87626-5_6

models for image synthesis in an unsupervised manner. It consists of a generator network that learns to produce realistic images, and a discriminator network that seeks to discern between real and generated images. This framework has since successfully been applied to numerous applications such as (unconditional and conditional) image synthesis [2,13,21], image editing [26], text-to-image translation [12,35], image-to-image translation [19], image super-resolution [25], and representation learning [32]. Given the breakthroughs of deep learning enabled by convolutional neural networks (CNNs), GANs typically consist of CNN layers.

While CNNs have been the gold standard in the computer vision community, natural language processing (NLP) problems have recently been dominated by transformer-based architectures [40]. On a high level, transformer models consist of an encoder and decoder built from multiple self-attention heads and processes sequences of embedded (word) tokens. Due to their simple and general architecture, transformers are less restricted by inductive biases and hence well-suited to become universal models. Inspired by the developments in the field of NLP, researchers have started to apply transformers on image problems by representing an image as a sequence of image patches or pixels [5,31]. Since then, there have been major developments of using vision transformers for computer vision applications [4,8,20].

Given the success of adversarial training frameworks, the authors of [20] conducted the first pilot study to investigate whether a GAN can be created purely from transformer-based architectures to generate images of similar quality. Their method, termed TransGAN, consists of a generator that progressively increases the feature resolution while decreasing the embedding dimension, and a patch-level discriminator [8]. However, the discriminator of TransGAN requires careful design choices to reach competitive performance because it seems to be an inferior counterpart unable to provide useful learning signals to the generator. Given that transformers typically require large datasets, the authors partially alleviate this issue through data augmentation. Furthermore, they introduce an auxiliary super-resolution task and construct a gradually increasing mask to limit the receptive field of the self-attention mechanism.

Although TransGAN achieves good results and is less restricted by inductive biases, the required design choices are cumbersome. On the other hand, CNNs have strong biases towards feature locality and spatial invariance induced by the convolutional layers which make them very efficient for problems in the image domain. Given the success of CNNs for vision problems, in this work we explore the combination of a purely transformer-based generator and CNN discriminator into a hybrid GAN for image synthesis. In particular, we show that the discriminator of SNGAN [27] is especially well-suited and leads to improved results on CIFAR-10. Moreover, our analysis of the frequency spectrum of generated images indicates that our model retains the benefits of a transformer-based generator. Figure 1 shows an illustration of our method. In summary, our contributions are:

- we combine a purely transformer-based generator and convolutional discriminator into a hybrid GAN thereby achieving better results on CIFAR-10;

– we benchmark several convolutional discriminators, ablate the size of the generator and show that our hybrid method is more robust;
– we analyze the frequency spectrum of generated images and show that our hybrid model retains the benefits of the attention-based generator.

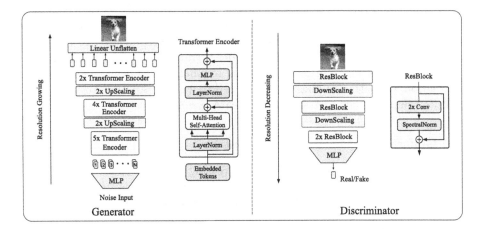

Fig. 1. Illustration of our proposed hybrid model consisting of a transformer-based generator and convolutional discriminator. While the transformer consists of multiple up-sampling stages combined with transformer encoder blocks, the discriminator consists of down-sampling stages combined with ResBlocks.

2 Related Work

The goal of generative models is to approximate a real data distribution with a generated data distribution. To that end, the model is trained to automatically discover and learn the regularities and patterns in the real data assigning a probability to each possible combination of these features. Eventually, this procedure will encourage the system to mimic the real distribution. Until recently, most generative models for image synthesis were exclusively built using convolutional layers. However, with the uprising of transformers, new topologies started to break the convolution hegemony.

2.1 Generative Models Using CNNs

Generative adversarial network (GAN) [15] is one of the most successful generative framework based on convolutional layers. They are trained to minimize the distance between the real and generated distributions by optimizing the Jensen-Shannon divergence. From a game theoretical point of view, this optimization problem can be seen as a minimax game between two players, represented by the discriminator and generator model. While the generator is trained to generate plausible data, the discriminator's goal is to distinguish between generated and real data, and to penalize the generator for producing unrealistic results.

Variational Autoencoder (VAE) [23] is another very popular framework to train generative models. Unlike GANs, VAEs explicitly estimate the probability density function of real data by minimizing the Kullback-Leibler (KL) divergence between the two probability distributions. Similar to an autoencoder, VAEs consist of an encoder and decoder. The encoder maps the input (e.g., an image) to a latent representation, which usually has a lower dimensionality, to fit a predefined probability distribution. The decoder is trained to reconstruct the input from the latent representation thereby approximating the original probability distribution. Once the training has converged to a stable solution, one can sample from the predefined distribution to create new samples.

2.2 Generative Models Using Attention

As previously mentioned, there is an increasing tendency pushing attention mechanisms towards visual tasks. Image Transformer [31] is one of the first approaches to generalize transformers [40] to a sequence modeling formulation of image generation with a tractable likelihood such as in [29,39].

Another recent approach is ImageGPT [5] which was designed to leverage unsupervised representation learning by pre-training a transformer on the image generation task. As a result, the representations learned by ImageGPT can be used for downstream tasks such as image classification. The architecture is based on GPT-2 [33] which trains sequence transformers to auto-regressively predict pixels without incorporating knowledge of the 2D input structure.

Finally, TransGAN [20] introduced a new GAN paradigm completely free of convolutions and based on pure self-attention blocks. This transformer-based architecture introduces a novel generator that combines transformer encoders with up-sampling modules consisting of a reshaping and pixelshuffle module [37] in a multi-level manner. The discriminator is based on the ViT architecture [8] which was originally developed for image classification without using convolutions.

2.3 Hybrid Models

Given the benefits of convolutions and transformers, finding a way to combine both technologies is an interesting and important research question One successful example of this symbiosis is DALL-E [34]. DALL-E is a text-to-image generative model that produces realistic-looking images based on short captions that can specify multiple objects, colors, textures, positions, and other contextual details such as lighting or camera angle. It has two main blocks: a pre-trained VQ-VAE [30] built from convolutional layers which allows the model to generate diverse and high quality images, and a GPT-3 transformer [3] which learns to map between language and images. VQGAN [11] is a similar architecture but uses images instead of text as input for conditional image synthesis. GANs-former [18] is a novel approach based on StyleGAN [21] that employs a bipartite transformer structure coined duplex-attention. In particular, this model sequentially stacks convolutional layer together with transformer blocks throughout the whole architecture. This attention mechanism achieves a favorable balance between modeling global phenomena and long-range interaction across the image while maintaining linear efficiency.

3 Model Architecture

Our proposed hybrid model is a type of generative model using the GAN framework which involves a generator and discriminator network. Traditionally, both networks consist of multiple layers of stacked convolutions. In contrast to previous hybrid models [11,18,34], in our approach the generator is purely transformer-based and the discriminator only contains convolutions. See Fig. 1 for an illustration of our model.

3.1 Transformer Generator

Originally, transformers were designed for NLP tasks, where they treat individual words as sequential input. Modelling pixels as individual tokens, even for low-resolution images such as 32×32, is infeasible due to the prohibitive cost (quadratic w.r.t. the sequence length) [20]. Inspired by [20], we leverage their proposed generator to build our hybrid model. The generator employs a memory-friendly transformer-based architecture that contains transformer encoders and up-scaling blocks to increase the resolution in a multi-level manner. The transformer encoder [40] itself is made of two blocks. The first is a multi-head self-attention module, while the second is a feed-forward MLP with GELU non-linearity [16]. Both blocks use residual connections and layer normalization [1]. Additionally, an up-sampling module after each stage based on pixelshuffle [37] is inserted.

3.2 Convolutional Discriminator

Unlike the generator which has to synthesize each pixel precisely, the discriminator is typically only trained to distinguish between real and fake images. We benchmark various well-known convolutional discriminators [22,27,32,41] and find that the discriminator of SNGAN [27] performs particularly well in combination with the transformer-based generator. It consists of residual blocks (Res-Block) followed by down-sampling layers using average pooling. The ResBlock itself consists of multiple convolutional layers stacked successively with residual connections, spectral layer normalization [27] and ReLU non-linearity [28].

4   Experiments

We first provide a detailed description of the experimental setup. Next, we benchmark various discriminators to investigate their influence on the final performance on the CIFAR-10 dataset. Then, we ablate the size of the transformer-based generator to assess the effect of the generator's capacity. Next, we train our proposed method on other datasets and compare with fully convolutional and fully transformer-based architectures. Finally, we analyze the impact of our proposed method on the frequency spectrum of generated images.

4.1   Setup

Models: For our empirical investigations, we carry out a benchmark and analyse the impact of different discriminator architectures: DCGAN [32], SNGAN [27], SAGAN [41], AutoGAN [14], StyleGANv2 [22] and TransGAN. Furthermore, we ablate the size of the transformer-based generator using the scaled-up models of TransGAN [20] by varying the dimension of the input embedding and/or the number of transformer encoder blocks in each stage. We built upon the existing codebase[1] from [20] with default training procedure and hyperparamters.

Datasets: We train our models on four commonly used datasets: CIFAR-10 [24], CIFAR-100 [24], STL-10 [6] resized to 48×48, and tiny ImageNet [7] resized to 32×32.

Metrics: The two most common evaluation metrics are Inception Score (IS) [36] and Fréchet Inception Distance (FID) [17]. While IS computes the KL divergence between the conditional class distribution and the marginal class distribution over the generated data, FID calculates Fréchet distance between multivariate Gaussian fitted to the intermediate activations of the Inception-v3 network [38] of generated and real images.

4.2   Results

We first study the role and influence of the discriminator topology on the final performance using the CIFAR-10 dataset. To that end, the generator architecture remains fixed, while the discriminator architecture is swapped with various standard CNN discriminators. Table 1 contains the scores for combination, where we can see that the discriminator of SNGAN leads to the best IS and FID and, unlike TransGAN, our model does not require data augmentation, auxiliary tasks nor any kind of locality-aware initialization for the attention blocks. However, we can observe an influence of the number of parameters on the final results. If the discriminator is strong, such as in StyleGANv2 [22], our transformer-based generator is not able to improve as quickly and consequently results in poor performance. If the discriminator is too small, such as in DCGAN [32], it will not be able to provide good learning signals to the generator. Finally, we ablate

---

[1] https://github.com/VITA-Group/TransGAN/tree/7e5fa2d.

the impact of Spectral Normalization (SN) on the discriminator and observe just slightly worse results which indicates that SN is not the main contributor to the good overall performance of this combination.

Table 1. Benchmark results on CIFAR-10 using different discriminator architectures. ✗ indicates unavailable scores due to a collapsed model during training. Using the SNGAN discriminator, we can achieve better scores without the need of data augmentation, auxilifoldary tasks and mask guidance.

Discriminator	Params. (M)	IS ↑	FID ↓
DCGAN [32]	0.6	✗	✗
StyleGANv2 [22]	21.5	4.19	127.25
SAGAN [41]	1.1	7.29	26.08
AutoGAN [14]	9.4	8.59	13.23
TransGAN [20]	12.4	8.63	11.89
SNGAN w/o SN	9.4	8.79	9.45
SNGAN [27]	9.4	**8.81**	**8.95**

Table 2. Benchmark results on CIFAR-10 using different generator sizes together with the convolutional SNGAN discriminator. Our hybrid model achieves consistently better scores when compared to the full transformer-based GAN, especially for small transformer-based generators. Note that our approach does not employ any additional mechanisms during training.

Generator	Params. (M)	Discriminator	IS ↑	FID ↓
TransGAN-S	18.6	TransGAN	8.22	18.58
		SNGAN	**8.79**	**9.95**
TransGAN-M	33.1	TransGAN	8.36	16.27
		SNGAN	**8.80**	**9.53**
TransGAN-L	74.3	TransGAN	8.50	14.46
		SNGAN	**8.81**	**8.97**
TransGAN-XL	133.6	TransGAN	8.63	11.89
		SNGAN	**8.81**	**8.95**

After benchmarking the discriminator topology, we ablate the size of the transformer-based generator using the scaled-up models of [20]. Table 2 contains the scores for each configuration where we can see how our approach systematically outperforms the fully transformer-based version. Additionally, we observe how a bigger capacity leads to better results, but with marginal gains above

TransGAN-L size. This behaviour indicates a saturation in the generative model and hence adding more capacity might not further improve the results.

Table 3 contains results on other commonly used datasets. Our method, consisting of a transformer-based generator and SNGAN discriminator achieved similar or better results without requiring data augmentation, auxiliary tasks or mask guidance. Figure 2 shows random generated samples which appear to be natural, visually pleasing and diverse in shape and in texture.

Table 3. FID results on various datasets. Our hybrid model achieves similar or better scores when compared to either a full convolutional or full transformer-based GAN.

FID ↓	CIFAR-10	CIFAR-100	STL-10	ImageNet
SNGAN [27]	22.16	27.13	43.75	29.30
TransGAN [20]	11.89	–	**25.32**	–
Ours	**8.95**	**14.29**	31.30	**14.53**

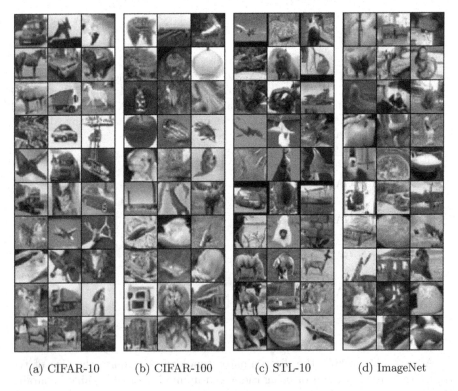

(a) CIFAR-10   (b) CIFAR-100   (c) STL-10   (d) ImageNet

Fig. 2. Random generated samples of our method trained on different datasets. The images are visually pleasing and diverse in shape and in texture.

4.3   Frequency Analysis

While a good score on the chosen image metric is one way to assess the performance of a given model, there are other, equally important properties, that need to be evaluated. Recently, [9] observed that commonly used convolutional up-sampling operations might lead to the inability to learn the spectral distribution of real images, especially their high-frequency components. Furthermore, these artifacts seem to be present in all kinds of convolutional based models, independently of their topology. Following prior works [9,10], we also employ the azimuthal integration over the Fourier power spectrum to analyze the spectral properties of generated images, and we extend the evaluation to non-convolutional based systems. In particular, we conduct experiments on pure attention, pure convolutional and hybrid architectures trained on CIFAR-10.

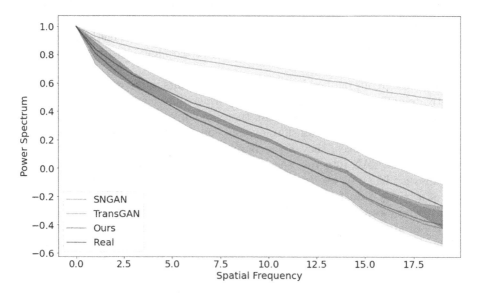

Fig. 3. Power spectrum results of real and generated images on CIFAR-10. Statistics (mean and variance) after azimuthal integration over the power spectrum of real and generated images. Our hybrid model displays good spectral properties indicated by a response similar to the real data.

Figure 3 displays the power spectrum of real data and images generated by three different models. Among them, one is based on convolutions (SNGAN), one is based on transformers (TransGAN), and one is a hybrid model (ours). Notice how the pure CNN approach has a significantly worse power spectrum indicated by an unmatched frequency response when compared to real data. TransGAN and our method are much more aligned with the real spectrum, but still there is a substantial gap. By using the transformer-based generator and a strong CNN discriminator, our model achieves better results in terms of IS and

FID without the additional data augmentation, auxiliary loss and masking prior while retaining a good frequency spectrum.

5 Discussion

Our method successfully combines transformers with convolutions into a hybrid GAN model and achieves similar or better results compared to its fully convolutional and fully attentional baselines. Furthermore, our method removes the need of data augmentation, auxiliary learning tasks, and masking priors to guide the self-attention mechanism. Additionally, images generated by our hybrid approach retain the benefits of the attention-based TransGAN in terms of frequency spectrum.

By benchmarking several discriminator topologies and differently-sized generators, we found that the capacity of the convolutional discriminator must be aligned to the capacity of the transformer-based generator and cannot be too big or too small to achieve good performance. Moreover, our method performs much more reliable across generators of different sizes and consistently achieves better scores.

Even though our method leads to promising results, more work is required to investigate optimal ways to combine transformers and convolutions into strong GANs. To the best of our knowledge, there are currently only two other GAN approaches that use both transformers and convolutions, GANsformer [18] and VQGAN [11]. However, they have completely different setups. While GANsformer and VQGAN integrate self-attention layers in-between the architecture in a sandwich like way, we keep them separated. In particular, our approach consists of a purely transformer-based generator, and a fully CNN-based discriminator, thereby constraining the interaction between attention and convolutions. Hence, our approach maintains relaxed inductive biases that characterize transformers in the generator, while leveraging the useful ones in the discriminator. Last but not least, our frequency spectrum analysis has brought new insights regarding the impact of transformers on the generated images. It shows, how a pure transformer based GAN framework, such as in TransGAN [20], seems to learn the frequency components in a more accurate manner. Our hybrid model is able to maintain the well-matched spectrum, while achieving better or similar scores without requiring additional training constraints. We think that these findings can lead to a new paradigm, where both transformers and convolutions are used to generate images.

6 Conclusion

Motivated by the desire to obtain the best from transformers and convolutions, in this work we proposed a hybrid model using a pure transformer-based generator, and a standard convolutional discriminator. Typically, transformers rely on relaxed inductive biases thereby making them universal models. As a consequence, they require vast amounts of training data. However, our method leverages the benefits of convolutions through the discriminator feedback, while retaining the advantages of transformers in the generator. Our hybrid approach achieves competitive scores across multiple common datasets, and does not need data augmentation, auxiliary learning tasks, and masking priors for the attention layers to successfully train the model. Additionally, it inherits the well-matched spectral properties from its transformer-based generator baseline. We hope this approach can pave the way towards new architectural designs, where the benefits of different architectural designs can successfully be combined into one. Possible future research directions could be investigating the importance of including inductive biases into the architectures of the generator and discriminator, respectively, as well as scaling our hybrid approach to higher resolutions.

References

1. Ba, J.L., Kiros, J.R., Hinton, G.E.: Layer normalization. arXiv:1607.06450 (2016)
2. Brock, A., Donahue, J., Simonyan, K.: Large scale GAN training for high fidelity natural image synthesis. In: International Conference on Learning Representations (2018)
3. Brown, T.B., et al.: Language models are few-shot learners. In: Advances in Neural Information Processing Systems (2020)
4. Carion, N., Massa, F., Synnaeve, G., Usunier, N., Kirillov, A., Zagoruyko, S.: End-to-end object detection with transformers. In: Vedaldi, A., Bischof, H., Brox, T., Frahm, J.-M. (eds.) ECCV 2020. LNCS, vol. 12346, pp. 213–229. Springer, Cham (2020). https://doi.org/10.1007/978-3-030-58452-8_13
5. Chen, M., et al.: Generative pretraining from pixels. In: International Conference on Machine Learning, pp. 1691–1703 (2020)
6. Coates, A., Ng, A., Lee, H.: An analysis of single-layer networks in unsupervised feature learning. In: Proceedings of the International Conference on Artificial Intelligence and Statistics, pp. 215–223 (2011)
7. Deng, J., Dong, W., Socher, R., Li, L.J., Li, K., Fei-Fei, L.: ImageNet: a large-scale hierarchical image database. In: Proceedings of the IEEE Computer Vision and Pattern Recognition, pp. 248–255 (2009)
8. Dosovitskiy, A., et al.: An image is worth 16x16 words: transformers for image recognition at scale. In: International Conference on Learning Representations (2021)
9. Durall, R., Keuper, M., Keuper, J.: Watch your up-convolution: CNN based generative deep neural networks are failing to reproduce spectral distributions. In: Proceedings of the IEEE Computer Vision and Pattern Recognition, pp. 7890–7899 (2020)
10. Durall, R., Keuper, M., Pfreundt, F.J., Keuper, J.: Unmasking deepfakes with simple features. arXiv:1911.00686 (2019)
11. Esser, P., Rombach, R., Ommer, B.: Taming transformers for high-resolution image synthesis. arXiv:2012.09841 (2020)
12. Frolov, S., Hinz, T., Raue, F., Hees, J., Dengel, A.: Adversarial text-to-image synthesis: a review. arXiv:2101.09983 (2021)
13. Frolov, S., Sharma, A., Hees, J., Karayil, T., Raue, F., Dengel, A.: AttrLost-GAN: attribute controlled image synthesis from reconfigurable layout and style. arXiv:2103.13722 (2021)

14. Gong, X., Chang, S., Jiang, Y., Wang, Z.: AutoGAN: neural architecture search for generative adversarial networks. In: Proceedings of the IEEE International Conference on Computer Vision, pp. 3224–3234 (2019)

15. Goodfellow, I.J., et al.: Generative adversarial networks. In: Advances in Neural Information Processing Systems (2014)

16. Hendrycks, D., Gimpel, K.: Gaussian error linear units (GELUs). arXiv:1606.08415 (2016)

17. Heusel, M., Ramsauer, H., Unterthiner, T., Nessler, B., Hochreiter, S.: GANs trained by a two time-scale update rule converge to a local nash equilibrium. In: Advances in Neural Information Processing Systems (2017)

18. Hudson, D.A., Zitnick, C.L.: Generative adversarial transformers. arXiv:2103.01209 (2021)

19. Isola, P., Zhu, J.Y., Zhou, T., Efros, A.A.: Image-to-image translation with conditional adversarial networks. In: Proceedings of the IEEE Computer Vision and Pattern Recognition, pp. 1125–1134 (2017)

20. Jiang, Y., Chang, S., Wang, Z.: TransGAN: two transformers can make one strong GAN. arXiv:2102.07074v2 (2021)

21. Karras, T., Laine, S., Aila, T.: A style-based generator architecture for generative adversarial networks. In: Proceedings of the IEEE Computer Vision and Pattern Recognition, pp. 4401–4410 (2019)

22. Karras, T., Laine, S., Aittala, M., Hellsten, J., Lehtinen, J., Aila, T.: Analyzing and improving the image quality of StyleGAN. In: Proceedings of the IEEE Computer Vision and Pattern Recognition, pp. 8110–8119 (2020)

23. Kingma, D.P., Welling, M.: Auto-encoding variational bayes. In: International Conference on Learning Representations (2013)

24. Krizhevsky, A., Hinton, G., et al.: Learning multiple layers of features from tiny images. Technical report, University of Toronto (2009)

25. Ledig, C., et al.: Photo-realistic single image super-resolution using a generative adversarial network. In: Proceedings of the IEEE Computer Vision and Pattern Recognition, pp. 4681–4690 (2017)

26. Lee, C.H., Liu, Z., Wu, L., Luo, P.: MaskGAN: towards diverse and interactive facial image manipulation. In: Proceedings of the IEEE Computer Vision and Pattern Recognition, pp. 5549–5558 (2020)

27. Miyato, T., Kataoka, T., Koyama, M., Yoshida, Y.: Spectral normalization for generative adversarial networks. In: International Conference on Learning Representations (2018)

28. Nair, V., Hinton, G.E.: Rectified linear units improve restricted Boltzmann machines. In: International Conference on Machine Learning (2010)

29. van den Oord, A., Kalchbrenner, N., Vinyals, O., Espeholt, L., Graves, A., Kavukcuoglu, K.: Conditional image generation with PixelCNN decoders. In: Advances in Neural Information Processing Systems (2016)

30. van den Oord, A., Vinyals, O., Kavukcuoglu, K.: Neural discrete representation learning. In: Advances in Neural Information Processing Systems (2017)

31. Parmar, N., et al.: Image transformer. In: International Conference on Machine Learning, pp. 4055–4064 (2018)

32. Radford, A., Metz, L., Chintala, S.: Unsupervised representation learning with deep convolutional generative adversarial networks. In: International Conference on Learning Representations (2015)

33. Radford, A., Wu, J., Child, R., Luan, D., Amodei, D., Sutskever, I.: Language models are unsupervised multitask learners. OpenAI blog 1(8), 9 (2019)

34. Ramesh, A., et al.: Zero-shot text-to-image generation. arXiv:2102.12092 (2021)
35. Reed, S., Akata, Z., Yan, X., Logeswaran, L., Schiele, B., Lee, H.: Generative adversarial text to image synthesis. In: International Conference on Machine Learning, pp. 1060–1069 (2016)
36. Salimans, T., Goodfellow, I., Zaremba, W., Cheung, V., Radford, A., Chen, X.: Improved techniques for training GANs. In: Advances in Neural Information Processing Systems (2016)
37. Shi, W., et al.: Real-time single image and video super-resolution using an efficient sub-pixel convolutional neural network. In: Proceedings of the IEEE Computer Vision and Pattern Recognition, pp. 1874–1883 (2016)
38. Szegedy, C., Vanhoucke, V., Ioffe, S., Shlens, J., Wojna, Z.: Rethinking the inception architecture for computer vision. In: Proceedings of the IEEE Computer Vision and Pattern Recognition, pp. 2818–2826 (2016)
39. Van Oord, A., Kalchbrenner, N., Kavukcuoglu, K.: Pixel recurrent neural networks. In: International Conference on Machine Learning, pp. 1747–1756 (2016)
40. Vaswani, A., et al.: Attention is all you need. In: Advances in Neural Information Processing Systems, pp. 5998–6008 (2017)
41. Zhang, H., Goodfellow, I., Metaxas, D., Odena, A.: Self-attention generative adversarial networks. In: International Conference on Machine Learning, pp. 7354–7363 (2019)

Explanation as a Process: User-Centric Construction of Multi-level and Multi-modal Explanations

Bettina Finzel[1(✉)], David E. Tafler[1], Stephan Scheele[2], and Ute Schmid[1]

[1] Cognitive Systems, University of Bamberg, Bamberg, Germany
{bettina.finzel,ute.schmid}@uni-bamberg.de,
david-elias.tafler@stud.uni-bamberg.de
[2] Sensory Perception & Analytics, Fraunhofer Institute for Integrated Circuits IIS, Erlangen, Germany
stephan.scheele@iis.fraunhofer.de
https://www.uni-bamberg.de/en/cogsys

Abstract. In the last years, XAI research has mainly been concerned with developing new technical approaches to explain deep learning models. Just recent research has started to acknowledge the need to tailor explanations to different contexts and requirements of stakeholders. Explanations must not only suit developers of models, but also domain experts as well as end users. Thus, in order to satisfy different stakeholders, explanation methods need to be combined. While multi-modal explanations have been used to make model predictions more transparent, less research has focused on treating explanation as a process, where users can ask for information according to the level of understanding gained at a certain point in time. Consequently, an opportunity to explore explanations on different levels of abstraction should be provided besides multi-modal explanations. We present a process-based approach that combines multi-level and multi-modal explanations. The user can ask for textual explanations or visualizations through conversational interaction in a drill-down manner. We use Inductive Logic Programming, an interpretable machine learning approach, to learn a comprehensible model. Further, we present an algorithm that creates an explanatory tree for each example for which a classifier decision is to be explained. The explanatory tree can be navigated by the user to get answers of different levels of detail. We provide a proof-of-concept implementation for concepts induced from a semantic net about living beings.

Keywords: Multi-level explanations · Multi-modal explanations · Explanatory processes · Semantic net · Inductive logic programming

The work presented in this paper is part of the BMBF ML-3 project Transparent Medical Expert Companion (TraMeExCo), FKZ 01IS18056 B, 2018-2021.

The original version of this chapter was revised: Figure 5 has been updated. The correction to this chapter is available at https://doi.org/10.1007/978-3-030-87626-5_28

© Springer Nature Switzerland AG 2021, corrected publication 2021
S. Edelkamp et al. (Eds.): KI 2021, LNAI 12873, pp. 80–94, 2021.
https://doi.org/10.1007/978-3-030-87626-5_7

1 Introduction

In order to develop artificial intelligence that serves the human user to perform better at tasks, it is crucial to make an intelligent system comprehensible to the human user [20,24]. This requires giving the user an understanding of how an underlying algorithm works (mechanistic understanding) on the one hand and whether the intelligent system fulfills its purpose (functional understanding) on the other hand [27]. Explanations can foster both types of understanding. For example, developers and experts can gain insights into the decision making process and validate the system. Users who have no in depth technical understanding in a field could use explainable systems for training, for instance as implemented in intelligent tutoring systems [26].

Methods to generate explanations are developed in Explainable Artificial Intelligence (XAI) research [10]. A variety of techniques have been proposed, namely approaches that generate post-hoc explanations for deep learned models [1], solutions based on interpretable symbolic approaches [30] as well as a combination of both in hybrid systems [5]. As existing methods are refined and new methods are developed, voices are growing louder about the need for more user-centric solutions (see for example [17,27,30]). Explanations need to fit into the context of the user, meaning the task and level of expertise. However, there is no *one-size-fits-all* explanation method, thus approaches have to be combined.

Current research proposes multi-modal explanations to serve the user's varying need for information [2,8,15], in particular a combination of different explanation strategies (inductive, deductive, contrastive) with explanation modalities (text, image, audio) to represent information accordingly and involve cognitive processes adequately for establishing effective XAI methods. Recent studies show that presenting explanations with different modalities can have a positive influence on the comprehensibility of a decision. Existing approaches combine visual, textual or auditory explanations in multi-modal settings [12,39].

Less focus is given to explanation as a process. Substantial work exists in the area of argumentation, machine learning and explanation [13,20,22,38], where conversations between systems and users follow certain patterns. However, we found that in the current literature not enough attention is given to the fact that functional or mechanistic understanding is developed over a period of time and that users may need different depths and types of information depending on where in the process they are and which level of expertise they have [8]. Template-based explanation approaches that allow humans to drill down into an explanation and to explore its sub-problems in terms of a hierarchical structure have previously been applied to assist ontology engineers in understanding inferences and to correct modelling flaws in formal ontologies [18] as well to justify results from semantic search [29]. Studies have shown that users prefer abstract and simple explanations over complex ones [19], but may ask for more detailed and complex information [40] as well, which should ideally be presented through the best possible and comprehensible explanation strategy. Therefore, involving them in a dialogue, where users can get more detailed explanations if needed, and providing multi-modal explanations at the same time to reveal different aspects of a prediction and its context, seems to be a promising step towards more comprehensible decision-making in human-AI-partnerships.

Our contribution, presented in this paper, is an approach that allows users to understand the classification of a system in a *multi-modal* way and to explore a system's decision step by step through *multi-level* explanations. Multi-modality is implemented in a way such that explanations can be requested by the user as textual statements and pictures that illustrate concepts and examples from the domain of interest. Multiple levels of explanation are implemented in such a way that the user can pose three types of requests to the system, which then returns explanations with three different levels of detail: a *global* explanation to explain a target class, a *local* explanation to explain the classification of an example with respect to the learned classification model and *drill-down* explanations that reveal more in-depth reasons for the classification of an example. Thus, users can ask for different explanation modalities and details at any point in time in the explanation process in accordance with their understanding of the system's decision that was gained until this point in time.

In a proof-of-concept implementation of our proposed approach, we represent a domain of interest as a semantic net with additional rules to reason about the domain. We train a model based on Inductive Logic Programming (ILP), since it is a method that allows for generating interpretable models [30] for relational, potentially highly complex, domains, where it may be beneficial for the understanding of a user to explain them in a step-by-step manner. In contrast to other interpretable approaches, ILP allows for integrating knowledge and learning relations. It has already been applied to concrete application fields, such as medicine [31] or more abstract examples, like family trees [9], but not yet with a combination of multi-level and multi-modal explanations. In order to generate these explanations, we produce a so-called *explanatory tree* for each example that is to be explained. Each tree is derived from a proof for the classification of an example and extended by references to images that illustrate concepts in the hierarchy. Finally, we allow for interaction in natural language with the explanatory tree through a dialogue interface. Thus, we contribute a concept for multi-level and multi-modal explanations, present an algorithm to construct such explanations and provide a proof-of-concept implementation to realize the explanation process accordingly.

The sections of our paper are organized as follows. In Sect. 2, we first describe our running example, i.e., the data basis from a relational domain, which consists of a semantic net, reasoning rules and examples. In Sect. 3, we show how the chosen ILP approach is used to generate an interpretable model by generalizing from the data basis. We proceed with describing our approach to multi-level and multi-modal explanations in Sect. 4. How to generate an explanatory tree for an example to be explained, is introduced and formalized in Subsect. 4.1. The proof-of-concept implementation is presented in Subsect. 4.2 and discussed in Subsect. 4.3. Finally, we show which research aspects and extensions of the system appear to be of interest for future work in Sect. 5.

2   A Relational Knowledge Domain

For simple domains, where the model consists just of conjunctions of feature values, it might be sufficient to give a single explanation in one modality. For instance, the prediction that *Aldo plays tennis, if the outlook is sunny and the humidity is normal* (see PlayTennis example from [21]) can be plausibly explained by presenting a verbal statement of the learned constraints. In contrast, if a model is more complex, for instance involving relational structures, multi-level and multi-modal explanations might be helpful to foster understanding.

In the following we introduce a running example that we will refer to throughout the paper to illustrate our approach. We assume the reader is familiar with first-order logic and Prolog (see [35]), but we will restate the key terminology. The main constructs in Prolog are facts, rules and queries. Basic Prolog programs consist of a finite set of Horn clauses, where each is a finite conjunction of literals with at most one positive literal, written in the form

$$A_0 \leftarrow A_1 \wedge A_2 \wedge \ldots \wedge A_n, \text{ where } n \geq 0.$$

Each A_i is an atomic formula of the form $p(t_1, \ldots, t_m)$, consisting of a predicate p and terms t_i, that are either a constant symbol, a variable or a composite expression. The atom A_0 is called the *head* and the conjunction of elements $\bigwedge_{i=1}^n A_i$ is called the *body* of a clause. Horn clauses with an empty body are denoted as *facts* and express unconditional statements, otherwise they are called *rules* and express conditional statements. Semantically, we can read a clause as "the conclusion (or *head*) A_0 is true if every A_i in the body is true". Facts are literals with constant terms. Rules express a logical implication to describe that a condition holds if a combination of literals holds, supported by given facts. *Queries* can be used to retrieve information from a Prolog program. Queries can be either facts, to check for their truth or falsity or they can be composite expressions to retrieve terms that make those expressions true. Note that Prolog uses :- to denote ←, "," for conjunction ∧ and every clause ends in a full stop.

Semantic nets are a well-known formalism to represent relational and hierarchical knowledge. They are constructed from a set of nodes and a set of directed, labeled edges, where nodes represent concepts and edges denote the semantic relationships between concepts [6,11]. A semantic network serves as a schema to represent facts in a declarative way and can therefore be implemented, for example in Prolog using predicates to represent relations between concepts.

Figure 1a represents knowledge about living beings and their relations to each other. The nodes in the semantic net represent concepts and their subset hierarchy is expressed through edges via the is relationship, e.g., birds belong to class animal. The has relation denotes properties of a concept, e.g., bird *has* feathers. Both relations are transitive, e.g., a carnivore is an animal, because it is a mammal which is an animal. Figure 1b shows the corresponding Prolog encoding, where facts consist of a predicate (is_a or has_property) with one or more *constants* as terms, e.g., is_a(plant,being) denotes that plant is a being.

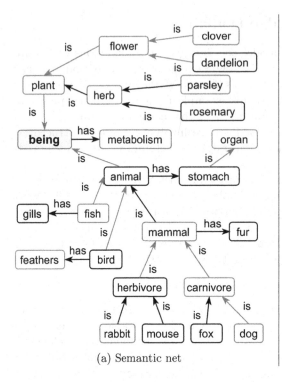

```
is_a(plant,being).
is_a(animal,being).
is_a(flower,plant).
is_a(clover,flower).
is_a(dandelion,flower).
is_a(herb,plant).
is_a(parsley,herb).
is_a(rosemary,herb).
is_a(fish,animal).
is_a(bird,animal).
is_a(mammal,animal).
is_a(herbivore,mammal).
is_a(carnivore,mammal).
is_a(mouse,herbivore).
is_a(rabbit,herbivore).
is_a(fox,carnivore).
is_a(dog,carnivore).
is_a(stomach,organ).

has_p(being,metabolism).
has_p(animal,stomach).
has_p(fish,gills).
has_p(bird,feathers).
has_p(mammal,fur).
```

(a) Semantic net   (b) Prolog representation

Fig. 1. Semantic net of living beings and its representation in Prolog.

Reasoning over a Prolog program P is based on the inference rule *modus ponens*, i.e., from B and $A \leftarrow B$ one can deduce A, and the first-order resolution principle and *unification* (the reader may refer to [3,35] for more details). For a query q it verifies whether logical variables can be successfully substituted with constants from existing facts or some previously implied conditions from P. That means, an existentially quantified query q is a logical consequence of a program P if there is a clause in P with a ground instance $A \leftarrow B_1, ..., B_n, n \geq 0$ such that $B_1, ..., B_n$ are logical consequences of P, and A is an instance of q. Thus, to answer query A, the conjunctive query $\bigwedge_{i=1}^{n} B_i$ is answered first, since A follows from it. For instance, the first reasoning rule from our running example, denoting that is(A,B) $\leftarrow$ is_a(A,B) can be used to query the semantic net. If we pose the query is(animal,being) accordingly, it will be *true*, since the predicate is_a(animal,being) is present in the facts. With the second reasoning rule is(A,B) (see below) and the query is(fox,being) we could, for example, find out that a fox is a living being, due to transitivity.

Additionally, we introduce inheritance and generalization for both relationships, e.g., to express that concept rabbit inherits *has* relationships from mammal. For instance, a rabbit *has* fur, since it *is* a mammal that *has* fur. Generalisation, on the other hand, allows us to express properties in a more abstract way, e.g., that an animal *has* a stomach and since the more general concept of stomach *is* organ, it follows that animal *has* organ. Transitivity and inheritance as well as generalisation are expressed by the following reasoning rules:

```
is(A,B)  :-  is_a(A,B).        is(A,B)  :-  is_a(A,C), is(C,B).
has(A,X) :-  has_p(A,X).       has(X,Z) :-  has_p(X,Y), has(Y,Z).
has(A,X) :-  is(A,B), has(B,X). has(A,X) :-  has_p(A,Y), is(Y,X).
```

We will show later how successful unifications resulting from this step-wise reasoning procedure can be stored in a data structure, which we call *explanatory trees*, to generate explanations with different levels of detail.

```
is_a(bobby,rabbit).
is_a(fluffy,rabbit).
is_a(bella,fox).
is_a(samson,dog).
is_a(argo,dog).
is_a(tipsie,mouse).
is_a(dandelion,flower).
is_a(clover,flower).
is_a(parsley,herb).
is_a(rosemary,herb).
```

Bobby   Fluffy   Bella   Samson   Argo

Tipsie   dandelion   clover   parsley   rosemary

Fig. 2. Background knowledge T with corresponding example images.

```
tracks_down(bobby,dandelion).     tracks_down(argo,argo).
tracks_down(fluffy,clover).       tracks_down(dandelion,bobby).
tracks_down(samson,fluffy).       tracks_down(bobby,bobby).
tracks_down(bella,bobby).         tracks_down(blubbly,samson).
tracks_down(bella,tipsie).        tracks_down(fluffy,argo).
tracks_down(bobby,parsley).       tracks_down(clover,clover).
tracks_down(fluffy,rosemary).     tracks_down(tipsie,bella).
tracks_down(tipsie,rosemary).     tracks_down(rosemary,tipsie).
```

Fig. 3. Positive (E^+) and negative (E^-) training examples.

The definition of the semantic net and the reasoning rules represent a so-called background theory T [7], about living beings in this case, but it does not include examples yet. In order to represent knowledge about examples, entries for each example can be added to T by including respective predicates such as shown in Fig. 2, e.g., to express that bobby is an instance of the concept rabbit.

Having the background theory complemented by knowledge about concrete examples, which describes relational and hierarchical knowledge, we proceed to take this as input to learn a classification model for a given target class. From a user's perspective, the target class can be understood as a concept, which we want to explain to the user. For our running example, we define a relational classification task, where the model has to learn if and under which conditions a living being would *track down* another living being.

Consider the set of training examples in Fig. 3. First, we define a set E^+ of *positive* examples that belong to the target class. For example, the rabbit bobby would track down dandelion. Secondly, we define a set E^- of *negative* examples that do not belong to the target class, i.e., we define cases that exclude reflexivity, inverse transitivity within species and inverses among all species. For instance, consider the dog argo that would not track down itself and obviously also the flower dandelion would not track down the rabbit bobby.

3   Learning an Interpretable Model with ILP

Inductive Logic Programming (ILP) will be applied to induce a classification model in terms of inferred rules from the given examples and background theory as introduced before. For our running example, the model shall learn whether one living being would track down another living being. ILP is capable of learning a model over hierarchical and non-hierarchical relations that separates positive from negative examples. The basic learning task of ILP (see e.g., [3] and [23]) is described in Algorithm 1 and defined as follows:

An ILP problem is a tuple (T, E^+, E^-) of ground atoms, where the background theory T is a finite set of Horn clauses, and E^+ and E^- are disjoint finite sets of positive and negative example instances. The goal is to construct a first-order clausal theory M we call *model*, which is a set of definite clauses that consistently explains the examples w.r.t. the background theory. Specifically, it must hold that the model M is *complete* and *consistent*, i.e.,

$$\forall p \in E^+ : T \cup M \vDash p, \text{and } \forall n \in E^- : T \cup M \nvDash n,$$

where symbol $\vDash$ denotes the semantic entailment relation and we assume the examples to be noise-free, i.e., this excludes false positives and false negatives.

In particular, it can be seen from Algorithm 1 that it learns in a top-down approach a set of clauses which cover the positive examples while not covering the negative ones. A model is induced by iteratively generating new clauses C using the function $GenerateNewClause$ [9] with T, E^+ and E^-, such that for each C there exists a positive example p that is entailed by $C \cup T$, i.e., $C \cup T \vDash p$, while no negative example n is entailed by $C \cup T$. Furthermore, it is of interest to find clauses such that each C is optimal with respect to some *quality criterion* $A(C)$, such as the total number of entailed positive examples. Such *best* clauses are added to model M.

In our approach we use the *Aleph* framework with default settings for the quality criterion [34] to generalize clauses (rules) from (T, E^+, E^-). A well-structured overview on ILP and Aleph in particular is given in Gromowski et al. [9]. Given the examples as well as the background theory for our running example, Aleph learns a model consisting of two rules (see Fig. 4). According to these rules, a living being A tracks down another living being B either if A is a carnivore and B is a herbivore, or A is a herbivore and B is a plant.

Note that in our running example, we disregarded carnivorous plants as well as cannibals. Since ILP works based on the *closed world* assumption, these cases do not hold given T.

Algorithm 1: Basic ILP algorithm

Input:
(T, E^+, E^-): an ILP problem
Output:
M: a classification model
Begin:
    $M \leftarrow \varnothing$, initialise the model
    $C \leftarrow \varnothing$, temporary clause
    $Pos \leftarrow E^+$, the set of positive training examples
       While $Pos \neq \varnothing$ **do**
          $C \leftarrow GenerateNewClause(Pos, E^-, T)$
             such that $\exists p \in E^+ : T \cup C \vDash p$
             and $\forall n \in E^- : T \cup C \nvDash n$
             and C is optimal w.r.t. quality criterion $A(C)$
          $Pos \leftarrow Pos \smallsetminus \{p\}$
          $M \leftarrow M \cup \{C\}$
       End
       Return M
End

```
tracks_down(A,B) :- is(A,carnivore), is(B,herbivore).
tracks_down(A,B) :- is(A,herbivore), is(B,plant).
```

Fig. 4. Learned model

4   Multi-level and Multi-modal Explanations

Having the model induced from a relational background theory and training examples, we can now proceed to explain the model's prediction for an individual example with our proposed multi-level and multi-modal approach that is presented and discussed in the following subsections. We define and explain how our proposed approach generates explanations and how the user can enter into a dialogue with the system to receive them.

4.1   Explanation Generation

Explanations produced by our approach cover three different levels, which can be described as follows.

- The **first level** reveals a *global* explanation, thus an explanation for the target class (e.g., What does *tracks_down* mean?). This level of detail gives the most shallow explanation for a target class of positive examples.
- The **second level** gives a *local* explanation for the classification of an example by instantiating the global model.
- The **third level** allows for a theoretically endless amount of detail/drill-down. The drill-down follows each clause's body, which can consist of literals that

constitute heads of further clauses. Thus producing explanations continues as long as the user asks follow-up questions. However, if the dialogue reaches a fact, the drill-down ends. The user can then ask for an image in order to receive a visual explanation.

This means, the user can ask for the class of an example, for an explanation for the class decision as well as ask for explanations for the underlying relational concepts and features in a step-by-step manner. We define the terminology and different kinds of explanations more formally in the following paragraphs.

Let $P = M \cup T$ be a Prolog program, which we can query to explain the classification of a positive example $p \in E^+$. We can create a tree ε for each clause in $C \in M$ with $C \vDash p$, which we call an *explanatory tree*. This tree is created as part of performing a proof for example p, given a clause $C \in M$ and the corresponding background theory T such as introduced in [3]. We extend the proof computation by storing ε consisting of successful query and sub-query unifications. We check, whether an example $p \in E^+$ can be proven to be entailed by $T \cup C$, where $C \in M$, all generated by Algorithm 1.

The tree can be traversed to yield explanations of different levels of detail for our proposed dialogue approach. In order to generate a *global* explanation for a target class c (see Definition 1), the set of all clauses from model M of that target class are presented. In order to explain a positive example p globally, only the clauses from M that entail p are presented. The global explanation corresponds to the body of each clause C from M, while the target class is encoded in the heads of all clauses in M. In order to generate a *local* explanation (see Definition 2), a ground clause $C\theta$ has to be found for C taken from M or T, under substitution θ of the terms in C. A local explanation is derived from a successful proof of q initialized to the head of $C\theta$, where the body of the clause $C\theta$ is entailed by M and T. The *drill-down* is applied to a local explanation $C\theta$ (see Definition 3), and is defined as the creation of a subsequent local explanation for some ground literal $B_i\theta$ from the set of all literals from the body of $C\theta$, given that the body of $C\theta$ is not empty. If the head of $C\theta$ is a fact and consequently the body of $C\theta$ is empty, the drill-down stops.

Definition 1 (Global explanation). *A* global *explanation for a target class c is given by the set M of all clauses in the learned model.*

Definition 2 (Local explanation). *A* local *explanation for a query q is a ground clause $C\theta$ where $C \in M \cup T$ such that $q = head(C\theta)$ and $M \cup T \vDash body(C\theta)$.*

Definition 3 (Drill down of a local explanation). *A* drill down *for a local explanation $C\theta$ is given by some literal in $body(C\theta) = B_1, B_2, \ldots, B_n$ where $n \geq 0$ such that either $head(C\theta)$ is a fact, i.e., $head(C\theta) \vdash true$ $(body(C\theta) = \varnothing)$; or otherwise $body(C\theta) \neq \varnothing$ and we create a local explanation for some $B_i\theta$, where $1 > i \leq n$.*

Accordingly, the explanatory tree ε is constructed such that, for each successful unification of a query q, ground q is the parent node of ground clauses resulting from the proof of q. The explanatory tree ε can be traversed up and down in a dialogue to get explanations at all defined levels of detail in the form of natural language expressions or images at leaf nodes.

4.2   Explanatory Dialogue

As presented above, our multi-level and multi-modal explanation approach allows the user to enter into a dialogue with the system and ask for explanations on three different levels. Accordingly, users can pose various types of questions, depending on the need for information and detail.

The input, internal program structure as well as the output of an ILP program is represented in expressive first-order predicate logic, in Prolog. Nevertheless, although its output is readable for humans, it is not necessarily comprehensible, due to factors like the complexity of the domain of interest and the unusual syntax. We therefore realize the explanatory dialogue by generating natural language expressions.

Template-based generation is commonly used to generate natural language explanations for logic-based models, e.g., see Siebers et al. [32] and Musto et al. [25] or [18]. Our template consists of domain-specific as well as domain-independent transformation rules. For example the *has_a* and *is_a* relations can be easily translated for any kind of data set, which is structured as a semantic net. For binary predicates we connect the first argument with the second argument through a transformed version of the predicate. In case of a n-ary predicate, arguments are added by *and*. Each parent node from the explanatory tree is connected to its direct children through the word *because*, since giving a reason is at the core of implication. Consider the first rule of our learned model, presented in Sect. 3. Transforming this rule to formulate for example a *global* explanation in natural language results in the sentence: "A tracks down B, because A is a carnivore and B is a herbivore.". For a *local* explanation, the sentence is, e.g.: "Bella tracks down Bobby, because Bella is a carnivore and Bobby is a herbivore.". Beyond this template-based expression generation, our dialogue provides some static content, such as introductory content, advice and an epilogue, when the user quits the program.

An example of an explanatory dialogue for the classification of the relationship between *Bobby* and *dandelion* is presented in Fig. 5. The different levels of explanations correspond to the levels of the previously generated explanatory tree. The user can explore the whole tree, following the paths up and down, depending on the type of request (see Fig. 5). Due to space restrictions we are only presenting the dialogue for local explanations and drill-down requests. The user could ask for a global explanation by posing the question: "What does tracks_down mean?". The system would return an answer based on the verbalization of the predicate is and the constants carnivore and herbivore to explain the first rule of the learned model from Sect. 3.

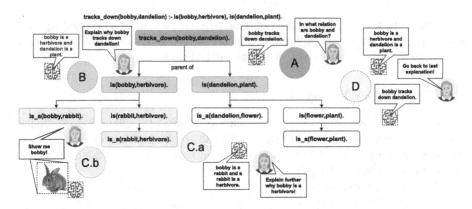

Fig. 5. An explanatory tree for `tracks_down(bobby,dandelion)`, that can be queried by the user to get a *local* explanation why Bobby tracks down dandelion (steps A and B). A dialogue is realized by different *drill-down* questions, either to get more detailed verbal explanations or visual explanations (steps C.a and C.b)). Furthermore, the user can return to the last explanation (step D).

4.3   Proof-of-Concept Implementation

The dialogue presented in Sect. 4.2 illustrates the proof-of-concept implementation of our approach. The code is accessible via gitlab[1]. In general, the approach is not only applicable to the domain presented here. Any Prolog program including a model learned with ILP can be explained with our approach. The only precondition is, that the template-based verbalization of the nodes from the explanatory tree can be performed by the domain-independent transformation rules. Otherwise, domain-specific transformation rules must be defined first. Furthermore, we want to point out that the introduced algorithm fulfills correctness, since it is complete and consistent with respect to the ILP problem solution. Finally, first empirical investigations show that humans perform better in decision-making and trust more into the decisions of an intelligent system, if they are presented with visual as well as verbal explanations [37].

5   Conclusion and Outlook

Explanations of decisions made by intelligent systems need to be tailored to the needs of different stakeholders. At the same time there exists no *one-size-fits-all* explanation method. Consequently, an approach that combines explanation modalities and that provides explanation as a step-by-step process, is promising to satisfy various users. We presented an approach that combines textual and visual explanations, such that the user can explore different kinds of explanations

---

[1] Gitlab repository of the proof-of-concept implementation: https://gitlab.rz.uni-bamberg.de/cogsys/public/multi-level-multi-modal-explanation.

by posing requests to the system through a dialogue. We introduced an algorithm as well as our proof-of-concept implementation of it.

In comparison to other explainable state-of-the-art systems that present explanations rather as static content [1], our approach allows for step-by-step exploration of the reasons behind a decision of an intelligent system. Since our approach is interpretable, it could help users in the future to uncover causalities between data and a system's prediction. This is especially important in decision-critical areas, such as medicine [4,14,31].

Other recent interactive systems enable the user to perform corrections on labels and to act upon wrong explanations, such as implemented in the CAIPI approach [36], they allow for re-weighting of features for explanatory debugging, like the EluciDebug system [16] and correcting generated verbal explanations and the underlying model through user-defined constraints, such as implemented in the medical-decision support system LearnWithME [31]. Our approach could be extended by correction capabilities in the future, in addition to requesting information from the system to better understand its operation or purpose. In that way, explanations would be bi-directional.

We presented a proof-of-concept implementation of our approach that could be technically extended in the future by combining explanations with linked data, e.g., to integrate formal knowledge from ontologies combined with media from open data repositories, which would allow for more flexibility in the presentation of content based on semantic search[2]. Furthermore, we envisage to explain decisions of deep neural networks using ILP, as presented in [28].

In future work, we aim to systematically evaluate our approach with empirical user studies, recognizing design dimensions of XAI put forth by Sperrle et al. [33]. In this context, our multi-modal and multi-level approach allows for precise control and manipulation of experimental conditions. For instance, we are currently preparing an empirical study to evaluate the effectiveness of the combination of multi-level and multi-modal explanations with respect to user performance and understanding of a model. It is planned to apply the proposed approach to a decision-critical scenario, in particular to asses pain and emotions in human facial expressions for a medical use case.

In order to meet a user-centric explanation design and to close the semantic gap between data, model and explanation representation, the use of hybrid approaches seems promising as a future step. Especially in the field of image-based classification, it is an exciting task to consider sub-symbolic neural networks as sensory components and to combine them with symbolic approaches as drivers of knowledge integration. In this way, models can be validated and corrected with the help of expert knowledge. Furthermore, hybrid approaches allow for modeling the context of an application domain in a more expressive and complex manner and, in addition, taking into account users' context and individual differences. Our approach is a first step towards this vision.

---

[2] Retrieval through semantic search can be performed for example over semantic *mediawiki*: https://www.semantic-mediawiki.org/wiki/Help:Semantic_search.

Acknowledgements. The authors would like to thank the anonymous referees, who provided useful comments on the submission version of the paper.

References

1. Arrieta, A.B., et al.: Explainable artificial intelligence (XAI): concepts, taxonomies, opportunities and challenges toward responsible AI. Inf. Fus. **58**, 82–115 (2020)
2. Baniecki, H., Biecek, P.: The grammar of interactive explanatory model analysis. CoRR abs/2005.00497 (2020)
3. Bratko, I.: Prolog Programming for Artificial Intelligence. Addison-Wesley Longman Publishing Co., Inc., Boston (1986)
4. Bruckert, S., Finzel, B., Schmid, U.: The next generation of medical decision support: a roadmap toward transparent expert companions. Front. Artif. Intell. **3**, 75 (2020)
5. Calegari, R., Ciatto, G., Omicini, A.: On the integration of symbolic and subsymbolic techniques for XAI: a survey. Intelligenza Artificiale **14**(1), 7–32 (2020)
6. Chein, M., Mugnier, M.L.: Graph-Based Knowledge Representation: Computational Foundations of Conceptual Graphs. Springer, London (2008). https://doi.org/10.1007/978-1-84800-286-9
7. De Raedt, L., Lavrač, N.: The many faces of inductive logic programming. In: Komorowski, J., Raś, Z.W. (eds.) ISMIS 1993. LNCS, vol. 689, pp. 435–449. Springer, Heidelberg (1993). https://doi.org/10.1007/3-540-56804-2_41
8. El-Assady, M., et al.: Towards XAI: structuring the processes of explanations. In: Proceedings of the ACM CHI Conference Workshop on Human-Centered Machine Learning Perspectives at CHI'19, p. 13 (2019)
9. Gromowski, M., Siebers, M., Schmid, U.: A process framework for inducing and explaining datalog theories. ADAC **14**(4), 821–835 (2020). https://doi.org/10.1007/s11634-020-00422-7
10. Gunning, D., Aha, D.: DARPA's explainable artificial intelligence (XAI) program. AI Mag. **40**(2), 44–58 (2019)
11. Hartley, R.T., Barnden, J.A.: Semantic networks: visualizations of knowledge. Trends Cogn. Sci. **1**(5), 169–175 (1997)
12. Hendricks, L.A., Hu, R., Darrell, T., Akata, Z.: Grounding visual explanations. In: Ferrari, V., Hebert, M., Sminchisescu, C., Weiss, Y. (eds.) ECCV 2018. LNCS, vol. 11206, pp. 269–286. Springer, Cham (2018). https://doi.org/10.1007/978-3-030-01216-8_17
13. Hilton, D.J.: A conversational model of causal explanation. Eur. Rev. Soc. Psychol. **2**(1), 51–81 (1991)
14. Holzinger, A., Langs, G., Denk, H., Zatloukal, K., Müller, H.: Causability and explainability of artificial intelligence in medicine. WIREs Data Min. Knowl. Discov. **9**(4), e1312 (2019)
15. Holzinger, A., Malle, B., Saranti, A., Pfeifer, B.: Towards multi-modal causability with graph neural networks enabling information fusion for explainable AI. Inf. Fus. **71**, 28–37 (2021)
16. Kulesza, T., et al.: Explanatory debugging: Supporting end-user debugging of machine-learned programs. In: 2010 IEEE Symposium on Visual Languages and Human-Centric Computing, pp. 41–48. IEEE (2010)
17. Langer, M., et al.: What do we want from explainable artificial intelligence (XAI)? - a stakeholder perspective on XAI and a conceptual model guiding interdisciplinary XAI research. Artif. Intell. **296**, 103473 (2021)

18. Liebig, T., Scheele, S.: Explaining entailments and patching modelling flaws. Künstliche Intell. **22**(2), 25–27 (2008)
19. Lombrozo, T.: Simplicity and probability in causal explanation. Cogn. Psychol. **55**(3), 232–257 (2007)
20. Miller, T.: Explanation in artificial intelligence: insights from the social sciences. Artif. Intell. **267**, 1–38 (2019)
21. Mitchell, T.M.: Machine Learning. McGraw-Hill, New York (1997)
22. Možina, M., Žabkar, J., Bratko, I.: Argument based machine learning. Artif. Intell. **171**(10), 922–937 (2007)
23. Muggleton, S., de Raedt, L.: Inductive logic programming: theory and methods. J. Logic Program. **19–20**, 629–679 (1994)
24. Muggleton, S.H., Schmid, U., Zeller, C., Tamaddoni-Nezhad, A., Besold, T.: Ultrastrong machine learning: comprehensibility of programs learned with ILP. Mach. Learn. **107**(7), 1119–1140 (2018). https://doi.org/10.1007/s10994-018-5707-3
25. Musto, C., Narducci, F., Lops, P., De Gemmis, M., Semeraro, G.: ExpLOD: a framework for explaining recommendations based on the linked open data cloud. In: Proceedings of the 10th ACM Conference on Recommender Systems, pp. 151–154. ACM, Boston (2016)
26. Putnam, V., Conati, C.: Exploring the need for explainable artificial intelligence (XAI) in intelligent tutoring systems (ITS), Los Angeles p. 7 (2019)
27. Páez, A.: The pragmatic turn in explainable artificial intelligence (XAI). Mind. Mach. **29**(3), 441–459 (2019). https://doi.org/10.1007/s11023-019-09502-w
28. Rabold, J., Siebers, M., Schmid, U.: Explaining black-box classifiers with ILP – empowering LIME with aleph to approximate non-linear decisions with relational rules. In: Riguzzi, F., Bellodi, E., Zese, R. (eds.) ILP 2018. LNCS (LNAI), vol. 11105, pp. 105–117. Springer, Cham (2018). https://doi.org/10.1007/978-3-319-99960-9_7
29. Roth-Berghofer, T., Forcher, B.: Improving understandability of semantic search explanations. Int. J. Knowl. Eng. Data Min. **1**(3), 216–234 (2011)
30. Rudin, C.: Stop explaining black box machine learning models for high stakes decisions and use interpretable models instead. Nat. Mach. Intell. **1**(5), 206–215 (2019)
31. Schmid, U., Finzel, B.: Mutual explanations for cooperative decision making in medicine. KI-Künstliche Intelligenz, pp. 1–7 (2020)
32. Siebers, M., Schmid, U.: Please delete that! Why should I? KI - Künstliche Intelligenz **33**(1), 35–44 (2018). https://doi.org/10.1007/s13218-018-0565-5
33. Sperrle, F., El-Assady, M., Guo, G., Chau, D.H., Endert, A., Keim, D.: Should we trust (X)AI? Design dimensions for structured experimental evaluations. arXiv:2009.06433 [cs] (2020)
34. Srinivasan, A.: The Aleph Manual. http://www.cs.ox.ac.uk/activities/machinelearning/Aleph/
35. Sterling, L., Shapiro, E.: The Art of Prolog: Advanced Programming Techniques. MIT Press, Cambridge (1986)
36. Teso, S., Kersting, K.: Explanatory interactive machine learning. In: Proceedings of the 2019 AAAI/ACM Conference on AI, Ethics, and Society, pp. 239–245 (2019)
37. Thaler, A., Schmid, U.: Explaining machine learned relational concepts in visual domains-effects of perceived accuracy on joint performance and trust. In: Proceedings of the 43rd Annual Conference of the Cognitive Science Society (CogSci'21, Vienna). Cognitive Science Society (to appear)

38. Walton, D.: A dialogue system for evaluating explanations. In: Argument Evaluation and Evidence. LGTS, vol. 23, pp. 69–116. Springer, Cham (2016). https://doi.org/10.1007/978-3-319-19626-8_3

39. Weitz, K., Schiller, D., Schlagowski, R., Huber, T., André, E.: "Let me explain!" exploring the potential of virtual agents in explainable AI interaction design. J. Multimod. User Interfaces **15**, 87–98 (2020)

40. Zemla, J.C., Sloman, S., Bechlivanidis, C., Lagnado, D.A.: Evaluating everyday explanations. Psychonomic Bull. Rev. **24**(5), 1488–1500 (2017). https://doi.org/10.3758/s13423-017-1258-z

Multi-Type-TD-TSR – Extracting Tables from Document Images Using a Multi-stage Pipeline for Table Detection and Table Structure Recognition: From OCR to Structured Table Representations

Pascal Fischer[✉][iD], Alen Smajic[iD], Giuseppe Abrami[iD],
and Alexander Mehler[iD]

Text Technology Lab, Goethe University Frankfurt, Frankfurt, Germany
`{s4191414,s0689492}@stud.uni-frankfurt.de`
`{abrami,mehler}@em.uni-frankfurt.de`
`https://www.texttechnologylab.org`

Abstract. As global trends are shifting towards data-driven industries, the demand for automated algorithms that can convert images of scanned documents into machine readable information is rapidly growing. In addition to digitization there is an improvement toward process automation that used to require manual inspection of documents. Although optical character recognition (OCR) technologies mostly solved the task of converting human-readable characters from images, the task of extracting tables has been less focused on. This recognition consists of two sub-tasks: table detection and table structure recognition. Most prior work on this problem focuses on either task without offering an end-to-end solution or paying attention to real application conditions like rotated images or noise artefacts. Recent work shows a clear trend towards deep learning using transfer learning for table structure recognition due to the lack of sufficiently large datasets. We present a multistage pipeline named *Multi-Type-TD-TSR*, which offers an end-to-end solution for table recognition. It utilizes state-of-the-art deep learning models and differentiates between three types of tables based on their borders. For the table structure recognition we use a deterministic non-data driven algorithm, which works on all three types. In addition, we present an algorithm for non-bordered tables and one for bordered ones as the basis of our table structure detection algorithm. We evaluate Multi-Type-TD-TSR on a self annotated subset of the ICDAR 2019 table structure recognition dataset [5] and achieve a new state-of-the-art. Source code is available under https://github.com/Psarpei/Multi-Type-TD-TSR.

Keywords: Multi-Type-TD-TSR · Table detection · Table structure recognition · Multi-stage pipeline · OCR

© Springer Nature Switzerland AG 2021
S. Edelkamp et al. (Eds.): KI 2021, LNAI 12873, pp. 95–108, 2021.
https://doi.org/10.1007/978-3-030-87626-5_8

1   Introduction

OCR based on digitized documents in general and OCR post-correction in particular remains a desideratum, especially in the context of historical documents when they have already been subjected to OCR. In the case of such texts, incorrect or incomplete recognition results often occur due to the application of mostly purely letter-oriented methods. Considerable methodological progress has been made in the recent past, with the focus of further developments being in the area of neural networks. However, special attention must be paid to the recognition of tables, where performance tends to be poor. In fact, the scores in this area are so poor that downstream NLP approaches are still practically incapable of automatically evaluating the information contained in tables. Better recognition of table structures is precisely the task to which this work relates.

Rang	Team		Rang	Team		Rang	Team
1	Centurion		1	Centurion		1	Centurion
2	Pinbu$taz		2	Pinbu$taz		2	Pinbu$taz
3	Kugelblitz		3	Kugelblitz		3	Kugelblitz
4	Cosinus phi		4	Cosinus phi		4	Cosinus phi
5	Rattlesnake on Tour		5	Rattlesnake on Tour		5	Rattlesnake on Tour
6	Dark Pins		6	Dark Pins		6	Dark Pins
7	Strike Sharkattack		7	Strike Sharkattack		7	Strike Sharkattack
8	Holy Wings		8	Holy Wings		8	Holy Wings
9	Alfi und die Chipmunk		9	Alfi und die Chipmunk		9	Alfi und die Chipmunk
a)			b)			c)	

Fig. 1. Types of tables based on how they utilize borders: a) tables without borders, b) tables with partial borders, c) tables with borders.

Tables are used to structure information into rows and columns to compactly visualize multidimensional relationships between information units. In order to convert an image of a table, i.e. a scanned document that contains a table into machine readable characters, it is important to structure the information in such a way that the original relationships between the information units and their semantics is preserved. Developing algorithms that can handle such conversion tasks is a major challenge, since the appearance and layout of tables can vary widely and depends very much on the style of the table author. The already mentioned row and column structure of tables goes hand in hand with different sizes and layouts of table elements, changing background colors and fonts per cell, row or column and changing borders of the table as a whole or its individual entries. All these properties must be taken into account in order to achieve sufficient applicability of OCR, especially in the area of historical documents. Otherwise information represented in tables is only insufficiently available or not available at all for downstream tasks of *Natural Language Processing* (NLP) and related approaches.

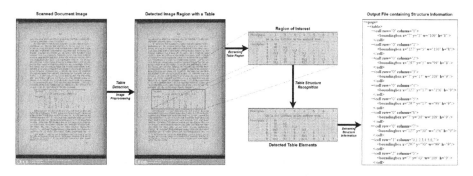

Fig. 2. Schematic depiction of the staged process of *Table Detection* (TD) and *Table Structure Recognition* (TSR) starting from table images, i.e. digitized document pages containing tables.

Consequently, we are faced with a *computer vision task* for mapping table images to structured, semantically interpreted table representations. For this task, table borders are of particular importance because they serve as a direct visualization of the table structure and act as a frame for the elementary cell elements that are ultimately input to NLP. In order to address this scenario, we distinguish between three types of tables. Figure 1a) shows a table without any table borders, Fig. 1b) a partially bordered table and Fig. 1c) a fully bordered one. We refer to tables without any borders as *unbordered tables*, tables that are completely bordered as *bordered tables* and tables that contain some borders as *partially bordered tables*. It should be mentioned that *partially bordered tables* also include unbordered and bordered tables.

The task of converting an image of a table into machine readable information starts with the digital image of a document, which is created using a scanning device. Obviously, this process is crucial for the later conversion, since small rotations of the document during scanning or noise artifacts generated by the scanning device can have a negative impact on recognition performance. The conversion itself involves two steps, namely *Table Detection* (TD) inside a document image and *Table Structure Recognition* (TSR). TD is performed to identify all regions in images that contain tables, while TSR involves identifying their components, i.e. rows, columns, and cells, to finally identify the entire table structure - see Fig. 2 for a schematic depiction of this two-step recognition process. In general, these two tasks involve detecting some sort of bounding boxes that are correctly aligned with the table elements to be identified. However, without proper alignment of the entire table image, it is not possible to generate accurate bounding boxes, which reduces the overall performance of table representation. Thus, the correct alignment of table images is to be considered as a constitutive step of the computer vision task addressed here.

In this paper, we present a multistage pipeline named *Multi-Type-TD-TSR* which solves the task of extracting tables from table images and representing their structure in an end-to-end fashion. The pipeline consists of four main modules that have been developed independently and can therefore be further developed in a modular fashion in future work. Unlike related approaches, our pipeline starts by addressing issues of rotation and noise that are common when scanning documents. For TD we use a fully data-driven approach based on a *Convolutional Neural Network* (CNN) to localize tables inside images and forward them to TSR. For the latter we use a deterministic algorithm in order to address all three table types of Fig. 1. Between TD and TSR, we perform a pre-processing step to create font and background color invariance so that the tables contain only black as the font color and white as the background color. In addition, we present two specialized algorithms for bordered tables and unbordered tables, respectively. These two algorithms form the basis for our table type-independent algorithm for recognizing table structures. Our algorithm finally represents recognized table elements by means of a predefined data structure, so that the table semantics can finally be processed further as a structured document – for example in NLP pipelines.

For table detection we use the state-of-the-art deep learning approach proposed by Li *et al.* [12], which was evaluated on the TableBank [12] dataset. For the task of table structure recognition we evaluate Multi-type-TD-TSR on a self-annotated subset of the ICDAR 2019 dataset (Track B2) [5].

The paper is structured as follows: In Sect. 2, we summarize related work. Then the pipeline of Multi-type-TD-TSR is explained in Sect. 3 and in detail in Sect. 4. After that, the evaluation and comparison with state-of-the-art techniques is presented in Sect. 5. Finally, we draw a conclusion in Sect. 6.

2   Related Work

Several works have been published on the topic of extracting table semantics and there are comprehensive surveys available describing and summarizing the state-of-the-art in the field since 1997 when P. Pyreddy and, W. B. Croft [15] proposed the first approach of detecting tables using heuristics like character alignment and gaps inside table images. To further improve accuracy, Wonkyo Seo *et al.* [21] used an algorithm to detect junctions, that is, intersections of horizontal and vertical lines inside bordered tables. T. Kasar *et al.* [10] also used junction detection, but instead of heuristics he passed the junction information to a SVM [4] to achieve higher detection performance.

With the advent of *Deep Learning* (DL), advanced object recognition algorithms, and the first publicly available datasets, the number of fully data-driven approaches continued to grow. Azka Gilani *et al.* [7] was the first to propose a DL-based approach for table detection by using Faster R-CNN [16]. Currently, there are three primary datasets used for TD and TSR. The first one is provided by the ICDAR 2013 table competition [9], which is a benchmark for TD and TSR. The dataset contains a total of 150 tables: 75 tables in 27 excerpts from the EU and 75 tables in 40 excerpts from the US Government. Its successor, the ICDAR 2019 competition on Table Detection and Recognition (cTDaR) [5] features two datasets. The first one consists of modern documents with modern tables, while the other consists of archival documents with presence of hand-drawn tables and handwritten text. In general this dataset includes 600 documents for each of the two datasets with annotated bounding boxes for the image regions containing a table. In 2020, Li *et al.* [12] published the TableBank dataset, the latest available dataset. It consists of Word and LaTeX documents and is the first to be generated completely automatically. The TableBank dataset includes 417.234 annotated tables for TD and 145.463 for TSR. Unfortunately, the dataset for TSR contains only information about the number of rows and columns, but no information about the location or size of table elements. Li *et al.* [12] proposed a ResNeXt-152 [23] model trained on TableBank for TD, which represents the current state-of-the-art for type-independent TD.

Riba *et al.* [18] introduce an approach based on Graph Neural Networks (GNNs) to detect tables in invoice documents. In contrast to methods that rely on DL-based approaches coupled with transfer learning on representative datasets, the method of Riba *et al.* models documents as graphs and treats table detection as a node classification problem. This approach works well on invoice table layouts. However, its generalizability to other tabular layouts remains to be proven. A more general approach is presented by Lu and Dooms [13] who develop a probabilistic framework for document segmentation, which also uses Gestalt patterns to identify text regions in the context of (non-)text classification.

In web-based table detection, a number of approaches exist that evaluate features from HTML code in addition to visual features of tables [3,6]. An extension to this comes from Buehler and Paulheim [2], who present a CNN-based approach to table classification based on rendered images. They show that classification based only on visual features can achieve results comparable to feature engineering based on HTML code. Moreover, they reach a new state of the art in web table classification by combining both methods using random forests.

In 1998, Kieninger and Dengel [11], introduced the first approach to TSR by means of clubbing text into chunks and dividing chunks into cells based on column border. The low number of annotated tables with bounding-boxes for TSR enforces the use of transfer learning and leads to a high risk of overfitting. Schreiber *et al.* [20] addressed TD and TSR in a single approach using a two-fold system based on Faster R-CNN [16] for TD and DL-based semantic segmentation for TSR that utilizes transfer learning. Mohsin *et al.* [17] generalized the model by combining a GAN [8] based architecture for TD with a SegNet [1] based encoder-decoder architecture for TSR. Recently, Prasad *et al.* [14] presented an end-to-end TD and TSR model based on transfer learning. It is the first approach that distinguishes between different types of tables and solves each type with a different algorithm. First, an object detection model is used to identify tables inside a document and to classify them as either bordered or unbordered. In a second step, TSR is addressed with a CNN for non-bordered tables and with a deterministic algorithm based on the vertical and horizontal table borders for bordered tables. For the development of Multi-Type-TD-TSR we utilize the TD approach proposed by Li *et al.* [12], since it offers the state-of-the-art model for type-independent TD, which is crucial for our TSR approach. For the task of TSR we use the architecture proposed by Prasad *et al.* [14], who introduced the erosion and dilation operation for bordered tables, and extend this approach to implement a robust algorithm that can handle all table types.

3   End-to-End Multistage Pipeline

Fig. 3 shows our multi-stage, multi-type pipeline. It consists of two main parts, namely *Table Detection* (TD), which processes the full-size image, and *Table Structure Recognition* (TSR), which processes only the recognized sections from TD. In the first step, a pre-processing function is applied to the scanned document image to account for documents that were not properly aligned during scanning and to correct the digital image alignment before the scan is passed on to the next step. The aligned image is then fed into a ResNext152 model of the sort proposed by [12] in order to perform TD. Based on the predicted bounding boxes, the recognized tables are cropped from the image and successively passed to TSR. Here, our algorithm applies a second preprocessing step, which accounts for documents with graphical table features (e.g. table cells with varying background colors). The algorithm converts the foreground, which in this case contains information units such as lines and fonts, to black and the background to white, resulting in a color-variant image. In the next step, 3 branching options are available. The first one uses an algorithm specialized for unbordered tables. The second one utilizes a conventional algorithm based on [14] that is specialized for bordered tables. The third option is a combination of the latter two; it works on partially bordered tables, which includes fully bordered and fully unbordered tables, making the algorithm type-independent. Finally, the recognized table structure is exported per input table using a predefined data structure. It should be mentioned that our type-independent algorithm works only with rows and columns that span the entire table. Therefore, we consider recursive tables that contain nested rows and columns as out of scope.

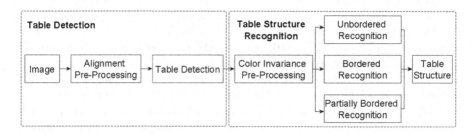

Fig. 3. The two-stage process of TD and TSR in Multi-Type-TD-TSR.

4   Methods

All three TSR algorithms used by us are based on the following two mathematical operations. The first operation is `dilation` defined as follows:

$$\texttt{dilation}(x, y) = \max_{(x', y'): K(x', y') \neq 0} I(x + x', y + y') \tag{1}$$

This operation involves filtering an image I with a kernel K, which can be of any shape and size, but in our case is a rectangle. K has a defined anchor point, in our case the center of the kernel. As K slides over the image, the maximum pixel value overlapped by K is determined and the image pixel value at the anchor point position is overwritten by this maximum value. Maximization causes bright areas within an image to be magnified.

The second operation named `erosion` is defined as follows:

$$\texttt{erosion}(x, y) = \min_{(x', y'): K(x', y') \neq 0} I(x + x', y + y') \tag{2}$$

It works analogously to `dilation`, but determines a local minimum over the area of the kernel. As K slides over I, it determines the minimum pixel value overlapped by K and replaces the pixel value under the anchor point with this minimum value. Conversely to `dilation`, `erosion` causes bright areas of the image to become thinner while the dark areas become larger.

Following the example of Prasad *et al.* [14], we use `erosion` on bordered tables to detect vertical and horizontal borders, which need to be retained, while removing the font and characters from the table cells resulting in a grid-cell image. `Dilation` is applied successively to restore the original table border structure, since `erosion` shortens the borders. Additionally we apply `erosion` on unbordered tables to add the missing borders producing a full grid-cell image.

4.1 Table Alignment Pre-processing

The first method of our Multi-Type-TD-TSR algorithm includes table alignment pre-processing, which is crucial for TSR since it ensures that the TD model is able to draw proper bounding boxes around the table regions. Currently, this pre-processing utilizes the text skew correction algorithm proposed by [19]. To remove all noise artifacts within an image, we apply a median filter of kernel size 5×5 pixels, which showed the best results in our experiments and produced the cleanest images. One by one, the algorithm converts the image to grayscale and flips the pixel values of the foreground (lines and characters) so that they have a white color and the background has a black color. In the next step we compute a single bounding box that includes all pixels that are not of black color and therefore represent the document content. Based on this bounding box we calculate the angle under which the content is presented inside the image and apply a deskew function, which rotates the whole bounding box along with its content to be orthogonal with respect to the horizontal image axis.

4.2 Table Detection

In the TD step, we extract the bounding-boxes for each table inside the image by using a *Convolutional Neural Network* (CNN) which does not distinguish between the three table types (see Fig. 1). We utilize the approach of Li *et al.* [12] who trained a ResNeXt-152 [23] model on the TableBank dataset [12]. The reason for this selection is that this model reaches the best results by only detecting bounding boxes for each table without classification. The state-of-the-art approach from Prasad *et al.* performs an additional classification of tables by borders. We decided against the approach of Prasad *et al.* [14], since their classification only considers two table types and also includes a slightly different definition of bordered and unbordered tables than ours.

4.3   Bordered TSR

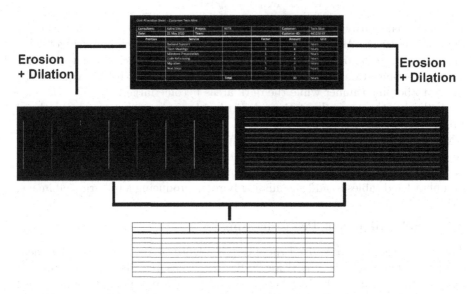

Fig. 4. Example of the erosion and dilation operations as performed by Multi-Type-TD-TSR for bordered tables.

The algorithm for bordered TSR is based on the same named algorithm from Prasad *et al.* [14], which utilizes the erosion and dilation operation for extracting the row-column grid cell image without any text or characters. The first step includes converting the image into a binary representation with pixel values of either zero (black) or one (white) and finally inverting these values to get a table image of white foreground (lines and characters) and black background as shown in the upper part of Fig. 4. The intuition behind this approach is that most documents use black (dark) color for font, lines and other information units, while the background color is white (bright). We also consider the case where dark colors are used as background with bright colored fonts in Sect. 4.6. In the next step, a horizontal and vertical erosion kernel $k_h, k_v \in \mathbb{R}^2$ are applied independently to the inverted image. It is worth mentioning that the kernel shape and size is not fixed and can be set for both erosion kernels. The erosion kernels are generally thin vertical and horizontal strips that are longer than the overall font size but shorter than the size of the smallest grid cell and, in particular, must not be wider than the smallest table border width. Using these kernel size constraints results in the erosion operation removing all fonts and characters from the table while preserving the table borders. Since the erosion operation is keeping the minimum pixel value from the kernel overlay, its application leads to shorter lines compared to the original table borders. In order to restore the original line shape, the algorithm applies the dilation operation using the same kernel size on each of the two eroded images like shown in the middle part of Fig. 4, producing an image with vertical and a second with horizontal lines. The dilation operation rebuilds the lines by keeping only the maximum pixel value from the kernel overlay of the image. Finally, the algorithm combines both images by using a *bit-wise or* operation and re-inverting the pixel values to obtain a raster cell image, as shown in the lower part of Fig. 4. We then use the contours function on the grid-cell image to extract the bounding-boxes for every single grid cell.

4.4 Unbordered TSR

The TSR algorithm for unbordered tables works similarly to the one for bordered tables. It also starts with converting the image to a binary representation. However, unlike the first algorithm it does not invert the pixel values straight away and also does not utilize the dilation operation. Furthermore, it uses a different kind of erosion compared to TSR for bordered tables. The erosion kernel is in general a thin strip with the difference that the horizontal size of the horizontal kernel includes the full image width and the vertical size of the vertical kernel the full image height. The algorithm slides both kernels independently over the whole image from left to right for the vertical kernel, and from top to bottom for the horizontal kernel. During this process it is looking for empty rows and columns that do not contain any characters or font. The resulting images are inverted and combined by a *bit-wise and* operation producing the final output as shown in the middle part of Fig. 5. This final output is a grid-cell image similar to the one from TSR for bordered tables, where the overlapping areas of the two resulting images represent the bounding-boxes for every single grid cell as shown in the right part of Fig. 5 which displays the grid cells produced by our TSR algorithm and the corresponding text.

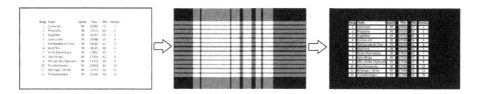

Fig. 5. Example of the erosion operation as performed by Multi-Type-TD-TSR for unbordered tables.

4.5   Partially Bordered TSR

To handle all types of tables, an algorithm for partially bordered tables is needed. The main goal of our algorithms for bordered and unbordered tables is to create a grid cell image by adding borders in the unbordered case and detecting lines in the bordered case. If a table is only partially bordered, then the unbordered algorithm is prevented to add borders in orthogonal direction to the existing borders, while the bordered algorithm can only find the existing borders. Both approaches result in incomplete grid cell images. So the question is how to obtain an algorithm that produces a grid cell image for partially bordered tables. The main idea is to detect the existing borders as done by the algorithm for bordered tables, but without using them to create a grid cell, but to delete the borders from the table image to get an unbordered table (see Fig. 6 for an example). This allows then for applying the algorithm for unbordered tables to create the grid-cell image and contours by analogy to the variants discussed above. A key feature of this approach is that it works with both bordered and unbordered tables: it is type-independent.

Rang	Team	Spiele	Pins	Pkt.	Vorwo.
1	Centurion	99	19082	72	1
2	Pinbu$taz	99	19016	64	2
3	Kugelblitz	99	18782	60	3
4	Cosinus phi	99	18588	56	4
5	Rattlesnake on Tour	99	18284	52	6
6	Dark Pins	99	18225	50	5
7	Strike Sharkattack	99	17902	42	7
8	Holy Wings	99	17350	32	8
9	Alfi und die Chipmunk	99	17358	26	9
10	Pinschutzverein	90	15968	26	12
11	Wittinger / Strike	99	17344	24	11
12	Tschalamangos	90	15760	24	10

Rang	Team	Spiele	Pins	Pkt.	Vorwo.
1	Centurion	99	19082	72	1
2	Pinbu$taz	99	19016	64	2
3	Kugelblitz	99	18782	60	3
4	Cosinus phi	99	18588	56	4
5	Rattlesnake on Tour	99	18284	52	6
6	Dark Pins	99	18225	50	5
7	Strike Sharkattack	99	17902	42	7
8	Holy Wings	99	17350	32	8
9	Alfi und die Chipmunk	99	17358	26	9
10	Pinschutzverein	90	15968	26	12
11	Wittinger / Strike	99	17344	24	11
12	Tschalamangos	90	15760	24	10

Fig. 6. Example of the erosion operation as performed by Multi-Type-TD-TSR for partially bordered tables

4.6   Color Invariance Pre-Processing

A main goal of this work is to create a multi-level pipeline for TD and TSR that works on all types of documents with tables. To this end, we addressed the problem of image rotation, detected tables in images, and developed an algorithm that can handle all three types of table margins. The quest is then whether this approach can handle different colors. In general, we do not need to treat colors with 3 different channels as in the case of RGB images, for example, because we convert table images to binary images based on the contrast of font and background colors. All algorithms proposed so far require a white background and a black font. But the resulting binary image could have a black background and white font, or cells with a black background and white font, while others have a white background and black font as shown in Fig. 7. Therefore, to obtain table images of the desired color type, we insert an additional image processing step between TD and TSR. This step also searches for contours, but now for counting black and white pixels per contour: if there are more black pixels than white pixels, the colors of the contour are inverted. This procedure results in backgrounds being white and fonts being black.

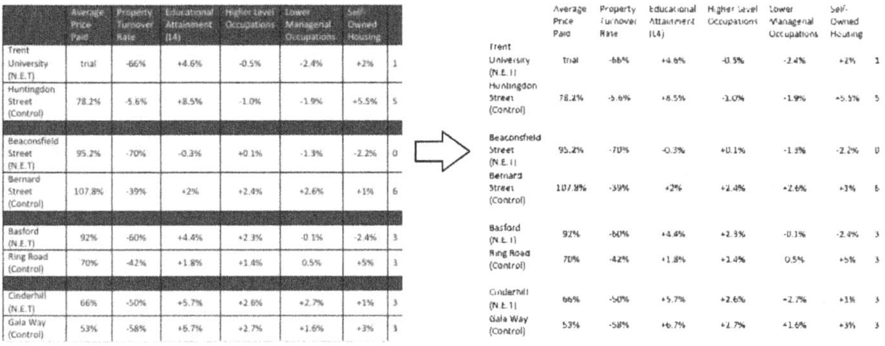

	Average Price Paid	Property Turnover Rate	Educational Attainment (14)	Higher Level Occupations	Lower Managerial Occupations	Self-Owned Housing	
Trent University (N.E.T)	trial	-66%	+4.6%	-0.5%	-2.4%	+2%	1
Huntingdon Street (Control)	78.2%	-5.6%	+8.5%	-1.0%	-1.9%	+5.5%	5
Beaconsfield Street (N.E.T)	95.2%	-70%	-0.3%	+0.1%	-1.3%	-2.2%	0
Bernard Street (Control)	107.8%	-39%	+2%	+2.4%	+2.6%	+1%	6
Basford (N.E.T)	92%	-60%	+4.4%	+2.3%	-0.1%	-2.4%	3
Ring Road (Control)	70%	-42%	+1.8%	+1.4%	0.5%	+5%	1
Cinderhill (N.E.T)	66%	-50%	+5.7%	+2.6%	+2.7%	+1%	3
Gala Way (Control)	53%	-58%	+6.7%	+2.7%	+1.6%	+3%	3

Fig. 7. Color invariance pre-processing example

5   Evaluation

To enable comparability of Multi-Type-TD-TSR with other state-of-the-art approaches [14], we reuse their datasets. Prasad et al. [14] randomly chose 342 images (out of 600) from the ICDAR 19 training set [5] to get 534 tables and 24,920 cells. They manually annotated all images accordingly in order to train their TSR model and also published these annotations to the research community. We reuse the same subset for hyperparameter tuning after we manually re-annotated the cells accordingly for Multi-type-TD-TSR, since our algorithm recognizes only cells as part of the overlap from recognized rows and columns. An annotation example of both annotation types is shown in Fig. 8. Because of the mentioned limitation, we had to remove all tables from the dataset that contained nested rows and columns, resulting in a total of 324 tables.

To validate our TSR algorithm, we had to determine the best kernel sizes for the horizontal and vertical kernel. For this purpose, we used a random search algorithm to find the best values for the width of the vertical kernel and the height of the horizontal kernel based on the 324 table images taken from ICDAR 2019 [5]. Our random search algorithm optimized the size values iteratively, based on the recognition performance on our train set from the last iteration. Finally, we determined the best width to be 8 and the best height to be 3 pixel units.

For the final evaluation, we used the type independent algorithm for partially bordered tables, since it is the one we would be deploying in a real world

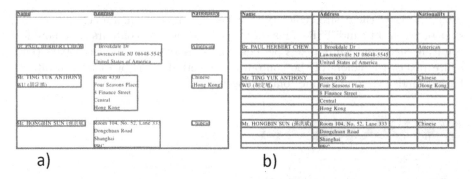

a)   b)

Fig. 8. Annotation example from: a) the original validation dataset of [14], b) the manually labeled validation dataset of Multi-Type-TD-TSR.

application where we do not have any information about the respective table types. For the test set, we used the same 100 document images from the cTDaR competition track B2 [5], that were used by Prasad et al. for the evaluation of CascadeTabNet [14]. However, it should be mentioned that our evaluation was only considering the TSR part for tables that do not contain any nested rows or columns since we consider them out of scope for this project iteration. For this purpose, we cut out the document regions containing the tables and re-annotated the cells accordingly (as shown in Fig. 8). We evaluated using F1-scores by analogy to [14] with IoU (*Intersection over Union* [22]) thresholds of 0.6, 0.7, 0.8, and 0.9, respectively and achieved the results shown in Table 1.

We achieved the highest F1-score by using a threshold of 0.6, 0.7 and 0.8. However, it should be mentioned that a possible reason for the high F1-scores is due to the fact that by re-annotating the data as shown in Fig. 8, the total amount of cells increased, diminishing the effect of failing to identify small, challenging cells. When using higher thresholds (0.8 and 0.9), we encounter a clear performance decrease, which also applies for the other two algorithms we are comparing with. According to the overall result, we conclude that Multi-Type-TD-TSR reaches the highest weighted average F1-score as well as the highest overall performance of 0.737, at least for the task of recognizing cells and columns on tables that do not contain nested columns and borders, thus representing a new state-of-the-art in the field for this subtask.

Table 1. F1-score performances on ICDAR 19 Track B2 (Modern) [5]

Team	IoU 0.6	IoU 0.7	IoU 0.8	IoU 0.9	Weighted Average
CascadeTabNet	0.438	0.354	0.19	0.036	0.232
NLPR-PAL	0.365	0.305	0.195	0.035	0.206
Multi-Type-TD-TSR	0.737	0.532	0.213	0.021	0.334

6   Conclusion

We presented a multistage pipeline for table detection and table structure recognition with document alignment and color invariance pre-processing. For this purpose, we distinguished three types of tables, depending on whether they are borderless or not. Because of the unavailability of large labeled datasets for table structure recognition we decided to use two conventional algorithms: The first one can handle tables without borders, the second one can handle tables with borders. Further, we combined both algorithms into a third, conventional table structure recognition algorithm that can handle all three types of tables. This algorithm achieves the highest F1-score among the systems compared here for an IoU threshold of 0.6, 0.7 and 0.8, but does not detect sharp borders, so the F1-score decreases rapidly for higher thresholds 0.8 and 0.9. However, the highest weighted averaged F1-scores obtained by our algorithm show the potential of our multi-type approach, which can handle all three table types considered here: it benefits from using one of the specialized algorithms to transform the input tables so that they can be optimally processed by the other specialized algorithm. This kind of multi-stage division of labor among otherwise conventional algorithms could help to finally bring such a difficult task as table structure recognition into domains that allow downstream NLP procedures to process linguistic table contents properly. This paper made a contribution to this difficult task.

References

1. Badrinarayanan, V., Kendall, A., Cipolla, R.: SegNet: a deep convolutional encoder-decoder architecture for image segmentation. IEEE Trans. Pattern Anal. Mach. Intell. **39**(12), 2481–2495 (2017)
2. Bühler, B., Paulheim, H.: Web table classification based on visual features. CoRR abs/2103.05110 (2021). https://arxiv.org/abs/2103.05110
3. Cohen, W.W., Hurst, M., Jensen, L.S.: A flexible learning system for wrapping tables and lists in html documents. In: Proceedings of the 11th International Conference on World Wide Web, WWW 2002, pp. 232–241. Association for Computing Machinery, New York (2002). https://doi.org/10.1145/511446.511477
4. Cortes, C., Vapnik, V.: Support vector machine. Mach. Learn. **20**(3), 273–297 (1995)
5. Gao, L., et al.: ICDAR 2019 competition on table detection and recognition (CTDAR). In: 2019 International Conference on Document Analysis and Recognition (ICDAR), pp. 1510–1515 (2019). https://doi.org/10.1109/ICDAR.2019.00243
6. Gatterbauer, W., Bohunsky, P., Herzog, M., Krüpl, B., Pollak, B.: Towards domain-independent information extraction from web tables. In: Proceedings of the 16th International Conference on World Wide Web, WWW 2007, pp. 71–80. Association for Computing Machinery, New York (2007). https://doi.org/10.1145/1242572.1242583
7. Gilani, A., Qasim, S.R., Malik, I., Shafait, F.: Table detection using deep learning. In: 2017 14th IAPR International Conference on Document Analysis and Recognition (ICDAR), vol. 1, pp. 771–776. IEEE (2017)

8. Goodfellow, I.J., et al.: Generative adversarial networks. arXiv preprint arXiv:1406.2661 (2014)
9. Göbel, M., Hassan, T., Oro, E., Orsi, G.: ICDAR 2013 table competition. In: 2013 12th International Conference on Document Analysis and Recognition, pp. 1449–1453 (2013). https://doi.org/10.1109/ICDAR.2013.292
10. Kasar, T., Barlas, P., Adam, S., Chatelain, C., Paquet, T.: Learning to detect tables in scanned document images using line information. In: 2013 12th International Conference on Document Analysis and Recognition, pp. 1185–1189. IEEE (2013)
11. Kieninger, T., Dengel, A.: The T-recs table recognition and analysis system. In: Lee, S.-W., Nakano, Y. (eds.) DAS 1998. LNCS, vol. 1655, pp. 255–270. Springer, Heidelberg (1999). https://doi.org/10.1007/3-540-48172-9_21
12. Li, M., Cui, L., Huang, S., Wei, F., Zhou, M., Li, Z.: TableBank: table benchmark for image-based table detection and recognition. In: Proceedings of the 12th Language Resources and Evaluation Conference, pp. 1918–1925. European Language Resources Association, Marseille (2020). https://www.aclweb.org/anthology/2020.lrec-1.236
13. Lu, T., Dooms, A.: Probabilistic homogeneity for document image segmentation. Pattern Recognit. **109**, 1–14 (2021). https://doi.org/10.1016/j.patcog.2020.107591
14. Prasad, D., Gadpal, A., Kapadni, K., Visave, M., Sultanpure, K.: CascadeTabNet: an approach for end to end table detection and structure recognition from image-based documents. In: Proceedings of the IEEE/CVF Conference on Computer Vision and Pattern Recognition Workshops, pp. 572–573 (2020)
15. Pyreddi, P., Croft, W.B.: A system for retrieval in text tables. In: ACM DL (1997)
16. Ren, S., He, K., Girshick, R., Sun, J.: Faster R-CNN: towards real-time object detection with region proposal networks. arXiv preprint arXiv:1506.01497 (2015)
17. Reza, M.M., Bukhari, S.S., Jenckel, M., Dengel, A.: Table localization and segmentation using GAN and CNN. In: 2019 International Conference on Document Analysis and Recognition Workshops (ICDARW), vol. 5, pp. 152–157. IEEE (2019)
18. Riba, P., Dutta, A., Goldmann, L., Fornés, A., Ramos, O., Lladós, J.: Table detection in invoice documents by graph neural networks. In: 2019 International Conference on Document Analysis and Recognition (ICDAR), pp. 122–127 (2019). https://doi.org/10.1109/ICDAR.2019.00028
19. Rosebrock, A.: Text skew correction with opencv and python (2017). pyImageSearch, https://www.pyimagesearch.com/2017/02/20/text-skew-correction-opencv-python/. Accessed 17 Feb 2021
20. Schreiber, S., Agne, S., Wolf, I., Dengel, A., Ahmed, S.: DeepDeSRT: deep learning for detection and structure recognition of tables in document images. In: 2017 14th IAPR International Conference on Document Analysis and Recognition (ICDAR), vol. 1, pp. 1162–1167. IEEE (2017)
21. Seo, W., Koo, H.I., Cho, N.I.: Junction-based table detection in camera-captured document images. Int. J. Doc. Anal. Recognit. (IJDAR) **18**, 1–11 (2014). https://doi.org/10.1007/s10032-014-0226-7
22. Subramanyam, V.S.: Iou (intersection over union) (2017). Medium. https://medium.com/analytics-vidhya/iou-intersection-over-union-705a39e7acef. Accessed 09 July 2021
23. Xie, S., Girshick, R., Dollár, P., Tu, Z., He, K.: Aggregated residual transformations for deep neural networks. In: Proceedings of the IEEE Conference on Computer Vision and Pattern Recognition, pp. 1492–1500 (2017)

A High-Speed Neural Architecture Search Considering the Number of Weights

Fuyuka Yamada[1]($\boxtimes$), Satoki Tsuji[1], Hiroshi Kawaguchi[1], Atsuki Inoue[1], and Yasufumi Sakai[2]

[1] Kobe University, Kobe, Japan
yamada.fuyuka@cs28.cs.kobe-u.ac.jp
[2] Fujitsu Laboratories Ltd., Kawasaki, Japan

Abstract. Neural architecture search (NAS) is a promising method to ascertain network architecture automatically and to build a suitable network for a particular application without any human intervention. However, NAS requires huge computation resources to find the optimal parameters of a network in the training phase of each search. Because a trade-off generally exists between model size and accuracy in deep learning models, the model size tends to increase in pursuit of higher accuracy. In applications with limited resources, such as edge AI, reducing the network weight might be more important than improving its accuracy. Alternatively, achieving high accuracy with maximum resources might be more important. The objective of this research is to find a model with sufficient accuracy with a limited number of weights and to reduce the search time. We improve the Differentiable Network Search (DARTS) algorithm, one of the fastest NAS methods, by adding another constraint to the loss function, which limits the number of network weights. We evaluate the proposed algorithm using three constraints. Compared to the conventional DARTS algorithm, the proposed algorithm reduces the search time by up to 40% when the model size range is set properly. It achieves comparable accuracy with that of DARTS.

Keywords: Deep learning · Deep neural network · Neural architecture search · Edge AI

1 Introduction and Related Works

Starting with speech recognition [1] in 2012, deep learning has marked great achievements in various fields in the past decade, such as image recognition [4] and automatic translation. However, the network architecture design difficulty is an extremely important issue that must be resolved. In deep learning, the network architecture plays a major role in performance. This network architecture has been designed manually every step of the way. Because of the necessary high level of expertise and repeated experimentation, a huge amount of time is needed to find the optimal network for the application. Edge AI, such as in automated driving, is also attracting attention. Edge AI must incorporate deep learning

© Springer Nature Switzerland AG 2021
S. Edelkamp et al. (Eds.): KI 2021, LNAI 12873, pp. 109–115, 2021.
https://doi.org/10.1007/978-3-030-87626-5_9

models that considering a trade-off between accuracy and computational complexity under a hardware resource constraint. In 2017, a method called Neural Architecture Search (NAS) was proposed [10]. It requires no expertise because it searches the network architecture automatically. However, because NAS algorithms are designed to train and compare numerous models, the computational complexity is huge. Therefore, strong demand exists for a method to build an optimal network in a shorter time. Good tradeoff between hardware resources and accuracy is also an important factor in edge AI. A network structure search method that takes such a trade-off into account is also needed.

Various approaches for NAS are used to design architectures automatically, such as EA-based and RL-based. These NAS have achieved comparable performance to those of human-designed models in image recognition. However, these methods are computationally intensive: AmoebaNet [7] (EA-based) requires 3150 GPUdays. NASNet [11] (RL-based) requires 1800 GPUdays of search time. Another method, PNAS [5], divides the network into cells and relaxes the search space into cells. In fact, PNAS is five times faster than RL-based NASnet. Another method, DARTS [6], proposes a differentiable NAS. It has search time of 1.5 GPUdays. Two other methods, FBNet [9] and MnasNet [8], respectively use latency-aware search and support mobile devices such as smartphones. As described herein, we aim to produce and use search algorithms with high accuracy considering the model size, and work to make NAS compatible with hardware. Specifically examining the number of weights in the model, we propose a search algorithm using both the number of weights and accuracy as indicators at the same time, and apply a method for search speed enhancement.

2 Proposed Method

2.1 DARTS Algorithm

For our method, we use the DARTS [6] algorithm as a baseline. DARTS defines the network structure as a differentiable problem and selects the best operation from multiple candidates such as convolution and pooling. In a normal learning algorithm for neural network, only the weights $w_{i,j}$ are trained in the gradient descent algorithm. In addition to the network weights, DARTS trains each operation parameter α_j, which is the probability of selecting each operation. Because they are defined as probabilities, DARTS can train them as well as the network weights in the conventional gradient descent algorithm using bilevel optimization. Finally, the operation with the highest probability is selected to ascertain the network architecture (Fig. 1). In the DARTS search, two forward and backward propagations are conducted in a single step. The first one is for updating the network weights $w_{i,j}$. The second one is for updating the architecture parameters α_j.

2.2 Loss Function with the Number of Weights

To improve the search method based on DARTS, we introduce the number of weights into the loss function in the search model. That is defined as the product of both losses L_{DARTS} and L_{params}, as shown in Fig. 1. One component

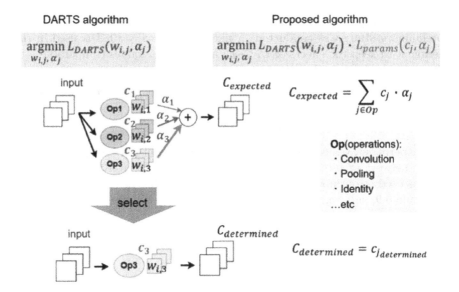

Fig. 1. Search algorithm overview. α_j is selection probability of Op, c_j is the number of weights for each operation. Many operation selections are shown here in the network. The values of $C_{expected}$ and $C_{determined}$ are actually the sum over all the selections in the network.

of that product, L_{DARTS}, is the original loss function used when updating the weights and operation parameters in the network. Also, L_{params} is the loss function related to the number of weights. It is defined from the number of effective weights $C_{expected}$, which is the sum of the product of c_j and α_j, where c_j represents the number of weights of each operation and α_j denotes the selection probability of each operation. (c_j is the number of weights of each operation and α_j is the selection probability of each operation.) In addition, $C_{determined}$ is defined as the total number of weights in network when the highest possible operation is selected. To limit the resources to be used in the network, we specify the lower limit of $C_{determined}$ as C_{min} and specify the upper limit as C_{max}. During training, L_{params} is determined as follows according to $C_{determined}$ so that $C_{determined}$ falls between C_{min} and C_{max}.

$$L_{params} = \begin{cases} \beta C_{expected} & (C_{determined} < C_{min}) \\ \dfrac{1}{\beta C_{expected}} & (C_{determined} > C_{max}) \\ 1 & (otherwise) \end{cases} \tag{1}$$

Because the training process always makes the total loss function $L_{DARTS} \cdot L_{params}$ smaller, then it makes the $C_{expected}$ smaller when $C_{determined}$ is less than C_{min}. However, it makes the $C_{expected}$ larger when $C_{determined}$ is more than C_{max}. When the current $C_{determined}$ is within the target range, only the original L_{DARTS} is regarded as the loss function. Then the weights w_i and operation parameters α_j in the network are trained as in the DARTS algorithm. β is a parameter introduced to regulate the balance between L_{DARTS} and L_{params}. A preliminary study was conducted. A fixed value of $\beta = 10^{-4}$ is used in this experiment to keep the effects of L_{DARTS} and L_{params} values comparable.

3 Experiments

3.1 Implementation Details

In this experiment, we use an image classification dataset to investigate and evaluate the network architecture. As a dataset, we used CIFAR-10 [3]. Momentum SGD was used to optimize the weights $w_{i,j}$, with initial learning rate $\eta = 0.025$, momentum 0.9, and weight decay 3×10^{-4}. Adam [2] was used as the optimizer for α_j.

3.2 Results

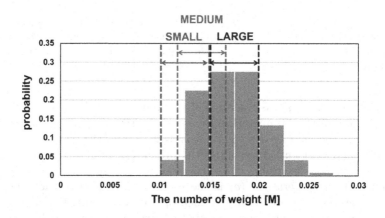

Fig. 2. Probability of the number of weights in the network, as searched by DARTS.

The numbers of weights in the original DARTS search results are distributed between 0.010 M and 0.025 M, depending on initial weights and architecture parameters, as shown in Fig. 2. Based on the distribution of the number of weights in DARTS, we set three ranges of the number of weights, which are targeted using the proposed method. The range between 0.010 M and 0.015 M is the small target range, 0.012 M and 0.017 M is the medium target range, and 0.015 M and 0.020 M is the large target range.

The distributions of the number of weights and accuracy of the networks explored using the proposed method and DARTS for the three conditions are shown respectively in Fig. 3, Fig. 4, and Fig. 5. From these results, one can infer that the accuracy of the network explored using the proposed method is not much different from that of the DARTS network.

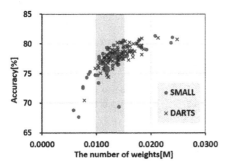

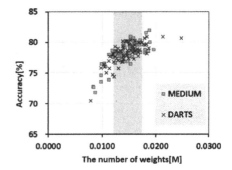

Fig. 3. Distribution of searched networks [small].

Fig. 4. Distribution of searched networks [medium].

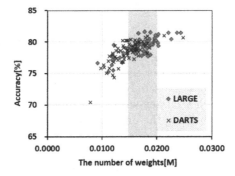

Fig. 5. Distribution of searched networks [large].

Table 1 presents a comparison of the accuracy of the networks explored in the proposed method and DARTS, as well as the search time. The accuracy is the accuracy of network when the network model size falls within the target range in each case. The search time is the time to find a network model that falls within the target range. The search time of proposed method is defined relative to that of DARTS. When we set the model size as small, we specifically examine hardware resources rather than accuracy. In this case, the proposed method reduces the search time by 21% compared to that of DARTS. This result shows that when we give restrictions on the resource during search, we can reduce the search time because we can explore the network intensively with limited resources. However, when setting the model size as large, we specifically examine accuracy rather than hardware resources in the search. The proposed method reduces the search time by as much as 40%. Moreover, because DARTS does not allow for hardware resource restrictions, it requires numerous searches until high accuracy is obtained. The proposed method explores a network with large resources and high accuracy more efficiently. When setting the target range medium, neither method has much difference in terms of accuracy or search time

Table 1. Average accuracy and search time. The search time defined relative to that of DARTS

Method	Small		Medium		Large	
	Accuracy (%)	Search time (relative)	Accuracy (%)	Search time (relative)	Accuracy (%)	Search time (relative)
DARTS	77.69 ± 0.26	1.00	78.41 ± 0.20	1.00	79.23 ± 0.18	1.00
Proposed	77.26 ± 0.27	0.79	78.46 ± 0.18	1.02	79.44 ± 0.15	0.60

because both methods are designed to explore a similar search space. When setting a proper target range, we can obtain a clear advantage in search time over DARTS.

4 Conclusions

Herein, we propose a new NAS algorithm that considers not only accuracy but also hardware resources. By adding a measure of the number of weights to the loss function, we can search the network with numerous weights intensively within the target range. This enables not only search to reduce network resources, but also search to achieve high accuracy with maximum resources. Compared to the conventional DARTS algorithm, the proposed algorithm reduces the search time by up to 40% when the model size range is set properly. The algorithm also achieves comparable accuracy to that of DARTS. The algorithm allows us more efficient search for the optimal network architecture used for the devices required for edge AI.

References

1. Hinton, G., et al.: Deep neural networks for acoustic modeling in speech recognition: the shared views of four research groups. IEEE Sig. Process. Mag. **29**(6), 82–97 (2012). https://doi.org/10.1109/MSP.2012.2205597
2. Kingma, D., Ba, J.: Adam: a method for stochastic optimization. In: International Conference on Learning Representations (2014)
3. Krizhevsky, A.: Learning multiple layers of features from tiny images. University of Toronto (2012)
4. Krizhevsky, A., Sutskever, I., Hinton, G.E.: ImageNet classification with deep convolutional neural networks. In: Proceedings of the 25th International Conference on Neural Information Processing Systems, NIPS 2012, vol. 1. pp. 1097–1105. Curran Associates Inc., Red Hook (2012)
5. Liu, C., et al.: Progressive neural architecture search. CoRR abs/1712.00559 (2017). http://arxiv.org/abs/1712.00559
6. Liu, H., Simonyan, K., Yang, Y.: Darts: differentiable architecture search (2019)
7. Real, E., et al.: Large-scale evolution of image classifiers. CoRR abs/1703.01041 (2017). http://arxiv.org/abs/1703.01041
8. Tan, M., Chen, B., Pang, R., Vasudevan, V., Le, Q.V.: MnasNet: platform-aware neural architecture search for mobile. CoRR abs/1807.11626 (2018). http://arxiv.org/abs/1807.11626

9. Wu, B., et al.: FbNet: hardware-aware efficient convnet design via differentiable neural architecture search. CoRR abs/1812.03443 (2018). http://arxiv.org/abs/1812.03443

10. Zoph, B., Le, Q.V.: Neural architecture search with reinforcement learning. CoRR abs/1611.01578 (2016). http://arxiv.org/abs/1611.01578

11. Zoph, B., Vasudevan, V., Shlens, J., Le, Q.V.: Learning transferable architectures for scalable image recognition. CoRR abs/1707.07012 (2017). http://arxiv.org/abs/1707.07012

Semantic Segmentation of Aerial Images Using Binary Space Partitioning

Daniel Gritzner$^{(\boxtimes)}$ (ID) and Jörn Ostermann

Institut für Informationsverarbeitung (TNT), Leibniz Universität Hannover,
Appelstr. 9A, 30167 Hannover, Germany
{gritzner,ostermann}@tnt.uni-hannover.de
https://www.tnt.uni-hannover.de

Abstract. The semantic segmentation of aerial images enables many useful applications such as tracking city growth, tracking deforestation, or automatically creating and updating maps. However, gathering enough training data to train a proper model for the automated analysis of aerial images is usually too labor-intensive and thus too expensive in most cases. Therefore, domain adaptation techniques are often necessary to be able to adapt existing models or to transfer knowledge from existing datasets to new unlabeled aerial images. Modern adaptation approaches make use of complex architectures involving many model components, losses and loss weights. These approaches are hard to apply in practice since their hyperparameters are hard to optimize for a given adaptation problem. This complexity is the result of trying to separate domain-invariant elements, e.g., structures and shapes, from domain-specific elements, e.g., textures. In this paper, we present a novel model for semantic segmentation, which not only achieves state-of-the-art performance on aerial images, but also inherently learns separate feature representations for shapes and textures. Our goal is to provide a model which can serve as the basis for future domain adaptation approaches which are simpler but still effective. Through end-to-end training our deep learning model learns to map aerial images to feature representations which can be decoded into binary space partitioning trees, a resolution-independent representation of the semantic segmentation, which can then be rendered into a pixelwise semantic segmentation in a differentiable way.

Keywords: Computer vision · Semantic segmentation · Deep learning · Spatial partitioning · Aerial images

1 Introduction

Modern deep learning-based computer vision techniques enable many useful applications based on aerial image analysis. Object detection can, e.g., be used to find vehicles and thus analyze traffic. Semantic segmentation can be used for tracking city growth [11], tracking deforestation [19], or automatically creating and updating maps [9]. A problem faced by these applications is usually

© Springer Nature Switzerland AG 2021
S. Edelkamp et al. (Eds.): KI 2021, LNAI 12873, pp. 116–134, 2021.
https://doi.org/10.1007/978-3-030-87626-5_10

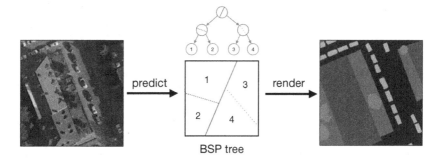

Fig. 1. Overview of our proposed approach: predict binary space partitioning trees which are then rendered into semantic segmentations. The inner nodes (blue) specify segment boundaries by defining lines (green) which partition a given region into two subregions. The leaf nodes (orange) then define the content, i.e., class, of each segment. (Color figure online)

the availability of sufficient amounts of labeled training examples. Annotating a large number of aerial images is very labor-intensive and thus expensive. To mitigate this cost, domain adaptation is used to transfer knowledge from an existing dataset to new unlabeled aerial images. Modern domain adaptation approaches try to separate domain-invariant elements, e.g., the shape of buildings, from their domain-specific elements, e.g., the texture or look of buildings [1]. However, these approaches make use of complex architectures involving many model components, losses and loss weights. This complexity makes these approaches hard to use in practice due to the required hyperparameter optimization.

In this paper, we present a novel model for semantic segmentation which shall serve as the basis for future domain adaptation approaches which are simpler, and thus easier to use, but still effective. Our model achieves state-of-the-art segmentation performance on aerial images and inherently learns separate feature representations for shapes and textures without the need to impose specific constraints with hyperparameters that need to be optimized. The learned features can be decoded into binary space partitioning (BSP) trees [8] which describe the desired semantic segmentation, as depicted in Fig. 1. The shape features are decoded into the inner nodes of the trees, thus describing the shape of each segment, while the texture features are decoded into the leaf nodes, which define the class of each segment. By implementing differentiable BSP tree rendering, our model is trainable end-to-end and learns to represent the ground truth as BSP trees by itself. These trees are inherently resolution-independent, though, of course, their precision is dependent on the resolution used during training. Our rendering also produces sharp, well-defined boundaries, whereas state-of-the-art models usually produce smoother, blurry boundaries.

The next section of this paper will discuss related work. This discussion is then followed by a section on our proposed model and an evaluation thereof. Our model is compared to several state-of-the-art models on multiple datasets. The paper then finishes with a conclusion in its final section.

2   Related Work

There are many modern deep learning-based semantic segmentation models [3,15,24,33,35]. A defining characteristic is, that they all follow an encoder-decoder architecture. First, an encoder maps the input image into a feature map. This feature map has a smaller spatial resolution than the input or the desired output and thus serves a bottleneck. The decoder part takes the feature map and computes the desired semantic segmentation from it. This approach implies that the encoder performs spatial downsampling, e.g., through max-pooling or strided convolutions, while the decoder performs spatial upsampling, e.g., through bilinear upsampling or transpose convolutions (also called deconvolutions).

A popular model following this pattern is U-Net [25]. Initially conceived for medical image analysis, it has also been applied to other data. There is also a variant for 3D data [7]. While U-Net's encoder and decoder are almost symmetrical, Fully Convolutional Networks for Semantic Segmentation (FCN) [20] uses a far more complex encoder than decoder. It relies on classification models, such as VGG, ResNet, MobileNetv2 or Xception [6,13,26,28], and modifies them to produce pixel-wise classifications, i.e., a semantic segmentation. DeepLabv3+ [4] also uses modified classification models as backbone/encoder. However, its decoder is more complex than that of FCN. Additionally, it adds atrous spatial pyramid pooling (ASPP) [2] to the encoder in order to take context information of each pixel at different scales into account. Other models are tuned to process videos instead of images [36] or add parallel branches to process specific information such as boundaries/edges [30].

Recent research also focuses on more sophisticated problems such as instance segmentation [12], i.e., detecting objects and finding their segmentation masks, and panoptic segmentation [17], which is a combination of instance segmentation of objects and semantic segmentation of the rest. Semantic segmentation models are still required for some approaches to solve these problems. As an example, AdaptIS [29] uses U-Net as a backbone for its instance segmentation approach and ResNet and DeepLabv3+ for its panoptic segmentation approach.

Our proposed model incorporates BSP trees, which are usually used in computer graphics applications such as video games [27]. To the best of our knowledge no other approach uses the prediction of BSP trees, which are resolution-independent and thus avoid the necessity of the model performing upsampling, for semantic segmentation. Other approaches making use of ideas from computer graphics for computer vision applications are PointRend [18] and models reconstructing 3D meshes [10,23,31,32]. PointRend uses a cascade of refinements to turn a coarse instance segmentation into a finer instance segmentation. BSPnet [5] also tries to predict BSP planes in order to reconstruct polygonal 3D models.

3   Semantic Segmentation

This section will first present the overall architecture of our proposed model before moving on to explain the differentiable BSP tree rendering in more detail. It will finish with a comparison of our model to state-of-the-art models.

3.1 BSP-based Segmentation Model

Figure 2 shows the architecture of BSPSegNet, the model we propose. It consists of four components: an encoder (or backbone), two decoders and a BSP tree renderer. An input image is first mapped by an encoder to two feature maps, which are then further processed by two parallel decoders. Their outputs, the parameters of BSP trees, are then rendered into a semantic segmentation.

Similarly to FCN or DeepLabv3+, the encoder is the feature extraction part of a classification model such as MobileNetv2 or Xception. The final classification layers of these models are replaced by a convolution layer to reduce number of features of the extracted feature map. This way, we introduce a bottleneck so that the number of features is smaller than the number of parameters in the BSP trees which get predicted later. We split this feature map into two parts, the shape feature map and the texture feature map.

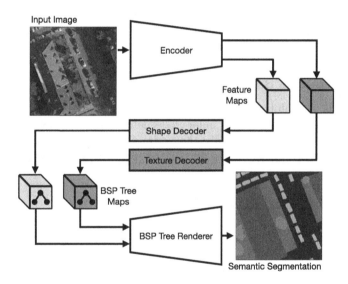

Fig. 2. Architecture of our proposed model, BSPSegNet. An encoder maps an input image to two separate feature maps, which in turn are processed by two parallel decoders. The decoders output parameters of BSP trees which are then rendered into the desired semantic segmentation. The blue shape path predicts the BSP trees' inner nodes, which describe each segments shape, while the orange texture path predicts the BSP trees' leaf nodes, which describe each segments class. (Color figure online)

From this point on we interpret each feature map such that each spatial unit corresponds to a small block in the input image. As an example, if the input image has a resolution of 224×224 pixels and the encoder, through max-pooling and/or strided convolutions, downsamples this to 28×28 spatial units, each spatial units corresponds to a 8×8 pixel block in the input image. This, in turn, means we have a feature vector for each such block. The length of these vectors is defined by the depth (= number of features) of the feature map.

In order to keep this interpretation, the two decoders consist of multiple convolution layers with a kernel size of 1×1. Effectively, this means each region's feature vector is processed by a multilayer perceptron. The two decoders have the same overall structure, but each decoder has its own trainable parameters. The shape decoder, which processes only the shape feature map, outputs the parameters of the inner nodes of the BSP trees, thus predicting the shape of the segments. The texture decoder, which processes only the texture feature map, outputs the parameters of the leaf nodes of the BSP trees, thus predicting the classes of each segment. All convolutions we added to our model are followed by a batch normalization layer and an activation function in that order.

Since every spatial unit corresponds to a small block in the input image, we effectively predict a separate BSP tree for each such small block. The BSP renderer computes the final semantic segmentation from the predicted BSP trees in a differentiable way. This enables end-to-end training without having to define any BSP trees in advance: they are learned instead. The BSP renderer, as opposed to the encoder and the decoders, does not have any trainable parameters.

3.2 Differentiable BSP Tree Rendering

A BSP tree is a resolution-independent representation of a semantic segmentation as outlined in Fig. 3. Each inner node defines a line which partitions the current segment, which is initially the entire region, into two parts. The leaf nodes do not partition the segments any further but instead define what the content of each segment is.

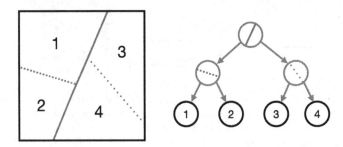

Fig. 3. A square region (left) partitioned into four segments by green lines. The BSP tree (right) encodes this segmentation. The blue inner nodes encode the shape of the segmentation, while the orange leaf nodes encode the content of each segment. (Color figure online)

To determine the corresponding leaf node for a pixel location $\mathbf{p}$ the signed distance function

$$f(\mathbf{p}) = \mathbf{n} \cdot \mathbf{p} - d \tag{1}$$

with the normal $\mathbf{n}$ of the root node's line and its distance d from the origin is computed. The sign of $f(\mathbf{p})$ determines which child node to proceed to as the sign encodes on which side of the line $\mathbf{p}$ is. $f(\mathbf{p}) = 0$ implies that $\mathbf{p}$ is exactly on the line. This process is repeated for each inner node until a leaf node is reached.

Our model's shape decoder outputs three parameters for each inner node: two for the normal $\mathbf{n}$ and one for the distance d. We do not normalize $\mathbf{n}$ but instead let the network learn appropriate magnitudes of $\mathbf{n}$ and d itself. The texture decoder outputs the logits, i.e., in each leaf node it predicts one value per output class.

To render a BSP tree we first pre-compute a matrix of sampling points $\mathbf{S}$. This matrix' size is equal to the block size which each BSP tree encodes. Each entry in $\mathbf{S}$ contains two coordinates ranging from $(0, 0)$ for the pixel in the top-left of the block to $(1, 1)$ for the pixel in the bottom-right. We also construct a region map $\mathbf{R}$, initialized with ones, which is a 3D array whose width and height are equal to the block size and whose depth is equal to the number of leaf nodes.

We then iterate over all inner nodes in order of depth, starting with the root node. For each inner node, we compute the signed distance function f for all sampling points $\mathbf{S}$, giving us the matrix $\mathbf{T}$ of signed distances. We map these signed distances to the interval $(0, 1)$ by applying a sigmoid activation σ:

$$\mathbf{T}' = \sigma \left(\lambda_C \cdot \mathbf{T} \right). \tag{2}$$

Signed distances near 0 will be mapped to values close to 0.5, which means there is region of uncertainty for small signed distances. We introduce λ_C to be able to scale the size of this region of uncertainty. We mostly want values either close to 0 or close to 1 in $\mathbf{T}'$. Then, we update the region map $\mathbf{R}$ by computing

$$\mathbf{R}[\mathbf{l}] = \mathbf{R}[\mathbf{l}] \odot \lambda_R \cdot \mathbf{T}' \tag{3}$$
$$\mathbf{R}[\mathbf{r}] = \mathbf{R}[\mathbf{r}] \odot \lambda_R \cdot (1 - \mathbf{T}') \tag{4}$$

with $\mathbf{l}$ and $\mathbf{r}$ being the indices of the leaf nodes potentially reachable by going to the left child node or right child node respectively. $\mathbf{R}[\mathbf{l}]$. and $\mathbf{R}[\mathbf{r}]$ are matrices of the same size as $\mathbf{T}'$ and $\odot$ is the Hadamard product. Assuming $\lambda_R = 1$, each spatial entry of $\mathbf{R}$, which corresponds to a pixel in the block, will be almost a one-hot encoding of the corresponding leaf node reached after iterating over all inner nodes. With $\lambda_R > 1$ we amplify the difference between the chosen leaf node, which will have a value close to λ_R^D with tree depth D, and all other leaf nodes, which will still have a value close to 0.

To finish the BSP tree rendering, we apply a softmax across the depth ($=$ leaf node index dimension) of $\mathbf{R}$. Then, for each pixel $\mathbf{p} = (y, x)$ in the block, we compute the weighted sum

$$g(\mathbf{p}) = \sum_{i=1}^{N} \mathbf{R}[i, y, x] \cdot \mathbf{v}_i \tag{5}$$

with $\mathbf{v}_i$ being the class logits in the i-th leaf node and N being the number of leaf nodes. g computes the class logits for each pixel.

All these operations are differentiable and can be computed in parallel for all blocks simultaneously. The result is a semantic segmentation with the same spatial resolution as the input image. This segmentation can then be used to compute a loss function, e.g., categorical cross entropy.

3.3 Comparison to State of the Art

State-of-the-art models such as U-Net, FCN or DeepLabv3+ follow a similar encoder/decoder architecture as BSPSegNet. However, they only use a single decoder which outputs the desired semantic segmentation directly without any need of further rendering. Due to using only one decoder, it is hard to assign semantics to their feature maps. As a consequence, approaches built on top of those models may need to resort to complex techniques to get additional semantics, such as [1], which tries to separate domain-invariant structure features from domain-specific texture features. Additionally, through the use of bilinear upsampling and/or transpose convolutions, the boundaries between segments may become smooth and even blurry, as opposed to the sharp boundaries produced by the inner nodes of a BSP tree. Furthermore, BSP trees are resolution-independent and can easily be rendered at a higher resolution. It is, however, fair to assume that the precision of the learned BSP trees is limited by the ground truth resolution used during training.

4   Evaluation

This section will describe the datasets and the training setup used to perform the evaluation first. It will then, in order, discuss the quality of the BSP tree representation of the ground truth, the actual semantic segmentation performance as well as investigate the confidence of the models' predictions.

4.1   Datasets

We used aerial images of five different German cities as datasets. We used the two ISPRS 2D Semantic Labeling Benchmark Challenge [14] datasets consisting of images from Vaihingen and Potsdam. Additionally, we used images of Hannover, Buxtehude and Nienburg. All images are true orthophotos. Table 1 contains details about the datasets. We only used the 16 images initially released as training set for the respective benchmark challenges for Vaihingen and Potsdam. The images of Hannover, Buxtehude and Nienburg were divided into 16 patches of 2500 × 2500 pixels. One such Hannover patch, containing almost exclusively trees, was omitted. The images or image patches of each dataset were randomly partitioned into a training set and a validation set by randomly drawing ten images as training images and using the remaining images as validation images. The ground truth segmentations contained the classes impervious surfaces, buildings, low vegetation, tree, car, and clutter/background. Detailed class distributions can be found in the appendix.

Table 1. Dataset details; 3Cities consists of the Hannover, Buxtehude and Nienburg.

Dataset	Vaihingen	Potsdam	3Cities
No. of images	33	38	1 per city
Image resolution [pixels]	2336 × 1281 to 3816 × 2550	6000 × 6000	10000 × 10000
Channels	Near-infrared, red, green, depth	Near-infrared, red, green, blue, depth	Near-infrared, red, green, blue, depth

4.2 Training and Test Setup

As augmentation we sampled 800 patches of 224 × 224 pixels from each of the ten training images. We used random translation, rotation and shearing. The validation images were partitioned into 224 × 224 patches without overlap except at the right and the bottom image boundaries. These validation image patches were then further split into 50% validation patches and 50% test patches. This split was performed s.t. the sets of images used for validation and test are mostly disjoint, except for one image, which was used for validation patches up to a certain point and from then on was only used for test patches. We performed the splitting into training, validation and test sets and the augmentation ten times. We trained each model on each of the dataset splits once, for a total of ten training runs per model. Unless otherwise noted, all quality metrics shown in this section are means or standard deviations across these ten runs. They show the metrics measured on the test data, after using the validation set performance, in particular the mean Intersection-over-Union (mIoU), for model selection and hyperparameter optimization. The later was performed for all models, including the state-of-the-art models we compare ourselves to.

We trained all models on nVidia GeForce RTX 2080 Ti GPUs using PyTorch v1.3. For models with MobileNetv2 [26] as backbone, we used a mini-batch size of 36. For all other models we used a size of 18. AdamW [16,22] with a cosine annealing learning rate schedule [21] was used as optimizer. As loss function we used categorical cross entropy with class weights set such that rarer classes have higher weights (computed from the training image patches).

For BSPSegNet, we used a two phase training: we first used our model as an autoencoder, to learn a BSP tree representation of the ground truth. We then trained a fresh instance of BSPSegNet to predict the just learned BSP trees using smooth L1 loss just after the two decoders but before the BSP tree rendering. This turned out to produce better results than direct end-to-end training but still avoids pre-processing of the data. This approach used the same data for training as the other models and simply learned an additional intermediate representation.

To optimize hyperparameters such as learning rates, λ_C, λ_R, the number of features of the shape and texture feature maps or the number of epochs, we used random search for 100 to 200 runs. We optimized each hyperparameter individually. The chosen values can be found in the appendix.

We made small modifications to the state-of-the-art models and backbones used which either produced slightly better results or made the models simpler while keeping their performance the same (validated through performance measurements on the validation data): we replaced all ReLU activations with LeakyReLUs [34], we used no atrous/dilated convolutions and we omitted the branches in DeepLabv3+'s pyramid pooling which use atrous/dilated convolutions. In accordance to DeepLabv3+'s approach, we set the strides of the last two convolutions with stride = 2 in the backbone to 1 instead, so that the spatial resolution in the bottleneck is only downsampled at most by a factor of 8. The exception was FCN, for which we kept the full downsampling factor of 32. Also, we trained all models from scratch. We modified the first convolution in each backbone s.t. it accepts images with more than three channels in order to be able to use all available channels for each dataset.

4.3   Ground Truth as BSP Trees

Table 2 shows the quality of the learned BSP tree representation of the ground truth. We tested two configurations with different tree depths, both using MobileNetv2 as a backbone. One configuration, called BSPSegNet2, used two layers of inner nodes resulting in four leaf nodes, while the other configuration, BSPSegNet3, used three layers of inner nodes resulting in eight leaf nodes. Overall, the BSP trees encoded the ground truth precisely, even when using the shallower trees. As a reminder, each tree only encodes an 8×8 pixel block, i.e., there are rarely, if ever, more than four different segments in each such block. In fact, most blocks of this size contain only a single segment. It is notable that the mIoU showed slightly higher variance. It was even significantly higher on Vaihingen for both model configurations and on Hannover for BSPSegNet3. This might be due to mispredictions of rare classes in some runs. These errors hardly affect pixelwise accuracy but may significantly affect the IoU of these rare classes and thus affect the mIoU. For further experiments, we used the BSP tree

Table 2. Quality of the learned BSP tree representation of the ground truth. Two BSPSegNet configurations with a tree depth of two and three have been tested. Means and standard deviations across ten runs are shown.

	BSPSegNet2		BSPSegNet3	
	Accuracy	mIoU	Accuracy	mIoU
Vaihingen	99.8% ±0.1%	97.4% ±4.9%	99.8% ±0.1%	97.4% ±4.8%
Potsdam	99.8% ±0.0%	99.3% ±0.1%	99.8% ±0.0%	99.4% ±0.1%
Buxtehude	99.7% ±0.1%	98.5% ±0.4%	99.8% ±0.1%	98.8% ±0.4%
Hannover	99.7% ±0.1%	98.5% ±0.4%	99.8% ±0.0%	97.3% ±5.0%
Nienburg	99.8% ±0.0%	98.6% ±0.3%	99.8% ±0.0%	98.6% ±0.7%

representations learned by the autoencoder model with the highest validation mIoU in each run. This new ground truth was used to train the BSPSegNets for the semantic segmentation of aerial images.

4.4   Semantic Segmentation

Tables 3 and 4 show the semantic segmentation quality of BSPSegNet (same configurations as in the previous section), DeepLabv3+, FCN and U-Net. For all models except U-Net, we tested two backbones, MobileNetv2 and Xception [6]. Neither table shows a significant difference between the models. While there are differences in the mean performance, these differences are smaller than the standard deviations. The variance in mIoU, especially for the 3Cities datasets, is generally higher than it is for the accuracy. Due to the class imbalance, the former is a better metric for measuring the performance though. Even ignoring the standard deviations, there is no clear best model. U-Net performs best (in terms of mIoU) on Buxtehude and Nienburg, BSPSegNet with the Xception backbone performs best on Potsdam and Hannover, while DeepLabv3+ and FCN, both using the Xception backbone, share the victory on Vaihingen. Generally, the performance improves slightly when using the much larger Xception backbone or U-Net, which is also quite large by itself, but these improvements are again dwarfed by the standard deviation. Also, despite a tree depth of two already seeming to be sufficient for BSPSegNet judging from Table 2, BSPSegNet3 performed slightly better than BSPSegNet2. Again, within the standard deviation.

Table 3. Semantic segmentation accuracy. Unmarked models use MobileNetv2 as a backbone, while models marked with a star use Xception instead. Exception: U-Net is a fixed architecture without interchangeable backbones. Means and standard deviations across ten runs are shown.

	Vaihingen	Potsdam	Buxtehude	Hannover	Nienburg
BSPSegNet2	83.2% ±1.3%	83.2% ±2.1%	86.8% ±1.1%	85.0% ±1.3%	86.2% ±1.1%
BSPSegNet3	83.0% ±2.0%	83.1% ±2.0%	86.7% ±1.0%	85.4% ±1.2%	86.2% ±1.3%
DeepLabv3+	83.1% ±2.5%	83.2% ±1.9%	86.9% ±1.2%	85.1% ±1.8%	86.7% ±1.1%
FCN	84.0% ±1.7%	82.9% ±2.1%	87.0% ±1.4%	85.5% ±0.9%	86.2% ±1.1%
BSPSegNet2*	84.1% ±1.8%	83.6% ±1.9%	87.2% ±0.8%	85.4% ±1.3%	86.4% ±1.1%
BSPSegNet3*	84.1% ±2.3%	83.7% ±2.0%	87.4% ±1.1%	86.0% ±1.2%	86.6% ±1.1%
DeepLabv3+*	84.8% ±1.4%	83.7% ±2.0%	87.4% ±1.1%	85.2% ±2.2%	86.9% ±1.1%
FCN*	85.1% ±1.9%	83.8% ±2.0%	87.3% ±1.0%	85.6% ±0.9%	86.6% ±1.0%
U-Net	83.3% ±2.9%	83.5% ±2.1%	87.6% ±0.9%	84.6% ±2.4%	87.0% ±1.1%

Some qualitative samples of the predicted segmentations are shown in Fig. 4. Again, there is no clear best model, rather each model has its own issues. Overall, the predictions are rather good, however, there are some issues, such as the segmentations of different cars merging into one large region, or outright mispredictions such as confusing low vegetation and impervious surfaces (streets)

Table 4. Same as Table 3 but showing mIoU instead of accuracy.

	Vaihingen	Potsdam	Buxtehude	Hannover	Nienburg
BSPSegNet2	56.6% ±1.9%	64.8% ±2.7%	70.5% ±5.5%	57.5% ±3.6%	65.8% ±6.0%
BSPSegNet3	56.7% ±2.7%	64.7% ±2.6%	71.0% ±5.5%	57.7% ±3.4%	66.3% ±6.3%
DeepLabv3+	56.5% ±3.2%	64.8% ±2.7%	71.6% ±5.3%	58.3% ±4.2%	68.5% ±6.2%
FCN	58.3% ±1.8%	64.4% ±2.8%	72.2% ±5.7%	60.0% ±5.2%	67.9% ±6.2%
BSPSegNet2*	57.8% ±2.5%	65.9% ±2.8%	72.0% ±5.0%	59.6% ±4.3%	66.9% ±6.0%
BSPSegNet3*	58.1% ±2.3%	65.9% ±3.1%	72.6% ±5.3%	62.0% ±5.6%	67.2% ±6.4%
DeepLabv3+*	59.4% ±1.9%	65.8% ±3.4%	73.0% ±5.2%	59.4% ±5.2%	69.3% ±6.4%
FCN*	59.4% ±2.4%	65.5% ±3.6%	72.7% ±5.3%	60.8% ±6.7%	68.2% ±6.2%
U-Net	57.0% ±4.5%	65.6% ±3.1%	73.9% ±5.1%	57.8% ±7.8%	69.9% ±6.4%

with each other. Sometimes, the boundaries of the 8×8 blocks are visible in BSPSegNet's prediction.

The lack of performance differences may be due to ambiguities in the datasets. Every models may already achieve the best possible performance on these datasets.

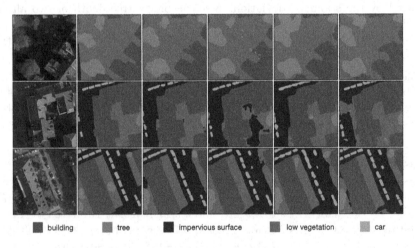

■ building   ■ tree   ■ impervious surface   ■ low vegetation   ■ car

Fig. 4. Qualitative segmentation samples from Hannover. In order from left to right: input image, ground truth, BSPSegNet3, DeepLabv3+, FCN, U-Net.

4.5   Prediction Confidence

Figure 5 compares the models' confidences. It shows

$$p_{GT} - \max_{i \neq GT} p_i$$

on the x-axis, i.e., the difference in probability assigned to the ground truth class in a prediction and the highest probability assigned to any other class. Thus, positive values indicate a correct prediction while negative values indicate an incorrect prediction. Higher absolute values indicate higher confidence in the prediction made. As can be seen, BSPSegNet has sharper boundaries between segments, as it is more confident in its predictions, indicated by showing a curve closer to being parallel to x-axis in the interval $(-1, 1)$. This is especially true for boundary pixels. Since all models have basically the same value at $x = 0$, their accuracy is also the same. More details concerning just the confidence without also looking at the accuracy at the same time can be found in the appendix.

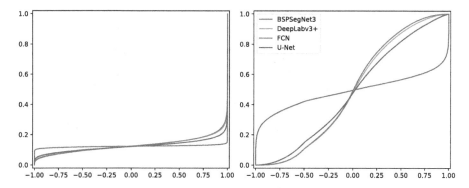

Fig. 5. Difference in probability of the ground truth class vs. the probability of the non-ground truth class with the highest probability (x-axis). The y-axis is the cumulative ratio of pixels with that difference or lower. The right-hand figure is restricted to pixels at the segment boundaries.

5   Conclusion

In this paper we presented a novel model predicting binary space partitioning trees which can be rendered in a differentiable way into semantic segmentations. Our model achieves state-of-the-art performance, but produced sharper segment boundaries than other models. Furthermore, it also inherently separates shape features from texture features, a fact we aim to make use of in future domain adaptation work. Additional future work also includes testing our approach on other image types, e.g., street scenes. This may necessitate using a different signed distance function in the BSP trees' inner nodes, as linear approximations are suitable for objects in aerial images, but may not be suitable for more organic image content from close-up. Additionally, we want to expand our model to perform instance and/or panoptic segmentation.

Appendix

A   Dataset Class Distributions

The class distributions of the datasets are shown in Fig. 6. While Vaihingen is closer in size to Buxtehude and Nienburg, its class distribution is more similar to Potsdam. Hannover, which is the largest city, has more buildings than the rest. The most low vegetation can be found in Buxtehude and Nienburg. Potsdam has a surprising amount of clutter. Cars and clutter are rare across all datasets. While there are many individual cars, there are still only few pixels showing cars since the area of each car in these images is small.

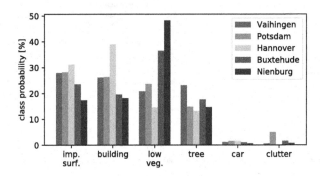

Fig. 6. Class distribution of the datasets

B   Hyperparameters and Model Details

The hyperparameters used for training BSPSegNet and additional model details can be found in Table 5. The hyperparameters for the other models' training can be found in Table 6. The random search ranges for shape and texture features of BSPSegNet were from 2 to $n - 1$ where n is the total number of parameters of the BSP trees inner node and leaf nodes respectively. The search range for λ_C was from .25 to 16 and the search range for λ_R was from 1 to 8. The random search for the learning rates was performed by randomly choosing an exponent $k \in [-5, -1]$ and then setting the learning rate to 10^k. There was a 50% chance to set the minimum learning rate to 0.

The random translations for augmentation were chosen s.t. the patches could be samples from the entire image. The random shearings were uniformly randomly sampled from $[-16°, 16°]$ (individually for both axes) while the random rotations were sampled in the same way from $[-45°, 45°]$. When the augmentation caused sampling outside the image, reflection padding was used. We used bilinear filtering for sampling. For the ground truth patches, when interpolating between pixels, we used the coefficients of the bilinear interpolation as weights for a vote to find the discrete class of each output pixel.

Table 5. Hyperparameters used for training BSPSegNet.

	BSPSegNet2	BSPSegNet3	BSPSegNet2*	BSPSegNet3*
backbone	MobileNetv2	MobileNetv2	Xception	Xception
# of conv. layers in decoders	3	3	3	3
# of hidden features in decoders	256	256	256	256
# of model parameters	2.12M	2.14M	21.17M	21.22M
tree depth	2	3	2	3
# of shape features	8	16	8	16
# of texture features	16	24	16	24
λ_C	8	8	8	8
λ_R	1	1	1	1
# of autoencoder epochs	200	200	200	200
# of epochs	120	120	120	120
mini-batch size	36	36	18	18
max. learning rate	$2.4 \cdot 10^{-3}$	$2.4 \cdot 10^{-3}$	$2.4 \cdot 10^{-3}$	$2.4 \cdot 10^{-3}$
min. learning rate	0	0	0	0

Table 6. Hyperparameters used for training DeepLabv3+, FCN, and U-Net.

	DeepLabv3+	FCN	DeepLabv3+*	FCN*	U-Net
backbone	MobileNetv2	MobileNetv2	Xception	Xception	—
# of model parameters	2.28M	1.84M	22.18M	20.87M	31.39M
# of epochs	80	120	80	120	80
mini-batch size	36	36	18	18	18
max. learning rate	$8 \cdot 10^{-3}$	$13 \cdot 10^{-3}$	$8 \cdot 10^{-3}$	$13 \cdot 10^{-3}$	$0.15 \cdot 10^{-3}$
min. learning rate	0	0	0	0	0

C   Metrics

We use two metrics to evaluate the performance of the models we trained. First, we are using the pixel level accuracy. Given a ground truth segmentation $y : L \rightarrow C$ mapping pixel locations $l \in L$ to classes $c \in C$ and a prediction $\hat{y} : L \times C \rightarrow \mathbb{R}$ of the same segmentation, we first compute $\hat{y}^* : L \rightarrow C$ using the equation

$$\hat{y}^*(l) = \arg \max_{c \in C} \hat{y}(l, c). \tag{6}$$

The accuracy is then defined as

$$Acc(y, \hat{y}^*) = \frac{|\{l \in L \mid y(l) = \hat{y}^*(l)\}|}{|L|}, \tag{7}$$

i.e., the fraction of pixel positions whose class has been predicted correctly.

As a second metric we compute the mean intersection-over-union (mIoU). The intersection-over-union (IoU) for a given class $c \in C$ is defined as

$$IoU(y, \hat{y}^*, c) = \frac{|\{l \in L \mid y(l) = c \wedge \hat{y}^*(l) = c\}|}{|\{l \in L \mid y(l) = c \vee \hat{y}^*(l) = c\}|}, \tag{8}$$

i.e., it is the number of pixel positions $l \in L$, which both segmentations assign to class c (intersection), over the number of pixel positions, which at least one segmentation assigns to class c (union). The mIoU is then defined as

$$mIoU(y, \hat{y}^*) = \frac{1}{|C|} \sum_{c \in C} IoU(y, \hat{y}^*, c), \tag{9}$$

i.e., the mean IoU over all classes $c \in C$.

Both metrics assign values in $[0, 1]$ to every pair of segmentations, with higher values meaning that the two segmentations are more alike. This, in turn, means values as close to 1 as possible are desirable as that means that the predicted segmentation is close to the ground truth segmentation.

Note: We do not use eroded boundaries when computing these metrics as opposed to metrics used by some other researchers, e.g., as (partially) used in the benchmark results of the ISPRS Vaihingen 2D Semantic Labeling Test.

D   Additional Sample Images

Figure 7 shows additional prediction samples, similarly to Fig. 4.

E   Confidence

Figure 8 shows only the prediction confidence at boundaries, without also encoding the accuracy, i.e., it shows the absolute difference between the highest two predicted class probabilities. Again, BSPScgNet produces sharper, less blurry boundaries. This is due to BSPSegNet not including any kind of upsampling. Instead, the resolution-independent BSP trees are merely rendered at the appropriate resolution.

The boundary is defined as those pixels which have at least one direct neighbor with a different class.

When computing $1 - A$, with A being the area below the curve in Fig. 8, for all ten runs for all models, we found values between 69.7% and 87% for BSPSegNet, while we found values between 10.7% and 47% for all the other models. Even the worst BSPSegNet run had significantly sharper boundaries between segments than the best run of any other model.

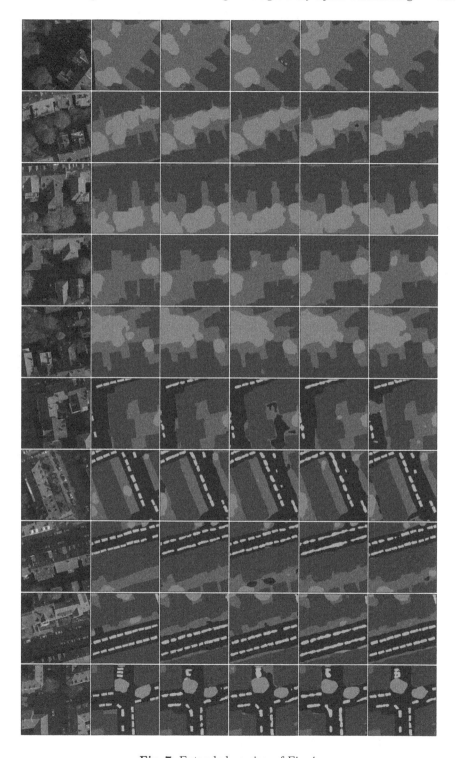

Fig. 7. Extended version of Fig. 4.

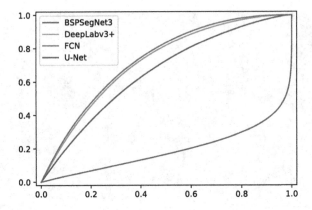

Fig. 8. Similar to the right-hand side of Fig. 5 but the x-axis shows the prediction confidence (highest probability vs. second highest probability).

References

1. Chang, W.L., Wang, H.P., Peng, W.H., Chiu, W.C.: All about structure: adapting structural information across domains for boosting semantic segmentation, In: CVPR. pp. 1900–1909 (2019)
2. Chen, L.C., Papandreou, G., Kokkinos, I., Murphy, K., Yuille, A.L.: Deeplab: semantic image segmentation with deep convolutional nets, Atrous convolution, and fully connected CRFs. IEEE Trans. Pattern Anal. Mach. Intell. **40**(4), 834–848 (2017)
3. Chen, L.C., Papandreou, G., Schroff, F., Adam, H.: Rethinking atrous convolution for semantic image segmentation. arXiv preprint arXiv:1706.05587 (2017)
4. Chen, L.-C., Zhu, Y., Papandreou, G., Schroff, F., Adam, H.: Encoder-decoder with atrous separable convolution for semantic image segmentation. In: Ferrari, V., Hebert, M., Sminchisescu, C., Weiss, Y. (eds.) ECCV 2018. LNCS, vol. 11211, pp. 833–851. Springer, Cham (2018). https://doi.org/10.1007/978-3-030-01234-2_49
5. Chen, Z., Tagliasacchi, A., Zhang, H.: BSP-NET: generating compact meshes via binary space partitioning. In: Proceedings of the IEEE/CVF Conference on Computer Vision and Pattern Recognition, pp. 45–54 (2020)
6. Chollet, F.: Xception: deep learning with depthwise separable convolutions. In: Proceedings of the IEEE Conference on Computer Vision and Pattern Recognition, pp. 1251–1258 (2017)
7. Çiçek, Ö., Abdulkadir, A., Lienkamp, S.S., Brox, T., Ronneberger, O.: 3D U-Net: learning dense volumetric segmentation from sparse annotation. In: Ourselin, S., Joskowicz, L., Sabuncu, M.R., Unal, G., Wells, W. (eds.) MICCAI 2016. LNCS, vol. 9901, pp. 424–432. Springer, Cham (2016). https://doi.org/10.1007/978-3-319-46723-8_49
8. Fuchs, H., Kedem, Z.M., Naylor, B.F.: On visible surface generation by a priori tree structures. In: Proceedings of the 7th Annual Conference on Computer Graphics and Interactive Techniques, pp. 124–133 (1980)
9. Girard, N., Charpiat, G., Tarabalka, Y.: Aligning and updating cadaster maps with aerial images by multi-task, multi-resolution deep learning. In: Jawahar, C.V., Li, H., Mori, G., Schindler, K. (eds.) ACCV 2018. LNCS, vol. 11365, pp. 675–690. Springer, Cham (2019). https://doi.org/10.1007/978-3-030-20873-8_43

10. Gkioxari, G., Malik, J., Johnson, J.: Mesh R-CNN. In: Proceedings of the IEEE/CVF International Conference on Computer Vision, pp. 9785–9795 (2019)
11. Gómez, J.A., Patiño, J.E., Duque, J.C., Passos, S.: Spatiotemporal modeling of urban growth using machine learning. Remote Sens. **12**(1), 109 (2020)
12. He, K., Gkioxari, G., Dollár, P., Girshick, R.: Mask R-CNN. In: Proceedings of the IEEE International Conference on Computer Vision, pp. 2961–2969 (2017)
13. He, K., Zhang, X., Ren, S., Sun, J.: Deep residual learning for image recognition. In: Proceedings of the IEEE Conference on Computer Vision and Pattern Recognition, pp. 770–778 (2016)
14. ISPRS: 2D Semantic Labeling - ISPRS (2020). http://www2.isprs.org/commissions/comm3/wg4/semantic-labeling.html. Accessed 28 Jan 2020
15. Jégou, S., Drozdzal, M., Vazquez, D., Romero, A., Bengio, Y.: The one hundred layers tiramisu: Fully convolutional densenets for semantic segmentation. In: Proceedings of the IEEE Conference on Computer Vision and Pattern Recognition Workshops, pp. 11–19 (2017)
16. Kingma, D.P., Ba, J.: Adam: a method for stochastic optimization. arXiv preprint arXiv:1412.6980 (2014)
17. Kirillov, A., He, K., Girshick, R., Rother, C., Dollár, P.: Panoptic segmentation. In: Proceedings of the IEEE/CVF Conference on Computer Vision and Pattern Recognition, pp. 9404–9413 (2019)
18. Kirillov, A., Wu, Y., He, K., Girshick, R.: PointRend: image segmentation as rendering. In: Proceedings of the IEEE/CVF Conference on Computer Vision and Pattern Recognition, pp. 9799–9808 (2020)
19. Lee, S.H., Han, K.J., Lee, K., Lee, K.J., Oh, K.Y., Lee, M.J.: Classification of landscape affected by deforestation using high-resolution remote sensing data and deep-learning techniques. Remote Sens. **12**(20), 3372 (2020)
20. Long, J., Shelhamer, E., Darrell, T.: Fully convolutional networks for semantic segmentation. In: CVPR, pp. 3431–3440 (2015)
21. Loshchilov, I., Hutter, F.: SGDR: stochastic gradient descent with warm restarts. arXiv preprint arXiv:1608.03983 (2016)
22. Loshchilov, I., Hutter, F.: Decoupled weight decay regularization. arXiv preprint arXiv:1711.05101 (2017)
23. Mescheder, L., Oechsle, M., Niemeyer, M., Nowozin, S., Geiger, A.: Occupancy networks: Learning 3d reconstruction in function space. In: Proceedings of the IEEE/CVF Conference on Computer Vision and Pattern Recognition, pp. 4460–4470 (2019)
24. Papandreou, G., Chen, L.C., Murphy, K., Yuille, A.: Weakly-and semi-supervised learning of a DCNN for semantic image segmentation. arXiv:1502.02734 (2015)
25. Ronneberger, O., Fischer, P., Brox, T.: U-Net: convolutional networks for biomedical image segmentation. In: Navab, N., Hornegger, J., Wells, W.M., Frangi, A.F. (eds.) MICCAI 2015. LNCS, vol. 9351, pp. 234–241. Springer, Cham (2015). https://doi.org/10.1007/978-3-319-24574-4_28
26. Sandler, M., Howard, A., Zhu, M., Zhmoginov, A., Chen, L.C.: Mobilenetv 2: Inverted residuals and linear bottlenecks. In: CVPR, pp. 4510–4520 (2018)
27. Sanglard, F.: Game Engine Black Book: DOOM v1.1. Sanglard, Fabien (2019)
28. Simonyan, K., Zisserman, A.: Very deep convolutional networks for large-scale image recognition. arXiv preprint arXiv:1409.1556 (2014)
29. Sofiiuk, K., Barinova, O., Konushin, A.: Adaptis: adaptive instance selection network. In: Proceedings of the IEEE/CVF International Conference on Computer Vision, pp. 7355–7363 (2019)

30. Takikawa, T., Acuna, D., Jampani, V., Fidler, S.: Gated-SCNN: gated shape CNNs for semantic segmentation. In: Proceedings of the IEEE/CVF International Conference on Computer Vision, pp. 5229–5238 (2019)
31. Tatarchenko, M., Dosovitskiy, A., Brox, T.: Octree generating networks: efficient convolutional architectures for high-resolution 3D outputs. In: Proceedings of the IEEE International Conference on Computer Vision, pp. 2088–2096 (2017)
32. Wang, N., Zhang, Y., Li, Z., Fu, Y., Liu, W., Jiang, Y.G.: Pixel2Mesh: generating 3D mesh models from single RGB images. In: Proceedings of the European Conference on Computer Vision (ECCV), pp. 52–67 (2018)
33. Wu, H., Zhang, J., Huang, K., Liang, K., Yu, Y.: FastFCN: rethinking dilated convolution in the backbone for semantic segmentation. arXiv preprint arXiv:1903.11816 (2019)
34. Xu, B., Wang, N., Chen, T., Li, M.: Empirical evaluation of rectified activations in convolutional network. arXiv preprint arXiv:1505.00853 (2015)
35. Yu, F., Koltun, V.: Multi-scale context aggregation by dilated convolutions. arXiv preprint arXiv:1511.07122 (2015)
36. Zhu, Y., et al.: Improving semantic segmentation via video propagation and label relaxation. In: Proceedings of the IEEE/CVF Conference on Computer Vision and Pattern Recognition, pp. 8856–8865 (2019)

EVARS-GPR: EVent-Triggered Augmented Refitting of Gaussian Process Regression for Seasonal Data

Florian Haselbeck[1,2] and Dominik G. Grimm[1,2,3(✉)]

[1] TUM Campus Straubing for Biotechnology and Sustainability, Bioinformatics, Technical University of Munich, Schulgasse 22, 94315 Straubing, Germany
{florian.haselbeck,dominik.grimm}@hswt.de
[2] Weihenstephan-Triesdorf University of Applied Sciences, Bioinformatics, Petersgasse 18, 94315 Straubing, Germany
[3] Department of Informatics, Technical University of Munich, Boltzmannstr. 3, 85748 Garching, Germany

Abstract. Time series forecasting is a growing domain with diverse applications. However, changes of the system behavior over time due to internal or external influences are challenging. Therefore, predictions of a previously learned forecasting model might not be useful anymore. In this paper, we present **EV**ent-triggered **A**ugmented **R**efitting of Gaussian Process Regression for **S**easonal Data (EVARS-GPR), a novel online algorithm that is able to handle sudden shifts in the target variable scale of seasonal data. For this purpose, EVARS-GPR combines online change point detection with a refitting of the prediction model using data augmentation for samples prior to a change point. Our experiments on simulated data show that EVARS-GPR is applicable for a wide range of output scale changes. EVARS-GPR has on average a 20.8% lower RMSE on different real-world datasets compared to methods with a similar computational resource consumption. Furthermore, we show that our algorithm leads to a six-fold reduction of the averaged runtime in relation to all comparison partners with a periodical refitting strategy. In summary, we present a computationally efficient online forecasting algorithm for seasonal time series with changes of the target variable scale and demonstrate its functionality on simulated as well as real-world data. All code is publicly available on GitHub: https://github.com/grimmlab/evars-gpr.

Keywords: Gaussian process regression · Seasonal time series · Change point detection · Online time series forecasting · Data augmentation

1 Introduction

Time series forecasting is an emerging topic with applications in diverse domains, e.g. business, medicine or energy. These approaches make use of time series data, which describes a system behavior by a sequence of observations within a certain time period and try to predict future values. However, sudden changes of the system behavior over

© Springer Nature Switzerland AG 2021
S. Edelkamp et al. (Eds.): KI 2021, LNAI 12873, pp. 135–157, 2021.
https://doi.org/10.1007/978-3-030-87626-5_11

time are common issues in time series analysis. These sudden changes can be either caused by external or internal influences, e.g. due to operational or strategic decisions. For instance, currently many sales forecasting systems are affected by the SARS-CoV-2 pandemic and energy demand predictions might be impeded by energetic optimizations of big consumers. Some but probably not all of the influential factors can be captured by features. Nevertheless, after a change of the generative data distribution, which reflects the relation between explanatory features and the target variable, predictions of a previously learned model might not be useful anymore. As a result, decisions based on these could cause damage such as a financial loss if e.g. an underestimated demand leads to missed sales [2, 13].

A common but computationally exhaustive approach to handle this problem is to periodically retrain a prediction model during the productive operation [13]. Furthermore, several methods combine change point detection (CPD), i.e. the problem of identifying a change of the generative data distribution, and Gaussian Process Regression (GPR). Some of them work offline and are therefore not suitable for changing data distributions during the online phase [9, 16]. Existing online approaches are either not event-triggered [21, 22], require a certain number of samples of a new generative distribution [12] or are based on *a priori* assumptions in terms of potentially changing time series properties [17]. Furthermore, none of them apply data augmentation (DA) on samples prior to a detected change point to reuse these augmented samples for model retraining.

In this work, we present **EV**ent-triggered **A**ugmented **R**efitting of Gaussian Process Regression for **S**easonal Data (EVARS-GPR), for which we provide an overview in Fig. 1. This novel online algorithm combines change point monitoring with a refitting of the prediction model using data augmentation. Compared to existing approaches, the main focus of our algorithm is on seasonal data with sudden changes of the target variable scale while values of explanatory features remain approximately equal, which is a common issue in seasonal time series forecasting. The data augmentation step is triggered after the detection of a change point and a deviation of the target variable scale compared to a certain threshold. This step updates known samples prior to a change point with new information on the changed target variable scale. Consequently, we gain potential useful data for the refitting of the prediction model. Hence, EVARS-GPR is event-triggered and as a result more efficient than a periodical refitting strategy. Furthermore, the algorithm reacts immediately after a detected change point and *a priori* assumptions on the output scale changes are not required. As prediction model we use Gaussian Process Regression (GPR), see Appendix A for an overview. GPR is a flexible and non-parametric Bayesian method including uncertainties of a prediction value, which seems profitable with regard to the practical use of forecasts. Moreover, we evaluate the integration of different approaches for online CPD and DA, two essential parts of EVARS-GPR. We further analyze EVARS-GPR using simulated data and evaluate the performance on real-world datasets including different comparison partners.

The remainder of this paper is organized as follows. In Sect. 2, we describe the related work. Afterwards, we provide the problem formulation in Sect. 3. Then, we outline EVARS-GPR in Sect. 4 followed by the experimental setup in Sect. 5. The experimental results are shown and discussed in Sect. 6, before we draw conclusions.

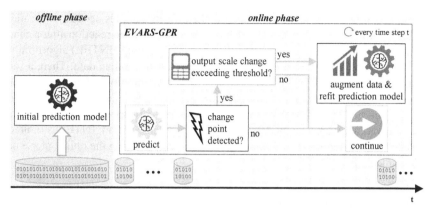

Fig. 1. Overview of EVARS-GPR during the online phase and the preconditions in the offline phase. The initial prediction model is trained offline. During the online phase, the prediction of the next target value is followed by a change point detection. If a change point is detected, the output scaling factor, which sets the target values of the current season in relation to previous seasons, is calculated. If the deviation between the current and last output scaling factor exceeds a threshold, then an augmented refitting of the prediction model is triggered. In case one of the two conditions is not fulfilled, EVARS-GPR continues using the current prediction model.

2   Related Work

Methods enabling GPR models to work with nonstationary data distributions can be divided into offline and online techniques. A common offline approach is to switch between kernel functions, e.g. by multiplication with sigmoid functions [9]. For some technical processes, multiple steady states can be determined. This enables the association of a corresponding model. For inference, the one associated with the current state is selected [16]. However, these approaches are limited to scenarios for which change points respectively steady states can be defined *a priori*. Furthermore, change points occurring abruptly at a single point can be treated as a hyperparameter of a nonstationary covariance function [11]. A further possibility of handling nonstationary data distributions is to augment the input using time-related functions. One option is the introduction of a forgetting factor, which leads to a lower influence of the information contained in older samples. Another common technique is to periodically update the hyperparameters of a GPR model using samples within a specified moving window [22]. A more elaborate approach is Moving-Window GPR (MWGPR). This method discards the oldest sample after a new one becomes available. Moreover, a dual preprocessing and dual updating strategy is performed. This introduces a recursive bias term, which depends on past model errors and is added to the model's prediction to get the final forecast value [21]. All these approaches have the drawback of losing potentially useful information from earlier samples even if the data distribution did not change [22]. GP-non-Bayesian clustering (GP-NBC) is focused on computational efficiency with the goal of making it suitable for resource-constrained environments, e.g. robotic platforms. Based on online-trained GP models, likelihood ratio tests are performed in order to determine whether a new candidate model or a previously stored one should be used in the further process. A disadvantage of GP-NBC is that a certain number of new samples needs to be available to enable the training of a new model. This may lead to a delayed reaction after a change point occurred [12]. The INstant TEmporal structure Learning (INTEL) algorithm was recently proposed. First, a template model is learned using offline data. Then, a set of candidate models with varying hyperparameters due to assumptions of potential changes during the productive operation is constructed based on the template model. For the final prediction, all models are combined using weights that correspond to the likelihood of a new observation given each model. In its current implementation, INTEL is limited to univariate data. Furthermore, possible changes happening during the online phase need to be assumed *a priori* [17].

3 Problem Formulation

We define a multivariate time series $\mathcal{D} = \{x_t, y_t\}^n$ as a sequence of n samples consisting of d-dimensional explanatory variables called covariates $x_t \in \mathbb{R}^d$ and a corresponding target value $y_t \in \mathbb{R}$ at time step t. The target value at time step t, y_t, is drawn from a distribution $p_i(y|x_t)$, i.e. it is dependent on the covariates x_t. In this work, we consider seasonal data, meaning data that follows a certain periodicity of length n_{seas}. We assume that periodicity is present for the target variable y as well as for at least some of the covariates X. Thus, the target variable at time step t can be decomposed in a seasonal component s_t and a residual r_t summing up all other effects: $y_t = s_t + r_t$. Based on its periodicity of length n_{seas}, the seasonal component at time step t is similar to those of previous seasons: $s_t \approx s_{t-k \cdot n_{seas}}$ with $k \in \mathbb{N} \backslash \{0\}$. The covariates x_t respectively a subset $\chi_t \subseteq x_t$ of them can also be decomposed in a seasonal component $s_{\chi,t}$ and a residual $r_{\chi,t}$ into $\chi_t = s_{\chi,t} + r_{\chi,t}$, with similar periodicity characteristics regarding $s_{\chi,t}$. The strength of the seasonal pattern, i.e. the influence of the seasonal component on the final value, might vary for different covariates and target variables.

With n_{off} samples of $\mathcal{D}$, a model M, here a Gaussian Process Regression, can be trained offline using cross-validation to determine the hyperparameter configuration that delivers predictions $\hat{y}$ generalizing best to the true distribution $p_i(y|x)$. During the online phase, with a new input x_t provided at every time step t, the model M is used to deliver a prediction for the target variable value $\hat{y}_t$ based on x_t. However, it is a common issue in time series forecasting that the generative distribution $p_i(y|x)$ our predictor M was trained on might change to another distribution $p_j(y|x)$. The time step at which such a shift happens is called a change point. In this work, we focus on output scale shifts, meaning that the value range of the target variable y changes. Therefore, with regard to the periodicity of the covariates X and the target variable y, a similar covariate vector x_t corresponds to a different target variable y_t as the generative distribution changed. Consequently, the predictions produced by the previously trained model M might not be useful anymore. With EVARS-GPR, we address this problem by combining online change point monitoring of the target variable y and a refitting of the base model M using data augmentation in case a change point is detected. A list of symbols including those of subsequent sections is provided in Appendix B.

4   EVARS-GPR

EVARS-GPR is an online algorithm that is focused on changes resulting in an output scale shift of seasonal multivariate time series, as outlined in Sect. 3. In Fig. 1 and Algorithm 1, we give an overview of EVARS-GPR. Following the problem formulation, we assume an offline-trained model M, which we subsequently call the base model M_{base}. Prior to the online phase, the current prediction model $M_{current}$ is initialized with this offline-trained model M_{base}. As EVARS-GPR operates online, the main part starts with a new sample becoming available at time step t. As a first step, we retrieve the prediction of the next target value $\hat{y}_t$ using the covariates x_t as well as the current model $M_{current}$. Then, we run an online change point detection (CPD) algorithm, which is updated with the current target variable value y_t. In case we do not detect a shift of the generative distribution $p(y|x_t)$, the current prediction model $M_{current}$ stays unchanged and the algorithm waits for the next time step $t + 1$. However, if we determine a change point at time step t, the remaining procedures of EVARS-GPR are triggered. First, as EVARS-GPR is focused on changes of the output scale in seasonal time series data, the output scaling factor η is determined. For that purpose, the target values y prior to the change point and within a window of size n_w are considered. These are set in relation to the target values y within the corresponding window of n_η previous seasons with a season length of n_{seas}:

$$\eta = \frac{1}{n_\eta} \sum_{k=1}^{n_\eta} \frac{\sum_{i=t-n_w}^{t} y_i}{\sum_{j=t-k \cdot n_{seas}-n_w}^{t-k \cdot n_{seas}} y_j} \tag{1}$$

The nominator of Eq. (1) includes current target values y_i prior to the change point, whereas the denominator conveys information on the corresponding period of a previous season. This ratio is averaged over the number of seasons taken into account to retrieve the output scaling factor. Online CPD is prone to false alarms due to outliers. For this reason and to limit the amount of refittings for efficiency, we set a minimum threshold π_η for the deviation between the current output scaling factor η and the output scaling factor of the last augmented refitting η_{old}. If this threshold is exceeded, the augmented refitting of the current model $M_{current}$ is triggered. First, we generate an augmented set of samples $\mathcal{D}'$ based on the dataset prior to the change point at time step t. Thereby, we reuse known samples and update them with new information on the changed target variable scale. Consequently, we gain an augmented dataset $\mathcal{D}'$ for the refitting of the current model $M_{current}$. Furthermore, the last output scaling factor η_{old} is stored. Subsequently, the refitted current model is used for the predictions of the target value. With a new sample arriving at the next time step $t + 1$, the whole cycle of predicting, change point monitoring, potential data augmentation and model refitting starts again.

The goal of CPD is to find abrupt changes in data, in the context of this work resulting in a shift of the scale of the target variable y. A CPD method should ensure a quick reaction to a change point. Considering a real time operation, computationally efficient CPD methods are advantageous. Beyond that, for EVARS-GPR, the CPD and the prediction methods are separated in order to enable the output scale-dependent, augmented model refitting. For these reasons, we excluded approaches such as GPTS-CP [24] and BOCPD-MS [15]. Based on the outlined criteria, we evaluated Bayesian

Online Change Point Detection (BOCPD) and ChangeFinder (CF). More information on these two methods can be found in Appendix C. In both cases, we deseasonalize data via seasonal differencing in order to prevent false alarms due to seasonal effects [2].

Besides online CPD, DA is an essential part of EVARS-GPR. For this work, we focus on computationally efficient approaches ensuring a real time operation and consider small datasets as well. Therefore, we excluded generative models such as TimeGAN [28] or C-RNN-GAN [20]. First, we augmented the original dataset consisting of all samples prior to a change point at time step t, $\mathcal{D}_{0:t}$, by scaling the original target variable vector $y_{0:t}$. Thereby, we multiply the target variable vector $y_{0:t}$ with the output scaling factor η and leave the covariates $x_{0:t}$ unchanged, resulting in the augmented dataset $\mathcal{D}_{0:t}^{\eta}$. Considering the focus on shifts of the output scale, augmenting the dataset by scaling the target variable vector y is a reasonable and efficient approach. Second, we used two virtual sample generation techniques for imbalanced regression: Random Oversampling with the introduction of Gaussian Noise (GN) [26] and SMOGN, which combines the former and the Synthetic Minority Oversampling TEchnique for Regression (SMOTER) [5, 27]. Both methods are outlined in Appendix D.

Algorithm 1. EVARS-GPR

Inputs: $M_{base}, \mathcal{D}_{0:n_{off}}$

Parameters: $n_\eta, n_{seas}, n_w, \pi_\eta$, *CPD* and *DA* parameters

Results: $\hat{y}$

  1: $M_{current} = M_{base}$

  2: $\eta_{old} = 1$

  3: **for** *new sample at time step t* **do**

  4:      predict target value: $\hat{y}_t = M_{current}(x_t)$

  5:      perform online CPD: $online\_cpd(y_{0:t}, CPD\ parameters)$ ▷ App. 2

  6:      **if** *change point detected* **then**

  7:            calculate output scaling factor:

                   $\eta = calc\_output\_scaling\_factor(n_\eta, n_{seas}, n_w)$ ▷ Eq. (1)

  8:        **if** $|\eta - \eta_{old}| / \eta_{old} > \pi_\eta$ **then**

  9:            augment data:

                   $\mathcal{D}' = augment\_data(\mathcal{D}_{0:t}, DA\ parameters)$ ▷ App. 3

10:         refit current model: $refit(M_{current}, \mathcal{D}')$

11:         $\eta_{old} = \eta$

12:        **end if**

13:      **end if**

14: **end for**

---

5 Experimental Setup

Subsequently, we will first describe the simulated data we used to determine the configuration of EVARS-GPR and to analyze its behavior. Afterwards, we outline the real-world datasets and the performance evaluation.

5.1 Simulated Data

EVARS-GPR is focused on seasonal data with changes regarding the target variable scale during the online phase. In order to configure and parametrize the algorithm as well as to analyze its behavior, we generated simulated data fulfilling these properties. Figure 2 visualizes a simplified example of simulated data to explain its configuration. As we observe in Fig. 2a, the target variable y follows a periodical pattern with a season length n_{seas} and an amplitude a. Between t_{start} and t_{end} during the online phase, we manipulate y by a multiplication with a factor δ, which results in a change of the output scale. The characteristics of this manipulation factor are visualized in Fig. 2b. At t_{start}, we begin with δ_{base} and increase δ by a slope of κ at every time step t, up to a maximum manipulation factor δ_{max}. Then, the manipulation factor δ stays constant until its sequential decrease is triggered in order to reach δ_{base} at t_{end}. To meet the properties specified in Sect. 3, the covariates x are also periodical. Both x and y can be modified with additive random noise in order to model the seasonality more realistic.

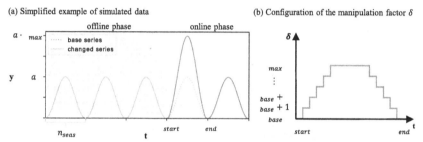

Fig. 2. (a) **Visualization of a simplified example of simulated data** with the base as well as the changed series, both with a season length of n_{seas}. Between t_{start} and t_{end}, the base series with its amplitude a is changed by multiplication with a manipulation factor δ. (b) **Configuration of the manipulation factor δ.** Starting from δ_{base} at t_{start}, the manipulation factor δ increases by a slope κ at every time step t. If a maximum manipulation factor δ_{max} is reached, δ stays constant. At t_{end}, the base factor δ_{base} is reached again after sequentially decreasing δ using κ.

In summary, the parameters n_{seas}, t_{start}, t_{end}, δ_{max} and κ enable us to simulate various settings of the output scale change. For instance, t_{start} and t_{end} modify the duration and time of occurrence. Furthermore, δ_{max} marks the maximum extent of the output scale change, whereas κ determines its increase at every time step t, thus the speed respectively abruptness. Based on this, we formulated 67 scenarios and evaluated the performance to select the online CPD and DA method for EVARS-GPR, see Sect. 6.1. Furthermore, the parametrization of EVARS-GPR is based on these scenarios, see Appendix E for an overview. For that purpose, we employed a random search with 100 different parameter settings for each combination of online CPD and DA method [3].

5.2 Real-World Datasets

We additionally evaluated EVARS-GPR on real-world datasets. Based on the algorithm's scope, we selected seasonal time series data, for which we provide more information in

Appendix F. For the horticultural sales prediction dataset *CashierData*[1], we observe a strong sales increase of potted plants (*PotTotal*) during the SARS-CoV-2 pandemic in 2020. Furthermore, we included the following common and publicly available datasets with changes of the output scale during the online phase: *DrugSales* [13], *VisitorNights* [13], *AirPassengers* [4] and *MaunaLoa* [10]. Beyond that, we used time series data without such changes to test the robustness of EVARS-GPR: *ChampagneSales* [18], *TouristsIndia* [7], *Milk* [19], *Beer* [13] and *USDeaths* [19]. We further applied mean imputation for missing values and added calendric as well as statistical features, e.g. lagged target variables, see Appendix F for an overview. Then, we used 80% of the data to determine the base model M_{base}, i.e. the configuration that leads to the best performance in a cross-validation setup. Thereby, we employed a random search over the model's hyperparameters such as the kernel function as well as preprocessing parameters, e.g. whether to perform a principal component analysis [3]. Finally, we evaluated EVARS-GPR in an online setting for the remaining left out 20% of the data.

5.3 Evaluation

To evaluate the performance on a set of n samples, we used the Root Mean Squared Error (RMSE), which is defined as $RMSE = \sqrt{1/n \sum_{i=1}^{n} (y_i - \hat{y}_i)^2}$ with the true value y_i and the prediction $\hat{y}_i$. As the RMSE is scale-dependent, we further applied a scaling by the RMSE value achieved with M_{base}, subsequently called RMSE-ratio. Thus, the performances on simulated scenarios with different scales are comparable.

We included several comparison partners for the real-world datasets. M_{base} applies the offline-trained model during the whole online phase. Furthermore, we employed common but computationally exhaustive periodical refits of the prediction model, which trigger a retraining at every (*PR1*) respectively every second (*PR2*) time step [13]. Moving-Window GPR (MWGPR) is included as an additional computational resource demanding comparison partner, because a refit is needed at every time step t [21]. Moreover, we defined methods with a computational resource consumption similar to EVARS-GPR. These methods also react after a valid change point was detected, so the number of refittings and thus the resource consumption is similar. *CPD_scaled* scales the predictions of M_{base} using the output scaling factor η, whereas *CPD_retrain* triggers a refitting of the current prediction model $M_{current}$ using all original samples prior to a change point. *CPD_MW* also leads to a refitting, but only uses data of the season before the detected change point. For an estimate of the resource consumption, we measured the process-wide CPU time of EVARS-GPR and the computationally exhaustive methods on a machine with two 2.1 GHz *Intel Xeon Gold 6230R* CPUs (each with 26 cores and 52 threads) and a total of 756 GB of memory.

6 Experimental Results

In this section, we will first describe the behavior on simulated data. Afterwards, we outline the results on real-world datasets, before we discuss them.

---

[1] https://github.com/grimmlab/HorticulturalSalesPredictions.

6.1 Behavior on Simulated Data

We determined the configuration and parameters of EVARS-GPR based on simulated data. Using CF for online CPD and a scaling of the original dataset for DA lead to the lowest RMSE-ratio averaged over all scenarios (0.549). Thereby, we experienced that EVARS-GPR is sensitive to hyperparameters, e.g. the window size n_w, see Appendix E regarding the final values. We further analyzed EVARS-GPR on different output scale changes regarding the extent (maximum manipulation factor δ_{max}), speed (slope κ), time of occurrence and duration (both via start t_{start} respectively end index t_{end}). Results are visualized in Fig. 3. The performance of EVARS-GPR was in all scenarios at least equal to M_{base} and outperformed it in most of the cases. Figure 3a and 3b show that the advantage of EVARS-GPR was larger for longer periods with an output change. However, there was also an improvement for shorter durations. EVARS-GPR was beneficial for several extents and speeds of the shift as well as robust for constant scenarios ($\delta_{max} = 1$), see Fig. 3c and 3d. For smaller slopes κ, the improvement tended to decrease with a higher maximum manipulation factor δ_{max}. We observe in Fig. 3d that EVARS-GPR's benefit was mostly smaller for maximum manipulation factors d_{max} close to one. We included further scenarios in Appendix G, which show similar results.

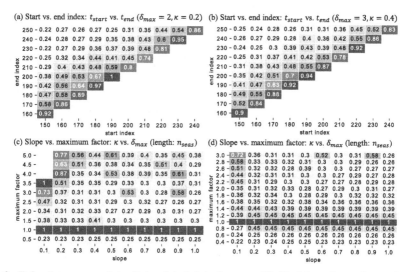

Fig. 3. Behavior on a variety of simulated data ($n_{seas} = 50$). Each box shows the result of the scenario parametrized with the values given on the x- and y- axis. Numbers are RMSE-ratios, lower values reflect a higher improvement compared to M_{base}. We analyzed the following factors of the output scale change: (**a**) time of occurrence and duration via start and end indices t_{start} respectively t_{end}, (**b**) same factors with a higher slope κ and maximum manipulation factor δ_{max}, (**c**) extent and speed of the change via κ and δ_{max}, (**d**) same factors on a finer grid for δ_{max}.

6.2 Results on Real-World Datasets

We further evaluated EVARS-GPR on several real-world datasets. In Table 1, we show the model performance in terms of RMSE compared to methods with a similar computational resource consumption for datasets with a changing target variable scale. As we observe, EVARS-GPR was superior on all datasets. Our algorithm outperformed M_{base} with an improvement of 37.9% averaged over all datasets and the second-best competing method among all datasets by 20.8%.

Table 1. Performance comparison based on RMSE for datasets with output scale changes during the online phase for EVARS-GPR and methods with a similar resource consumption. Numbers show the RMSE of the simulated online phase. The best results are printed bold.

	M_{base}	CPD_scaled	CPD_retrain	CPD_MW	EVARS-GPR
CashierData	1351.43	2266.57	1314.55	1683.11	**1125.34**
DrugSales	6.15	5.39	3.90	4.46	**2.75**
AirPassengers	171.58	101.61	108.79	174.31	**93.88**
MaunaLoa	34.37	32.01	31.22	33.50	**27.96**
VisitorNights	10.97	9.30	8.80	10.34	**5.11**

Beyond that, we compared EVARS-GPR to computationally exhaustive methods, for which we show the results as well as the process-wide CPU time in Table 2. EVARS-GPR outperformed all other methods with respect to the CPU time. In comparison to $PR2$, the method with the second lowest runtimes, the runtime of EVARS-GPR averaged over all datasets was more than six times lower.

Table 2. RMSE and CPU time compared to computationally exhaustive methods for datasets with output scale changes. Numbers show the RMSE and the CPU time averaged over ten runs. The best RMSE results and lowest CPU times excluding M_{base} are printed bold.

		M_{base}	PR1	PR2	MWGPR	EVARS-GPR
CashierData	RMSE	1351.43	1119.23	1185.82	**1098.16**	1125.34
	CPU time [s]	2.38	1443.80	741.71	1106.53	**166.06**
DrugSales	RMSE	6.15	**2.44**	2.54	2.86	2.75
	CPU time [s]	0.61	762.05	404.47	550.99	**52.40**
AirPassengers	RMSE	171.58	**69.06**	74.28	72.27	93.88
	CPU time [s]	0.93	587.70	303.31	514.53	**34.53**
MaunaLoa	RMSE	34.37	11.12	12.60	**9.88**	27.96
	CPU time [s]	3.60	27459.79	13790.61	19525.85	**78.99**
VisitorNights	RMSE	10.97	**5.08**	5.21	5.85	5.11
	CPU time [s]	0.35	40.85	22.28	33.87	**6.24**

It is not surprising that these comparison partners outperformed EVARS-GPR with respect to predictive power, however at the cost of computational runtime. Regarding *AirPassengers* and *MaunaLoa*, for which EVARS-GPR was outperformed in terms of RMSE, the CPU time of EVARS-GPR was 16 respectively 250 times more efficient. However, for *CashierData*, *DrugSales* and *VisitorNights*, the RMSE of EVARS-GPR was comparable to the leading ones, while being computationally much more efficient.

In Table 3, we see that EVARS-GPR was robust for datasets without an output scale change during the online phase as the results were identical to M_{base}.

Table 3. Robustness on datasets without output scale changes during the online phase. Numbers show the RMSE of the simulated online phase.

	ChampagneSales	*TouristsIndia*	*Milk*	*Beer*	*USDeaths*
M_{base}	1158.26	90707.30	15.16	16.88	276.72
EVARS-GPR	1158.26	90707.30	15.16	16.88	276.72

6.3 Discussion

We showed that EVARS-GPR is able to handle seasonal time series with changes of the target variable scale, both on simulated and real-world data. The performance on simulated data demonstrates a broad applicability regarding the time of occurrence, duration, speed and extent of the output scale change, with a higher advantage over M_{base} for longer durations. Shorter changes are more difficult to detect for online CPD methods, which is one reason for the lower improvement in such settings. Our results further indicate that EVARS-GPR can handle various speeds and extents of the output scale change, which can be seen as different abruptness levels. This applies both for increases as well as decreases. Experiments with smaller extents showed smaller improvements of EVARS-GPR, as it is more difficult to detect such changes. A similar effect can be observed for smaller speeds and larger extents of the output scale change. Nevertheless, EVARS-GPR was at least on par with M_{base} in all cases and outperformed it in most of the settings.

In addition, EVARS-GPR outperformed all methods with a similar computational resource consumption with respect to RMSE on real-world datasets, with a mean improvement of 20.8% compared to the second-best approaches. Regarding *AirPassengers* and *MaunaLoa*, the advantage of EVARS-GPR in terms of RMSE was 7.6% respectively 10.4%. For these datasets, the output scale changes at the detected change points were rather small. Consequently, the DA step did not enhance the performance that much, which might be a reason for the smaller improvements on RMSE in contrast to the other datasets. Furthermore, the difference to other periodical refitting strategies was largest for *AirPassengers* and *MaunaLoa*. This might indicate that not all possible change points were detected or that these datasets possess further data distribution shifts not resulting in an output scale change. With respect to the other three datasets, EVARS-GPR's results were comparable to the periodical refitting strategies, suggesting that all relevant change points could be detected. Moreover, we showed EVARS-GPR's efficiency in comparison with periodical refitting strategies with a more than six-fold reduction of the averaged runtime in relation to *PR2*. This advantage of EVARS-GPR was even bigger for *AirPassengers* and *MaunaLoa* with a 16 respectively 250 times lower runtime compared to the best performer. Finally, EVARS-GPR was robust for datasets without changes of the target variable scale.

The online detection of change points is an essential part of EVARS-GPR, as wrong or missed detections might lead to a performance decrease. We addressed the problem of misdetections due to outliers with the introduction of a threshold for the output scaling factor. Nevertheless, EVARS-GPR would probably benefit a lot from improvements of the online CPD method. Moreover, we observed lower RMSE values for periodical refitting strategies, especially on a dataset with more samples (*MaunaLoa*). Thus, a combination of EVARS-GPR and a periodical refitting strategy with a lower frequency is an interesting approach for future research. This might result in a computationally efficient algorithm, which is additionally able to capture changing data distributions that do not result in a target variable scale. We further determined the parameters of the whole pipeline based on simulated data. This might not be the best strategy for all settings and real-world applications. However, as the simulated scenarios were diverse and reflected the scope of this work with output scale changes, this is a reasonable approach. Nevertheless, another way for parameter optimization is a further potential for future research. One possibility is to integrate this into the cross-validation performed offline by simulating different manipulations of the real-world data. Beyond that, EVARS-GPR is model-agnostic. Therefore, it seems interesting to transfer this approach to other prediction models, e.g. XGBoost, which is limited to prediction values within the target value range of the training set [8].

7   Conclusion

In this paper, we presented EVARS-GPR, a novel online time series forecasting algorithm that is able to handle sudden shifts in the target variable scale of seasonal data by combining change point monitoring with an augmented refitting of a prediction model. Online change point detection and data augmentation are essential components of EVARS-GPR, for which we evaluated different approaches based on simulated scenarios. Using the resulting configuration and parameterization, we showed on simulated data that EVARS-GPR is applicable for a wide range of output scale changes. Furthermore, EVARS-GPR had on average a 20.8% lower RMSE on different real-world datasets compared to methods with a similar computational resource consumption. Moreover, we demonstrated its computational efficiency compared to periodical refitting strategies with a more than six-fold reduction of the averaged runtime.

Acknowledgments. This work is supported by funds of the Federal Ministry of Food and Agriculture (BMEL) based on a decision of the Parliament of the Federal Republic of Germany via the Federal Office for Agriculture and Food (BLE) under the innovation support program [grant number 2818504A18]. Furthermore, we acknowledge Maura John and Nikita Genze for fruitful discussions regarding the naming of the algorithm.

Competing Interests.   All authors declare that they have no competing interests.

Appendix A: Gaussian Process Regression

With regard to the practical use of forecasts, the uncertainty of a prediction value seems profitable. Providing those by its definition is a main advantage of the nonparametric Bayesian method GPR. To explain this approach, we use the linear model that is defined as

$$f(x) = x^T w, y = f(x) + \epsilon \tag{2}$$

with x being the input vector, w the vector of weights, the function value $f(x)$ and observed target value y with additive noise ϵ assumed to follow a zero-mean Gaussian. Combined with the independence assumption of the observation values, we get the likelihood, which reflects how probable the observed target values y are for the different inputs X and weights w:

$$p(y|X, w) = \prod_{i=1}^{j} p(y_i|x_i, w) \tag{3}$$

As usual for a Bayesian formulation, we define a prior over the weights, for which we again choose a zero-mean Gaussian. With the defined prior and the likelihood based on the observed data, we can use Bayes' rule to get the posterior of the weights given the data:

$$p(w|X, y) = \frac{p(y|X,w)p(w)}{p(y|X)} \tag{4}$$

This is also called the maximum a posteriori estimate, which - provided the data - delivers the most likely set of weights w. As $p(y|X)$ is independent of w, we can reformulate this equation expressing the posterior distribution with a Gaussian defined by a mean and covariance matrix:

$$p(w|X, y) \sim N\left(\overline{w}, A^{-1}\right) \tag{5}$$

During inference, we marginalize out w and as a result take the average based on all possible w weighted by their posterior probability:

$$\begin{aligned} p(y_{Test}|x_{Test}, X, y) &= \int p(y_{Test}|x_{Test}, w)p(w|X, y)dw \\ &= N\left(\frac{1}{\sigma^2}x_{Test}^T A^{-1}Xy, x_{Test}^T A^{-1}x_{Test}\right) \end{aligned} \tag{6}$$

Therefore, we do not only get an output value, but also an uncertainty. So far, we reached the Bayesian formulation of linear regression with its limited expressiveness. To overcome this constraint to linearity, we can project the inputs into a high-dimensional space and apply the linear concept there. This transformation can be accomplished using basis functions $\phi(x) : \mathbb{R}^d \to \mathbb{R}^i$ leading to the following model with i weights w:

$$f(x) = \phi(x)^T w \tag{7}$$

Conducting the same derivation as shown above results in a similar outcome:

$$p(y_{Test}|x_{Test}, X, y) = N\left(\frac{1}{\sigma^2}\phi(x_{Test})^T A^{-1}\Phi(X)y, \phi(x_{Test})^T A^{-1}\phi(x_{Test})\right) \tag{8}$$

The need of inverting the *ixi* matrix A possibly causes computational problems if the dimension of the feature space i becomes large. To solve this, we can reformulate the above using the so-called "kernel trick". This leads to the formulation of a Gaussian Process, which is completely specified by its mean and covariance function:

$$f(x) \sim GP\big(m(x), k\big(x, x'\big)\big) \tag{9}$$

$$m(x) = E\big[f(x)\big] \tag{10}$$

$$k\big(x, x'\big) = E\big[(f(x) - m(x))\big(f(x') - m(x')\big)\big] \tag{11}$$

$k(x, x')$ consists of the covariance value between any two sample points x and x' resulting in a nxn matrix for a training set length of n. The assumption is that the similarity between samples reflects the strength of the correlation between their corresponding target values. Therefore, the function evaluation can be seen as a draw from a multivariate Gaussian distribution defined by $m(x)$ and $k(x, x')$. Thus, Gaussian Processes are a distribution over functions rather than parameters, in contrast to Bayesian linear regression. For simplicity, the mean function is often set to zero or a constant value. There are many forms of kernel functions, which need to fulfill certain properties, e.g. being positive semidefinite and symmetric. Furthermore, they can be combined, e.g. by summation or multiplication. The choice of the covariance kernel function is a determining configuration of GPR and its parameters need to be optimized during training [15, 17].

Appendix B: List of Symbols

General Symbols

M	prediction model
t	current time step
$\mathcal{D}$	time series dataset
n	number of samples of the time series dataset $\mathcal{D}$
n_{off}	number of samples that are available during the offline phase
x_t	covariate vector at time step t
d	dimensionality of the covariate vector x_t
X	covariate matrix including all covariates vectors
χ_t	subset of the covariate vector x_t at time step t
$s_{\chi,t}$	seasonal component of the subset of the covariate vector χ_t at time step t
$r_{\chi,t}$	residual component of the subset of the covariate vector χ_t at time step t
y_t	true target value at time step t
s_t	seasonal component of y_t at time step t
r_t	residual component of y_t at time step t
n_{seas}	length of one season
$\hat{y}_t$	predicted target value at time step t
$p(y\|x_t)$	generative distribution of y.

EVARS-GPR

M_{base} offline-trained base model
$M_{current}$ current prediction model
η current output scaling factor
η_{old} output scaling factor of last augmented refitting
n_w window size for the calculation of the output scaling factor η
n_η number of previous seasons considered for the calculation of the output scaling factor η
π_η minimum threshold for the deviation between the current η and the last output scaling factor η_{old}
$\mathcal{D}'$ augmented set of samples.

Simulated Data

a amplitude
n_{seas} length of a season
t_{start} start index of the output scale change
t_{end} end index of the output scale change
δ multiplicative manipulation factor for the output scale change
δ_{base} starting manipulation factor
δ_{max} maximum manipulation factor for the output scale change
κ slope, i.e. increase per time step t, for the manipulation factor δ.

Appendix C: Online Change Point Detection

The goal of CPD is to find abrupt changes in data, in the context of this work resulting in a shift of the scale of the target variable y. Based on the criteria outlined in Sect. 4, we selected Bayesian Online Change Point Detection and ChangeFinder.

Bayesian Online Change Point Detection (BOCPD) is a common probabilistic technique. BOCPD assumes that a sequence of observations $y_1, y_2, \ldots, y_T$ can be divided into non-overlapping partitions ρ within which the data is i.i.d. from a distribution $p(y_t | \theta_\rho)$, with the parameters θ_ρ being i.i.d. as well. A central aspect of BOCPD is the definition of the run length at time step t, r_t, i.e. the time since the last change point. The posterior distribution of the run length r_t can be determined using Bayes' theorem with $y_t^{(r)}$ denoting the observations associated with r_t:

$$p(r_t | y_{1:t}) = \frac{\sum_{r_{t-1}} p(r_t | r_{t-1}) p(y_t | r_{t-1}, y_t^{(r)}) p(r_{t-1}, y_{1:t-1})}{\sum_{r_t} p(r_t, y_{1:t})} \tag{12}$$

The conditional prior $p(r_t|r_{t-1})$ is defined to be nonzero only for $r_t = 0$ and $r_t = r_{t-1}+1$ making the algorithm computationally efficient:

$$p(r_t|r_{t-1}) = \begin{cases} H(r_{t-1} + 1) & \text{if } r_t = 0 \\ 1 - H(r_{t-1} + 1) & \text{if } r_t = r_{t-1} + 1 \\ 0 & \text{otherwise} \end{cases} \tag{13}$$

$H(\tau) = \frac{p_{gap}(g=\tau)}{\sum_{t=\tau}^{\infty} p_{gap}(g=t)}$ is the so-called hazard function with the *a priori* probability distribution over the interval between between change points $p_{gap}(g)$. To apply BOCPD, a hazard function needs to be provided. With $p_{gap}(g)$ being a discrete exponential distribution with timescale λ, the hazard function is constant at $H(\tau) = 1/\lambda$, which is a common assumption. Finally, using the posterior distribution of the run length r_t, a change point can be determined [1, 2].

Another type of online CPD techniques suitable for our purposes are likelihood ratio methods, which declare a change point if the probability distributions before and after a candidate point differ significantly. ChangeFinder is a common approach of this kind, which employs a two-stage learning and smoothing strategy using Sequentially Discounting Auto-Regression (SDAR) model learning. In the first stage, we fit an SDAR model for each new sample at time step t to represent the statistical behavior of the data. The model parameters are updated sequentially with a reduction of the influence of older samples. Thereby, we obtain a sequence of probability densities $p_1, p_2, \ldots, p_t$ for each y_t. Based on these, we assign an outlier score to each data point, which is defined as $score(y_t) = -\log p_{t-1}(y_t)$. This enables the formulation of an auxiliary time series o_t by building moving averages of the outlier scores within a time window T for each time step t:

$$o_t = \frac{1}{T}\sum_{i=t-T+1}^{t} score(y_i) \tag{14}$$

After this first smoothing, the second stage starts. Thereby, another SDAR model is fitted using o_t, also resulting in a sequence of probability densities $q_1, q_2, \ldots, q_t$. Finally, we get a change point score z_t after a second smoothing step within a time window T:

$$z_t = \frac{1}{T}\sum_{i=t-T+1}^{t} - \log q_{t-1}(o_t) \tag{15}$$

A higher value of z_t corresponds to a higher probability of a change point at time step t. Hence, a threshold π_{cf} at which a change point is declared, needs to be defined [2, 14, 25].

Appendix D: Data Augmentation

As outlined in Sect. 4, we used Virtual Sample Generation approaches for imbalanced regression besides a scaling of the original dataset for data augmentation. These methods are suitable for continuous target variables and small datasets. We therefore selected the two following approaches: Random Oversampling with the introduction of Gaussian Noise (GN) [26] and SMOGN, which combines the former and the Synthetic Minority Oversampling TEchnique for Regression (SMOTER) [5, 27]. Both methods start with the assignment of a relevance value to every sample (x_i, y_i) of a dataset $\mathcal{D}_{vsg}$ using a relevance function $\phi : y \rightarrow [0, 1]$. Based on these and a specified threshold π_{rel}, the dataset $\mathcal{D}_{vsg}$ is splitted into a subset of normal and rare cases, $\mathcal{D}_N$ respectively $\mathcal{D}_R$. We employed a relevance function, which proposes an inverse proportionality of the relevance value and the probability density function of y [23]. Therefore, extreme cases have a higher relevance value. Furthermore, we tested two compositions of $\mathcal{D}_{vsg}$. In the first case, $\mathcal{D}_{vsg}$ was equal to the original dataset up to the change point at time step t, $\mathcal{D}_{0:t}$, and in the second one $\mathcal{D}_{0:t}$ and the output scaled dataset $\mathcal{D}_{0:t}^{\eta}$ were concatenated. Both GN and SMOGN then apply a Random Undersampling strategy for the normal cases $\mathcal{D}_N$, meaning that a specified share of these is randomly selected to get $\mathcal{D}_{us}$.

Furthermore, GN generates new samples $\mathcal{D}_{os}$ based on the rare cases $\mathcal{D}_R$ by adding Gaussian Noise to the target variable as well as the numeric covariates. Values for nominal attributes are randomly selected with a probability proportional to their frequency in the dataset. Finally, for GN, the undersampled and oversampled cases are concatenated to the augmented dataset $\mathcal{D}^{GN} = \{\mathcal{D}_{us}, \mathcal{D}_{os}\}$.

SMOGN instead employs two different oversampling techniques: GN and SMOTER. Prior to the sample generation, the k-nearest neighbors of a seed sample are determined. If a randomly selected k-nearest neighbor is within a specified maximum distance, SMOTER is performed resulting in a set of new samples $\mathcal{D}_{os}^{SMOTER}$. With SMOTER, values of numeric attributes are interpolated and nominal ones are randomly selected. The target value is determined by a weighted average with weights that are inversely proportional to the distance between the seed samples and the new generated one. In case the maximum distance is exceeded, GN is performed, leading to a second oversampling dataset $\mathcal{D}_{os}^{GN}$. The final augmented dataset for SMOGN therefore consists of three sets: $\mathcal{D}^{SMOGN} = \{\mathcal{D}_{us}, \mathcal{D}_{os}^{SMOTER}, \mathcal{D}_{os}^{GN}\}$ [5, 6, 23].

Appendix E: EVARS-GPR Parameters

Table 4 provides an overview of EVARS-GPR's parameters including all applied CPD and DA methods.

Table 4. Overview of EVARS-GPR's parameters with all analyzed methods CPD and DA.

Category	Parameter	Explanation
General parameters	scale_window(_factor)	Size of window prior to detected change point for calculation of output scaling factor, alternatively formulated as a factor of the season length
	scale_window_minimum	Minimum window size for output scaling factor
	scale_seasons	Number of seasons considered for output scaling factor
	scale_thr	Minimum threshold for the deviation between the current and last output scaling factor to trigger augmented refitting
CPD parameters	*BOCPD*	
	const_hazard(_factor)	Constant of the hazard function, alternatively formulated as a factor of the season length
	ChangeFinder	
	cf_r	Forgetting factor of the SDAR models
	cf_order	Order of the SDAR models
	cf_smooth	Window size for the smoothing step
	cf_thr_perc	Percentile threshold of the anomaly score during the offline phase to declare a change point
DA parameters	max_samples(_factor)	Maximum number of samples for DA, alternatively formulated as number of seasons
	GN	
	gn_operc	Oversampling percentage
	gn_uperc	Undersampling percentage
	gn_thr	Threshold to determine normal and rare values
	append	Specify if scaled dataset version is appended prior to sample generation
	SMOGN	
	smogn_relthr	Threshold to determine normal and rare values
	smogn_relcoef	Box plot coefficient for relevance function
	smogn_under_samp	Specify if undersampling is performed
	append	Specify if scaled dataset version is appended prior to sample generation

Based on the results over all 67 simulated scenarios, we selected CF for online CPD and a scaling of the original dataset for DA. Furthermore, our experiments yielded the following parameters: scale_window_factor = 0.1, scale_window_minimum = 2, scale_seasons = 2, scale_thr = 0.1, cf_r = 0.4, cf_order = 1, cf_smooth = 4, cf_thr_perc = 70. For efficiency, we set max_samples_factor = 10.

Appendix F: Real-World Datasets

Tables 5 and 6 show an overview of the real-world datasets used for evaluation as well as the additionally derived features.

Table 5. Overview of the used real-world datasets.

Dataset	Explanation	Samples
Datasets with a changing output scale during the online phase		
CashierData	Weekly sales of a horticultural retailer	195
DrugSales	Sales of antidiabetic drugs per month	204
VisitorNights	Visitor nights per quarter in millions in Australia	68
AirPassengers	Total number of US airline passengers per month	144
MaunaLoa	Monthly averaged parts per million of CO2 measured at Mauna Loa observatory, Hawaii	751
Datasets without a changing output scale during the online phase		
ChampagneSales	Sales of perrin freres champagne	105
TouristsIndia	Foreign tourist arrivals per quarter in India	48
Milk	Average milk production per cow and month	168
Beer	Australian monthly beer production	56
USDeaths	Accidental deaths in the US per month	72

Table 6. Overview of additional calendric and statistical features. Not all features are applicable for all datasets, e.g. due to the temporal resolution. Features are added to existing ones.

Category	Features	Explanation
Calendric features	Date based features	Hour, day of month, weekday, month, quarter
	Working day	Flag showing if the day is a working day
Statistical features	Lagged variables	Prior values of the target variable/features
	Seasonal lagged variables	Prior values of the preceding season
	Rolling statistics	Rolling mean and maximum within a window
	Seasonal rolling statistics	Seasonal rolling mean and maximum within a window
	Rolling weekday statistics	Rolling mean and maximum within a window calculated for each weekday

Appendix G: Further Simulated Scenarios

Figures 4, 5 and 6 show further simulated scenarios. Each box shows the result of the scenario parametrized with the value given on the x- and y- axis. Numbers are RMSE-ratios, lower values reflect a higher improvement compared to M_{base}.

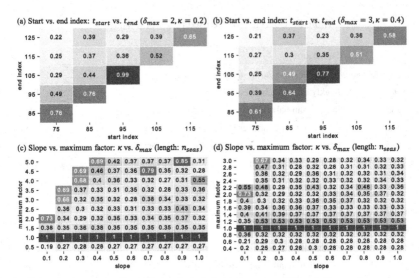

Fig. 4. Behavior on a variety of simulated data ($n_{seas} = 25$). (a) time of occurrence and duration via start and end indices t_{start} respectively t_{end}, **(b)** same factors with a higher slope κ and maximum manipulation factor δ_{max}, **(c)** extent and speed of the change via κ and δ_{max}, **(d)** same factors on a finer grid for δ_{max}.

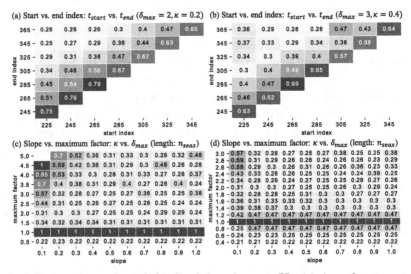

Fig. 5. Behavior on a variety of simulated data ($n_{seas} = 75$). (a) time of occurrence and duration via start and end indices t_{start} respectively t_{end}, **(b)** same factors with a higher slope κ and maximum manipulation factor δ_{max}, **(c)** extent and speed of the change via κ and δ_{max}, **(d)** same factors on a finer grid for δ_{max}.

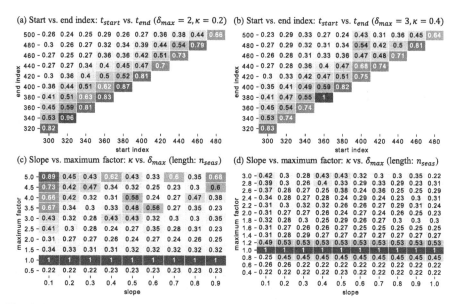

Fig. 6. Behavior on a variety of simulated data ($n_{seas} = 100$). (a) time of occurrence and duration via start and end indices t_{start} respectively t_{end}, (b) same factors with a higher slope κ and maximum manipulation factor δ_{max}, (c) extent and speed of the change via κ and δ_{max}, (d) same factors on a finer grid for δ_{max}.

References

1. Adams, R.P., MacKay, D.J.C.: Bayesian online changepoint detection (2007)
2. Aminikhanghahi, S., Cook, D.J.: A survey of methods for time series change point detection. Knowl. Inf. Syst. **51**(2), 339–367 (2016). https://doi.org/10.1007/s10115-016-0987-z
3. Bergstra, J., Bengio, Y.: Random search for hyper-parameter optimization. J. Mach. Learn. Res. **13**(10), 281–305 (2012)
4. Box, G.E.P., Jenkins, G.M., Reinsel, G.C., Ljung, G.M.: Time Series Analysis. Forecasting and Control. Wiley Series in Probability and Statistics. Wiley, Hoboken (2016)
5. Branco, P., Torgo, L., Ribeiro, R.P.: SMOGN: a pre-processing approach for imbalanced regression. In: Torgo, L., Krawczyk, B., Branco, P., Moniz, N. (eds.) Proceedings of the First International Workshop on Learning with Imbalanced Domains: Theory and Applications, pp. 36–50. PMLR, Skopje (2017)
6. Branco, P., Torgo, L., Ribeiro, R.P.: Pre-processing approaches for imbalanced distributions in regression. Neurocomputing **343**, 76–99 (2019). https://doi.org/10.1016/j.neucom.2018.11.100
7. Chakrabarty, N.: Quarterly foreign tourist arrivals in India. Determinants of Foreign Tourism Demand and Foreign Tourist Arrivals (2005–2016). https://www.kaggle.com/navoneel/fta-data. Accessed 14 May 2021
8. Chen, T., Guestrin, C.: XGBoost: A scalable tree boosting system. In: Krishnapuram, B., Shah, M., Smola, A., Aggarwal, C., Shen, D., Rastogi, R. (eds.) KDD 2016. 22nd ACM SIGKDD Conference on Knowledge Discovery and Data Mining, pp. 785–794. Association for Computing Machinery Inc. (ACM), New York (2016). https://doi.org/10.1145/2939672.2939785

9. Duvenaud, D.: Automatic model construction with Gaussian processes. Doctoral thesis, University of Cambridge (2014)

10. Earth System Research Laboratory: CO_2 PPM - Trends in Atmospheric Carbon Dioxide. Atmospheric Carbon Dioxide Dry Air Mole Fractions at Mauna Loa, Hawaii. https://datahub.io/core/co2-ppm-daily#data. Accessed 14 May 2021

11. Garnett, R., Osborne, M.A., Reece, S., Rogers, A., Roberts, S.J.: Sequential Bayesian prediction in the presence of changepoints and faults. Comput. J. **53**(9), 1430–1446 (2010). https://doi.org/10.1093/comjnl/bxq003

12. Grande, R.C., Walsh, T.J., Chowdhary, G., Ferguson, S., How, J.P.: Online regression for data with changepoints using gaussian processes and reusable models. IEEE Trans. Neural Netwo. Learn. Syst. **28**(9), 2115–2128 (2017). https://doi.org/10.1109/TNNLS.2016.2574565

13. Hyndman, R.J., Athanasopoulos, G.: Forecasting: Principles and Practice, 2nd edn. OTexts, Melbourne (2018)

14. Iwata, T., Nakamura, K., Tokusashi, Y., Matsutani, H.: Accelerating online change-point detection algorithm using 10 GbE FPGA NIC. In: Mencagli, G., et al. (eds.) Euro-Par 2018. LNCS, vol. 11339, pp. 506–517. Springer, Cham (2019). https://doi.org/10.1007/978-3-030-10549-5_40

15. Knoblauch, J., Damoulas, T.: Spatio-temporal Bayesian on-line changepoint detection with model selection. In: Dy, J., Krause, A. (eds.) Proceedings of the 35th International Conference on Machine Learning, pp. 2718–2727. PMLR (2018)

16. Liu, Y., Chen, T., Chen, J.: Auto-switch Gaussian process regression-based probabilistic soft sensors for industrial multigrade processes with transitions. Ind. Eng. Chem. Res. **54**(18), 5037–5047 (2015). https://doi.org/10.1021/ie504185j

17. Liu, B., Qi, Y., Chen, K.-J.: Sequential online prediction in the presence of outliers and change points: an instant temporal structure learning approach. Neurocomputing **413**, 240–258 (2020). https://doi.org/10.1016/j.neucom.2020.07.011

18. Makridakis, S., Wheelwright, S.C.: Forecasting Methods for Management, 5th edn. Wiley, New York (1989)

19. Makridakis, S.G., Wheelwright, S.C., Hyndman, R.J.: Forecasting. Methods and Applications, 3rd edn. Wiley, Hoboken (1998)

20. Mogren, O.: C-RNN-GAN: A continuous recurrent neural network with adversarial training. In: Constructive Machine Learning Workshop (CML) at NIPS 2016 (2016)

21. Ni, W., Tan, S.K., Ng, W.J., Brown, S.D.: Moving-window GPR for nonlinear dynamic system modeling with dual updating and dual preprocessing. Ind. Eng. Chem. Res. **51**(18), 6416–6428 (2012). https://doi.org/10.1021/ie201898a

22. Perez-Cruz, F., van Vaerenbergh, S., Murillo-Fuentes, J.J., Lazaro-Gredilla, M., Santamaria, I.: Gaussian processes for nonlinear signal processing: an overview of recent advances. IEEE Signal Process. Mag. **30**(4), 40–50 (2013). https://doi.org/10.1109/MSP.2013.2250352

23. Ribeiro, R.P.: Utility-based regression. Doctoral thesis, University of Porto (2011)

24. Saatçi, Y., Turner, R., Rasmussen, C.E.: Gaussian process change point models. In: Proceedings of the 27th International Conference on International Conference on Machine Learning, pp. 927–934. Omnipress, Madison (2010)

25. Takeuchi, J., Yamanishi, K.: A unifying framework for detecting outliers and change points from time series. IEEE Trans. Knowl. Data Eng. **18**(4), 482–492 (2006). https://doi.org/10.1109/TKDE.2006.1599387

26. Torgo, L., Ribeiro, R.: Utility-based regression. In: Kok, J.N., Koronacki, J., Lopez de Mantaras, R., Matwin, S., Mladenič, D., Skowron, A. (eds.) PKDD 2007. LNCS (LNAI), vol. 4702, pp. 597–604. Springer, Heidelberg (2007). https://doi.org/10.1007/978-3-540-74976-9_63

27. Torgo, L., Ribeiro, R.P., Pfahringer, B., Branco, P.: SMOTE for regression. In: Correia, L., Reis, L.P., Cascalho, J. (eds.) EPIA 2013. LNCS (LNAI), vol. 8154, pp. 378–389. Springer, Heidelberg (2013). https://doi.org/10.1007/978-3-642-40669-0_33
28. Yoon, J., Jarrett, D., van der Schaar, M.: Time-series generative adversarial networks. In: Wallach, H., Larochelle, H., Beygelzimer, A., d'Alché-Buc, F., Fox, E., Garnett, R. (eds.) Advances in Neural Information Processing Systems (NeurIPS 2019), vol. 32, pp. 5508–5518. Curran Associates, Inc. (2019)

Selective Pseudo-Label Clustering

Louis Mahon[(✉)] and Thomas Lukasiewicz

Department of Computer Science, University of Oxford, Oxford, UK
`louis.mahon@linacre.ox.ac.uk`

Abstract. Deep neural networks (DNNs) offer a means of addressing the challenging task of clustering high-dimensional data. DNNs can extract useful features, and so produce a lower dimensional representation, which is more amenable to clustering techniques. As clustering is typically performed in a purely unsupervised setting, where no training labels are available, the question then arises as to how the DNN feature extractor can be trained. The most accurate existing approaches combine the training of the DNN with the clustering objective, so that information from the clustering process can be used to update the DNN to produce better features for clustering. One problem with this approach is that these "pseudo-labels" produced by the clustering algorithm are noisy, and any errors that they contain will hurt the training of the DNN. In this paper, we propose selective pseudo-label clustering, which uses only the most confident pseudo-labels for training the DNN. We formally prove the performance gains under certain conditions. Applied to the task of image clustering, the new approach achieves a state-of-the-art performance on three popular image datasets.

1 Introduction

Clustering is the task of partitioning a dataset into clusters such that data points within the same cluster are similar to each other, and data points from different clusters are different to each other. It is applicable to any set of data for which there is a notion of similarity between data points. It requires no prior knowledge, neither the explicit labels of supervised learning nor the knowledge of expected symmetries and invariances leveraged in self-supervised learning.

The result of a successful clustering is a means of describing data in terms of the cluster that they belong to. This is a ubiquitous feature of human cognition. For example, we hear a sound and think of it as an utterance of the word "water", or we see a video of a biomechanical motion and think of it as a jump. This can be further refined among experts, so that a musician could describe a musical phrase as an English cadence in A major, or a dancer could describe a snippet of ballet as a right-leg fouette into arabesque. When clustering high-dimensional data, the curse of dimensionality [2] means that many classic algorithms, such as k-means [29] or expectation maximization [10], perform poorly. The Euclidean distance, which is the basis for the notion of similarity in the Euclidean space, becomes weaker in higher dimensions [51]. Several solutions to this problem have been proposed. In this paper, we consider those termed deep clustering.

© Springer Nature Switzerland AG 2021
S. Edelkamp et al. (Eds.): KI 2021, LNAI 12873, pp. 158–178, 2021.
https://doi.org/10.1007/978-3-030-87626-5_12

Deep clustering is a set of techniques that use a DNN to encode the high-dimensional data into a lower-dimensional feature space, and then perform clustering in this feature space. A major challenge is the training of the encoder. Much of the success of DNNs as image feature extractors (including [24, 46]) has been in supervised settings, but if we already had labels for our data, then there would be no need to cluster in the first place. There are two common approaches to training the encoder. The first is to use the reconstruction loss from a corresponding decoder, i.e., to train it as an autoencoder [47]. The second is to design a clustering loss, so that the encoding and the clustering are optimized jointly. Both are discussed further in Sect. 2.

Our model, *selective pseudo-label clustering (SPC)*, combines reconstruction and clustering loss. It uses an ensemble to select different loss functions for different data points, depending on how confident we are in their predicted clusters.

Ensemble learning is a function approximation where multiple approximating models are trained, and then the results are combined. Some variance across the ensemble is required. If all individual approximators were identical, there would be no gain in combining them. For ensembles composed of DNNs, variance is ensured by the random initializations of the weights and stochasticity of the training dynamics. In the simplest case, the output of the ensemble is the average of each individual output (mean for regression and mode for classification) [36].

When applying an ensemble to clustering problems (referred to as consensus clustering; see [3] for a comprehensive discussion), the sets of cluster labels must be aligned across the ensemble. This can be performed efficiently using the Hungarian algorithm. SPC considers a clustered data point to be confident if it received the same cluster label (after alignment) in each member of the ensemble. The intuition is that, due to random initializations and stochasticity of training, there is some non-zero degree of independence between the different sets of cluster labels, so the probability that all cluster labels are incorrect for a particular point is less than the probability that a single cluster label is incorrect.

Our main contributions are briefly summarized as follows.

- We describe a generally applicable deep clustering method (SPC), which treats cluster assignments as pseudo-labels, and introduces a novel technique to increase the accuracy of the pseudo-labels used for training. This produces a better feature extractor, and hence a more accurate clustering.
- We formally prove the advantages of SPC, given some simplifying assumptions. Specifically, we prove that our method does indeed increase the accuracy of the targets used for pseudo-label training, and this increase in accuracy does indeed lead to a better clustering performance.
- We implement SPC for image clustering, with a state-of-the-art performance on three popular image clustering datasets, and we present ablation studies on its main components.

The rest of this paper is organized as follows. Section 2 gives an overview of related work. Sections 3 and 4 give a detailed description of SPC and a proof of correctness, respectively. Section 5 presents and discusses our experimental results, including a comparison to existing image clustering models and ablation studies on main components of SPC. Finally, Sect. 6 summarizes our results and gives an outlook on future work. Full proofs and further details are in the appendix.

2   Related Work

One of the first deep image clustering models was [19]. It trains an autoencoder (AE) on reconstruction loss (rloss), and then clusters in the latent space, using loss terms to make the latent space more amenable to clustering.

In [44], the training of the encoder is integrated with the clustering. A second loss function is defined as the distance of each encoding to its assigned centroid. It then alternates between updating the encoder and clustering by k-means. A different differentiable loss is proposed in [43], based on a soft cluster assignment using Student's t-distribution. The method pretrains an AE on rloss, then, like [44], alternates between assigning clusters and training the encoder on cluster loss. Two slight modifications were made in later works: use of rloss after pretraining in [16] and regularization to encourage equally-sized clusters in [14].

This alternating optimization is replaced in [13] by a clustering loss that allows cluster centroids to be optimized directly by gradient descent.

Pseudo-label training is introduced by [6]. Cluster assignments are interpreted as pseudo-labels, which are then used to train a multilayer perceptron on top of the encoding DNN, training alternates between clustering encodings, and treating these clusters as labels to train the encoder.

Generative adversarial networks [15] (GANs) have produced impressive results in image synthesis [5,12,22]. At the time of writing, the most accurate GAN-based image clustering models [11,35] design a generator to sample from a latent space that is the concatenation of a multivariate normal vector and a categorical one-hot encoding vector, then recover latent vectors for the input images as in [9,28], and cluster the latent vectors. A similar idea is employed in [21], though not in an adversarial setting. For more details on GAN-based clustering, see [11,27,40,49,50] and the references therein.

Adversarial training is used for regularization in [33]. In [34], the method is developed. Conflicted data points are identified as those whose maximum probability across all clusters is less than some threshold, or whose max and next-to-max are within some threshold of each other. Pseudo-label training is then performed on the unconflicted points only. A similar threshold-based filtering method is employed by [7].

A final model to consider is [30], which uses a second round (i.e., after the DNN) of dimensionality reduction via UMAP [32], before clustering.

3   Method

Pseudo-label training is an effective deep clustering method, but training on only partially accurate pseudo-labels can hurt the encoder's ability to extract relevant features. Selective pseudo-label clustering (SPC) addresses this problem

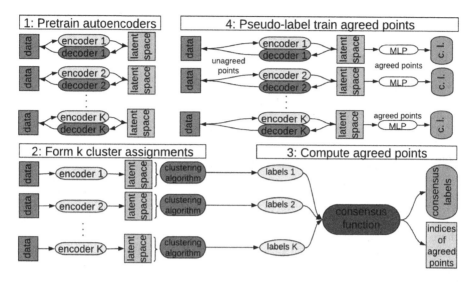

Fig. 1. The complete SPC method. (1) Pretrain autoencoders. (2) Perform multiple clusterings independently. (3) Identify agreed points as those that receive the same label in all ensemble members. (4) Perform pseudo-label training on agreed points and autoencoder training on unagreed points. Steps (2)–(4) are looped until the number of agreed points stops increasing.

by selecting only the most confident pseudo-labels for training, using the four steps shown in Fig. 1.

1. Train K autoencoders in parallel.
2. Cluster in the latent space of each, to obtain K sets of pseudo-labels.
3. Select for pseudo-label training, those points are those that received the same label in all K sets of pseudo-labels, after the labellings have been aligned using the Hungarian algorithm.
4. Train on the selected pseudo-labels. Go back to (2).

Training ends when the number of agreed points stops increasing. Then, each data point is assigned its most common cluster label across the (aligned) ensemble.

3.1 Formal Description

Given a dataset $\mathcal{X} \subseteq \mathbb{R}^n$ of size N with C true clusters, let $(f_j)_{1 \leq j \leq K}, f_j : \mathbb{R}^n \to \mathbb{R}^m$, and $(g_j)_{1 \leq j \leq K}, g_j : \mathbb{R}^m \to \mathbb{R}^n$ be the K encoders and decoders, respectively. Let $\psi : \mathbb{R}^{N \times m} \to \{0, \ldots, C-1\}^N$ be the clustering function, which takes the N encoded data points as input, and returns a cluster label for each. We refer to the output of ψ as a labelling. Let $\Gamma : \{0, \ldots, C-1\}^{K \times N} \to \{0, \ldots, C-1\}^N \times \{0, 1\}^N$ be the consensus function, which aggregates K different labellings of $\mathcal{X}$ into a single labelling, and also returns a Boolean vector indicating agreement. Then,

---

Algorithm 1. Training algorithm for SPC

for $j = 1, \ldots, K$ **do**
    Update parameters of f_j and g_j using autoencoder reconstruction
end for
while number of agreed points increases **do**
    compute $(c_1, \ldots, c_N), (a_1, \ldots, a_N)$ as in (1)
    for $j = 1, \ldots, K$ **do**
        Update parameters of f_j and h_j to minimize (2)
    end for
end while

$$(c_1, \ldots, c_N), (a_1, \ldots, a_N) = \Gamma(\psi(f_1(\mathcal{X})) \circ \cdots \circ \psi(f_K(\mathcal{X}))), \tag{1}$$

where $(c_1, \ldots, c_N)$ are the consensus labels, and $a_i = 1$ if the i-th data point received the same cluster label (after alignment) in all labellings, and 0 otherwise. The consensus function is the ensemble mode average, c_i is the cluster label that was most commonly assigned to the i-th data point.

Define K pseudo-classifiers $(h_j)_{1 \le j \le K}, h_j : \mathbb{R}^m \to \mathbb{R}^C$, and let

$$\mathcal{L} = \frac{1}{N} \sum_{i=1}^{N} \sum_{j=1}^{K} \begin{cases} CE(h_j(f_j(x_i)), c_i) & a_i = 1 \\ \|g_j(f_j(x_i)) - x_i\| & \text{otherwise,} \end{cases} \tag{2}$$

where CE denotes categorical cross-entropy:

$$CE : \mathbb{R}^C \times \{0, \ldots, C-1\} \to \mathbb{R}$$
$$CE(x, n) = -\log(x[n]).$$

First, we pretrain the autoencoders, then compute $(c_1, \ldots, c_N), (a_1, \ldots, a_N)$ and minimize $\mathcal{L}$, recompute, and iterate until the number of agreed points stops increasing. The method is summarized in Algorithm 1.

Figure 2 shows the training dynamics. Agreed points are those that receive the same cluster label in all members of the ensemble. As expected, the agreed points' accuracy is higher than the accuracy on all points. Initially, the agreed points will not include those that are difficult to cluster correctly, such as an MNIST digit 3 that looks like a digit 5. Some ensemble members will cluster it as a 3 and others as a 5. The training process aims to make these difficult points into agreed points, thus increasing the fraction of agreed points, without decreasing the agreed points' accuracy. Figure 2 shows that this aim is achieved. As more points become agreed (black dotted line), the total accuracy approaches the agreed accuracy. The agreed accuracy remains high, decreasing only very slightly (blue line). The result is that the total accuracy increases (orange line). We end training when the number of agreed points plateaus.

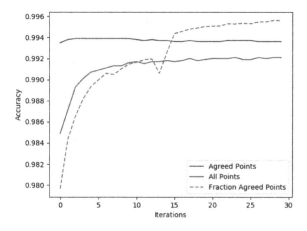

Fig. 2. Iterations of (2)–(4) in Fig. 1 on MNIST.

3.2   Implementation Details

Encoders are stacks of convolutional and batch norm layers; decoders of transpose convolutional layers. Decoders have a *tanh* activation on their output layer, all other layers use leaky ReLU. The MLP pseudo-classifier has a hidden layer of size 25. The latent space of the autoencoders has the size 50 for MNIST and FashionMNIST, and 20 for smaller USPS. We inject noise from a multivariate normal into the latent space as a simple form of regularization. As suggested in [48], the reconstruction loss is ℓ_1. The architectures are the same across the ensemble, diversity comes from random initialization and training dynamics.

The clustering function (ψ above) is a composition of UMAP [32] and either HDBSCAN [31] or a Gaussian mixture model (GMM). As in previous works, we set the number of clusters to the ground truth. UMAP uses the parameters suggested in the clustering documentation clustering, *n_neighbours* is 30 for MNIST and scaled in proportion to the dataset size for the others. HDBSCAN uses all default parameters. We cut the linkage tree at a level that gives the correct number of clusters. On the rare occasions when no such cut can be found, the clustering is excluded from the ensemble. The GMM uses all default parameters.

Consensus labels are taken as the most common across the ensemble, after alignment with the Hungarian algorithm (called the "direct" method in [3]).

4   Proof of Correctness

Proving correctness requires proving that the expected accuracy of the agreed pseudo-labels is higher than that of all pseudo-labels, and that training with more accurate pseudo-labels makes the latent vectors easier to cluster correctly.

4.1   Agreed Pseudo-Labels Are More Accurate

Given that each member of the ensemble is initialized independently at random, and undergoes different stochastic training dynamics, we can assume that each cluster assignment contains some unique information. Formally, there is strictly positive conditional mutual information between any one assignment in the ensemble and the true cluster labels, conditioned on all the other assignments in the ensemble. From this assumption, the reasoning proceeds as follows.

Choose an arbitrary data point x_0 and cluster c_0. Let X be a random variable (r.v.), indicating the true cluster of x_0, given that n members of the ensemble have assigned it to c_0, and other assignments are unknown, $n \geq 0$. Thus, the event $X = c_0$ is the event that x_0 is correctly clustered. Let Y be a Boolean r.v. indicating that the $(n+1)$-th member of the ensemble also assigns it to c_0. Assume that, if n ensemble members have assigned x_0 to c_0, and other assignments are unknown, then x_0 belongs to c_0 with probability at least $1/C$ and belongs to all other clusters with equal probability, i.e.,

$$p(X = c_0) = t$$
$$\forall c \neq c_0, p(X = c) = (1 - t)/(C - 1),$$

for some $1/C \leq t \leq 1$. It follows that the entropy $H(X)$ is a strictly decreasing function of t (see appendix for proof). Thus, the above assumption on conditional mutual information, written $I(X; Y) > 0$, is equivalent to $p(X = c_0 | Y) > p(X = c_0)$. This establishes that the accuracy of the agreed labels is an increasing function of ensemble size. Standard pseudo-label training uses $n = 1$, whereas SPC uses $n > 1$ and so results in more accurate pseudo-labels for training.

4.2   Increased Pseudo-Label Accuracy Improves Clustering

Problem Formulation. Let $\mathcal{D}$ be a dataset of i.i.d. points from a distribution over $\mathcal{S} \in \mathbb{R}^n$, where $\mathcal{S}$ contains C true clusters $c_1, \ldots, c_C$. Let T be the r.v. defined by the identity function on $\mathcal{S}$ and $f : \mathcal{S} \to \mathbb{R}^m$, an encoding function parametrized by θ, whose output is an r.v. X. The task is to recover the true clusters conditional on X, and we are interested in choosing θ such that this task is as easy as possible. Pseudo-label training applies a second function $h : \mathbb{R}^m \to \{0, \ldots, C - 1\}$ and trains the composition $h \circ f : \mathbb{R}^n \to \{0, \ldots, C - 1\}$ using gradient descent (g.d.), with cluster assignments as pseudo-labels. The claim is that an increased pseudo-label accuracy facilitates a better choice of θ.

To formalize "easy", recall the definition of clustering as a partition that minimizes intra-cluster variance and maximizes inter-cluster variance. We want the same property to hold of the r.v. X. Let $y : \mathcal{D} \to \{0, \ldots, C - 1\}$ be the true cluster assignment function and Y the corresponding random variable, then ease of recovering the true clusters is captured by a high value of d, where

$$d = \text{Var}(\mathbb{E}[X|Y]) - \mathbb{E}[\text{Var}(X|Y)].$$

High d means that a large fraction of the variance of X is accounted for by cluster assignment, as, by Eve's law, we can decompose:

$$\text{Var}\,(X) = \mathbb{E}[\text{Var}(X|Y)] + \text{Var}(\mathbb{E}[X|Y]), \tag{3}$$

In the following, we assume that f and g are linear, $C = 2$, $h \circ f(\mathcal{D}) \subseteq (0,1)$, and $\mathbb{E}[T] = \overrightarrow{0}$. The proof proceeds by expressing the value of d in terms of expected distances between encoded points after a training step with correct labels and with incorrect labels, and hence proving that the value is greater in the former case. We show that the expectation is greater in each coordinate, from which the claim follows by linearity (see appendix for details).

Lemma 1. *Let $x, x' \in \mathcal{D}$ be two data points, and consider the expected squared distance between their encodings under f. Let u_{same} and u_{diff} denote the value of this difference after a g.d. update in which both labels are the same and after a step in which both labels are different, respectively. Then, $u_{same} < u_{diff}$.*

If $w \in \mathbb{R}^m$ and $w' \in \mathbb{R}$ are, respectively, the vector of weights mapping the input to the i-th coordinate of the latent space, and the scalar mapping the i-th coordinate of the latent space to the output, then the expected squared distance in the i-th coordinate of the latent vectors before the g.d. update is

$$\mathop{\mathbb{E}}_{x,x' \sim T}[(w^T x - w^T x')^2] = \mathop{\mathbb{E}}_{x,x' \sim T}[(w^T(x - x'))^2].$$

When the two labels are the same, assume w.l.o.g. that $y = y' = 0$. Then, with step size η, the update for w and following expected squared difference u_{same} is

$$w \leftarrow w - \eta(w'(x + x'))$$
$$u_{same} = \mathop{\mathbb{E}}_{x,x' \sim T}[((w - \eta w'(x + x'))^T(x - x'))^2]$$
$$= \mathop{\mathbb{E}}_{x,x' \sim T}[(w^T(x - x') - \eta w'(||x||^2 - ||x'||^2))^2].$$

When the two labels are different, assume w.l.o.g. that $y = 0$, $y' = 1$, giving

$$w \leftarrow w - \eta(w'(x - x'))$$
$$u_{diff} = \mathop{\mathbb{E}}_{x,x' \sim T}[((w - \eta(w'(x - x'))^T)(x - x')])^2]$$
$$= \mathop{\mathbb{E}}_{x,x' \sim T}[(w^T(x - x') - \eta w'||x - x'||^2)^2].$$

It can then be shown (see appendix) that $u_{same} < u_{diff}$.

Lemma 2. *Let z be a third data point, $z \in \mathcal{D}, z \neq x, x'$, and consider the expected squared distance of the encodings, under f, of x and z. Let v_{same} and v_{diff} denote, respectively, the value of this difference after a g.d. update with two of the same labels, and with two different labels. Then, $v_{same} = v_{diff}$.*

Lemma 3. *Let s and r denote, respectively, the expected squared distance between the encodings, under f, of two points in the same cluster and between two points in different clusters. Then, there exist $\lambda_1, \lambda_2 > 0$ whose values do not depend on the parameters of f, such that $d = \lambda_1 r - \lambda_2 s$.*

For simplicity, assume that the clusters are equally sized. The argument can easily be generalized to clusters of arbitrary sizes. We then obtain

$$d = \frac{C-1}{2C}r - \frac{2C-1}{2C}s,$$

where C is the number of clusters (see appendix for proof).

Definition 1. *Let $\tilde{y} : \mathcal{D} \to \{0, \ldots, C-1\}$ be the pseudo-label assignment function. For $d_i, d_j \in \mathcal{D}$, the pseudo-labels are* pairwise correct *iff $y(x_i) = y(x_j)$ and $\tilde{y}(x_i) = \tilde{y}(x_j)$, or $y(x_i) \neq y(x_j)$ and $\tilde{y}(x_i) \neq \tilde{y}(x_j)$.*

Theorem 1. *Let d_T and d_F denote, respectively, the value of d after a g.d. step from two pairwise correct labels and from two pairwise incorrect labels, and let $x, x' \in \mathcal{D}$ as before. Then, $d_T > d_F$.*

Proof. Let r_T, s_T, and r_F, s_F be, respectively, the values of r and s after a g.d. step from two pairwise correct labels and from two pairwise incorrect labels. Consider two cases. If $y(x) = y(x')$, then $r_T = r_F$, by Lemma 2, and $s_T < s_F$, by Lemmas 1 and 2, so by Lemma 3, $d_T > d_F$. If $y(x) \neq y(x')$, then $s_T = s_F$, by Lemma 2, and $r_T > r_F$, by Lemmas 1 and 2, so again $d_T > d_F$, by Lemma 3.

The fraction of pairwise correct pairs is one measure of accuracy (Rand Index). Thus, training with more accurate pseudo-labels facilitates better clustering.

5   Experimental Results

Following previous works, we measure accuracy and normalized mutual information (NMI). Accuracy is computed by aligning the predicted cluster labels with the ground-truth labels using the Hungarian algorithm [25] and then calculating as in the supervised case. NMI, as in [41], is defined as $2I(\tilde{Y}; Y)/(H(\tilde{Y}) + H(Y))$, where $\tilde{Y}$, Y, $I(\cdot, \cdot)$, and $H(\cdot)$ are, respectively, the cluster labels, ground truth labels, mutual information, and Shannon entropy. We report on two handwritten digits datasets, MNIST (size 70000) [26] and USPS (size 9298) [20], and Fashion-MNIST (size 70000) [42] of clothing items. Table 1 shows the central tendency for five runs and the best single run.

We show results for two different clustering algorithms: Gaussian mixture model and the more advanced HDBSCAN [31]. Both perform similarly, showing robustness to clustering algorithm choice. SPC-GMM performs slightly worse on USPS and FashionMNIST (though within margin of error), suggesting that HDBSCAN may cope better with the more complex images in FashionMNIST and the smaller dataset in USPS. In Table 1, 'SPC' uses HDBSCAN.

Table 1. Accuracy and NMI of SPC compared to other top-performing image clustering models. The best results are in bold, and the second-best are emphasized. We report the mean and standard deviation (in parentheses) for five runs.

	MNIST		USPS		FashionMNIST	
	ACC	NMI	ACC	NMI	ACC	NMI
SPC-best	**99.21**	**97.49**	**98.44**	**95.44**	*67.94*	**73.48**
SPC	99.03 (.1)	97.04 (.25)	98.40 (.94)	95.42 (.15)	65.58 (2.09)	72.09 (1.28)
SPC-GMM	99.05 (.2)	97.10 (.47)	98.18 (.14)	94.93 (.32)	65.03 (1.54)	69.51 (1.21)
DynAE [34]†	*98.7*	*96.4*	*98.1*	94.8	59.1	64.2
ADC [33]†	98.6	96.1	*98.1*	94.8	58.6	66.2
DDC [39]†	98.5	96.1	97.0	*95.3*	57.0	63.2
n2d [30]	97.9	94.2	95.8	90.0	67.2	*68.4*
DLS [11]	97.5	93.6	–	–	**69.3**	66.9
JULE [45]	96.4	91.3	95.0	91.3	56.3*	60.8*
DEPICT [14]	96.5	91.7	96.4	92.7	39.2*	39.2*
DMSC [1]†	95.15	92.09	95.15	92.09	–	–
ClusterGAN [35]	95	89	-	-	63	64
VADE [21]	94.5	87.6*	56.6*	51.2*	57.8*	63.0*
IDEC [16]	88.06	86.72	76.05	78.46	52.9*	55.7*
CKM [13]	85.4	81.4	72.1	70.7	–	–
DEC [43]	84.3	83.4*	76.2*	76.7*	51.8*	54.6*
DCN [44]	83	81	68.8*	68.3*	50.1*	55.8*

† = uses data augmentation * = results taken from [34]

SPC (using either clustering algorithm) outperforms all existing approaches for both metrics on MNIST and USPS, and for NMI on FashionMNIST. The disparity between the two metrics, and between HDBSCAN and GMM, on FashionMNIST is due to the variance in cluster size. Many of the errors are lumped into one large cluster, and this hurts accuracy more than NMI, because being in this large cluster still conveys some information about what the ground truth cluster label is (see appendix for full details).

The most accurate existing methods use data augmentation. This is to be expected, given the well-established success of data augmentation in supervised learning [18]. More specifically, [17] have shown empirically that adding data augmentation to deep image clustering models improves performance in virtually all cases. Here, its effect is especially evident on the smaller dataset, USPS. For example, on MNIST, n2d [30] (which does not use data augmentation) is only 0.6 and 1.9 behind DDC [39], which does on ACC and NMI, respectively, but is 1.2 and 5.3 behind on USPS. SPC could easily be extended to include data augmentation, and even without using it, outperforms models that do.

5.1 Ablation Studies

Table 2 shows the effect of removing each component of our model. All settings use HDBSCAN. Particularly relevant are rows 2 and 3. As described in Sect. 3, we produce multiple labellings of the dataset and select for pseudo-label train-

Table 2. Ablation results, central tendency for three runs. A1=w/o label filtering; A2 = w/o label sharing; A3 = w/o ensemble; A4 = pseudo-label training only; A5 = UMAP+AE; A6 = UMAP. Both A1 and A2 train on all data points. The former trains each member of the ensemble on their own labels, and the latter uses the consensus labels. A3 sets $K = 1$, in the notation of Sect. 3.1.

	MNIST		USPS		FashionMNIST	
	ACC	NMI	ACC	NMI	ACC	NMI
SPC	**99.03 (.1)**	**97.04 (.25)**	**98.40 (.94)**	**95.42 (.15)**	**65.58 (2.09)**	**72.09 (1.28)**
A1	98.01 (.04)	94.46 (.11)	97.03 (.65)	92.43 (1.29)	63.12 (.16)	70.59 (.01)
A2	98.18 (.05)	94.86 (.09)	97.31 (.89)	92.99 (1.84)	60.60 (4.45)	68.77 (.48)
A3	98.02 (.19)	94.45 (.43)	95.85 (.80)	89.77 (1.65)	59.23 (3.58)	67.09 (3.77)
A4	97.88 (.72)	94.8 (.85)	87.49 (7.93)	82.68 (2.6)	61.2 (4.28)	67.28 (1.72)
A5	96.17 (.26)	91.07 (.23)	87.00 (8.88)	80.79 (7.43)	55.29 (3.54)	66.07 (1.04)
A6	70.24	77.42	70.46	71.11	42.08	49.22

Table 3. Ablation studies on the size of the ensemble.

	MNIST		USPS		FashionMNIST	
	ACC	NMI	ACC	NMI	ACC	NMI
25	98.48	95.60	97.70	93.82	67.67	73.25
20	98.49	95.64	97.87	94.21	67.52	73.13
15	99.03 (.10)	97.04 (.25)	98.40 (.94)	95.42 (.15)	65.58 (2.09)	72.09 (1.28)
12	98.82	96.54	98.20	95.02	67.77	73.13
10	98.78	96.42	98.39	95.47	62.93	69.89
8	98.75	96.32	98.41	95.44	67.45	71.99
6	98.61	95.90	98.40	95.39	63.84	70.62
5	98.56	95.82	98.30	95.19	67.91	73.46
4	98.47	95.60	98.27	95.18	67.90	73.38
3	98.44	95.50	98.15	94.84	63.36	70.88
2	98.27	95.07	97.98	94.40	62.9	70.41
1	98.02 (.19)	94.45 (.43)	95.85 (.80)	89.77 (1.65)	59.23 (3.58)	67.09 (3.77)

ing only those data points that received the same label in all labellings. We perform two different ablations on this method: A1 and A2. Both use all data points for training, but A1 trains each ensemble on all data points using the labels computed in that ensemble member, and A2 uses the consensus labels. At inference, both use consensus labels. The significant drop in accuracy in both settings demonstrates that the strong performance of SPC is not just due to the application of an ensemble to existing methods, but rather to the novel method of label selection.

It is interesting to observe that A1 performs worse than A2 on MNIST and USPS. Combining approximations in an ensemble has long been observed to give higher expected accuracy [4,8,37,38], so the training targets would be more accurate in A1 than in A2. We hypothesize that the reason that this fails to translate to improved clustering is a reduction in ensemble variance. On MNIST and USPS, high accuracy across the ensemble means high agreement. Giving the same training signal for every data point reduces variance further. Especially, compared with A2, the reduction is greatest on incorrectly clustered data points, because most incorrectly clustered data points are non-agreed points, and as argued in [23], high ensemble variance in the errors is important for performance.

A4 clusters in the latent space of one untrained encoder and then pseudo-label trains (essentially the method in [6]). It performs significantly worse than SPC, showing the value of the decoder, and of SPC's label selection technique.

A3 omits the ensemble entirely. Comparing with A2 again shows that the ensemble itself only produces a small improvement. Alongside SPC's label selection method, the improvement is much greater.

5.2 Ensemble Size

The number of autoencoders in the ensemble, K in the terminology of Sect. 3.1, is a hyperparameter. We add the concatenation of all latent spaces as an additional element. Table 3 shows the performance for smaller ensemble sizes. In MNIST and USPS, where the variance is reasonably small, there is a discernible trend of the performance increasing with K, then plateauing and starting to decrease. For FashionMNIST, where the variance is higher, the pattern is less clear. For all three datasets, however, we can see a significant difference between an ensemble of size two and an ensemble of size one (i.e., no ensemble). We hypothesize that the decrease for $K = 20, 25$ is due to a decrease in the number of agreed points, and so fewer pseudo-labels to train the encoders.

6   Conclusion

This paper has presented a deep clustering model, called selective pseudo-label clustering (SPC). SPC employs pseudo-label training, which alternates between clustering features extracted by a DNN, and treating these clusters as labels to train the DNN. We have improved this framework with a novel technique for preventing the DNN from learning noise. The method is formally sound and achieves a state-of-the-art performance on three popular image clustering datasets. Ablation studies have demonstrated that the high accuracy is not merely the result of applying an ensemble to existing techniques, but rather is due to SPC's novel filtering method. Future work includes the application to other clustering domains, different from images, and an investigation of how SPC combines with existing deep clustering techniques.

Acknowledgments. This work was supported by the Alan Turing Institute under the UK EPSRC grant EP/N510129/1 and by the AXA Research Fund. We also acknowledge the use of the EPSRC-funded Tier 2 facility JADE (EP/P020275/1) and GPU computing support by Scan Computers International Ltd.

A   Appendix A: Full Proofs

This appendix contains the full proofs of the results in Sect. 4.

A.1   More Accurate Pseudo-Labels Supplement

The only part omitted from the argument in the main paper is a proof for the claim about the entropy of the random variable X. This is supplied by the following proposition.

Proposition 1. *Given a categorical random variable X of the form*

$$p(X = c_0) = t$$
$$\forall c \neq c_0, p(X = c) = \frac{1-t}{C-1},$$

for some $1/C \leq t \leq 1$, the entropy $H(X)$ is a strictly decreasing function of t.

Proof.

$$H(X) = -t \log t - (1 - t) \log \frac{1-t}{C-1}$$

$$\frac{d(H(X))}{dt} = -\log t - 1 - \frac{1}{1-t} + \log \frac{1}{C-1}$$

$$+ \frac{t}{1-t} + \log 1 - t$$

$$= -2 - \log t - \log C - 1 + \log t - 1$$

$$= -2 - \log \left(\frac{t}{1-t}(C-1) \right).$$

The argument to the log is clearly an increasing function of t for $t > 1$. Therefore, for $1/C \leq t < 1$, it is lower-bounded by setting $t = 1/C$. This gives

$$\frac{d(H(X))}{dt} \leq -2 - \log \left(\frac{1/C}{1-1/C}(C-1) \right)$$

$$< -\log \left(\frac{1/C}{1-1/C}(C-1) \right) = -\log 1 = 0.$$

The derivative is always strictly negative with respect to t, so, as a function of t, $H(X)$ is always strictly decreasing.

A.2   Lemma 1 Supplement

The following is a proof for the claim that $u_{same} < u_{diff}$, as stated in Sect. 4.

Decomposing u_{same} according to the definition of variance (as the expectation of the square minus the square of the expectation) gives

$$\mathop{\mathbb{E}}_{x,x'\sim T}[w^T(x-x') - \eta w'(||x||^2 - ||x'||^2)]^2$$
$$+ \text{Var}(w^T(x-x') - \eta w'(||x||^2 - ||x'||^2)).$$

The expectation term equals 0, as

$$w^T \mathop{\mathbb{E}}_{x,x'\sim T}[(x-x')] - \eta w' \mathop{\mathbb{E}}_{x,x'\sim T}[(||x||^2 - ||x'||^2)]$$
$$= (w\mathbb{E}[T] - \mathbb{E}[T]) - \eta w'(\mathbb{E}[||T||^2] - \mathbb{E}[||T||^2]) = 0.$$

By symmetry, we can replace covariances involving x' with the same involving x. The remaining term can then be rearranged to give

$$u_{same} = 2\text{Var}(w^T x - \eta w'||x||^2)$$
$$= 2w^T Cov(T)w + 2\eta w' Var(||x||^2) - 4\text{Cov}(w^T x, \eta w'||x||^2).$$

Now rewrite u_{diff}. Decomposing as above gives

$$\mathop{\mathbb{E}}_{x,x'\sim T}[w^T(x-x') - \eta w'(||x-x'||^2)]^2$$
$$+ \text{Var}(w^T(x-x') - \eta w'(||x-x'||^2)),$$

and here the expectation term does not equal 0:

$$(w^T \mathop{\mathbb{E}}_{x,x'\sim T}[(x-x')] - \eta w' \mathop{\mathbb{E}}_{x,x'\sim T}[(||x-x'||^2)])^2$$
$$= (\eta w')^2 \mathop{\mathbb{E}}_{x,x'\sim T}[||x-x'||^2]^2.$$

The variance term can be expanded to give:

$$\text{Var}(w^T(x-x') - \eta w'(||x-x'||^2))$$
$$= 2w^T Cov(T)w + 2\eta w' \text{Var}(||x-x'||^2)$$
$$- 4\text{Cov}(w^T x, \eta w'||x-x'||^2).$$

By comparing terms, we can see that this expression is at least as large as u_{same}. First, consider the covariance terms.

Claim. $\text{Cov}(w^T x, \eta w' ||x - x'||^2) = \text{Cov}(w^T x, \eta w' ||x||^2)$.

$$\text{Cov}(w^T x, \eta w' ||x - x'||^2)$$
$$= \mathbb{E}[w^T x \eta w' ||x - x'||^2] - \mathbb{E}[w^T x]\mathbb{E}[\eta w' ||x - x'||^2]$$
$$= \eta w' \mathbb{E}[w^T x ||x - x'||^2] - 0\mathbb{E}[\eta w' ||x - x'||^2]$$
$$= \eta w' \mathbb{E}[w^T x ||x - x'||^2]$$
$$= \eta w' \mathbb{E}[w^T x \sum_k x^2 - 2xx' + x'^2]$$
$$= \eta w' \sum_k \mathbb{E}[w^T x x_k^2] - 2\mathbb{E}[w^T x x_k]\mathbb{E}[x'] + \mathbb{E}[w^T x]\mathbb{E}[x'^2]$$
$$= \eta w' \sum_k \mathbb{E}[w^T x x_k^2] - 2\mathbb{E}[w^T x x_k]0 + 0\mathbb{E}[x'^2]$$
$$= \eta w' \sum_k \mathbb{E}[w^T x x_k^2]$$
$$= \eta w' \mathbb{E}[w^T x \sum_k x_k^2]$$
$$= \eta w' \mathbb{E}[w^T x ||x||^2]$$
$$= \eta w' \mathbb{E}[w^T x ||x||^2] - 0\mathbb{E}[\eta w' ||x||^2]$$
$$= \mathbb{E}[w^T x \eta w' ||x||^2] - \mathbb{E}[w^T x]\mathbb{E}[\eta w' ||x||^2]$$
$$= \text{Cov}(w^T x, \eta w' ||x||^2).$$

So, we see the covariance terms are equal.
    Next, compare the second variance terms

Claim. $\text{Var}(||x - x'||^2) \geq \text{Var}(||x||^2)$.

$$\text{Var}(||x - x'||^2)$$
$$= \text{Var}\left(\sum_{k=0}^{nz}(x)_k^2 + (x')_k^2 - 2(x)_k(x')_k\right)$$
$$= \text{Var}\left(\sum_{k=0}^{nz}(x)_k^2\right) + \text{Var}\left(\sum_{k=0}^{nz}(x')_k^2\right) + 2\,\text{Var}\left(\sum_{k=0}^{nz}x_k x'_k\right)$$
$$= 2\text{Var}\left(\sum_{k=0}^{nz}(x)_k^2\right) + 2\,\text{Var}\left(\sum_{k=0}^{nz}x_k x'_k\right)$$
$$= 2(\text{Var}(||x||^2) + \text{Var}(x^T x'))$$
$$\geq \text{Var}(||x||^2).$$

Assuming that the data are not all identical, this implies that u_{diff} is strictly greater than u_{same}.

$$u_{diff} - u_{same}$$
$$= (\eta w')^2 \mathop{\mathbb{E}}_{x,x'\sim T}[||x - x'||^2]^2 + 2w^T \text{Cov}(T)w$$
$$+ 2\eta w' \text{Var}(||x - x'||^2) - 4\text{Cov}(w^T x, \eta w'||x - x'||^2)$$
$$- ((2w^T \text{Cov}(T)w + 2\eta w' Var(||x||^2)$$
$$- 4\text{Cov}(w^T x, \eta w'||x||^2)))$$
$$= (\eta w')^2 \mathop{\mathbb{E}}_{x,x'\sim T}[||x - x'||^2]^2$$
$$+ 2\eta w' \left(\text{Var}(||x - x'||^2) - \text{Var}(||x||^2)\right)$$
$$- 4\left(\text{Cov}(w^T x, \eta w'||x - x'||^2) - \text{Cov}(w^T x, \eta w'||x||^2)\right)$$
$$= (\eta w')^2 \mathop{\mathbb{E}}_{x,x'\sim T}[||x - x'||^2]^2$$
$$+ 2\eta w' \left(\text{Var}(||x - x'||^2) - \text{Var}(||x||^2)\right)$$
$$\geq (\eta w')^2 \mathop{\mathbb{E}}_{x,x'\sim T}[||x - x'||^2]^2 > 0.$$

A.3   Lemma 2 Supplement

The following is the complete proof of Lemma 2, which was omitted from the main paper.

Proof. $v_{diff} - v_{same}$

$$= \mathbb{E}[(w^T(x - z) - w'(x - x')(x - z))^2]$$
$$- \mathbb{E}[(w^T(x - z) - w'(x + x')(x - z))^2]$$
$$= \mathbb{E}[(w^T(x - z) - w'(x - x')^T(x - z))^2$$
$$- (w^T(x - z) - w'(x + x')^T(x - z))^2]$$
$$= \mathbb{E}[(w^T(x - z) - w'(x - x')^T(x - z)$$
$$+ w^T(x - z) - w'(x + x')^T(x - z))$$
$$(w^T(x - z) - w'(x - x')^T(x - z)$$
$$- w^T(x - z) - w'(x + x')^T(x - z))]$$
$$= \mathbb{E}[(2w^T(x - z) - w'(x - z)^T(x - x' + x + x'))$$
$$(-w'(x - z)^T(x - x' - x - x'))]$$
$$= \mathbb{E}[(2w^T(x - z) - 2w'(x - z)^T(x))(2w'(x - z)^T(x'))]$$
$$= 2\mathbb{E}[(w^T(x - z) - w'(x - z)^T(x))w'(x - z)^T]\mathbb{E}[x']$$
$$= 2\mathbb{E}[(w^T(x - z) - w'(x - z)(x))w'(x - z)^T]\overrightarrow{0} = 0.$$

A.4   Lemma 3 Supplement

The following is the complete proof of Lemma 3, which was omitted from the main paper.

Proof.

$$
\begin{aligned}
\mathrm{Var}(T) &= \tfrac{1}{2} \mathop{\mathbb{E}}_{x,x' \sim T}[(x - x')^2] \\
&= \tfrac{1}{2}\Big(\mathop{\mathbb{E}}_{x,x' \sim T}[(x - x')^2 | y(x) = y(x')] P(y(x) = y(x')) \\
&\quad + \mathop{\mathbb{E}}_{x,x' \sim T}[(x - x')^2 | y(x) \neq y(x')] P(y(x) \neq y(x')) \\
&= \tfrac{1}{2}(s P(y(x) = y(x')) + r P(y(x) \neq y(x')) \\
&= \frac{1}{2}\left(s\frac{1}{C} + r\frac{C-1}{C} \right).
\end{aligned}
$$

Noting that $s = 2\mathbb{E}[\mathrm{Var}(T|C)]$, and using Eve's law, we have

$$
\begin{aligned}
d &= \mathrm{Var}(T) - s \\
&= \frac{1}{2}\left(s\frac{1}{C} + r\frac{C-1}{C} \right) - s \\
&= \frac{C-1}{2C}r - \frac{2C-1}{2C}s.
\end{aligned}
$$

A.5   Theorem 5 Supplement

The following is a more detailed version of the argument given in the main paper.

If $y(x) = y(x')$, then Lemma 2 means that the expected distance of the encodings of x and x' to any data point from another cluster is unchanged by whether the update was from points with the same or with different labels. Similarly, the distance between any two other points is unchanged by whether the update was from points with the same or with different labels. This establishes that $r_T = r_F$. As for the intra-cluster variance, it is smaller after the update with the same labels than with different labels. Lemma 1 shows that the expected distance between the encodings of the two points themselves is smaller if the labels were the same, and the same argument as above shows that all other expected distances within clusters are unchanged.

If $y(x) \neq y(x')$, then Lemma 2 means that the expected distance of the encodings of x and any data point from the same cluster is unchanged by whether the update was from points with the same or with different labels (and the same for x'). Similarly, the distance between any two other points is unchanged by whether the update was from points with the same or with different labels. This establishes that $s_T = s_F$. As for the *inter*-cluster variance, it is larger after the update with the same labels than with different labels. Lemma 1 shows that the expected distance between the encodings of the two points themselves is larger if the labels were different, and the same argument as above shows that all other expected distances within clusters are unchanged.

Table 4. Sizes of predicted clusters for MNIST.

	Zero	One	Two	Three	Four	Five	Six	Seven	Eight	Nine
HDBSCAN	6923	7878	6979	7095	6802	6290	6911	7384	6776	6962
GMM	6942	6958	6791	7885	6976	7096	7350	6294	6906	6802
Ground Truth	7000	7000	7000	7000	7000	7000	7000	7000	7000	7000

Table 5. Sizes of predicted clusters for USPS.

	Zero	One	Two	Three	Four	Five	Six	Seven	Eight	Nine
HDBSCAN	1565	1272	933	819	856	706	833	787	693	834
GMM	1271	834	785	833	690	835	862	930	699	1559
Ground Truth	1553	1269	929	824	852	716	834	792	708	821

Table 6. Sizes of predicted clusters for FashionMNIST.

	Top	Trouser	Pullover	Dress	Coat	Sandal	Shirt	Sneaker	Bag	Boot
HDBSCAN	7411	6755	56	6591	21333	6046	3173	5666	3711	9258
GMM	6700	3111	16379	6807	6753	9127	7389	4482	8814	438
Ground Truth	7000	7000	7000	7000	7000	7000	7000	7000	7000	7000

B   Appendix C: Extended Results

The results in the main paper report the central tendency of five different training runs for each dataset. Tables 4, 5, and 6 show the sizes of the clusters predicted by SPC for one randomly selected run out of these five. On MNIST and USPS, where the accuracy of SPC is >98%, the predicted sizes are close to the true sizes. On FashionMNIST, where the accuracy is ∼65%, there is a much greater variance. This accounts for the discrepancy in ACC and NMI for FashionMNIST. Most of the errors are put into one large cluster, specifically the cluster that was aligned to 'coat' is over three times larger than it should be. This hurts accuracy more than NMI, because the incorrect data points in the 'coat' cluster count for zero when calculating the accuracy, but they are not randomly distributed among the other classes, so the conditional entropy of a data point that was mis-clustered as a coat is $< \log(10)$. Actually, most of the mistakes in the 'coat' cluster are pullovers or shirts, and almost none of them are, for examples, boots or tops. Comparing the cluster sizes for SPC-HDBSCAN and SPC-GMM also accounts for the differences across ACC and NMI between these two settings on FashionMNIST: SPC-GMM produces more uniformly-sized clusters, so the difference between ACC and NMI is smaller.

References

1. Abavisani, M., Patel, V.M.: Deep multimodal subspace clustering networks. IEEE J. Sel. Top. Signal Process. **12**(6), 1601–1614 (2018)

2. Bellman, R.: Dynamic programming. Science **153**(3731), 34–37 (1966)
3. Boongoen, T., Iam-On, N.: Cluster ensembles: a survey of approaches with recent extensions and applications. Comput. Sci. Rev. **28**, 1–25 (2018)
4. Breiman, L.: Bagging predictors. Mach. Learn. **24**(2), 123–140 (1996)
5. Brock, A., Donahue, J., Simonyan, K.: Large scale GAN training for high fidelity natural image synthesis. arXiv:1809.11096 (2018)
6. Caron, M., Bojanowski, P., Joulin, A., Douze, M.: Deep clustering for unsupervised learning of visual features. In: Proceedings of ECCV, pp. 132–149 (2018)
7. Chang, J., Wang, L., Meng, G., Xiang, S., Pan, C.: Deep adaptive image clustering. In: Proceedings of ICCV, pp. 5879–5887 (2017)
8. Clemen, R.T.: Combining forecasts: a review and annotated bibliography. Int. J. Forecast. **5**(4), 559–583 (1989)
9. Creswell, A., Bharath, A.A.: Inverting the generator of a generative adversarial network. IEEE Trans. Neural Netw. Learn. Syst. **30**(7), 1967–1974 (2018)
10. Dempster, A.P., Laird, N.M., Rubin, D.B.: Maximum likelihood from incomplete data via the EM algorithm. J. R. Stat. Soc.: Ser. B (Methodol.) **39**(1), 1–22 (1977)
11. Ding, F., Luo, F.: Clustering by directly disentangling latent space. arXiv:1911.05210 (2019)
12. Elgammal, A., Liu, B., Elhoseiny, M., Mazzone, M.: CAN: Creative adversarial networks, generating art by learning about styles and deviating from style norms. arXiv:1706.07068 (2017)
13. Gao, B., Yang, Y., Gouk, H., Hospedales, T.M.: Deep clustering with concrete k-means. In: Proceedings of ICASSP, pp. 4252–4256. IEEE (2020)
14. Ghasedi Dizaji, K., Herandi, A., Deng, C., Cai, W., Huang, H.: Deep clustering via joint convolutional autoencoder embedding and relative entropy minimization. In: Proceedings of ICCV (2017)
15. Goodfellow, I., et al.: Generative adversarial nets. In: Proceedings of NIPS, pp. 2672–2680 (2014)
16. Guo, X., Gao, L., Liu, X., Yin, J.: Improved deep embedded clustering with local structure preservation. In: Proceedings of IJCAI, pp. 1753–1759 (2017)
17. Guo, X., Zhu, E., Liu, X., Yin, J.: Deep embedded clustering with data augmentation. In: Proceedings of Asian Conference on Machine Learning, pp. 550–565 (2018)
18. Hinton, G.E., Srivastava, N., Krizhevsky, A., Sutskever, I., Salakhutdinov, R.R.: Improving neural networks by preventing co-adaptation of feature detectors. arXiv:1207.0580 (2012)
19. Huang, P., Huang, Y., Wang, W., Wang, L.: Deep embedding network for clustering. In: Proceedings of ICPR, pp. 1532–1537. IEEE (2014)
20. Hull, J.J.: A database for handwritten text recognition research. TPAMI **16**(5), 550–554 (1994)
21. Jiang, Z., Zheng, Y., Tan, H., Tang, B., Zhou, H.: Variational deep embedding: an unsupervised and generative approach to clustering. arXiv:1611.05148 (2016)
22. Karras, T., Laine, S., Aila, T.: A style-based generator architecture for generative adversarial networks. In: Proceedings of CVPR (2019)
23. Kittler, J., Hatef, M., Duin, R.P., Matas, J.: On combining classifiers. TPAMI **20**(3), 226–239 (1998)
24. Krizhevsky, A., Sutskever, I., Hinton, G.E.: ImageNet classification with deep convolutional neural networks. In: Proceedings of NIPS, pp. 1097–1105 (2012)
25. Kuhn, H.W.: The Hungarian method for the assignment problem. Naval Res. Logist. Q. **2**(1–2), 83–97 (1955)

26. LeCun, Y., Bottou, L., Bengio, Y., Haffner, P.: Gradient-based learning applied to document recognition. Proc. IEEE **86**(11), 2278–2324 (1998)
27. Liang, J., Yang, J., Lee, H.-Y., Wang, K., Yang, M.-H.: Sub-GAN: an unsupervised generative model via subspaces. In: Ferrari, V., Hebert, M., Sminchisescu, C., Weiss, Y. (eds.) ECCV 2018. LNCS, vol. 11215, pp. 726–743. Springer, Cham (2018). https://doi.org/10.1007/978-3-030-01252-6_43
28. Lipton, Z.C., Tripathi, S.: Precise recovery of latent vectors from generative adversarial networks. arXiv:1702.04782 (2017)
29. Lloyd, S.: Least square quantization in PCM. IEEE Trans. Inf. Theory (1957/1982) **18**, 129–137 (1957)
30. McConville, R., Santos-Rodriguez, R., Piechocki, R.J., Craddock, I.: N2D:(not too) deep clustering via clustering the local manifold of an autoencoded embedding. arXiv:1908.05968 (2019)
31. McInnes, L., Healy, J., Astels, S.: HDBSCAN: hierarchical density based clustering. J. Open Sour. Softw. **2**(11), 205 (2017)
32. McInnes, L., Healy, J., Melville, J.: UMAP: uniform manifold approximation and projection for dimension reduction. arXiv:1802.03426 (2018)
33. Mrabah, N., Bouguessa, M., Ksantini, R.: Adversarial deep embedded clustering: on a better trade-off between feature randomness and feature drift. arXiv:1909.11832 (2019)
34. Mrabah, N., Khan, N.M., Ksantini, R., Lachiri, Z.: Deep clustering with a dynamic autoencoder: From reconstruction towards centroids construction. arXiv:1901.07752 (2019)
35. Mukherjee, S., Asnani, H., Lin, E., Kannan, S.: ClusterGAN: latent space clustering in generative adversarial networks. arXiv:1809.03627 (2019)
36. Opitz, D.W., Maclin, R.F.: An empirical evaluation of bagging and boosting for artificial neural networks. In: Proceedings of ICNN, vol. 3, pp. 1401–1405. IEEE (1997)
37. Pearlmutter, B.A., Rosenfeld, R.: Chaitin-Kolmogorov complexity and generalization in neural networks. In: Proceedings of NIPS, pp. 925–931 (1991)
38. Perrone, M.P.: Improving regression estimation: averaging methods for variance reduction with extensions to general convex measure optimization. Ph.D. thesis (1993)
39. Ren, Y., Wang, N., Li, M., Xu, Z.: Deep density-based image clustering. Knowl.-Based Syst. **197**, 105841 (2020)
40. Wang, Y., Zhang, L., Nie, F., Li, X., Chen, Z., Wang, F.: WeGAN: deep image hashing with weighted generative adversarial networks. IEEE Trans. Multimed. **22**, 1458–1469 (2019)
41. Witten, I.H., Frank, E.: Data mining: practical machine learning tools and techniques with Java implementations. ACM SIGMOD Rec. **31**(1), 76–77 (2002)
42. Xiao, H., Rasul, K., Vollgraf, R.: Fashion-MNIST: a novel image dataset for benchmarking machine learning algorithms. arXiv:1708.07747 (2017)
43. Xie, J., Girshick, R., Farhadi, A.: Unsupervised deep embedding for clustering analysis. In: Proceedings of ICML, pp. 478–487 (2016)
44. Yang, B., Fu, X., Sidiropoulos, N.D., Hong, M.: Towards k-means-friendly spaces: simultaneous deep learning and clustering. In: Proceedings of ICML, vol. 70, pp. 3861–3870. JMLR.org (2017)
45. Yang, J., Parikh, D., Batra, D.: Joint unsupervised learning of deep representations and image clusters. In: Proceedings of CVPR, pp. 5147–5156 (2016)

46. Zeiler, M.D., Fergus, R.: Visualizing and understanding convolutional networks. In: Fleet, D., Pajdla, T., Schiele, B., Tuytelaars, T. (eds.) ECCV 2014. LNCS, vol. 8689, pp. 818–833. Springer, Cham (2014). https://doi.org/10.1007/978-3-319-10590-1_53

47. Zemel, R.S., Hinton, G.E.: Developing population codes by minimizing description length. In: Proceedings of NIPS, pp. 11–18 (1994)

48. Zhao, H., Gallo, O., Frosio, I., Kautz, J.: Loss functions for neural networks for image processing. arXiv:1511.08861 (2015)

49. Zhao, W., Wang, S., Xie, Z., Shi, J., Xu, C.: GAN-EM: GAN based EM learning framework. arXiv:1812.00335 (2018)

50. Zhou, P., Hou, Y., Feng, J.: Deep adversarial subspace clustering. In: Proceedings of CVPR (2018)

51. Zimek, A., Schubert, E., Kriegel, H.P.: A survey on unsupervised outlier detection in high-dimensional numerical data. Stat. Anal. Data Min.: ASA Data Sci. J. 5(5), 363–387 (2012)

Crop It, but Not Too Much: The Effects of Masking on the Classification of Melanoma Images

Fabrizio Nunnari[1(✉)] [ID], Abraham Ezema[1] [ID], and Daniel Sonntag[1,2] [ID]

[1] German Research Center for Artificial Intelligence (DFKI),
Stuhlsatzenhausweg 3, Campus D3.2, 66123 Saarbrücken, Germany
[2] Oldenburg University, Oldenburg, Germany
{fabrizio.nunnari,abraham_obinwanne.ezema,daniel.sonntag}@dfki.de

Abstract. To improve the accuracy of convolutional neural networks in discriminating between nevi and melanomas, we test nine different combinations of masking and cropping on three datasets of skin lesion images (ISIC2016, ISIC2018, and MedNode). Our experiments, confirmed by 10-fold cross-validation, show that cropping increases classification performances, but specificity decreases when cropping is applied together with masking out healthy skin regions. An analysis of Grad-CAM saliency maps shows that in fact our CNN models have the tendency to focus on healthy skin at the border when a nevus is classified.

Keywords: Skin cancer · Convolutional neural networks · Image segmentation · Masking · Preprocessing · Reducing bias

1 Introduction

As reported in the 2019 USA cancer statistics, skin diseases have been steadily increasing over the years, whereby skin cancer (with more than 100k cases) represents 7% of the total cancer cases, of which more than 90% are classified as melanoma. The importance of detecting skin cancer is evident from the high percentage of survival (92%) after surgery resulting from early detection [21].

The classification of skin lesions using computer vision algorithms has been a subject of recent research (e.g., [6,11,14]). One of the breakthroughs is the work of Esteva et al. [8], who report a better performance than expert dermatologists (on carefully selected cases) using a deep convolutional neural network (CNN).

Given the promising progress of computer vision algorithms in aiding skin lesion classification, the ISIC [10] hosts a competition for the automated analysis of skin lesions. In the years from 2016 to 2018 (see [4,5,13]), the challenge included three tasks: segmentation, attribute extraction, and classification. These tasks replicate the procedure usually followed by dermatologists: identify the contour of the skin lesion, highlight the areas in the lesion that suggest malignancy, and classify the specific type of lesion.

S. Edelkamp et al. (Eds.): KI 2021, LNAI 12873, pp. 179–193, 2021.
https://doi.org/10.1007/978-3-030-87626-5_13

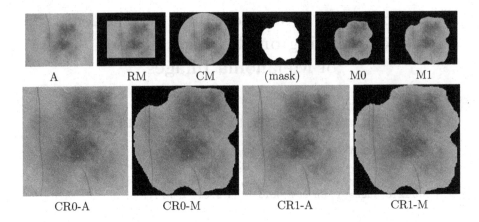

Fig. 1. Example for each of the masking policies.

Masking skin lesion images, i.e., using segmentation to remove the pixels of the healthy skin while retaining the pixels belonging to the lesion, is an image pre-processing technique that is supposed to help the classification of skin lesions not only because it helps the systems to focus on the lesion itself, but also because it removes image artifacts. In fact, Winkler et al. [25] found that the presence of *gentian violet* ink, often used by dermatologists to mark the skin in proximity to suspicious lesions, can disrupt the correct classification and lower the specificity of commercial Diagnosis Support Systems (DSS). Moreover, recently Bissoto et al. [2] found a strong bias in the ISIC 2018 dataset; by removing 70% of the central part of the images (hence likely removing the totality of pixels containing the skin lesions), the CNN model was still able to reach 0.74 AUC (the Area Under the Curve of the *receiver operating characteristic*), with respect to 0.88 AUC reached with full images. This suggests a strong bias of the dataset and image borders.

To date, while there seem to be clear advantages of masking out the skin surrounding the lesion area, it is not clear to what extent masking images influences (positively or negatively) the quality of classification (e.g., by removing bias). Likewise, what are the other consequences for the process of training classifiers when for example learning the wrong, and medically irrelevant, concept?

In this paper, we present a detailed investigation and discussion on image masking by, first, assessing the presence of biases at the dataset images' borders, and, second, comparing the classification performances when applying several types of masks. Third, we analyse the CNN attention patterns through a visual inspection by Grad-CAM [20] saliency maps to take (at least) visual explanations into account that account for medically relevant spatial regions (though not the semantic medical concepts behind). This analysis employs four basic types of *masks* (see Fig. 1, top):

1. Rectangular Mask (RM) removes 30% of the image surface around the border. This is the opposite of the masking utilized by Bissoto et al. [2] to prove a bias at the image borders.
2. Circular Mask (CM) draws a circle at the middle of images. Here, we evaluate if removing the corners of the images and inspecting only its central part retains model performance.
3. Full Mask (M0) reveals only the lesion pixels. It is used to reveal whether completely removing the skin surrounding a lesion improves prediction performance.
4. Extended Mask (M1) applies a mask extended by a factor 1.1 around its center, thus showing lesion pixels together with a fraction of the surrounding skin. It is used to check if providing information about the surrounding healthy skin improves prediction performances.

In addition, we investigate the change in performances when cropping the images with a rectangle circumscribing masks of type M0 and M1 (see Fig. 1, bottom):

- In condition CR0-A, the images are cropped at mask M0 and show the pixels of the surrounding skin.
- In condition CR0-M, the images are cropped at mask M0, but outside pixels are blacked out.
- In condition CR1-A, the images are cropped at mask M1 and show the pixels of the surrounding skin.
- Finally, in condition CR1-M, the images are cropped at mask M1, but outside pixels are blacked out.

In the rest of this paper, we conduct experiments on three popular skin lesion image datasets (ISIC 2016, ISIC 2018, and MedNode), each evaluated through a 10-fold cross validation approach to overcome biases due to randomization.

To our knowledge, this is the first work measuring with such detail the role of masking and reporting that an excessive masking can in fact deteriorate performances, rather than improve them.

2 Related Work

Following the popular approach presented by Esteva et al. [8], all performant neural-network-based solutions for skin lesion classification are based on a transfer learning approach [23], where a baseline deep CNN is pre-trained for example on the ImageNet dataset [7], and the transfer-learning step consists of substituting the final fully-connect layers of the network with a few randomly initialized ones, then to continue training the model on skin lesion images. In our work, we perform transfer learning using pre-trained versions of the VGG16 architecture [22].

Kawahara et al. [11] pointed out that much work focuses on improving benchmarks. Differently, our goal in this contribution is to investigate the change in performance when using plain images with respect to segmented ones for a classification task. To train our classifiers, we rely on three publicly available datasets:

ISIC 2016 [13], ISIC 2018 [4], and MedNode [9]; all of which are used to train several models on a number of masking conditions (see Sect. 3).

Burdick et al. [3] performed a systematic study on the importance of masking skin lesion images. They measured the performance of a CNN using the full images compared to applying masks on several levels; from fully masking out the surrounding skin to exposing some portion of the skin surrounding the lesion. Tests show best results when only a limited portion of the surrounding skin is kept for training. The hypothesis is that masking the healthy skin helps in classification while showing too much of the healthy skin in the image "confuses" the network, that is, it becomes more probable that the network learns image artifacts.

In general, an *image mask* is a binary black/white image wherein white is associated with pixels of interest, and black is associated with the non-interesting or the confounding part of the image to be discarded in subsequent processing steps. In skin lesion pre-processing, the identification of the contour of the contiguous area of lesioned skin is also known as *segmentation*. Ronnenberg et al. [19] first proposed the application of the convolution-deconvolution network (U-Net) for medical image segmentation. Variants of this model have shown to be very effective in past ISIC segmentation challenges, with a Jaccard index score of 0.765 and 0.802 in the ISIC2017 and ISIC2018 editions, respectively (see [1,18]). In this paper, we implement a segmentation model to show the effects of masking in melanoma images by using a variation of the Ronnenberg's method described by Nguyen et al. [15].

3   Method Overview

The experimental method is composed of three phases: preparation of the segmentation model, masked images construction, training of classification models.

As **segmentation model** we utilize the images from Task 1 of the ISIC 2018 to train a masking model based on the U-Net architecture [19] using the method of Nguyen et al. [15]. The train dataset comprised 2594 RGB skin lesion images, and for each sample the ground truth is a binary mask in the same resolution as the input image.

Figure 2 shows the U-Net architecture together with a sample input and output (binary mask). The architecture is composed of 9 convolution blocks, where each of them is a pair of 2D *same* convolution with a kernel size of 3 × 3 × 3. Downsampling is the result of a max-pooling with size 2 × 2. Upsampling is the result of a 2 × 2 transposed 2D *same* convolution. After each upsampling step, the deconvolution is performed on the concatenation of the upsampling result and the output of the downsampling with corresponding resolution. The initial number of filters (32) doubles at each downsampling. For this work, we used an input/output resolution of 160 × 160 pixels.

The segmentation model described above is used to **extract the masks** for Melanoma and Nevus images of the ISIC 2018 Task 3, ISIC 2016, and MedNode datasets. From ISIC 2018 Task 3, we selected only nevus (NV) and melanoma

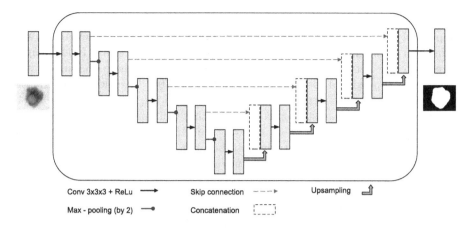

Fig. 2. The U-Net architecture used for lesion segmentation. The input image is 3-channel RGB, while the output image is 1-channel gray-scale with the same resolution.

(MEL) classes (the same used to train the segmentation model) because, after an initial visual inspection, we realized that applying the mask prediction to any of the other 6 classes often led to erroneous results.

In total, starting from the full images (condition A, containing all of the pixels), we generated the other eight datasets described in the introduction: RM, CM, M0, M1, CR0-A, CR0-M, CR1-A, CR1-M (See Fig. 1). For the M1 and CR1-* datasets, the mask is first scaled around its center by a factor of 1.1 to reveal a portion of the surrounding skin (as suggested by Burdick et al. [3]). For the CR*-* datasets, the mask is utilized to identify a rectangular cropping region containing the lesions contour. The CR*-* datasets contains a few less samples than the others because an initial visual inspection revealed that the masks of samples with a thin lesion–foreground pixel variation result in very small (mostly inaccurate) lesion blobs. Hence, we automatically filtered away images whose mask was less than $\frac{1}{8}$ of the picture area.

Finally, for each of the nine masking conditions, we trained 10 **binary classification models** using a 10-fold splitting strategy. Each fold was composed using 10% of the dataset for testing and another random 10% for validation. While splitting, we ensured to preserve the proportion between classes. In the rest of this paper, performance metrics are reported as the mean (and the standard deviation) among the 10 folds. The performance of the binary classifiers in discriminating *nevi* (negative case) from *melanomas* (positive case) are reported in terms of accuracy, specificity, sensitivity, and ROC AUC (Receiver Operating Curve - Area Under the Curve) on the test set.

As already successfully employed in previous research (e.g., [8]), all of the binary classifiers are based on the transfer learning approach with CNNs [23]. The base CNN model is the VGG16 architecture [22], which has been pre-trained on ImageNet [12]. We then substituted the original three final fully connected layers with a sequence of two 2048-node fully connected layers, each followed by a dropout of 0.5, and a final 2-class discrimination softmax layer. Each model was trained for a maximum of 100 epochs and optimized for accuracy. Input images were fed to the network with an 8x augmentation factor, where each image was horizontally flipped and rotated by 0, 90, 180, and 270°. To avoid the generation of black bands, images were rotated after scaling to the CNN input resolution (227×227) using a nearest neighbor filter. Other training parameters are: SGD optimizer, learning rate = 1e−5, decay = 1e−4, momentum = 0.9, nesterov = True. Class imbalance was taken into account using a compensation factor in the loss-function (parameter `class_weight` in the `fit` method of the Keras framework). All training was performed on Linux workstations using our toolkit for Interactive Machine Learning (TIML) [16]. Our reference Hardware is an 8-core Intel 9th-gen i7 CPU with 64 GB RAM and an NVIDIA RTX Titan 24 GB GPU.

4   Experiments

We report the details of the classification performances on the three datasets (ISIC2018, MedNode, and ISIC2016) for each of the nine masking conditions and the results of the statistical analyses comparing among masking conditions. The analysis focuses on determining a potential bias from the border of the images and the change in performances when masks are applied to the lesion border or are extended to reveal part of the healthy skin.

The **ISIC2018** dataset consisted of 7818 samples (7645 correctly cropped), of which 85.8% were nevi. Training a full model (6256 samples, 100 epochs) takes about 9 hours on our reference hardware. Table 1, left, show the results of the tests as mean (and standard deviation) over a 10-fold cross-validation.

In order to measure the statistical significance of the difference of the metrics among conditions, we run a set of t-tests for independent samples (N = 10) between the no-mask condition (A) against all the others. The results of the test are reported in Table 1, right. The table reports the compared conditions, followed by the compared metric, their absolute and relative difference, and the significance code for the p-value (+: $p < .1$; *: $p < .05$; **: $p < .01$; ***: $p < 0.001$).

Both rectangular (RM) and circular masks (CM) did not lead to any significant change. Differently, both the full (M0) and the extended masks (M1) lower the performances in accuracy and specificity. For M1 condition, also AUC is slightly decreasing.

This result seems to be in contrast with the observation of Bissoto et al. [2], who claims a positive bias at the border. In fact, by removing the 30% of the external image border (RM condition), we would have expected a drop in performance. We can't so far find an explanation for the loss of performances in the masking conditions M0 and M1, which could be caused by the imprecision of the segmentation algorithm or related to the following observations on the cropping conditions.

Table 1. Results for the ISIC2018 dataset. Left: classification performances in all masking conditions, indicating with **bold** the values significantly above the baseline (condition A) and with *italic* the values significantly below the baseline. Right: significantly different masking conditions and their mutual absolute and relative variations.

Condition	Metr.	Diff.	%	p
A vs. M0	ACC	-.0172	-1.91%	**
A vs. M0	SPEC	-.0217	-2.34%	*
A vs. M1	ACC	-.0168	-1.86%	**
A vs. M1	SPEC	-.0214	-2.31%	*
A vs. M1	AUC	-.0092	-0.97%	+
A vs. CR0-A	ACC	.0239	2.65%	**
A vs. CR0-A	SPEC	.0201	2.17%	*
A vs. CR0-A	SENS	.0485	6.45%	+
A vs. CR0-A	AUC	.0171	1.81%	**
A vs. CR0-M	ACC	-.0689	-7.64%	***
A vs. CR0-M	SPEC	-.0812	-8.76%	***
A vs. CR0-M	AUC	-.0299	-3.17%	***
A vs. CR1-A	ACC	.0201	2.23%	**
A vs. CR1-A	SPEC	.0211	2.28%	*
A vs. CR1-A	AUC	.0141	1.49%	**
A vs. CR1-M	ACC	-.0173	-1.92%	**
A vs. CR1-M	SPEC	-.0160	-1.73%	+
A vs. CR1-M	AUC	-.0236	-2.50%	***

set	testacc	testspec	testsens	testauc
A	.902 (.014)	.926 (.020)	.752 (.048)	.944 (.010)
RM	.898 (.011)	.920 (.012)	.768 (.053)	.940 (.012)
CM	.905 (.012)	.933 (.015)	.738 (.063)	.944 (.012)
M0	*.885 (.010)*	*.905 (.016)*	.762 (.060)	.936 (.012)
M1	*.885 (.010)*	*.905 (.012)*	.764 (.042)	*.935 (.010)*
CR0-A	**.926 (.013)**	**.947 (.016)**	**.801 (.054)**	**.961 (.009)**
CR0-M	*.833 (.018)*	*.845 (.027)*	.757 (.042)	*.915 (.010)*
CR1-A	**.922 (.007)**	**.948 (.012)**	.770 (.057)	**.958 (.009)**
CR1-M	*.884 (.008)*	*.911 (.013)*	.729 (.046)	*.921 (.014)*

For the cropping conditions we observe a clear pattern. When the cropping is applied leaving visible healthy skin (CR0-A and CR1-A) the performances increase, up to a +2.65% accuracy and +6.45% sensitivity. This can be explained by the fact that when images are cropped almost all of the 227×227 pixels sent to the CNN are covered by the lesion–hence increasing the quantity of details attributed to the lesioned skin.

However, when the cropping is combined with a masking of the healthy pixels, the performances drop in terms of specificity. This is especially notable in the CR0-M condition, where no healthy skin is supposed to be visible.

This leads us to a question. As we cannot state that there is a bias at the images border, and that by removing all of the healthy skin pixels from the image performances drop: can we state that indeed *healthy skin contains fundamental useful information for a better classification?* This will be discussed in Sect. 6 together with the results on the two other datasets, MedNode and ISIC2016, presented in the following.

The **MedNode** dataset consisted of 170 samples (169 correctly cropped), of which 58.8% were nevi. Training one fold of the full dataset (about 136 samples, 100 epochs) takes about 15 min on our reference hardware. Appendix A reports the results of the t-tests for independent samples between the no-mask condition (A) against all the others. The only notable performance difference is in the CR0-M condition, with a 10.85% drop in specificity, which is in line with the observation on ISIC2018, though with a limited significance ($p < 0.1$).

The **ISIC2016** dataset consisted of 900 samples (884 correctly cropped), of which 80.8% were nevi. Training one fold of the full dataset (722 samples, 100 epochs) takes about 1 h 30 m on our reference hardware. Appendix B reports the results of the t-tests for independent samples between the no-mask condition (A) against all the others. As for the ISIC2018 dataset, the masking conditions M0 and M1 lead to a drop in specificity. For this dataset, the drop is present also for the CM condition (essentially removing the angles of the images). Again in line with ISI2018, there is a significant drop in performances in the crop & mask conditions (CR0-M and CR1-M), both in accuracy and specificity.

In **summary**, for all of the three datasets, the application of a rectangular mask (RM) did not affect classification performances. As such, even though Bissoto et al. [2] claimed that the 30% of the border around the lesion is enough to reach an important classification result, with our experiments we could not state that removing the borders compromises the accuracy. In other words, although there is a bias in the images border, it is also true that when the lesioned skin is fully visible, this biased information are not affecting the performances as the network is fully concentrating on the lesioned area.

Another behavior common to the three datasets is that cropping and masking the images deteriorates performances. These are the conditions where all of the healthy skin pixels are blacked out (CR0-M, CR1-M). Hence, while it is true that removing some healthy skin pixels from the borders doesn't affect performances, removing all of the healthy skin negatively affect the classification. For the ISIC2018 dataset, we could also find that cropping but leaving healthy skin visible increases performance (CR0-A, CR1-A). This last finding couldn't be verified statistically on the MedNode and ISIC2016 datasets, possibly because of their lower amount of samples.

There seems hence to be contrast between the intuitive urge to help the neural network improving its performance by removing pixels of healthy skin, and the progressive degradation of performances as healthy skin pixels are less and less visible. To get a better understanding of this phenomenon, we ran a set of visual inspections and statistical analyses, which are presented in the next section.

5   Visual Inspection

In order to visually explain the characteristics that influenced model predictions, we leveraged the Grad-CAM method [20] to generate the saliency maps of *attention*. Figures 3 and 4 show the heatmaps of a correctly classified melanoma and a nevus in all masking conditions. All the saliency maps were extracted from the last convolutional layer of the VGG16 architecture (`block5_conv3`).

Two contrasting patterns emerge, thus giving additional details about the model's discrimination strategy. For images correctly predicted as melanoma (Fig. 3), the saliency is higher on the skin lesion pixels, focused towards the center of the image. In contrast, for pictures correctly classified as nevus (Fig. 4), the saliency is higher on the skin pixels, towards the borders. The opposite

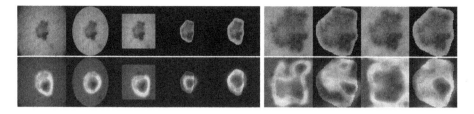

Fig. 3. Heatmaps of an ISIC2018 melanoma (ISIC_0032797) in all masking conditions. Notice how heatmaps concentrate towards the center of the image.

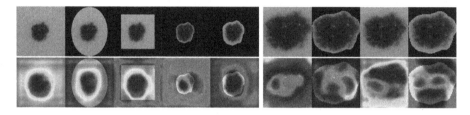

Fig. 4. Heatmaps of an ISIC2018 nevus (ISIC_0027548) in all masking conditions. Notice how heatmaps (except CR0-A) concentrate towards the border of the image.

happens when images are wrongly classified (not shown in the pictures), with the attention for wrongly classified nevus towards the center and the attention for wrongly classified melanomas towards the border.

From a closer look at conditions A, CM, RM, and M0 in Fig. 4, it seems that, as the healthy skin is progressively removed from the image, the network has the tendency to avoid black areas and tries to "justify" nevi by increasing its highest attention (red areas) towards the visible healthy skin pixels. This doesn't hold for condition M1, where the network is finally "discharging" its attention on the black borders. The same behaviour can be observed in the cropping conditions, especially for CR1-A.

Our intuition is that, in order to justify a nevus, the network needs an *area of alternative attention* to "motivate" its choice, otherwise it will be forced to look at the lesioned skin and might be induced in a wrong decision. This would explain the deterioration in terms of specificity observed in the ISIC2018 dataset when switching from CR*-A conditions to CR*-M conditions.

To confirm this intuition, we perform an analysis by measuring the degree of overlap between (thresholded) saliency maps and segmentation masks on the cropping conditions (CR0-A, CR0-M, CR1-A, CR1-M). For each of the four conditions, we apply the following procedure to each image:

1. Define $S_{0.5}$ as the saliency map thresholded at 0.5, where white pixels correspond to high saliency;
2. define L as the segmentation mask (as used for CR0-M or CR1-M), where white pixels mark the area with lesion pixels;
3. define B as the complement of L, hence the "masked-away" area at the border;

4. compute J_L as the Jaccard index between $S_{0.5}$ and L; and
5. compute J_B as the Jaccard index between $S_{0.5}$ and B.

This leads to the creation of four datasets, each of them associating images to two Jaccard indices: J_L, representing the degree of overlap between the saliency and the lesioned skin, and J_B, representing the degree of overlap between the saliency and the healthy skin (or the black area). Figure 5 shows the box-plots of the resulting Jaccard indices J_L and J_B, for each dataset, divided by lesion type (MEL/NV).

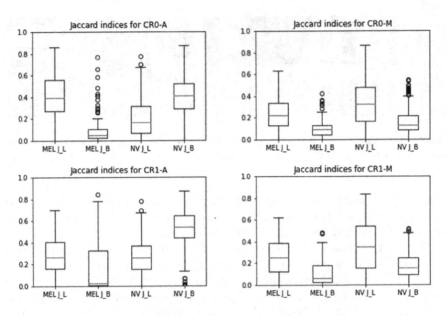

Fig. 5. Box plots of Jaccard indices between thresholded saliency and mask areas in all cropping (and masking) conditions.

The top-left boxplot (CR0-A, cropping but *no* black masking) shows that for melanoma (MEL), on average, J_L is higher than J_B, meaning that the saliency is more concentrated at the center. In contrast, for nevi (NV), saliency concentrates more at the border. However, for condition CR0-M (top-right, cropping and masking), for nevi (NV) the opposite happens, with the saliency more concentrated to the center. The two bottom plots report the same behavior for the condition pair CR1-A and CR1-M.

More formally, we formulated the following hypotheses:

- **H0** In all four conditions, for MEL, mean J_L is higher than mean J_B;
- **H1** In CR*-A conditions (healthy skin is visible), for NV, mean J_L is lower than mean J_B;
- **H2** In CR*-M conditions (healthy skin is masked to black), for NV, mean J_L is higher than mean J_B;

Table 2. Left: results of Mann-Whitney tests comparing J_L and J_B distributions. Right: results of Mann-Whitney tests comparing J_L and J_B distributions on the NV class between CR0-A and CR0-M (CR1-A vs. CR1-M, respectively).

Cond.	Class	$\bar{J_L}$	$\bar{J_B}$	U	Sig.
CR0-A	MEL	0.4010	0.1006	U=10662	***
CR0-A	NV	0.1997	0.4003	U=86403	***
CR0-M	MEL	0.2409	0.1020	U=9642	***
CR0-M	NV	0.3437	0.1562	U=336747	***
CR1-A	MEL	0.2844	0.1757	U=8692	***
CR1-A	NV	0.2662	0.5265	U=51450	***
CR1-M	MEL	0.2600	0.1182	U=9368	***
CR1-M	NV	0.3578	0.1631	U=321957	***

Crop	J	$\bar{A}$	$\bar{M}$	U	Sig.
CR0-	J_L	0.1997	0.3437	U=124265	***
CR0-	J_B	0.4003	0.1562	U=375561	***
CR1-	J_L	0.2662	0.3578	U=169012	***
CR1-	J_B	0.5265	0.1631	U=406799	***

- **H3** For NV, mean J_L in CR*-A is lower than mean J_L in CR*-M;
- **H4** For NV, mean J_B in CR*-A is higher than mean J_B in CR*-M.

A set of Mann-Whitney U tests (Table 2) confirmed a statistically significant difference for all tests with $p < .001$, thus baking all of our hypotheses. In other words, we can conclude that *when some skin is visible, the nevi classification is accumulating the saliency on the healthy skin pixels*. In contrast, when no healthy skin is visible, the CNN attention is forced towards the center of the image, thus compromising classification specificity.

6 Discussion

The metrics measurement performed on the image datasets (ISIC2016, MedNode, and ISIC2018) shows that, with respect to using full plain images, masking decreases the performances in terms of specificity. The results on ISIC2018 show that cropping can increase the performance of the network, but cropping and masking decreases specificity.

From the visual inspection of the saliency maps (Sect. 5), it appears that when images are classified as melanoma, the network concentrates most of its "attention" in the central part of the image, as a human practitioner would do.

In contrast, when images are to be classified as nevus, the saliency map is more spread towards the border. This last phenomenon is less pronounced in the CR0-M and CR1-M conditions, where most of the healthy skin is absent. It seems that, in absence of visual elements characterizing a melanoma, the network has the tendency to find a "reason" for the competing class (nevus) elsewhere in the image. Blacked-out areas, which are surely non-discriminating, are avoided and healthy skin areas are preferred. This leads us to re-interpret the conclusions of Burdick et al. [3], who found that (with respect to full masks) indeed extended masks increase performances, but explained it in terms of "taking advantage of the contrast between the lesioned and healthy skin". Differently, it seems that CNNs really need an "area of alternative attention", which could informally defined as the portions of the image on which the CNN needs to focus the activation of its layers when predicting a negative case (nevus).

7   Conclusions

In this paper, we presented a comprehensive investigation on the effect of masking on the classification of skin lesions between nevus and melanoma. We performed our statistical analyses on three datasets (ISIC 2018, MedNode, and ISIC 2016) using a 10-fold cross validation procedure to discard shallow conclusions due to the intrinsic randomness of CNN training procedures.

Our experiments show that the best strategy to improve performance is to crop images around the rectangular area containing the lesion segmentation mask. Likely, performances increase thanks to the higher image detail after zooming in the lesioned area. However, specificity decreases when cropping is performed together with masking to black the healthy surrounding skin.

To better explain this behavior, we conducted an automated analysis on saliency maps and formulated the hypothesis that CNNs are more effective when an *area of alternative attention* is available. In summary, while it is true that one should better maximize the area of the image with visual features able to identify a (positive) class, at the same time some of the pixels should be left free for the network to "justify" the complementary (negative) class.

As a result of our experiments, towards a process to standardize skin lesions image preprocessing in CNN contexts (like in the standardization roadmap for artificial intelligence [24]), we suggest to apply an automated process of segmentation and cropping, but avoiding masking to black surrounding healthy skin.

Future work might investigate if the hypothesis of "area of alternative attention" generalizes to other contexts by testing classification performances after cropping images on popular non-medical databases (e.g., ImageNet [7]). In fact, it is worth noticing that most of the research in image classification has been conducted on databases where the objects of interest occupy only a relatively small portion of an image. Consequently, visual explanation methods like GradCAM [20] and RISE [17] have been developed and tested with the goal of identifying the relatively small subset of pixels justifying a classification. Differently, in the domain of skin cancer detection, very often the majority (or all) of the pixels of an image are associated to a single entity, and this condition has received so far very little attention.

Another subject of investigation would be on understanding what CNNs see on healthy skin that is invisible to human eyes and can point to new medically-relevant features.

Acknowledgments. The research has been supported by the Ki-Para-Mi project (BMBF, 01IS19038B), the pAItient project (BMG, 2520DAT0P2), and the Endowed Chair of Applied Artificial Intelligence, Oldenburg University (see https://uol.de/aai/). We would like to thank all student assistants that contributed to the development of the platform (see https://iml.dfki.de/).

A   MedNode Results

Table 3 and Table 4 show the results of the experiments on the MedNode dataset.

Table 3. Classification performance on the MedNode dataset. Italic text indicates values significantly below the baseline (condition A).

Set	testacc	testspec	testsens	testauc
A	.806 (.123)	.870 (.100)	.714 (.181)	.869 (.131)
RM	.753 (.094)	.800 (.118)	.686 (.189)	.860 (.073)
CM	.818 (.140)	.830 (.135)	.800 (.194)	.890 (.114)
M0	.806 (.083)	.850 (.092)	.743 (.167)	.890 (.107)
M1	.806 (.112)	.830 (.090)	.771 (.214)	.880 (.111)
CR0-A	.768 (.144)	.820 (.087)	.700 (.328)	.843 (.120)
CR0-M	.739 (.085)	*.776 (.107)*	.686 (.154)	.823 (.092)
CR1-A	.823 (.111)	.870 (.090)	.757 (.203)	.882 (.093)
CR1-M	.764 (.069)	.809 (.104)	.700 (.149)	.816 (.090)

Table 4. Significant differences between masking conditions in the MedNode dataset.

Condition	Metr.	Diff.	Diff. %	Sig.
A vs. CR0-M	SPEC	−0.0944	−10.85%	+

B   ISIC2016 Results

Table 5 and Table 6 show the results of the experiments on the ISIC2016 dataset.

Table 5. Classification performance on the ISIC2016 dataset. Italic text indicates values significantly below the baseline (condition A).

Set	testacc	testspec	testsens	testauc
A	.806 (.028)	.898 (.031)	.416 (.163)	.773 (.074)
RM	.794 (.037)	.878 (.069)	.445 (.146)	.756 (.063)
CM	.788 (.026)	*.872 (.030)*	.432 (.151)	.790 (.059)
M0	.792 (.039)	*.860 (.056)*	.509 (.119)	.778 (.065)
M1	.781 (.033)	*.852 (.045)*	.486 (.152)	.773 (.065)
CR0-A	.803 (.056)	.885 (.057)	.467 (.140)	.776 (.088)
CR0-M	*.760 (.037)*	*.827 (.030)*	.485 (.091)	.754 (.060)
CR1-A	.796 (.028)	.890 (.028)	.410 (.115)	.772 (.068)
CR1-M	*.757 (.036)*	*.845 (.051)*	.391 (.148)	.732 (.080)

Table 6. Significant differences between masking conditions in the ISIC2016 dataset.

Condition	Metr.	Diff.	Diff. %	Sig.
A vs. CM	SPEC	−0.0262	−2.92%	+
A vs. M0	SPEC	−0.0384	−4.28%	+
A vs. M1	SPEC	−0.0465	−5.18%	*
A vs. CR0-M	ACC	−0.0453	−5.62%	**
A vs. CR0-M	SPEC	−0.0712	−7.93%	***
A vs. CR1-M	ACC	−0.0488	−6.06%	**
A vs. CR1-M	SPEC	−0.0529	−5.89%	*

References

1. Berseth, M.: ISIC 2017 - skin lesion analysis towards melanoma detection. CoRR abs/1703.00523 (2017). http://arxiv.org/abs/1703.00523
2. Bissoto, A., Fornaciali, M., Valle, E., Avila, S.: (De)constructing bias on skin lesion datasets. In: The IEEE Conference on Computer Vision and Pattern Recognition (CVPR) Workshops, June 2019
3. Burdick, J., Marques, O., Weinthal, J., Furht, B.: Rethinking skin lesion segmentation in a convolutional classifier. J. Digit. Imaging **31**(4), 435–440 (2017). https://doi.org/10.1007/s10278-017-0026-y
4. Codella, N., Rotemberg, V., Tschandl, P., Celebi, M.E., et al.: Skin lesion analysis toward melanoma detection 2018 (2019). http://arxiv.org/abs/1902.03368
5. Codella, N.C.F., Gutman, D., Celebi, M.E., Helba, B., et al.: Skin lesion analysis toward melanoma detection: a challenge at the 2017 International Symposium on Biomedical Imaging. In: 2018 IEEE 15th International Symposium on Biomedical Imaging (ISBI 2018), pp. 168–172. IEEE, Washington, DC, April 2018. https://doi.org/10.1109/ISBI.2018.8363547
6. Curiel-Lewandrowski, C., Novoa, R.A., Berry, E., Celebi, M.E., et al.: Artificial Intelligence Approach in Melanoma. In: Fisher, D., Bastian, B. (eds.) Melanoma, pp. 1–31. Springer, New York (2019). https://doi.org/10.1007/978-1-4614-7322-0_43-1
7. Deng, J., Dong, W., Socher, R., Li, L.J., et al.: ImageNet: a large-scale hierarchical image database. In: 2009 IEEE Conference on Computer Vision and Pattern Recognition, pp. 248–255. IEEE, Miami, June 2009. https://doi.org/10.1109/CVPR.2009.5206848
8. Esteva, A., Kuprel, B., Novoa, R.A., Ko, J., Swetter, S.M., et al.: Dermatologist-level classification of skin cancer with deep neural networks. Nature **542**, 115 (2017). https://doi.org/10.1038/nature21056
9. Giotis, I., Molders, N., Land, S., Biehl, M., et al.: MED-NODE: a computer-assisted melanoma diagnosis system using non-dermoscopic images. Expert Syst. Appl. **42**(19), 6578–6585 (2015). https://doi.org/10.1016/j.eswa.2015.04.034
10. ISIC: International Skin Imaging Collaboration. https://www.isic-archive.com/
11. Kawahara, J., Hamarneh, G.: Visual diagnosis of dermatological disorders: human and machine performance, June 2019. http://arxiv.org/abs/1906.01256

12. Krizhevsky, A., Sutskever, I., Hinton, G.E.: ImageNet classification with deep convolutional neural networks. In: Advances in Neural Information Processing Systems, vol. 25, pp. 1097–1105. Curran Associates, Inc. (2012)

13. Marchetti, M.A., Codella, N.C., Dusza, S.W., Gutman, D.A., et al.: Results of the 2016 international skin imaging collaboration international symposium on biomedical imaging challenge. J. Am. Acad. Dermatol. **78**(2), 270-277.e1 (2018). https://doi.org/10.1016/j.jaad.2017.08.016

14. Masood, A., Ali Al-Jumaily, A.: Computer aided diagnostic support system for skin cancer: a review of techniques and algorithms. Int. J. Biomed. Imaging **2013**, 1–22 (2013). https://doi.org/10.1155/2013/323268

15. Nguyen, D.M.H., Ezema, A., Nunnari, F., Sonntag, D.: A visually explainable learning system for skin lesion detection using multiscale input with attention U-net. In: Schmid, U., Klügl, F., Wolter, D. (eds.) KI 2020. LNCS (LNAI), vol. 12325, pp. 313–319. Springer, Cham (2020). https://doi.org/10.1007/978-3-030-58285-2_28

16. Nunnari, F., Sonntag, D.: A software toolbox for deploying deep learning decision support systems with XAI capabilities. In: Proceedings of the 13th ACM SIGCHI Symposium on Engineering Interactive Computing Systems. ACM (2021). https://doi.org/10.1145/3459926.3464753

17. Petsiuk, V., Das, A., Saenko, K.: RISE: randomized input sampling for explanation of black-box models. In: Proceedings of the British Machine Vision Conference (BMVC) (2018)

18. Qian, C., Liu, T., Jiang, H., Wang, Z., et al.: A detection and segmentation architecture for skin lesion segmentation on dermoscopy images. CoRR abs/1809.03917 (2018). http://arxiv.org/abs/1809.03917

19. Ronneberger, O., Fischer, P., Brox, T.: U-net: convolutional networks for biomedical image segmentation. In: Navab, N., Hornegger, J., Wells, W.M., Frangi, A.F. (eds.) MICCAI 2015. LNCS, vol. 9351, pp. 234–241. Springer, Cham (2015). https://doi.org/10.1007/978-3-319-24574-4_28

20. Selvaraju, R.R., Cogswell, M., Das, A., Vedantam, R., et al.: Grad-CAM: visual explanations from deep networks via gradient-based localization. In: The IEEE International Conference on Computer Vision (ICCV), October 2017

21. Siegel, R.L., Miller, K.D., Jemal, A.: Cancer statistics, 2019. CA: Cancer J. Clin. **69**(1), 7–34 (2019). https://doi.org/10.3322/caac.21551

22. Simonyan, K., Zisserman, A.: Very deep convolutional networks for large-scale image recognition, September 2014. http://arxiv.org/abs/1409.1556

23. Tan, C., Sun, F., Kong, T., Zhang, W., Yang, C., Liu, C.: A survey on deep transfer learning. In: Kůrková, V., Manolopoulos, Y., Hammer, B., Iliadis, L., Maglogiannis, I. (eds.) ICANN 2018. LNCS, vol. 11141, pp. 270–279. Springer, Cham (2018). https://doi.org/10.1007/978-3-030-01424-7_27

24. Wahlster, W., Winterhalter, C.: German standardization roadmap on artificial intelligence. Technical report, DIN e.V. and German Commission for Electrical, Electronic & Information Technologies of DIN and VDE (2020)

25. Winkler, J.K., Fink, C., Toberer, F., Enk, A., et al.: Association between surgical skin markings in dermoscopic images and diagnostic performance of a deep learning convolutional neural network for melanoma recognition. JAMA Dermatol. **155**(10), 1135 (2019). https://doi.org/10.1001/jamadermatol.2019.1735

A Demonstrator for Interactive Image Clustering and Fine-Tuning Neural Networks in Virtual Reality

Alexander Prange[1(✉)] and Daniel Sonntag[1,2]

[1] German Research Center for Artificial Intelligence (DFKI),
Saarland Informatics Campus, Saarbrücken, Germany
{alexander.prange,daniel.sonntag}@dfki.de
[2] German Research Center for Artificial Intelligence (DFKI), Oldenburg University,
Oldenburg, Germany

Abstract. We present a virtual reality (VR) application that enables us to interactively explore and manipulate image clusters based on layer activations of convolutional neural networks (CNNs). We apply dimensionality reduction techniques to project images into the 3D space, where the user can directly interact with the model. The user can change the position of an image by using natural hand gestures. This manipulation triggers additional training steps of the network, based on the new spatial information and new label of the image. After the training step is finished, the visualization is updated according to the new output of the CNN. The goal is to visualize and improve the cluster output of the model, and at the same time, to improve the understanding of the model. We discuss two different approaches for calculating the VR projection, a combined PCA/t-SNE dimensionality reduction based approach and a variational auto-encoder (VAE) based approach.

Keywords: Virtual Reality · Interactive image clustering · CNN

1 Introduction

Neural networks lack the interpretability and transparency needed to understand the underlying decision process and learned representations. Making sense of why a particular model misclassifies test data instances or behaves poorly at times is a challenging task for model developers and is an important problem to address [2]. Recent publications have shown the benefits of visualizing complex data in virtual reality (VR), e.g., in data visualization [1], and big data analytics [9]. We present an interactive image clustering method in VR, where the user can explore and then fine-tune the underlying machine learning model through intuitive hand gestures. Image clustering is the process of grouping similar images into clusters, which helps to understand large image data sets and improves labeling performance. We use a convolutional neural network (CNN) to perform an initial classification of the images and our first goal is to visualize these results, by projecting the output of the hidden layers into a 3D VR space. VR helps to visualize sizeable image data sets in an immersive way, which should allow users to understand the outputs of deep neural networks more easily and to provide feedback on the clusters towards an intended cluster formation and image labeling. The tied interaction cycle between machine learner and the human-in-the-loop should help to understand and optimize deep learning models while potentially requiring less human effort and fewer labeled instances.

In order to display image data in VR, we first need to calculate 3D positions for each image to be displayed in VR. Then, the user can interact with the VR system and thereby refine the model and output of the deep neural network. By using a drag-and-drop gesture the user can move images inside and between clusters, thereby triggering a re-training of the model based on the new spatial location of the image. Here we explore two methods on how to reduce the high dimensional output of the model to be displayed in 3D VR space: (1) Principal Component Analysis (PCA) and t-SNE dimensionality reduction [7], and (2) Variational Auto Encoders (VAE) [4]. We display the results of the second to last layer of the AlexNet [5] in the 3D VR space. Unfortunately, there is no quantitative benchmark available that measures the performance of the visualizations, which is why we focus on a qualitative comparison of the approaches.

2   Architecture

We base the selection of toolkits, data sets, and libraries on the survey conducted by Zacharias et al. [14]. In this contribution, we use two data sets: POET [11] and ILSVRC2013 [13], which provide diverse and complex image data and are commonly used in similar experiments [2]. Our architecture (Fig. 1) allows us to visualize any image data set with only slight modifications: we use a pre-trained AlexNet [5] deep convolutional neural network as the backbone of our image classifier. It consists of 5 convolutional layers and 3 fully connected layers, where the final layer has 1000 class labels (dimensions). We use the PyTorch[1] library for training and fine-tuning. Our distributed computing architecture (Fig. 2) consists of two GPU-accelerated machines: (1) a backend server responsible for training and fine-tuning the deep neural network, and (2) a computer running the front-end VR visualization. Both machines interact using a HTTP based REST API. The 3D reduction methods share the same architecture; for the experiments we just replace the visualization module. After the visualization component has computed the 3D coordinates of each image we send them over the network to be displayed in VR. Through user interaction with the images we receive new coordinates for the manipulated images, which are sent back to the backend server to trigger re-training and fine-tuning cycles. First, we load all the images and corresponding annotations from the data set. After cropping, corresponding object patches from the images are created. Preprocessing steps on the image follow, e.g., mean subtraction. The images are then fed to the network in

---

[1] https://pytorch.org/.

a feed forward manner. We extract feature maps from the *fc7* layer of the network because it provides the layer activations extracted from the convolutional network, right before the classification (includes the ReLU non-linearity).

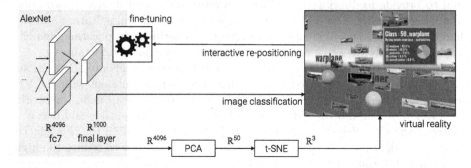

Fig. 1. Architecture of the first approach based on PCA and t-SNE dimensionality reduction. Based on a AlexNet we calculate 3D coordinates for each image. In VR, information related to a particular image is displayed if the user looks at that image.

3   Visualization in VR

Images are visualized in VR according to their 3D vectors. Projected 3D vectors are normalized so that distances in all dimensions are perceived in an explorable VR space. Then we calculate cluster centers for each class in the projected space. We discuss the aforementioned approaches.

3.1   PCA/t-SNE Approach

We first apply PCA on the feature maps of the *fc7* layer, reducing from 4096 dimensions to 50 dimensions. Next, we apply t-SNE dimensionality reduction [7], which maps the 50 dimensional vector to the 3D VR space. For each image we display the projected 3D VR position, the ground truth and the prediction scores (top-5 scores). Our VR environment is created with Unity3D and uses the Oculus Rift CV1 with Oculus Touch controllers for interaction. Each input image is displayed based on its corresponding 3D vector and color coded by label. The user can move around in the VR space and change image positions by using hand gestures. Displaying complex image sets in VR facilitates visual perception and spatial awareness and can be employed in different domains, such as viewing complex 3D medical image data in VR [12].

The focus of our use case is the clustering of images in 3D space. Although t-SNE is extremely useful for visualizing high-dimensional data, the choice of

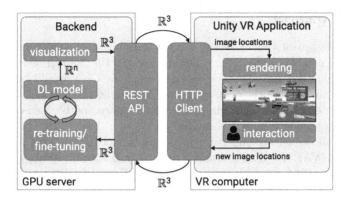

Fig. 2. Visualization of our distributed computing architecture used in all three approaches with varying *visualization* modules. Workload is shared between the GPU server machine, where the DL model is trained and the computer on which the VR application runs. We transmit only the 3D coordinates over the network using a REST API to communicate between server and client.

parameters is crucial for preserving adequate spatial clustering. We therefore conduct an experiment in which we adjust the parameters to receive a satisfactory visual representation. The POET data set was used to find the local optimum for the combination of the following t-SNE parameters: perplexity, iterations, learning rate and early exaggeration. Perplexity manipulates the balance attention between local and global aspects of our data, while the choice of iterations and learning rate can require different values for data sets to reach a stable configuration. The early exaggeration value controls how tightly natural clusters in the original space are positioned in the embedded space and how much space will be between them. For larger values, the space between natural clusters will be larger in the embedded space.

The procedure is as follows: during dimensionality reduction the classification of the CNN is not considered. As we aim for clustering images in the 3D space according to the visual properties, we optimize the t-SNE parameters in regard to the image clusters. The rationale of the t-SNE based clustering is as follows: (1) images from the same class label in the supervised dataset should be visualized in the same cluster in 3D and (2) similar images should move closer together. Figure 3 shows the 3D plot of the local optimum of t-SNE parameter combinations resulting from our experiment. We also conduct the experiment in 2D space (see Fig. 4) and find that the same parameters also result in a local 2D optimum. While comparing both 3D and 2D plots, we can clearly see that a visualization in 2D is not suitable for the image data sets under investigation, as the clusters highly overlap and cannot be distinguished. This supports the application of a 3D space for visualizing and exploring these image data sets.

3.2   VAE Approach

Due to the design of the PCA and t-SNE techniques, their main drawback is the lack of a precise method of projecting back to the high dimensional space. Ideally, the high dimensional layer activations of the CNN would be reduced to the 3D VR space, where they can be manipulated, and the new positional vector can be projected back into the high dimensional space and be used as new input for training the underlying CNN model.

Figure 5 shows the architecture of our approach which uses a variational auto encoder (VAE) for dimensionality reduction. Basically, we are replacing the PCA/t-SNE part of our architecture with a VAE, which is trained in reducing high dimensional vectors into 3D space. As before, this 3D vector v can then be manipulated in the VR space, leading to a new 3D vector v'. We project the new vector back into the high dimensional space, where it is used for training the CNN model. By design we implicitly train the decoder of the VAE to reverse this mapping and generate a high dimensional vector from the 3D vector.

We conduct a similar experiment to the t-SNE before and train our VAE on the MNIST data set [6]. For the experiment, each image is squashed to a single vector of 784 dimensions. Our VAE [4] consists of six fully connected layers (i.e., 784 - 512 - 256 - 3 - 256 - 512 - 784). ReLU is applied at all the hidden layers except at the bottleneck layer, whereas the sigmoid function is applied at the output layer. The network is trained using the Adam [3] optimizer with default parameters. After the network is trained, cluster centers for each class are found by averaging in the latent space using the label information provided in the training split. A validation split is then passed forward through the encoder to fetch the latent representation of each image. In this case, label information for the split can either come from the CNN classifier or can be calculated from the closest cluster center in the latent space. Resulting plots for 2D and 3D are displayed in Figs. 6 and 7.

4   Interactive Fine-Tuning

After the user has moved an image, the new location can be used as an input parameter to fine-tune the model. Due to the dimensionality reduction, we cannot infer the high dimensional output vector (4096 dimensions) of the deep convolutional neural network from the new 3D position. Therefore we distinguish between two cases: (1) the image was re-labeled because it was moved from one cluster to another, or (2) the image was moved inside a cluster without changing the label. In the first case we assume that the instance now belongs to a different class and re-train the model with this information as input. For the second case we approximate the re-positioning step through re-training the network with the same image and label, as it was not moved between clusters. Depending on the Euclidean distance of the new position to the cluster centroid we apply heuristics to decide how many times the image is used in the re-training step. If the image's original position was far away from the centroid, it will be selected multiple times as input using the new label. In either case, after re-training is done, all images are again processed by the network and moved to their updated position. Due to the nature of the fine-tuning process, it is not guaranteed that the image moved by the user will stay at its designated position, but we allow smooth animations in the 3D layout change. The entire fine-tuning process can be repeated iteratively.

5   Conclusion and Future Work

We presented an interactive clustering method that allows users to explore and fine-tune a convolutional neural network in VR, resulting in improved interpretability and transparency of the deep learning model. Our experiments show that the selection of 3D instead of 2D is not only motivated by the beneficial cognitive and immersive aspects of VR, but also on the fact that large image data sets are difficult to cluster and display in 2D. Currently we are investigating how different selections of the layer and dimensionality reduction method can improve the visualization in the VR space. Our experiments show that the proper selection of t-SNE parameters is highly dependent on the used data set and potentially needs to be adjusted to each image data set individually. We are working on the automatic selection of these parameters. Our approach to fine-tuning could be further improved by manipulating specific layers based on the new spatial location of the image or creating an additional layer that specifically addresses the interactive learning step. Also, we are looking into different visualization and interaction methods that could benefit from the interaction with virtual objects in VR [10], e.g., by leveraging the peripheral view of the user [8] and displaying additional information in an unobtrusive way.

Acknowledgments. This research is supported by the pAItient project (BMG, 2520DAT0P2), the Ophthalmo-AI project (BMBF), and the Endowed Chair of Applied Artificial Intelligence, Oldenburg University. We would like to thank all student assistants that contributed to the development of the platform, see iml.dfki.de.

A Appendix PCA and t-SNE Approach

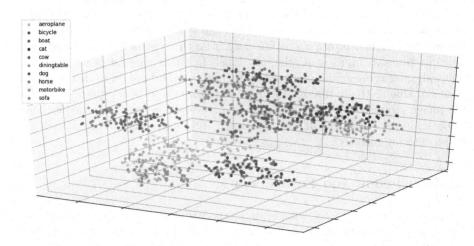

Fig. 3. Visualization of dimensionality reduction into 3D space using PCA and t-SNE on the POET data set. We used the following t-SNE parameters: perplexity = 25, iterations = 750, learning rate = 410, early exaggeration = 5. This selection of parameters yields the best clustering results (local optimum).

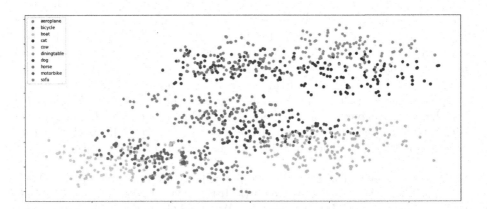

Fig. 4. Visualization of dimensionality reduction into 2D space using PCA and t-SNE on the POET data set. For t-SNE we used the same parameters as in the 3D projection (see Fig. 3): perplexity = 25, iterations = 750, learning rate = 410, early exaggeration = 5. This selection of parameters yields the best clustering results (local optimum) in 2D as well.

B Appendix VAE Approach

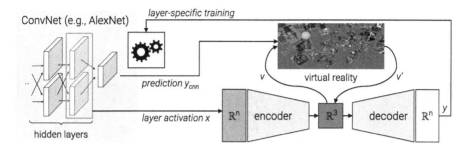

Fig. 5. Architecture of the second approach using a variational auto encoder for dimensionality reduction. In our case we reduce the 4096 dimensions of the layer activation vector to the 3D VR space. After user input in VR the new location can be decoded back into a 4096 dimensional vector and be used for layer-specific training.

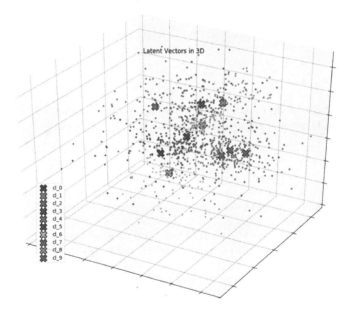

Fig. 6. Plot of the MNIST data set projected into 3D space using a VAE. Classes are color-coded and cluster centers are indicated.

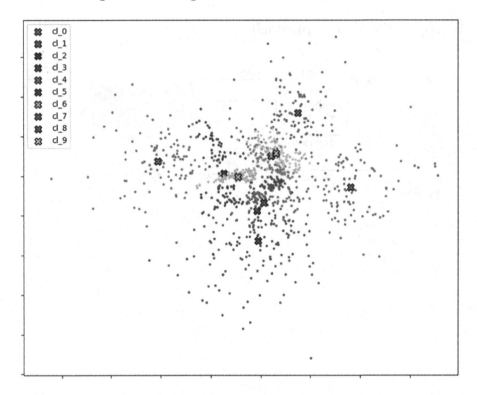

Fig. 7. Plot of the MNIST data set projected into 2D space using a VAE. Classes are color-coded and cluster centers are indicated.

References

1. Donalek, C., et al.: Immersive and collaborative data visualization using virtual reality platforms. In: 2014 IEEE International Conference on Big Data (Big Data), pp. 609–614, October 2014

2. Hohman, F., Kahng, M., Pienta, R., Chau, D.H.: Visual analytics in deep learning: an interrogative survey for the next frontiers. IEEE Trans. Vis. Comput. Graph. **25**, 2674–2693 (2018)

3. Kingma, D.P., Ba, J.: Adam: a method for stochastic optimization. arXiv preprint arXiv:1412.6980 (2014)

4. Kingma, D.P., Welling, M.: Auto-encoding variational bayes. arXiv preprint arXiv:1312.6114 (2013)

5. Krizhevsky, A., Sutskever, I., Hinton, G.E.: ImageNet classification with deep convolutional neural networks. In: Advances in Neural Information Processing Systems, pp. 1097–1105 (2012)

6. LeCun, Y., Bottou, L., Bengio, Y., Haffner, P., et al.: Gradient-based learning applied to document recognition. Proc. IEEE **86**(11), 2278–2324 (1998)

7. Van der Maaten, L, Hinton, G.: Visualizing data using t-SNE. J. Mach. Learn. Res. **9**(Nov), 2579–2605 (2008)

8. Moniri, M.M., Sonntag, D., Luxenburger, A.: Peripheral view calculation in virtual reality applications. In: Proceedings of the 2016 ACM International Joint Confer-

ence on Pervasive and Ubiquitous Computing, UbiComp Adjunct 2016, Heidelberg, Germany, 12–16 September 2016, pp. 333–336 (2016). https://doi.org/10.1145/2968219.2971391

9. Moran, A., Gadepally, V., Hubbell, M., Kepner, J.: Improving big data visual analytics with interactive virtual reality. In: 2015 IEEE High Performance Extreme Computing Conference (HPEC), pp. 1–6, September 2015

10. Orlosky, J., Toyama, T., Sonntag, D., Kiyokawa, K.: The role of focus in advanced visual interfaces. KI - Künstliche Intell. 301–310 (2015). https://doi.org/10.1007/s13218-015-0411-y

11. Papadopoulos, D.P., Clarke, A.D.F., Keller, F., Ferrari, V.: Training object class detectors from eye tracking data. In: Fleet, D., Pajdla, T., Schiele, B., Tuytelaars, T. (eds.) ECCV 2014. LNCS, vol. 8693, pp. 361–376. Springer, Cham (2014). https://doi.org/10.1007/978-3-319-10602-1_24

12. Prange, A., Barz, M., Sonntag, D.: Medical 3D images in multimodal virtual reality. In: Proceedings of the 23rd International Conference on Intelligent User Interfaces Companion, Tokyo, Japan, 07–11 March 2018, pp. 19:1–19:2 (2018). https://doi.org/10.1145/3180308.3180327

13. Russakovsky, O., et al.: ImageNet large scale visual recognition challenge. Int. J. Comput. Vis. **115**(3), 211–252 (2015)

14. Zacharias, J., Barz, M., Sonntag, D.: A survey on deep learning toolkits and libraries for intelligent user interfaces. CoRR abs/1803.04818 (2018)

HUI-Audio-Corpus-German: A High Quality TTS Dataset

Pascal Puchtler[✉], Johannes Wirth, and René Peinl

Hof University of Applied Sciences, Alfons-Goppel-Platz 1, 95028 Hof, Germany
{Pascal.Puchtler,Johannes.Wirth,Rene.Peinl}@iisys.de

Abstract. The increasing availability of audio data on the internet leads to a multitude of datasets for development and training of text to speech applications, based on deep neural networks. Highly differing quality of voice, low sampling rates, lack of text normalization and disadvantageous alignment of audio samples to corresponding transcript sentences still limit the performance of deep neural networks trained on this task. Additionally, data resources in languages like German are still very limited. We introduce the "HUI-Audio-Corpus-German", a large, open-source dataset for TTS engines, created with a processing pipeline, which produces high quality audio to transcription alignments and decreases manual effort needed for creation.

Keywords: Neural network · Corpus · Text-to-speech · German

1 Introduction

Performance of text to speech (TTS) systems has increased vastly over the past decade, primarily by leveraging deep neural networks (DNNs) [1], which in turn lead to higher acceptance by end-users [1, 2]. Globally operating companies have started to incorporate TTS engines for human machine interaction into their products, like home assistants, cars or smartphones [3]. State-of-the-art TTS consists of a two-stage process. An acoustic model, which generates mel spectrograms, intermediate audio representations from input characters or phonemes, and subsequently, a vocoder, which processes the previously created mel spectrograms and produces a final audio signal. Primarily the acoustic model requires large numbers of corresponding pairs of textual transcription and audio recordings to be successfully trained. Tacotron 2 is one of the most popular acoustic models and achieved a mean opinion score (MOS) of 4.53 on a five point scale for the English language [4] using a modified WaveNet [5] as vocoder. To achieve such good results, training data must be available in large enough quantity and high enough quality. For English language, there are high quality datasets like LJ Speech [6] and LibriTTS [7], which are commonly used for research and produce good results [8, 9]. However, the results are currently not suitable for a production-ready TTS system.

In languages other than English, high quality training data is scarce and creation of new datasets often requires unfeasibly high efforts as well as time. This is especially

© Springer Nature Switzerland AG 2021
S. Edelkamp et al. (Eds.): KI 2021, LNAI 12873, pp. 204–216, 2021.
https://doi.org/10.1007/978-3-030-87626-5_15

true for researchers in the domain of audio processing as well as smaller businesses so they mostly have to resort to freely available data, in order to utilize this technology.

In this paper we introduce a new, open-source dataset for TTS, called **HUI**-Audio-Corpus-German (**H**of University – Institute for information systems) for the German language, which consists of over 326 h of audio snippets with matching transcripts, gathered from librivox.org and processed in a fine-grained refinement pipeline. The dataset consists of five speakers with 32–96 h of audio each to construct single speaker TTS models, as well as 97 h of audio from additional 117 speakers for diversity in a multi-speaker TTS model. For every speaker, a clean version with high signal-noise-ratio has been generated additionally, further increasing quality. The underlying goal was to create a German dataset with the quality of LJ Speech [6] that is more comprehensive than the one from M-AILABS [10]. The dataset[1] as well as the source code[2] are open sourced under the Apache public license 2.0 and freely available.

The remainder of this article is organized as follows. We start discussing related work on freely available datasets in English and German and derive requirements for an own dataset from it in Sect. 2. We introduce the data processing pipeline that we used to create our own dataset in Sect. 3. We present our own dataset in Sect. 4 and discuss its advantages over existing datasets, before concluding the article with a summary and outlook.

2 Related Work

LJ Speech is a well-known audio dataset, that achieves good results in state-of-the-art TTS models [11]. Within this public domain dataset, there are nearly 24 h of speech recordings by a single female speaker who reads passages from seven non-fiction books. The 13,100 recordings, with an average length of 6.6 s, are used in many TTS research papers [8, 12, 13], although the recordings have some spatial reverberation [6].

Table 1. Dataset overview

Corpus	License	Duration (hours)	Sampling rate (kHz)	Total speakers
Thorsten-Voice neutral [14]	CC0	23	22.05	1
CCS10 – German [15]	CC0	17	22.05	1
M-AILABS – German [10]	BSD	237	16	5+[a]
MLS – German [16]	CC By 4.0	3,287	16	244
HUI-Audio-Corpus-German	CC0	326	44.1	122

[a] The data set consists of 5 named speakers plus others aggregated in mixed.

In contrast to this single-speaker dataset, LibriTTS is a popular dataset that can be used for multi-speaker training [7]. It consists of 585 h of speech data at 24 kHz sampling

[1] https://opendata.iisys.de/datasets.html#hui-audio-corpus-german.

[2] https://github.com/iisys-hof/HUI-Audio-Corpus-German.

rate from 2,456 speakers and the corresponding texts. It is derived from the LibriSpeech corpus [17], which is tailored for automatic speech recognition (ASR), but comes with a number of problems regarding its use for TTS. These are a low sample rate (16 kHz), removed punctuation and varying degrees of background noise [7]. While a selection of TTS-ready datasets already exists in German (see Table 1), most of them have similar quality issues, which is in turn reflected in output quality of trained models.

According to our demands, a TTS dataset of high quality should therefore fulfil at least the following requirements:

1. A minimum recording duration of 20 h per speaker (for single speaker dataset)
2. Audio recordings with sampling rates of at least 22,050 Hz (as suggested by [7])
3. Normalization of text (resolution of abbreviations, numbers etc., see [7])
4. Normalization of audio loudness
5. Average audio length between 5 and 10 s (inspired by [6], with ø 6.6 s)
6. Inclusion of pronunciation-relevant punctuation
7. Optional: Preservation of capitalization (as suggested by [7])

Thorsten-Voice neutral [14] is the only German dataset, which meets all our requirements, with 23 h of audio from a single speaker in good to medium quality and 22.05 kHz. However, it is read nearly over-emphasized leading to partly unnaturally sounding TTS results in our experiments. CSS10 - German [15] is a collection of single speaker speech datasets in ten languages. Its German part has a good text normalization as well as a sufficient sampling rate. However, the amount of data is quite low with not even 17 h of German speech from a single female speaker (Hokuspokus).

M-AILABS [10] have compiled speech data from five main speakers with 19, 24, 29, 40 and 68 h of speech. It contains mostly perfect text normalization, but the sampling rate of the recordings is only 16 kHz. Multi-lingual LibriSpeech (MLS) is an automatically generated dataset for multiple languages [16]. In the German variant with a massive 3,287 h of audio, however, errors have occurred in the normalization of the texts. Numbers are e.g., completely missing in the text. Additionally, the sampling rate is not sufficient. All these datasets, except Thorsten-Voice neutral, are derived from LibriVox.

3   Data Processing Pipeline

To create a high-quality TTS dataset fulfilling the previously described requirements, a fine-grained pre-processing pipeline was constructed, which generates audio-transcript pairs, featuring automated download of data, very precise alignment of audio files and transcripts with utilization of a deep neural network, audio/text normalization and further processing (see Fig. 1).

3.1   Acquisition of Suitable Audio Data

We use LibriVox, a web platform, offering "free public domain audiobooks"[3] in several languages, as a source for audio. The available audio files are read and created by volunteers in various lengths and recording qualities. All authors of the texts read aloud either

---

[3] https://librivox.org/.

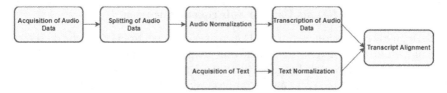

Fig. 1. Data processing pipeline overview.

passed away more than 70 years ago or their publishers agreed to a free publication. Thus, neither books nor recordings are subject to copyright claims. The LibriVox API[4] presents a convenient way to retrieve metadata about available audiobooks and is leveraged to create an automated download process for audiobooks. Audio files are available in different sampling rates on the platform. For data generation, only files with sampling rates of 44.1 kHz were considered, as generally higher sampling rates allow for greater flexibility in terms of further sampling rate adjustment.

3.2 Splitting of Audio Data

For training with neural networks, short audio snippets with lengths ranging from 10 to 20 s are preferred in comparable works such as [16]. Shorter recordings result in a worse sentence melody for longer inference outputs after training. Longer input data lead to slower loss convergences at training time and thereby to higher computational complexity. However, other successful TTS datasets like LJspeech have a range of 1–10 s of audio [6]. Therefore, the thresholds of recording duration were set to a range of 5 to 40 s in order to preserve emphasis on full sentences, mainly beginning and ending.

For this purpose, a decibel value of -70 dB was defined. Each audio signal was split at points where this value was undercut for at least 0.2 s. The longest resulting segment was then identified and used as an indicator for further steps. If its length exceeded the defined maximum length threshold, a new segmentation was carried out with the decibel limit corrected upwards by 5 dB. Afterwards, segments below the minimum length threshold were concatenated until all segments were within the previously defined length interval.

3.3 Audio Normalization

Audio normalization is hereinafter defined as adjustment of the volume of audio files to a uniform value. Experiments suggest that -20 dB is considered useful for filtering background noise. Moreover, the loudness of the majority of data we acquired already had a level close to this threshold. This is supported by the use of -24 dB in the Thorsten-Voice dataset [14]. Pyloudnorm[5] is used as an implementation here. Additionally, a fade in/out of 0.1 s is applied to the beginning and end of recordings to further filter out undesired sounds such as breathing.

---

[4] https://librivox.org/api/info.

[5] https://github.com/csteinmetz1/pyloudnorm.

3.4 Transcription of Audio Data for Subsequent Alignment

Each audio file is transcribed. A trained Deep Speech model from [19] in the most recent version[6] is utilized. Inferences are created in conjunction with a 3-g KenLM language model, which is as provided together with the Deep Speech model. The model uses 16 kHz as input sample rate. While the base model had achieved a word error rate (WER) of 21.5% on the combined Tuda-de, Voxforge and Common Voice DE dataset [19], the version used (based on a newer Deep Speech implementation) was trained with additional datasets, but no new benchmark data was published.

3.5 Acquisition of Text for Audio Data

For each audio book, LibriVox provides a link to the original text. For German, these are mainly hosted on projekt-guttenberg.de[7] and guttenberg.org[8], offering public domain books and literary prose works. Our solution downloads the texts automatically and parses them for further processing.

3.6 Text Normalization

Preparation of transcripts partially has to be conducted in manual processes, due to individual differences of the speakers. *An overview of the replacements used can be found in* Table 2.

Numbers. In German, the correct normalized form of ordinal numbers depends on grammatical gender, case as well as grammatical number. This increases the number of possible normalizations by a large factor at each occurrence, compared to e.g., English.

Abbreviations. Partially, abbreviations written in the same way have to be mapped to different normalized words, which significantly complicates automation.

Censorship. Parts of the texts were censored, e.g., because of German history, mainly terms and names from the national socialists era. Different speakers dealt with this kind of symbol sequences in various manners, which in turn leads to the need of manually comparing recordings with transcripts in order to gain best possible audio to transcript alignments.

Footnotes. Some of the texts contain footnotes. These are again treated differently by speakers. The most common ways are 1) omit completely 2) read the number and read the footnote at the end of the page 3) omit the number and read the footnote immediately. Additionally, in some cases the word "Fussnote" (footnote) is added by a speaker. In other cases, the word is explicitly written in the text.

Comments. The texts partly contain comments in round brackets. These are only partly read out loud. Depending on the speaker, "Kommentar Anfang" (comment beginning) and "Kommentar Ende" (comment end) are added.

---

[6] https://github.com/AASHISHAG/deepspeech-german#trained-models.

[7] https://www.projekt-gutenberg.org/.

[8] https://gutenberg.org.

Table 2. Replacements for text editing.

Original text	Normalized text	Type of normalization
XIII	Siebzehn	Roman numeral
III	der dritte	Roman ordinal number nominative case
51,197	einundfünfzig komma eins neun sieben	Decimal number
5½	fünf einhalb	Numbers with fractures
30	Dreißigsten	Ordinal number dative case
1793	Siebzehnhundertdreiundneunzig	Year
1804/05	achtzehnhundertvier fünf	Range of years
1885/86	achtzehnhundertfünfundachtzig bis sechsundachtzig	Range of years
50 000	Fünfzigtausend	Decimal number without separator
4,40 Mk	Vier Mark vierzig	Sum of money (in specific currencies)
E.Th.A. Hoffmann	Ernst Theodor Amadeus Hoffmann	Name complete
Prof. Dr. Sigm. Freud LL. D	Professor Doktor Sigmund Freud Doktor of Law	Name complete
Pf…sche	Pfffsche	Emphasis in the text
***	Punkt Punkt Punk	Censorship pronounced
St	Sankt	Abbreviation
a. D	a D	Abbreviation
=	Ist	Abbreviation

3.7 Transcript Alignment

At this step, the original text in its normalized form as well as artificially generated transcripts are present. These are needed to create the best possible automated alignment between read aloud words from audio snippets and the corresponding transcripts. The generated transcripts mostly follow the same order as the original text. Note that spoken intro and outro sequences do not have corresponding transcripts.

In the following step, a positional alignment between original and artificially generated transcript sentences is to be achieved. The original text is a long string without alignment to the recordings. However, it contains punctuation, capitalization and error-free words. The transcripts of the recordings are a list of texts with assignment to a recording. However, they contain partly incorrect text, because of the error rate of the German Deep Speech model [19] and come without punctuation and capitalization.

The first transcript is near the beginning of the original text, with means that the alignment search area can be clearly limited. In this search area, the distance between each possible subarea and the transcript is formed. The range with the smallest distance is called match and is kept as the ground truth alignment between the original text and the recording. As distance $d(s1, s2)$ with the strings s_1 and s_2 we use a modified version of the Levenshtein Distance [20]:

$$d(s1, s2) \stackrel{\text{def}}{=} \frac{Levenshtein - Distance(s_1, s_2)}{\max(length(s_1), length(s_1))} \tag{1}$$

After that, the search area is moved by the length of the match. There, the search for the next match is repeated.

Now we have an associated part of the original text for each generated snippet. Due to various possible problems, the quality of the hit may not be sufficient. This can be determined by the distance. By testing, we have found that hits above a value of 0.2 should be discarded.

The transitions from one text snippet to the next are always a problem, as words can appear twice or not at all. To overcome this problem, a transition is called perfect if both matches are exactly adjacent to each other.

A text snippet is of sufficient quality for us, if all the following conditions are met (values were heuristically estimated):

- The text snippet has a distance of less than 0.2
- The preceding and following text snippets have a distance of less than 0.2
- The transitions to the previous and following text snippets are perfect

This way, it can be guaranteed that all text snippets are assigned in the best possible way and that the final dataset has as few errors as possible. However, this also means that some of the text snippets are discarded.

4 Dataset Summary

4.1 Full Dataset

The dataset was statistically evaluated for each included speaker (see Table 3). The following aspects are considered:

Speakers. Number of Speakers.

Hours. Total audio data length in hours.

Count. Count of audio-transcript pairs.

MVA. In each audio snippet, the frame with the minimum volume (in dB) is determined. An average is calculated over the minimum volume values in all audio snippets. This is defined as Minimum Volume Average (MVA). The standard deviation is indicated in parentheses.

SPA. Each audio snippet can be divided into silence and speech, through root mean square (RMS). The proportion of silence is measured for each audio snippet and an average is formed over the dataset. This metric is defined as silence proportion average (SPA). The value in parentheses represents the standard deviation of the data.

UW@1. Count of all unique words that occur in the transcripts. UW@1 describes the diversity of the transcripts. A larger value is an indication for higher coverage of the German vocabulary.

UW@5. Count of all unique words that occur at least five times in the transcripts. Extension of the UW@1 metric. The higher the frequency of unique words within the dataset, the less impact one-time poorly pronounced words have on the training process of TTS models.

Table 3. Subset overview – full.

Subset	Speakers	Hours	Count	MVA	SPA	UW@1	UW@5
Bernd Ungerer ♂	1	97	35k	-60 (6.1)	20 (6.5)	33.5k	9.1k
Hokuspokus ♀	1	43	19k	-45 (14.3)	18 (10.4)	33.7k	5.9k
Friedrich ♂	1	32	15k	-52 (8.9)	27 (9.6)	26.6k	5.0k
Karlsson ♂	1	30	11k	-60 (4.4)	20 (7.0)	26.4k	4.5k
Eva K ♀	1	29	11k	-56 (4.9)	18 (7.6)	23.2k	4.4k
Other ♂/♀	117	96	38k	-55 (14.0)	20 (9.5)	60.9k	11.7k
Total	122	326	130k	-55 (11.5)	20 (8.9)	105k	25.4k

Table 4. Subset overview – clean.

Subset	Speakers	Hours	Count	MVA	SPA	UW@1	UW@5
Bernd Ungerer ♂	1	92	33k	-61 (5.6)	21 (6.0)	31.8k	8.8k
Hokuspokus ♀	1	27	11k	-57 (2.8)	22 (6.4)	24.4k	4.1k
Friedrich ♂	1	21	9.6k	-56 (5.8)	26 (7.6)	21.1k	3.6k
Karlsson ♂	1	29	11k	-60 (3.7)	21 (6.4)	25.4k	4.3k
Eva K ♀	1	22	8.5k	-57 (4.0)	19 (6.4)	18.8k	3.4k
Other ♂/♀	113	64	24k	-63 (9.1)	22 (7.0)	48.4k	8.6k
Total	118	253	97k	-60 (6.6)	21 (6.8)	87.9k	21.0k

4.2 Clean Dataset

The audio quality of the individual audio snippets may well vary, caused by e.g. background noise or poor recording quality. For this reason, a clean variant was created for each subset. Using thresholds for minimum volume and silence proportion, each dataset was filtered, the resulting datasets are considered "clean" sets. The following thresholds were used:

$$min\,volume < -50\,\mathrm{dB} \wedge 10\% < silence\,proportion < 45\% \tag{2}$$

The minimum volume can be seen as a simplified version of the signal-noise-ratio, since in silent parts, only background noise is generating sound. A statistical evaluation of the resulting clean variants is presented in Table 4.

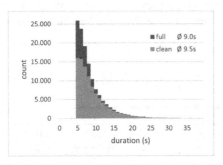

Fig. 2. Histogram of the audio duration for all speakers.

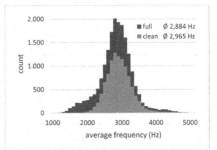

Fig. 3. Histogram of minimum volume for all speakers.

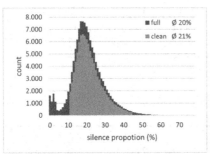

Fig. 4. Histogram of the silence proportion for all speakers.

Fig. 5. Histogram of the average frequency for the speaker "Hokuspokus".

Figures 2, 3 and 4 show histograms of the full and clean datasets for all speakers. Figure 2 shows the distribution of durations for all audio snippets. A strong tendency towards the 5–10 s range as well as the exclusion of any snippets under the length of 5 s can be observed. Furthermore, there are no audio snippets under 5 s. Figure 3 demonstrates a large variance with respect to minimum volume threshold, which is significantly lower within the clean dataset in comparison. Figure 4 shows the proportion of silence within the audio snippets. A concentration at 0% and no values above 70% can be detected. Furthermore, boundary values are recognizable for the clean dataset. Figure 5 depicts the average speech frequency of the audio snippets for speaker Hokuspokus. It shows that our normalization reduced the standard deviation of frequencies per speaker significantly.

Considering the described figures, it can be hypothesized that training a TTS model using the clean datasets will lead to a potentially better result, since audio snippets contained in the clean dataset show a higher coherence, primarily in terms of frequency spectrum, proportion of silence and minimum loudness. The duration of audio snippets is insignificantly higher within the clean dataset (Ø 9.5 s), compared to the full dataset (Ø 9.0 s).

4.3 Discussion

The generated HUI-Audio-Corpus-German is compared to the previously derived requirements for a state-of-the-art TTS dataset.

1) **Minimum duration of 20 h per speaker.** For the five main speakers, this goal is achieved. In addition, the "other" subset consists of several speakers, none of which has exceeded the set threshold of 20 h.
2) **Sampling rate of at least 22,050 Hz.** Each audio snippet in the HUI-Audio-Corpus-German has a sampling rate of 44.1 kHz.
3) **Normalization of text.** An automated check for digits, abbreviations and special characters as well as a thorough manual analysis of transcript samples confirmed the required grade of text normalization.
4) **Normalization of audio loudness.** All audio snippets are normalized according to the requirement.
5) **Average audio length of 5 to 10 s.** The full dataset as an average audio length of 9.0 s and the clean dataset of 9.5 s, thus averages of both sets are within the specified limits.
6) **Inclusion of pronunciation-relevant punctuation.** As punctuation relevant symbols, period (.), question mark (?) exclamation point (!), comma (,) and colon (:) were chosen. All other punctuations were either transformed or completely removed.
7) **Preservation of capitalization.** Capitalization of transcripts is preserved by default.

The statistics in Table 3 and Table 4 show, that even the longest single speaker dataset contains only 33.5k unique words, compared to 105k for the whole dataset. This is due to the focus of the books that were read and can be an issue for open domain TTS.

4.4 Evaluation with Tacotron 2

In order to verify and compare the overall quality of full and clean datasets as well as their effects on convergence of loss in a deep neural network for TTS, both variations of subsets by the speaker "Hokuspokus" were selected to be used for the training of multiple Tacotron 2 [21] models in conjunction with a Multi-band MelGAN [2] as vocoder. The Multi-band MelGAN is trained with the default configuration[9]. For comparability, all Tacotron 2 models were trained with identical configurations. As a grapheme-to-phoneme converter, we use a dictionary generated from the contents of Wiktionary[10]

---

[9] https://github.com/kan-bayashi/ParallelWaveGAN/blob/master/egs/vctk/voc1/conf/multi_band_melgan.v2.yaml.

[10] https://www.wiktionary.org/.

While training loss (Fig. 6) is similar between both datasets, validation loss (Fig. 7) strongly differs in favour of the full dataset. However, part of this difference may come from the reduced number of audio files. After training was completed, audio inferences of both networks were generated under the same conditions and compared manually. Subjectively, the evaluation indicated that the model trained using the clean dataset generated inferences with consistently less background noise and more stable stop token prediction, thus the subjective results are better than the objective ones. Samples are provided on the dataset's website[11].

A further, automated analysis of 105 generated audio inferences from both models shows large differences with regard to minimum volume. While inferences generated by the clean model have an MSA of −57 dB (MSA clean dataset −60 dB), those produced by the model trained on the full dataset have −45 dB (MSA full dataset −45 dB). These discrepancies support the previously conducted, subjective evaluation and also prove the effect of applying this metric in the creation of clean datasets.

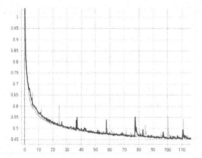 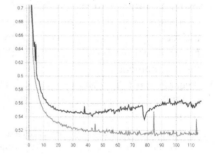

Fig. 6. Training loss Tacotron 2 Hokuspokus orange: full, blue: clean (Color figure online)   **Fig. 7.** Validation loss Tacotron 2 Hokuspokus orange: full, blue: clean (Color figure online)

5 Conclusion and Outlook

This paper described the HUI-German-Audio-Corpus, a freely available, high-quality dataset for TTS in German consisting of audio transcript pairs of several speakers with a total length of over 300 h. In addition, it contains a "clean" subset, which meets advanced quality criteria. While the audio to text alignment demonstrates a high degree of correctness, some manual steps such as normalization of ordinal numbers and abbreviations could be further assisted by a fitting deep neural network for POS tagging. We've demonstrated, that quality of the dataset is equally important as length. The higher frequency of 44.1 kHz compared to the 16 kHz of the MAILABs dataset makes a huge difference, although we've trained our samples only with 22.05 kHz. The fact, that we've normalized the text regarding numbers, which is especially demanding in German due to its different endings for numbers for different cases (e.g. genitive, dative), leads to good performance of the trained network models when reading numbers. Other datasets like the German part of MLS are completely missing the numbers and cannot be used for a

---

[11] https://opendata.iisys.de/datasets.html#hui-audio-corpus-german.

TTS model that should be able to read numbers. The fact that Thorsten Müller's dataset is somewhat overemphasized leads to fast convergence and an easy to understand output, but an unnatural reading style. The large amount of data available for the voice Bernd Ungerer leads to a very stable output that can cope with almost any speech situation, despite its limited vocabulary used for training. The fact that our datasets contain both short and large audio parts leads to TTS models that are able to read longer texts in one piece.

The usage of deep learning for the alignment of text and audio significantly increased the quality. TTS and automatic speech recognition (ASR) are closely related and can mutually benefit from each other. Training data for TTS can be reused for ASR as well. ASR can help to generate new training data for TTS. Sufficiently good TTS can on the other hand be used to generate additional training data for ASR, especially for words that are otherwise underrepresented in the training dataset. Generating statistics over the datasets and comparing the words present with manually curated lists like Wordnet can generate valuable insight for further tweaking. We envision to use TTS to generate audio for ASR that contains e.g. names, numbers and complex words in order to enhance existing audio datasets for ASR that are missing those. Finally, better text understanding can help splitting audio files at meaningful positions in the text, which would further enhance the already good training results.

References

1. Wang, Y., et al.: Tacotron: towards end-to-end speech synthesis. In: Proceedings of Interspeech 2017, pp. 4006–4010 (2017)
2. Yang, G., Yang, S., Liu, K., Fang, P., Chen, W., Xie, L.: Multi-band MelGAN: faster waveform generation for high-quality text-to-speech. arXiv preprint arXiv:2005.05106 (2020)
3. voicebot.ai: Hearables Consumer Adoption Report 2020. https://research.voicebot.ai/report-list/hearables-consumer-adoption-report-2020/. Accessed 12 May 2021
4. Shen, J., et al.: Natural TTS synthesis by conditioning wavenet on mel spectrogram predictions. In: 2018 IEEE International Conference on Acoustics, Speech and Signal Processing (ICASSP), pp. 4779–4783. IEEE (2018)
5. van den Oord, A., et al.: WaveNet: a generative model for raw audio. arXiv preprint arXiv: 1609.03499 (2016)
6. The LJ Speech Dataset. https://keithito.com/LJ-Speech-Dataset. Accessed 03 May 2021
7. Zen, H., et al.: LibriTTS: a corpus derived from LibriSpeech for text-to-speech. arXiv:1904. 02882 [cs, eess] (2019)
8. Kong, J., Kim, J., Bae, J.: HiFi-GAN: Generative adversarial networks for efficient and high fidelity speech synthesis. In: Advances in Neural Information Processing Systems, vol. 33 (2020)
9. Chen, N., Zhang, Y., Zen, H., Weiss, R.J., Norouzi, M., Chan, W.: WaveGrad: estimating gradients for waveform generation. arXiv preprint arXiv:2009.00713 (2020)
10. The M-AILABS Speech Dataset – caito. https://www.caito.de/2019/01/the-m-ailabs-speech-dataset/. Accessed 03 May 2021
11. Govalkar, P., Fischer, J., Zalkow, F., Dittmar, C.: A comparison of recent neural vocoders for speech signal reconstruction. In: Proceedings of 10th ISCA Speech Synthesis Workshop, pp. 7–12 (2019)

12. Kumar, K., et al.: MelGAN: generative adversarial networks for conditional waveform synthesis. In: Wallach, H., Larochelle, H., Beygelzimer, A., Alché-Buc, F., Fox, E., Garnett, R. (eds.) Advances in Neural Information Processing Systems, vol. 32, pp. 14910–14921. Curran Associates, Inc. (2019)
13. Prenger, R., Valle, R., Catanzaro, B.: WaveGlow: a flow-based generative network for speech synthesis. In: ICASSP 2019–2019 IEEE International Conference on Acoustics, Speech and Signal Processing (ICASSP), pp. 3617–3621. IEEE (2019)
14. Müller, T.: Thorsten Open German Voice Dataset. https://github.com/thorstenMueller/deep-learning-german-tts. Accessed 26 March 2021
15. Park, K., Mulc, T.: CSS10: a collection of single speaker speech datasets for 10 languages. arXiv preprint arXiv:1903.11269 (2019)
16. Pratap, V., Xu, Q., Sriram, A., Synnaeve, G., Collobert, R.: MLS: a large-scale multilingual dataset for speech research. arXiv preprint arXiv:2012.03411 (2020)
17. Panayotov, V., Chen, G., Povey, D., Khudanpur, S.: Librispeech: an ASR corpus based on public domain audio books. In: 2015 IEEE international conference on acoustics, speech and signal processing (ICASSP), pp. 5206–5210. IEEE (2015)
18. Goodfellow, I., Bengio, Y., Courville, A.: Deep learning. Das umfassende Handbuch: Grundlagen, aktuelle Verfahren und Algorithmen, neue Forschungsansätze. mitp, Frechen (2018)
19. Agarwal, A., Zesch, T.: German end-to-end speech recognition based on DeepSpeech. In: Proceedings of the 15th Conference on Natural Language Processing (2019)
20. Behara, K.N.S., Bhaskar, A., Chung, E.: A novel approach for the structural comparison of origin-destination matrices: levenshtein distance. Transp. Res. Part C: Emerg. Technol. **111**, 513–530 (2020). https://doi.org/10.1016/j.trc.2020.01.005
21. Wang, Y., et al.: Tacotron: towards end-to-end speech synthesis. arXiv preprint arXiv:1703.10135 (2017)

Negation in Cognitive Reasoning

Claudia Schon[1]([⊠])(iD), Sophie Siebert[2](iD), and Frieder Stolzenburg[2](iD)

[1] Institute for Web Science and Technologies, Universität Koblenz-Landau,
Universitätsstr. 1, 56070 Koblenz, Germany
`schon@uni-koblenz.de`
[2] Automation and Computer Sciences Department, Harz University of Applied
Sciences, Friedrichstr. 57–59, 38855 Wernigerode, Germany
`{ssiebert,fstolzenburg}@hs-harz.de`
`http://www.uni-koblenz.de/`
`http://artint.hs-harz.de/`

Abstract. Negation is both an operation in formal logic and in natural language by which a proposition is replaced by one stating the opposite, as by the addition of "not" or another negation cue. Treating negation in an adequate way is required for cognitive reasoning, which aims at modeling the human ability to draw meaningful conclusions despite incomplete and inconsistent knowledge. One task of cognitive reasoning is answering questions given by sentences in natural language. There are tools based on discourse representation theory to convert sentences automatically into a formal logic representation, and additional knowledge can be added using the predicate names in the formula and knowledge databases. However, the knowledge in logic databases in practice always is incomplete. Hence, forward reasoning of automated reasoning systems alone does not suffice to derive answers to questions because, instead of complete proofs, often only partial positive knowledge can be derived, while negative knowledge is used only during the reasoning process. In consequence, we aim at eliminating syntactic negation, strictly speaking, the negated event or property. In this paper, we describe an effective procedure to determine the negated event or property in order to replace it by its inverse. This lays the basis of cognitive reasoning, employing both logic and machine learning for general question answering. We evaluate our procedure by several benchmarks and demonstrate its practical usefulness in our cognitive reasoning system.

Keywords: Cognitive reasoning · Negation · Automated reasoning

1 Introduction

Negation is a very common operation in natural language. It reverses the meaning of a statement or parts of it. Especially in text comprehension, it is important

The authors gratefully acknowledge the support of the German Research Foundation (DFG) under the grants SCHO 1789/1-1 and STO 421/8-1 *CoRg – Cognitive Reasoning*.

© Springer Nature Switzerland AG 2021
S. Edelkamp et al. (Eds.): KI 2021, LNAI 12873, pp. 217–232, 2021.
https://doi.org/10.1007/978-3-030-87626-5_16

to correctly identify and process negation because negation can strongly alter the meaning of the overall contents of a statement. In this paper, we focus on solving commonsense reasoning tasks in natural language, which requires an adequate handling of negation.

Commonsense reasoning is the sort of everyday reasoning humans typically perform about the world [25]. It needs a vast amount of implicit background knowledge, such as facts about objects, events, space, time, and mental states. While humans solve commonsense reasoning tasks relatively easily and intuitively, they are rather difficult for a computer.

Most approaches that tackle commonsense reasoning and its benchmarks do not use any reasoning at all and rely mainly on machine learning and statistics on natural language texts. These often very successful approaches combine unsupervised pre-training on very large text corpora with supervised learning procedures [9,27]. However, the good results currently achieved, e.g., with BERT [9] should be critically questioned. [26] presents a system based on BERT that is only slightly below the average untrained human baseline on the Argument Reasoning Comprehension Task [11], but a close examination of the learned model by the authors of [26] shows that there are statistical cues in the dataset that have nothing to do with the represented problems. The good performance of BERT is explained by BERT exploiting these cues. Examples of those cues are the words "not", "is", "do", "are", "will not" and "cannot", with "not" being the strongest cue. After creating a version of the dataset without the bias of the cue "not", the authors find that performance of BERT drops to the random baseline. This illustrates that the system based on BERT in [26] has no underlying understanding of the tasks. This observation emphasizes the importance of explanations in commonsense reasoning and negation handling.

Therefore, we take a different way and rely on background knowledge represented in logic together with automated reasoning (cf. [29]). In a first step, the natural language representation of a benchmark problem is translated into a first-order logic formula using the KnEWS system [5] – a tool based on discourse representation theory [16]. Since many of the benchmark problems contain negations, it is important that they are treated correctly. Taking a look back at the detected bias from [26] it becomes clear that negation in particular is responsible for the majority of the biases. The word "not" is not only the strongest cue, but other cues are compound of it. This requires increased caution when dealing with negations.

By eliminating the word "not", additional technical advantages apply: While KnEWS can successfully detect negation, it often generates formulae with a large negation scope. Often it spans a whole sentence or subphrase. Our goal is to localize the negation as precisely as possible and thus to pinpoint the exact negated event or property, which can later be replaced by its non-negative counterpart or antonym – the inverse of the negated event or property. In many cases, the negation can even be completely removed from the formula in this way which often enables an automated reasoning system to derive more positive knowledge. In the CoRg system [28] (cf. Sect. 3.1), we use this knowledge as input for a neural network calculating a likelihood for each answer alternative to fit to the respective premise. A precisely determined (scope of the) negation in the formal representation also erases ambiguity and facilitates further processing.

In this paper, we therefore present an approach to automatically identify a negated event or property using a natural language sentence and the corresponding logical formula generated by KnEWS. Section 2 describes negation in logic as well as natural language and its importance in cognitive reasoning, which aims at modeling the human ability to draw meaningful conclusions despite incomplete and inconsistent knowledge [10]. In Sect. 3, we describe the cognitive reasoning system CoRg, in which this work is embedded, including challenges caused by negation. In Sect. 4, we present experimental results and demonstrate the usefulness of our approach for cognitive reasoning. Section 5 contains a summary, conclusions, and an outlook for future work.

2 Background and Related Works

2.1 Negation in Logic and Natural Language

Negation is a complex phenomenon in both logics and natural language [12]. In formal logics, the meaning of negation seems to be easy: It is a unary operation toggling the truth value of statements between true and false. In most classical logics, we have that double negation does not alter the original truth value, whereas this might not be true in other logics, e.g., multi-valued logics. In any case, the scope of a negation is the subformula that is affected by the negation. There are several types of negation in special logics: For instance, negation as failure or default negation is a non-monotonic inference rule in logic programming, used to derive *not p* for some statement p from the failure to derive p provided that this is consistent with the current knowledge [3].

In natural language, the meaning of negation often is not that clear, and it consists of several components (cf. [14]): Instead of precisely defined negation operators, there is a *negation cue*, that may be a syntactically independent negation marker like "never", "nor", "not" (syntactic negation), an affix expressing negation like "i(n)-" and "un-" (morphological negation), or a word whose meaning has a negative component like "deny" (lexical negation). The *scope* of a negation is the whole part of the sentence or utterance that is negated, i.e., affected by the negation cue.

Often the effect of negation shall be localized more precisely and reduced to only one part of the scope. On the one hand, there is the negated event or property, which we call *negatus* henceforth, usually a verb, noun, or adjective, that is directly negated. On the other hand, the *focus* is the part of the scope that is most prominently negated. It can also be defined as the part of the scope that is intended to be interpreted as false or whose intensity is modified [14]. By this, eventually a positive meaning may be implied. For example, the sentence "They didn't release the UFO files until 2008." has the negation cue "-n't". The pragmatic meaning of the sentence is probably a positive one, namely "The UFO files were released in 2008.", since "until 2008" is the negation focus [23].

Nevertheless, the negatus is "release" inducing the temporal negative meaning of the sentence: "They did not release the files before 2008".

2.2 Commonsense Reasoning and Negation

For automated commonsense reasoning, negation in natural language has to be treated in a formal manner. Traditional approaches tackle this problem by using Montague semantics together with Kripke semantics for modal logics [13]. Here, negation often is discussed in the context of performative verbs, e.g., "promise". So the two negations in "I do not promise not to assassinate the prime minister." [19] refer to different parts of the sentence and thus do not annihilate each other like double negation in classical logics. A more recent approach for formal negation detection comes from discourse representation theory and categorial grammars [16]. By means of the NLP toolchain [4], negation is detected on the basis of this theory. By means of further tools like KnEWS [5], complete sentences possibly including negation can be transformed eventually into a first-order logic formalization. Nevertheless, all these procedures and tools cannot hide the fact that the meaning of negation in natural language may be highly ambiguous. In languages like French or German, e.g., even the scope of negation may not be clear because of syntactic ambiguity. The German utterance "Ich verspreche dir nicht ruhig zu bleiben." may mean "I do not promise to stay calm." or "I promise not to stay calm."

As written in the introduction, the motivation to investigate negation is to treat it adequately in the context of cognitive reasoning. For this, it is important to identify a negation by its cue and assign the corresponding negatus correctly. For evaluation of our approach, there are numerous benchmark sets for commonsense reasoning and negation: The *COPA Challenge* (Choice of Plausible Alternatives) [20] or the *StoryClozeTest* [24] require causal reasoning in everyday situations, both without special focus on negation, however. In [23], *ConanDoyle-neg*, a corpus of stories by Conan Doyle annotated with negation information is presented. Here, the negation cues and their scope as well as the negatus have been annotated by two annotators in the CD-SCO dataset. The *SFU Opinion and Comments Corpus* [17] is a corpus for the analysis of online news comments. One of its focuses is how negation affects the interpretation of evaluative meaning in discourse.

3   Methods

3.1   A System for Cognitive Reasoning

The project CoRg (Cognitive Reasoning) [28] aims at solving commonsense reasoning benchmark tasks using extensive knowledge bases, automated reasoning, and neural networks. Benchmarks for commonsense reasoning often are multiple-choice natural language question-answering tasks. There, a premise together with answer alternatives is given, and the objective is to find the right alternative.

Premise: I think yesterday was when I realized I shouldn't be a mathematician. I was at the grocery store, restocking for next week. I had bought around twenty items, and thought I was under my budget. When I went to check out, I was ten dollars over!
Alternative 1: I then realized that I was not good at math.
Alternative 2: Then I knew that I was great at math!

Fig. 1. A StoryClozeTest example.

An example for such a task is given in Fig. 1. It is taken from the *StoryClozeTest* benchmark [24], which contains 3,744 problems in total.

Most systems tackling this type of problems rely on pre-trained neural networks and fine-tune their network for their specific problem. The natural language input is mapped to word embedding vectors (cf. [15]) and used as input for the neural network. In our approach, however, we enrich the input by knowledge derived through automated reasoning. The whole process is shown in Fig. 2: First, we translate the natural language input into a logical formula using KnEWS [5]. This is done for the premise as well as the answer candidates. Thus, we generate three logical formulae.

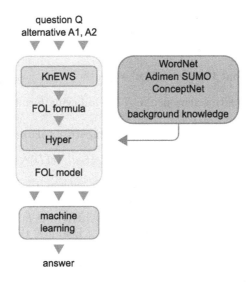

Fig. 2. The CoRg system.

In these formulae, the predicate names often correspond to words from the original sentence. Thus, the predicate names are used to look up synonyms from WordNet [21] and logically formalized background knowledge from different ontologies like AdimenSumo [2] and knowledge graphs like ConceptNet [18]. For each of the three formulae generated by KnEWS, the gathered knowledge together with the formula is used as input for the tableaux-based automated reasoning system Hyper [7] to perform inferences. In this process, we do not expect

Hyper to find a proof, but use it as an inference engine to derive new knowledge. Hyper thus computes a model or is terminated after a certain time and returns a tableau branch computed up to that point. Since there is the possibility that Hyper would still have closed this branch if it had run longer, we refer to this branch as a *potential partial model*. The information in the (potential partial) models represents knowledge that can be (potentially) deduced from the original sentence and the gathered background knowledge and thus provides more information than the original natural language sentence alone.

We extract all predicate names from the output of Hyper and use them as input for a two-channel neural network, pairing each answer candidate with the premise. Each word is mapped to a word embedding vector. Here we make use of the 300-dimensional word embeddings from ConceptNet Numberbatch [30] which has 400,000 entries. The neural network calculates a likelihood how much the pairs (consisting of question and answer candidate) correlate. Eventually, the answer with the highest likelihood is chosen as the correct answer. For further details about the system, the reader is referred to [28,29].

3.2 Negation Scope and the Negatus – Why Size Matters

An unnecessarily large scope of a negation in a formula induces a problem for the CoRg system. To see this, consider the following example (cf. first answer alternative in Fig. 1):

"I then realized that I was not good at math."

KnEWS translates this sentence into the following formula:

$$\exists A, B, C, D, E \Big(person(A) \wedge person(B) \wedge then(C) \wedge manner(D,C) \wedge$$
$$topic(D,E) \wedge actor(D,B) \wedge realize(D) \wedge$$
$$\neg \exists F, G \big(at(G,F) \wedge math(F) \wedge theme(G,A) \wedge good(G) \big) \Big) \quad (1)$$

We note that Formula (1), generated by KnEWS, is far from complete and how humans would formalize this sentence. For instance, the generated formula introduces two variables A and B, which refer to the two occurrences of the personal pronoun "I", but sound anaphora resolution would yield $A = B$. Furthermore, there is the singleton variable E, which actually refers to the subclause "that I was not good at math", but this is not formalized. Nevertheless, Formula (1) is still sufficient for our purposes. Developing a more suitable translation from natural language to logic would certainly be interesting but is beyond the scope of our project.

The subformula affected by the negation obviously includes the predicates *at*, *math*, *theme* and *good*. It is easy to see that this scope is unnecessarily large, since the word "math" is clearly not negated in the sentence. Actually, it would be sufficient to only negate the word "good". Nevertheless, "not good" may have a different meaning than "bad" for humans, which could be investigated by direct experiments with humans. However, this is again beyond the scope of our project. The big negation scope is not only unpleasant from a theoretical point of view, but leads to major problems in the CoRg system when the generated formula is fed into the automated reasoning system Hyper.

Before we take a closer look at these problems, let us assume that the selected background knowledge contains the information that math is a school subject. In fact, ConceptNet contains the triple (*Math*, *IsA*, *school subject*) which can be translated into:

$$\forall X \big(math(X) \rightarrow school\_subject(X) \big) \tag{2}$$

In the CoRg system, this background knowledge together with Formula (1) is passed to the Hyper theorem prover. In a preprocessing step, Hyper converts all input formulae to clause normal form. For Formulae (1) and (2), this includes the following clauses:

$$at(G, F) \wedge math(F) \wedge theme(G, A) \wedge good(G) \rightarrow \bot. \tag{3}$$

$$math(X) \rightarrow school\_subject(X). \tag{4}$$

Since Hyper is based on the hypertableau calculus [6], it can use Formula (3) only to close branches. More precisely, forward reasoning performed by Hyper is quite capable of using negative knowledge during the reasoning process, but the inferred knowledge always contains only positive statements. This means that the predicate name *math* can never appear in an open branch of a tableau constructed by Hyper. Moreover, Formula (4), created from the background knowledge, can not be used to infer that the person in question is not good at a school subject. Therefore, the predicate names *math* and *school subject* will not appear in (potential partial) models or inferences of Hyper. As we have seen above, the machine learning component of the CoRg system uses predicate names that occur in the models and inferences of Hyper to decide which of the given alternatives provides the right answer. Therefore, for us it is important that the output of Hyper contains as much knowledge as possible from the natural language input together with inferred knowledge from background knowledge.

In summary, the unnecessarily large scope of the negation in Formula (1) results in the fact that important information is withheld from the machine learning component of the CoRg system. Not all types of negation lead to this problem and need to be addressed by our approach: KnEWS is able to handle lexical and morphological negations, as they are directly translated into a single predicate without logical negation. Therefore, our approach only needs to address syntactic negation like "not good". But syntactic negation is common in natural language: 127 of the first 310 examples of the StoryClozeTest [24] contain syntactic negation.

Since the way KnEWS handles syntactic negation leads to the above mentioned problems in cognitive reasoning, we aim at determining the negatus for a given negation and to reduce the scope of the negation in the formula to include only the negatus. In the example, the subformula *good(G)* represents the desired negatus "good". The reduction of the scope of the negation in Formula (1) to the negatus leads to the following formula:

$$\exists A, B, C, D, E\Big(person(A) \wedge person(B) \wedge then(C) \wedge manner(D,C)\wedge$$
$$topic(D,E) \wedge actor(D,B) \wedge realize(D)\wedge$$
$$\exists F, G(at(G,F) \wedge math(F) \wedge theme(G,A) \wedge \neg good(G))\Big) \quad (5)$$

We are aware that moving the negation in the formula to the predicate representing the negatus does not preserve logical equivalence. But in our practical application context of commonsense reasoning, this is not mandatory. In addition, ordinary equivalence transformations such as De Morgan's rule do not help to restrict the scope of the negation in the formula to the negatus. But after reducing the scope of the negation of the formula to the negatus, in many cases it is even possible to remove the negation completely by determining an *inverse* (antonym) for the predicate symbol of the negated subformula. The negated subformula can be replaced by a non-negated subformula with the inverse as predicate symbol. For the example above, we determine the inverse *bad* of the predicate symbol *good* of the negated subformula $\neg good(G)$ with the help of WordNet and substitute the negated subformula $\neg good(G)$ in Formula (5) by $bad(G)$.

Clausification of the resulting formula leads to a set of clauses consisting only of unit clauses. Hence Hyper can use the background knowledge and infer that *math* is a *school_subject*. All this information will become available to the machine learning component of the CoRg system. Of course, one could argue that "being not good at math" is not the same as "being bad at math", but since our goal is to allow the theorem prover to draw as many inferences as possible, we accept this imprecision and consider the replacement by an antonym as an approximation.

3.3   Approach to Negation Treatment for Cognitive Reasoning

Now, after having described our motivation for the determination of the exact negatus, we describe the implementation and evaluation of this approach. For a given text T and its corresponding first-order logic representation F, Algorithm 1 describes how we treat negations. In the beginning, some preprocessing is performed (Lines 1 and 2): For the formula F, this means the removal of double negations. For the text T, this step includes lemmatization, tokenization, part-of-speech (POS) tagging and removal of certain stopwords like "the" or "he".

Then (in Lines 3 to 10) the negation cues $x_1, \ldots, x_n$ occurring in the text T as well as the logical negations $y_1, \ldots, y_m$ in the formula F are considered. For each negation cue x_i, the set $M(x_i)$ of all words in a word window of size k around (usually after) the negation cue are determined. In our evaluation we use $k = 3$ which has been established by manually determining the position of the negatus relative to the position of the negation cue from 486 example negations of the CD-SCO train dataset. Other choices are possible and will be considered

---

Algorithm 1: Treat negations

Input:
T: natural language text (input from benchmark sample)
F: first-order logic formula for T (output from KnEWS)
k: size of word window
strategy: to determine the negatus

Result:
A: assignments $x_i \leftrightarrow y_j$ between negation cues and logical negations
N: negatus for each assignment A

1 preprocess formula F (remove double negations)
2 preprocess text T (lemmatization, tokenization, POS tagging, removal of stopwords)

3 $x_1, \ldots, x_n$ = negation cues in text T
4 **for** $i = 1, \ldots, n$ **do**
5 $\quad M(x_i)$ = word window (set) of size k around negation cue x_i (depends on *strategy*)
6 **end**
7 $y_1, \ldots, y_m$ = logical negations in first-order formula F
8 **for** $j = 1, \ldots, m$ **do**
9 $\quad M(y_j)$ = set of predicates occurring in the scope of negation y_j
10 **end**
11 **for** $i = 1, \ldots, n$ **do**
12 $\quad j = \operatorname{argmax}_\ell \left\{ |M(x_i) \cap M(y_\ell)| : \ell \in \{1, \ldots, m\} \right\}$
13 $\quad i' = \operatorname{argmax}_\ell \left\{ |M(x_\ell) \cap M(y_j)| : \ell \in \{1, \ldots, n\} \right\}$
14 $\quad$ **if** $i' = i \wedge M(x_i) \cap M(y_j) \neq \emptyset$ **then**
15 $\quad\quad A_{ij}$ = assignment $x_i \leftrightarrow y_j$
16 $\quad\quad N_{ij}$ = word w in $M(x_i)$ (negatus) according to *strategy*
17 $\quad$ **end**
18 **end**

---

in future work. Depending on the strategy we consider the word preceding the negation cue to the word window. Similarly, for each logical negation y_j, the set $M(y_j)$ of predicates occurring in the scope of negation y_j is determined.

Texts may contain several negations. In general, the number n of negation cues in the text does not coincide with the number m of logical negations in the formula. Therefore, it can happen that for some negation in the text no corresponding negation can be found in the formula or vice versa. Since in addition the order of the information in the text does not always coincide with the order of the information in the generated formula, the first negation in the text does not necessarily correspond to the first negation in the formula. Hence, it is necessary to determine a mapping between both kinds of negation. We do this as follows: The negation cue x_i and the logical negation y_j are assigned to each other if the intersection of $M(x_i)$ and $M(y_j)$ is non-empty and has maximal cardinality with respect to both indexes i and j (cf. Lines 11 to 18).

Finally, for each assignment $x_i \leftrightarrow y_j$, the negatus N_{ij} is determined. Which word is selected as negatus, depends on the specified strategy and thus on the word types of the words in the word window, including possibly the negation cue. The strategies considered are:

- *baseline:* For a negation cue that is a negated modal verb ("can't", "couldn't", "should not"), the modal verb is chosen as the negatus (i.e., "can", "could", "should"). For all other cases, the negatus is the first non-stopword in the word window. The baseline strategy was determined after manually examining the position of the negatus relative to the position of the negation cue.
- *first non-stopword strategy (FNS):* Negatus is the first non-stopword in the word window.
- *first verb strategy (FV):* Negatus is the first verb in the word window.
- *first verb or non-stopword strategy (FNS+FV):* Negatus is the first verb in the word window. Use *first non-stopword strategy* if no negatus was determined this way.
- *combination strategy (Comb):* Determine negatus word according to Table 1.

All strategies use a word window consisting of the first k non-stopwords following the negation cue – with one exception: The combination strategy uses a word window of size k which starts from the first non-stopword left of the negation cue. The negation cue is not included in the word window. Afterwards, if the determined negatus corresponds to a predicate name in the scope of the negation, formula F is adapted such that the scope only includes this predicate. Further, if possible, the negatus predicate is replaced by its inverse, i.e., an antonym, such that eventually the negation is completely removed. Antonyms are looked up in WordNet.

Table 1. Procedure to determine the negatus in the *combination strategy* for syntactic negation. For each negation cue, the table is scanned from top to bottom and the first row matching the cue is selected and applied.

Negation Cue	Negatus
can't, cannot, can not	can
couldn't, could not	could
shouldn't, should not	should
nothing, isn't, is not, aren't, are not, wasn't, was not,	
weren't, were not	first non-stopword in word window
no	first noun after negation
not, never, all other negation cues	first verb in word window
any cues, if no negatus has been determined yet	first non-stopword in word window

4   Experiments

To evaluate our approach, we use the *SEM 2012 Negation Task [22,23] as benchmark, where negations in some books by Conan Doyle are annotated (cf. Section 2.2), more precisely CD-SCO, the corpus with scope annotation that additionally provides a negatus. The sentences of the corpus are split into words which are POS-tagged. Furthermore the stem of the word and a syntax-tree for the sentence is given.

However, the *SEM 2012 Negation Task does not entirely fit to our problem. Since we only want to address syntactic negation (cf. Section 3.2), we manually created a filtered version of CD-SCO: Lexical and morphological negations are deleted, while the syntactic ones remain. This process resulted in 132 deleted samples in the train dataset, 32 deleted samples in the development (dev) dataset and 32 deleted samples in the test dataset. Additionally, we manually created an own benchmark based on the StoryClozeTest [24], taking the first 100 tasks of the StoryClozeTest that contain a syntactic negation. Each StoryClozeTest task consists of six sentences. We generated one negation task for each negation we found (126) and the second and third author of this paper annotated the negatus for each negation. We denote these benchmarks as *Cloze-NEG*. In addition to that, we evaluated our approach within the CoRg system using all problems from the StoryClozeTest.[1]

Next, we present experimental results of our approach on the CD-SCO benchmarks and compare them with results achieved by different systems in the *SEM 2012 negation task on scope resolution where also the negatus has been determined. For the *SEM 2012 Shared Task, it was possible to enter systems in two tracks: the closed and the open track. The systems in the closed track did not use any external resources. In contrast to this, the systems in the open track were allowed to use external resources as well as tools. Since our approach relies on the KnEWS system which is built on top of Boxer [8], our approach belongs to the open track and we thus compare our approach to the systems from the open track in the following. Furthermore, we use evaluation measure B of the *SEM 2012 competition where precision is computed as the number of true positives divided by the total number of a systems predictions.

4.1   Data Preparation and Evaluation

Table 2 shows the results of our approach using different strategies and results of systems in the open track of *SEM 2012 Task 1. Since we do not use machine learning in this procedure, we present our results for the training and development set as well. For the systems of *SEM 2012 Task 1, only the results on the CD-SCO test set are shown.

In the CD-SCO benchmarks, a significant proportion of examples with negation have a cue and a scope in the gold standard, but no negatus. So, the train

---

[1] All used benchmark sets, our implementation in Python, and an extended version of this paper are available at http://arxiv.org/abs/2012.12641.

Table 2. Results of our approach using the strategies described in Sect. 3.3 on the CD-SCO dataset in the upper part of the table. The lower part of the table depicts the result of the systems in the open track of *SEM 2012 Task 1.

	Train			Dev			Test		
	Prec.	Rec.	F_1	Prec.	Rec.	F_1	Prec.	Rec.	F_1
Baseline	24.56	34.31	28.63	26.17	31.97	28.78	23.14	32.37	26.99
FNS	24.56	34.31	28.63	26.17	31.98	28.78	23.14	32.37	26.99
FV	19.75	20.65	20.19	22.52	20.49	21.46	24.42	24.28	24.35
FV+FNS	22.47	31.38	26.19	26.85	32.79	29.52	23.55	32.95	27.47
Comb.	35.39	49.43	41.25	34.90	42.62	38.38	34.71	48.55	40.48
UiO2							63.82	57.40	60.44
UGroningen r2							55.22	65.29	59.83
UGroningen r1							52.66	52.05	52.35
UCM-1							66.67	12.72	21.36
UCM-2							44.44	21.18	28.69

dataset contains 3,643 text passages with a total of 3,779 lines in the gold standard data. Of these lines, 983 contain a negation. However, in only 615 of these cases a negatus is specified in the gold standard. In contrast to this, our approach often finds a negatus in these cases. We report numbers for the CD-SCO benchmarks in Table 3 for the filtered CD-SCO benchmarks where only negations with negatus specification in the gold standard are considered. Of course, sometimes there are cases where indeed no negatus should be specified like in direct speech and elliptic utterances, where negations refer back to the previous sentence.

Table 3. Results of our approach using the strategies described in Sect. 3.3 on the filtered CD-SCO dataset. For the calculation of precision cases where our approach found a negatus but the gold standard did not specify a negatus were not included.

	Train Filtered			Dev Filtered			Test Filtered		
	Prec.	Rec.	F_1	Prec.	Rec.	F_1	Prec.	Rec.	F_1
Baseline	44.56	43.83	44.19	44.09	44.09	44.09	42.25	41.10	41.67
FNS	44.56	43.38	44.19	44.09	44.09	44.09	42.25	41.10	41.67
FV	36.71	26.13	30.53	42.86	29.03	34.62	44.21	28.77	34.85
FV+FNS	40.79	40.12	40.46	47.31	47.31	47.31	42.96	41.78	42.36
Comb.	64.02	62.96	63.49	58.06	58.06	58.06	61.97	60.27	61.11

Although the CD-SCO benchmarks do not exactly reflect what we are trying to achieve with our approach, the option combination strategy still ranks in the midfield of the systems that participated in *SEM 2012. In addition to that, we tested our approach on the 100 manually labeled StoryClozeTest tasks, the Cloze-NEG benchmarks. The results are depicted in Table 4. To check whether our approach is suitable for our purpose of identifying the negatus, the Cloze-NEG benchmarks are the most suitable ones. This is because only these benchmarks aim to determine a word in the scope of the negation that, when replaced by its antonym, leads to the removal of the negation. The results on the StoryClozeTest benchmarks show that the option combination strategy is often able to identify the negatus. Furthermore, we observe that for all considered benchmarks, the option combination strategy seems to be the most suitable for identifying the negatus.

Table 4. Results of our approach on the 100 manually labeled StoryClozeTest tasks.

	Cloze-NEG		
	Prec.	Rec.	F_1
Baseline	59.52	59.52	59.52
FNS	57.85	55.56	56.68
FV	54.33	49.21	51.67
FV+FNS	56.35	56.35	56.35
Comb.	66.67	66.67	66.67

As explained above, an unnecessarily large scope of a negation in a formula belonging to a commonsense reasoning problem causes the Hyper reasoner in the CoRg system to perform only few inferences and, in the extreme case, to return an empty model. To evaluate the benefit of our approach within the CoRg system, we integrated our approach into the system and used it on the whole set of problems in the StoryClozeTest. By this, the amount of completely empty models was reduced by 71.95% from 164 to 46. Overall, the negation treatment resulted in an increase in the average number of distinct predicate names per model from 18.83 to 19.35 with an overall gain of distinct predicate names of 5,726 in 11,119 models. This demonstrates that our negation handling enables the theorem prover to derive additional information, which in return can be used by further processing, in our case the neural network. We hope that these encouraging results will facilitate using automated reasoning in commonsense reasoning.

5   Summary, Conclusions, and Future Work

In this paper, we presented a way to detect syntactic negation in natural language using KnEWS, which is important in cognitive reasoning systems. This is why we want to replace negative information through a positive counterpart, its inverse. To achieve this, the negatus has to be identified and later on be replaced by its inverse. Our approach detects syntactic negation and identifies the negatus by combining the information from the generated KnEWS formula and from the natural language input itself.

We apply different strategies for identifying the negatus. The combination strategy apparently works best and ranks in the midfield of the *SEM 2012 negation task. Our evaluation of the StoryClozeTest yields comparable results. With the help of our approach for negation handling, we improved the input of the theorem prover Hyper in the CoRg system. This resulted in a decrease of the number of empty models by 71.95% and an average increase of 0.53 distinct predicates per model. This demonstrates an information gain which is useful for later processing in the CoRg system.

In future work, we aim to improve our negation handling by applying other strategies in more detail. Furthermore we shall use the inverse of the negatus in commonsense reasoning. So far, we implemented a first approach looking up the antonyms of the detected negatus from WordNet. Since eventually we work with neural networks and word embeddings (cf. [29]), another idea is to directly generate word embeddings by using an inverse operator. The overall goal is to implement a cognitive reasoning system with an adequate treatment of syntactic negation.

References

1. Agirre, E., Bos, J., Diab, M., Manandhar, S., Marton, Y., Yuret, D. (eds.): *SEM 2012: the first joint conference on lexical and computational semantics - volume 1: Proceedings of the main conference and the shared task, and Volume 2: Proceedings of the Sixth International Workshop on Semantic Evaluation (SemEval 2012). Association for Computational Linguistics, Montréal, Canada (2012). http://www.aclweb.org/anthology/volumes/S12-1/

2. Álvez, J., Lucio, P., Rigau, G.: Adimen-SUMO: reengineering an ontology for first-order reasoning. Int. J. Semant. Web Inf. Syst. 8(4), 80–116 (2012). http://doi.org/10.4018/jswis.2012100105

3. Antoniou, G.: A tutorial on default logics. ACM Comput. Surv. 31(4), 337–359 (1999). http://doi.org/10.1145/344588.344602

4. Basile, V., Bos, J., Evang, K., Venhuizen, N.: UGroningen: negation detection with discourse representation structures. In: Agirre et al. [1], pp. 301–309. http://www.aclweb.org/anthology/S12-1040

5. Basile, V., Cabrio, E., Schon, C.: KNEWS: using logical and lexical semantics to extract knowledge from natural language. In: Proceedings of the European Conference on Artificial Intelligence (ECAI) (2016). http://hal.inria.fr/hal-01389390

6. Baumgartner, P., Furbach, U., Pelzer, B.: The hyper tableaux calculus with equality and an application to finite model computation. J. Log. Comput. 20(1), 77–109 (2010). http://doi.org/10.1093/logcom/exn061

7. Bender, M., Pelzer, B., Schon, C.: System description: E-KRHyper 1.4. In: Bonacina, M.P. (ed.) CADE 2013. LNCS (LNAI), vol. 7898, pp. 126–134. Springer, Heidelberg (2013). https://doi.org/10.1007/978-3-642-38574-2_8

8. Bos, J.: Wide-coverage semantic analysis with Boxer. In: Semantics in Text Processing. STEP 2008 Conference Proceedings, pp. 277–286. College Publications (2008). http://www.aclweb.org/anthology/W08-2222

9. Devlin, J., Chang, M., Lee, K., Toutanova, K.: BERT: pre-training of deep bidirectional transformers for language understanding. In: Burstein, J., Doran, C., Solorio, T. (eds.) Proceedings of the 2019 Conference of the North American Chapter of the Association for Computational Linguistics: Human Language Technologies, NAACL-HLT, Volume 1 (Long and Short Papers), pp. 4171–4186. Association for Computational Linguistics (2019). http://aclweb.org/anthology/papers/N/N19/N19-1423/

10. Furbach, U., Hölldobler, S., Ragni, M., Schon, C., Stolzenburg, F.: Cognitive reasoning: a personal view. KI **33**(3), 209–217 (2019). http://link.springer.com/article/10.1007/s13218-019-00603-3

11. Habernal, I., Wachsmuth, H., Gurevych, I., Stein, B.: SemEval-2018 task 12: the argument reasoning comprehension task. In: Proceedings of The 12th International Workshop on Semantic Evaluation. pp. 763–772. Association for Computational Linguistics, New Orleans, Louisiana (June 2018). http://www.aclweb.org/anthology/S18-1121

12. Horn, L.R., Wansing, H.: Negation. In: Zalta, E.N. (ed.): Stanford Encyclopedia of Philosophy. Metaphysics Research Lab, Stanford University (2020). http://plato.stanford.edu/entries/negation/

13. Janssen, T.M.V., Zimmermann, T.E.: Montague semantics. In: Zalta, E.N. (ed.): Stanford Encyclopedia of Philosophy. Metaphysics Research Lab, Stanford University (2021). http://plato.stanford.edu/archives/sum2021/entries/montague-semantics/

14. Jiménez-Zafra, S.M., Morante, R., Teresa Martín-Valdivia, M., Ureña-López, L.A.: Corpora annotated with negation: an overview. Comput. Linguist. **46**(1), 1–52 (2020). http://doi.org/10.1162/coli_a_00371

15. Jurafsky, D., H. James, M.: Vector semantics and embeddings. In: Speech and Language Processing: an Introduction to Natural Language Processing, Computational Linguistics, and Speech Recognition, chap. 6, pp. 96–126. Prentice Hall, Upper Saddle River, N.J., 3rd edn. (2020). http://web.stanford.edu/~jurafsky/slp3/ed3book.pdf. Draft

16. Kamp, H., Reyle, U.: From discourse to logic: an introduction to modeltheoretic semantics of natural language, formal logic and discourse representation theory. Springer, Dordrecht (1993). http://www.springer.com/de/book/9780792310280

17. Kolhatkar, V., Wu, H., Cavasso, L., Francis, E., Shukla, K., Taboada, M.: The SFU opinion and comments corpus: a corpus for the analysis of online news comments. Corpus Pragmat. **4**, 155–190 (2020). http://link.springer.com/article/10.1007/s41701-019-00065-w

18. Liu, H., Singh, P.: ConceptNet - a practical commonsense reasoning tool-kit. BT Technol. J. **22**(4), 211–226 (2004). http://doi.org/10.1023/B:BTTJ.0000047600.45421.6d

19. Lyons, J.: Semantics, vol. 2. Cambridge University Press, Cambridge, New York, Melbourne, Madrid (1977). http://doi.org/10.1017/CBO9780511620614

20. Maslan, N., Roemmele, M., Gordon, A.S.: One hundred challenge problems for logical formalizations of commonsense psychology. In: Twelfth International Symposium on Logical Formalizations of Commonsense Reasoning, Stanford, CA (2015). http://www.aaai.org/ocs/index.php/SSS/SSS15/paper/viewFile/10252/10080

21. Miller, G.A.: WordNet: a lexical database for English. Commun. ACM **38**(11), 39–41 (1995). http://doi.org/10.1145/219717.219748

22. Morante, R., Blanco, E.: *SEM 2012 shared task: resolving the scope and focus of negation. In: Agirre et al. [1], pp. 265–274. http://www.aclweb.org/anthology/S12-1035

23. Morante, R., Daelemans, W.: ConanDoyle-neg: annotation of negation cues and their scope in Conan Doyle stories. In: Proceedings of the Eighth International Conference on Language Resources and Evaluation (LREC'12). pp. 1563–1568. European Language Resources Association (ELRA), Istanbul, Turkey (2012). http://www.lrec-conf.org/proceedings/lrec2012/pdf/221_Paper.pdf

24. Mostafazadeh, N., Roth, M., Louis, A., Chambers, N., Allen, J.: LSDSem 2017 shared task: the story cloze test. In: Proceedings of the 2nd Workshop on Linking Models of Lexical, Sentential and Discourse-level Semantics, pp. 46–51 (2017). http://doi.org/10.18653/v1/w17-0906

25. Mueller, E.T.: Commonsense Reasoning. Morgan Kaufmann, San Francisco, 2nd edn. (2014). http://dl.acm.org/doi/book/10.5555/2821577

26. Niven, T., Kao, H.Y.: Probing neural network comprehension of natural language arguments. In: Proceedings of the 57th Annual Meeting of the Association for Computational Linguistics, pp. 4658–4664. Association for Computational Linguistics, Florence, Italy (July 2019). http://www.aclweb.org/anthology/P19-1459

27. Radford, A., Narasimhan, K., Salimans, T., Sutskever, I.: Improving language understanding by generative pre-training. Technical report, Open AI (2018). http://openai.com/blog/language-unsupervised/

28. Schon, C., Siebert, S., Stolzenburg, F.: The CoRg project: cognitive reasoning. KI **33**(3), 293–299 (2019). http://link.springer.com/article/10.1007/s13218-019-00601-5

29. Siebert, S., Schon, C., Stolzenburg, F.: Commonsense reasoning using theorem proving and machine learning. In: Holzinger, A., Kieseberg, P., Tjoa, A.M., Weippl, E. (eds.) CD-MAKE 2019. LNCS, vol. 11713, pp. 395–413. Springer, Cham (2019). https://doi.org/10.1007/978-3-030-29726-8_25

30. Speer, R., Chin, J., Havasi, C.: ConceptNet 5.5: an open multilingual graph of general knowledge. In: AAAI Conference on Artificial Intelligence, pp. 4444–4451 (2017). http://aaai.org/ocs/index.php/AAAI/AAAI17/paper/view/14972

Learning to Detect Adversarial Examples Based on Class Scores

Tobias Uelwer[1]([⊠]), Felix Michels[1], and Oliver De Candido[2]

[1] Department of Computer Science, Heinrich Heine University Düsseldorf,
Düsseldorf, Germany
{tobias.uelwer,felix.michels}@hhu.de
[2] Department of Electrical and Computer Engineering,
Technical University of Munich, Munich, Germany
oliver.de-candido@tum.de

Abstract. Given the increasing threat of adversarial attacks on deep neural networks (DNNs), research on efficient detection methods is more important than ever. In this work, we take a closer look at adversarial attack detection based on the class scores of an already trained classification model. We propose to train a support vector machine (SVM) on the class scores to detect adversarial examples. Our method is able to detect adversarial examples generated by various attacks, and can be easily adopted to a plethora of deep classification models. We show that our approach yields an improved detection rate compared to an existing method, whilst being easy to implement. We perform an extensive empirical analysis on different deep classification models, investigating various state-of-the-art adversarial attacks. Moreover, we observe that our proposed method is better at detecting a combination of adversarial attacks. This work indicates the potential of detecting various adversarial attacks simply by using the class scores of an already trained classification model.

Keywords: Adversarial example detection · Class scores · Image classification models · Deep learning

1 Introduction

In recent years, deep neural networks (DNNs) have demonstrated exemplary performance on image classification tasks [9,18,20]. However, in their seminal work, Goodfellow et al. [7] have shown that these deep models can easily be deceived into misclassifying inputs by using adversarial examples (i.e., perturbed input images). These perturbed images can be crafted in a white-box setting where the attacker is given access to the (unnormalized) class scores of the DNN classifier, and is able to calculate gradients with respect to the input image. In contrast, in the black-box setting, the attacker is only able to observe the models final decision and cannot perform any gradient calculations. In this work, we consider the white-box setting as well as the black-box setting.

© Springer Nature Switzerland AG 2021
S. Edelkamp et al. (Eds.): KI 2021, LNAI 12873, pp. 233–240, 2021.
https://doi.org/10.1007/978-3-030-87626-5_17

The importance of adversarial defenses is evident, if we consider the wide variety of safety-critical domains where DNNs are employed, e.g., in medical imaging [15], in autonomous driving [5,19], or in face recognition [4]. As defined in [21], there are three main adversarial defense mechanisms: (i) gradient masking, (ii) robust optimization, and (iii) adversarial example detection. In this paper, we focus on the latter mechanism, and propose a method to detect adversarial examples based on the output class scores.

1.1 Related Work

One of the first methods to robustify the optimization of DNNs was proposed by Goodfellow et al. in [7]. The main idea is to adopt adversarial training by augmenting the training dataset with adversarial examples. This robustifies the model and it has been shown that adversarial training makes the model less susceptible to adversarial attacks of the same type. Grosse et al. [8] suggest adversarial retraining with an additional class for the adversarial examples. These retraining methods, however, are very time consuming as one not only has to generate many adversarial examples to train on, but one also needs to retrain the whole DNN.

To overcome the computational costs required to robustify optimization via adversarial training, researchers have focused on adversarial example detection instead. On the one hand, one can attempt to detect the adversarial examples in the input domain. Thereby, training an additional model to classify whether the input image is clean or not [13]. Another possibility is to detect the adversarial examples in the input space using a smaller DNN classifier, which is easier to train than the original DNN.

On the other hand, one can investigate the latent representations within the DNN to detect adversarial examples. Papernot and McDaniel [14] propose training a k-nearest neighbors classifier on the representations in each layer of a DNN to estimate whether a given input conforms with the labels of the surrounding representations. They show that this method provides a better estimate for the confidence of the DNN, and can also detect adversarial examples. In the limit, one can use the output class scores to detect adversarial examples. Kwon et al. [12] propose a method to detect adversarial examples by thresholding the difference of the highest and second highest class scores at the output of the DNN.

1.2 Contributions

The contributions of this work can be summarized as follows:

1. We propose to train a support vector machine (SVM) [3] with a radial basis function (RBF) kernel on the class scores to detect adversarial examples.
2. We empirically evaluate our method against the adversarial detection method by Kwon et al. [12], and show that our method improves the detection performance of different adversarial attacks on various deep classification models.

3. Furthermore, we observe that our method is better at detecting a combination of two adversarial attacks, compared with [12].

2   Detecting Adversarial Examples from Class Scores

For an input image x we denote the class scores that the attacked classification model F predicts by $F(x)$. Instead of retraining the whole model from scratch, we take advantage of the fact that adversarial attacks can be detected by classifying the class scores predicted by F. To this end, we train an SVM [3] with an RBF kernel on the class scores to detect whether unseen images have been altered or not. In order to perform adversarial example detection we proceed as follows:

1. We construct a dataset $X_{\mathrm{adv}} = \{\tilde{x}_1, \ldots, \tilde{x}_n\}$ that contains a perturbed instance of each image in the training dataset $X_{\mathrm{train}} = \{x_1, \ldots, x_n\}$.
2. We train the SVM on $X_{\mathrm{scores}} = \{F(x_1), \ldots, F(x_n), F(\tilde{x}_1), \ldots, F(\tilde{x}_n)\}$ to predict the label 1 for samples coming from X_{train} and -1 for samples from X_{adv} based on the outputs of F.
3. At test time, the trained SVM can then be used to detect adversarial examples based on the class score $F(x_{\mathrm{new}})$ where x_{new} is a new (possibly adversarial) input image.

To the best of our knowledge, only Kwon et al. [12] also use class scores to classify adversarial and non-adversarial inputs. In contrast to our method, they solely threshold the difference between the two largest scores. We argue that this approach discards valuable information contained in the class scores. Moreover, they choose the threshold value by hand, instead of optimizing for it. Our approach can be seen as a generalization to this method as we classify adversarial and non-adversarial input images by taking all of the class scores into account.

3   Experimental Setup

We calculate adversarial examples on three different pre-trained DNN architectures. Namely, the VGG19 [18], GoogLeNet [20], and ResNet18 [9]. All models were trained on the CIFAR-10 image recognition dataset [10]. To evaluate the efficiency of our proposed detection method, we consider adversarial examples produced by the basic iterative method (BIM) [11], the fast gradient sign method (FGSM) [7], the boundary attack [1], and the Carlini-Wagner (CW) method [2]. BIM, FGSM and CW are white-box attacks, whereas the boundary attack is a black-box attack. We use the implementations provided by the Python 3 package Foolbox [16, 17].

Moreover, we analyze the detection performance on a combination of two different attacks at the same time, i.e., we also consider detecting adversarial perturbations produced by CW and BIM, CW and FGSM, boundary attack and BIM, and boundary attack and FGSM. When detecting a single attack, the training dataset consists of original images and adversarial images in the ratio

1 : 1, whereas when detecting two attacks the ratio is 2 : 1 : 1 for original images, adversarial images from the first attack and adversarial images from the second attack, respectively.

For FGSM, we choose the step size ϵ individually for each model in a way that the attack is successful in 50% of the cases. We run BIM for 100 steps with a relative step size of 0.2 while allowing random starts. Again, we tune the maximum Euclidean norm of the perturbation for each model to achieve a success rate of approximately 95%. For the CW method we tune the step size and the number of steps for each model until all perturbed inputs were misclassified. We run the boundary attack for 25 000 steps which is the default value of the parameter in the Foolbox implementation.

To determine the threshold used in the detection method from Kwon et al. [12], we use a decision stump trained using the Gini index [6]. The regularization parameter C of the SVM and the kernel-bandwidth γ of the RBF kernel are optimized using a coarse-to-fine gridsearch.

4   Results

On the original test dataset (in absence of adversarial examples), the VGG19 achieves a classification accuracy of 93.95%, the GoogLeNet 92.85%, and the ResNet18 93.07%. In Table 1, we summarize the performance of the adversarial attacks, i.e., the classification accuracy on the test dataset after the attack. It also shows the average Euclidean norm of the perturbations for each classification model with the classification performance in the unattacked setting. In our experiments, the CW method and the boundary method produced images with the lowest average perturbation norm across all pre-trained DNN classifiers. Moreover, the CW method is more consistent at lowering the classification accuracy and strictly lower than the other attacks for each DNN. These advantages, however, come at the price of higher computational effort.

Table 1. Comparison of the classification accuracies on the adversarial examples for each model and the average Euclidean norm of the added perturbations.

Attack	Accuracy on adversarial examples			Average perturbation norm		
	VGG19	GoogLeNet	ResNet18	VGG19	GoogLeNet	ResNet18
FGSM	39.97%	39.85%	40.18%	17.6232	0.2575	2.7183
BIM	5.17%	4.29%	4.49%	8.9903	0.0484	0.2303
Boundary	8.99%	25.75%	1.39%	0.0515	0.0209	0.0849
CW	4.75%	0.55%	0.30%	0.2461	0.0140	0.0559

In Fig. 1, we visualize eight randomly selected, perturbed images from attacks on the ResNet18. Most of the adversarial examples are unnoticeable to the human eye compared to the original image, especially those produced by the

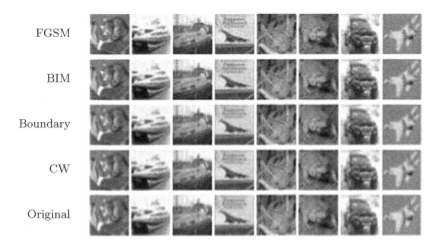

Fig. 1. Adversarial perturbations calculated for the ResNet18.

Table 2. Comparison of adversarial attack classification performance for single attacks.

Model	Attack	Accuracy		F_1 score	
		Kwon et al. [12]	Ours	Kwon et al. [12]	Ours
VGG19	FGSM	71.60%	**82.08%**	68.43%	**82.05%**
	BIM	85.20%	**98.70%**	84.47%	**98.69%**
	Boundary	**97.53%**	96.30%	**97.44%**	96.25%
	CW	89.90%	**90.05%**	89.99%	**90.16%**
GoogLeNet	FGSM	72.60%	**76.05%**	73.69%	**74.48%**
	BIM	81.50%	**83.60%**	77.88%	**82.38%**
	Boundary	**96.50%**	95.50%	**96.35%**	95.45%
	CW	93.65%	**93.80%**	93.58%	**93.76%**
ResNet18	FGSM	70.40%	**72.58%**	69.23%	**71.37%**
	BIM	85.48%	**89.48%**	83.68%	**88.96%**
	Boundary	**97.20%**	96.28%	**97.10%**	96.19%
	CW	93.53%	**93.58%**	93.63%	**93.65%**

CW and the boundary methods. However, the perturbations calculated by the FGSM are more recognizable since the backgrounds of the images are altered. Similar conclusions can be made when observing the perturbed images generated from the other DNNs, i.e., VGG19 and GoogLeNet.

Ultimately, we are interested in detecting these adversarial examples, i.e., classifying whether an input sample is adversarial or not. To this end, we compare the classification performance of our proposed SVM-based method to the method introduced in [12]. As described in Sect. 2, their method only thresholds

Table 3. Comparison of adversarial attack classification performance for combined attacks.

Model	Attack	Accuracy		F_1 Score	
		Kwon et al. [12]	Ours	Kwon et al. [12]	Ours
VGG19	CW+BIM	67.38%	**89.90%**	54.80%	**90.08%**
	CW+FGSM	80.75%	**83.65%**	79.90%	**83.14%**
	Boundary+BIM	73.45%	**95.88%**	63.73%	**95.85%**
	Boundary+FGSM	82.45%	**85.80%**	81.92%	**84.85%**
GoogLeNet	CW+BIM	70.93%	**84.08%**	59.66%	**83.92%**
	CW+FGSM	79.68%	**82.35%**	79.28%	**81.37%**
	Boundary+BIM	73.60%	**84.93%**	63.89%	**84.57%**
	Boundary+FGSM	78.93%	**80.93%**	78.53%	**79.58%**
ResNet18	CW+BIM	70.45%	**88.30%**	60.49%	**88.40%**
	CW+FGSM	78.68%	**79.33%**	79.03%	**79.52%**
	Boundary+BIM	72.73%	**90.05%**	62.16%	**89.61%**
	Boundary+FGSM	77.93%	**78.85%**	**78.31%**	77.76%

the difference between the highest and second highest class score and therefore disregards important information. The classification performance, i.e., the binary classification accuracy and the F_1 score, for the various attacks on the different models are depicted in Table 2. We observe that our method outperforms theirs in all cases except for the boundary attack, however, the difference is small for all DNNs. This could be explained by the fact that the boundary attack is a black-box attack which only considers the predicted class and not the class scores. On the other hand, we observe that our method increases the performance of detecting adversarial images produced by BIM and FGSM by more than 10% for the pre-trained VGG19. It is also able to better detect adversarial examples generated by BIM and FGSM on GoogLeNet and ResNet18.

Since the defender might not know a priori which attack the attacker will use, it would be useful for an adversarial example detection method to be capable of detecting a combination of different attacks. To this end, we simulate combinations of attacks and summarize the classification performance in Table 3. We observe that our SVM-based method performs better in almost all cases. In combinations of attacks which include BIM, our method improves the detection performance both in terms of the binary classification accuracy and the F_1 score.

5   Conclusion

In this paper, we propose a SVM-based method that detects adversarial attacks using the class scores of a DNN. Our detection method does not require one to retrain the model and achieves reasonable detection performance. Moreover, we are able to show that our method is capable to detect adversarial images produced by different attacks at the same time. These results indicate the potential of training adversarial example detection methods only using the class scores. This is a simple and effective measure to help defend against adversarial attacks, which is especially important in safety-critical applications.

References

1. Brendel, W., Rauber, J., Bethge, M.: Decision-based adversarial attacks: reliable attacks against black-box machine learning models. In: International Conference on Learning Representations (2018). https://openreview.net/forum?id=SyZIOGWCZ
2. Carlini, N., Wagner, D.: Towards evaluating the robustness of neural networks. In: 2017 IEEE Symposium on Security and Privacy (sp), pp. 39–57. IEEE (2017)
3. Cortes, C., Vapnik, V.: Support-vector networks. Mach. Learn. **20**(3), 273–297 (1995)
4. Dong, Y., et al.: Efficient decision-based black-box adversarial attacks on face recognition. In: Proceedings of the IEEE/CVF Conference on Computer Vision and Pattern Recognition, pp. 7714–7722 (2019)
5. Eykholt, K., et al.: Robust physical-world attacks on deep learning visual classification. In: Proceedings of the IEEE Conference on Computer Vision and Pattern Recognition, pp. 1625–1634 (2018)
6. Friedman, J.: Greedy function approximation: a gradient boosting machine. Ann. Stat. **29**(5), 1189–1232 (2001). http://www.jstor.org/stable/2699986
7. Goodfellow, I.J., Shlens, J., Szegedy, C.: Explaining and harnessing adversarial examples. arXiv preprint arXiv:1412.6572 (2014)
8. Grosse, K., Manoharan, P., Papernot, N., Backes, M., McDaniel, P.: On the (statistical) detection of adversarial examples. arXiv preprint arXiv:1702.06280 (2017)
9. He, K., Zhang, X., Ren, S., Sun, J.: Deep residual learning for image recognition. In: Proceedings of the IEEE Conference on Computer Vision and Pattern Recognition, pp. 770–778 (2016)
10. Krizhevsky, A., Hinton, G., et al.: Learning multiple layers of features from tiny images (2009)
11. Kurakin, A., Goodfellow, I., Bengio, S.: Adversarial examples in the physical world. arXiv preprint arXiv:1607.02533 (2016)
12. Kwon, H., Kim, Y., Yoon, H., Choi, D.: Classification score approach for detecting adversarial example in deep neural network. Multimed. Tools Appl. **80**(7), 10339–10360 (2020). https://doi.org/10.1007/s11042-020-09167-z
13. Metzen, J.H., Genewein, T., Fischer, V., Bischoff, B.: On detecting adversarial perturbations. arXiv preprint arXiv:1702.04267 (2017)
14. Papernot, N., McDaniel, P.: Deep k-nearest neighbors: Towards confident, interpretable and robust deep learning. arXiv preprint arXiv:1803.04765 (2018)
15. Paschali, M., Conjeti, S., Navarro, F., Navab, N.: Generalizability vs. robustness: investigating medical imaging networks using adversarial examples. In: Frangi, A.F., Schnabel, J.A., Davatzikos, C., Alberola-López, C., Fichtinger, G. (eds.) MICCAI 2018. LNCS, vol. 11070, pp. 493–501. Springer, Cham (2018). https://doi.org/10.1007/978-3-030-00928-1_56
16. Rauber, J., Brendel, W., Bethge, M.: Foolbox: a python toolbox to benchmark the robustness of machine learning models. In: Reliable Machine Learning in the Wild Workshop, 34th International Conference on Machine Learning (2017). http://arxiv.org/abs/1707.04131
17. Rauber, J., Zimmermann, R., Bethge, M., Brendel, W.: Foolbox native: fast adversarial attacks to benchmark the robustness of machine learning models in pytorch, tensorflow, and jax. J. Open Sour. Softw. **5**(53), 2607 (2020). https://doi.org/10.21105/joss.02607
18. Simonyan, K., Zisserman, A.: Very deep convolutional networks for large-scale image recognition. arXiv preprint arXiv:1409.1556 (2014)

19. Sitawarin, C., Bhagoji, A.N., Mosenia, A., Chiang, M., Mittal, P.: Darts: deceiving autonomous cars with toxic signs. arXiv preprint arXiv:1802.06430 (2018)
20. Szegedy, C., et al.: Going deeper with convolutions. In: Proceedings of the IEEE Conference on Computer Vision and Pattern Recognition, pp. 1–9 (2015)
21. Xu, H., et al.: Adversarial attacks and defenses in images, graphs and text: a review. Int. J. Autom. Comput. **17**(2), 151–178 (2020)

An Agent Architecture for Knowledge Discovery and Evolution

Tezira Wanyana[1,2]([✉]) [iD] and Deshendran Moodley[1,2] [iD]

[1] Department of Computer Science, University of Cape Town (UCT),
Cape Town, South Africa
{twanyana,deshen}@cs.uct.ac.za
[2] Center for Artificial Intelligence Research (CAIR),
Cape Town, South Africa

Abstract. The abductive theory of method (ATOM) was recently proposed to describe the process that scientists use for knowledge discovery. In this paper we propose an agent architecture for knowledge discovery and evolution (KDE) based on ATOM. The agent incorporates a combination of ontologies, rules and Bayesian networks for representing different aspects of its internal knowledge. The agent uses an external AI service to detect unexpected situations from incoming observations. It then uses rules to analyse the current situation and a Bayesian network for finding plausible explanations for unexpected situations. The architecture is evaluated and analysed on a use case application for monitoring daily household electricity consumption patterns.

Keywords: Agent architecture · BDI · Knowledge discovery and evolution · Abductive theory of method

1 Introduction

With the advent of low cost sensors, and advances in wireless and broad band technology there is an increasing interest in software agents as a paradigm for modeling and developing intelligent monitoring applications among others, for ambient assisted living and wellness, entertainment, logistics, energy management and industrial automation [23]. Continuous observations from the physical systems being monitored may contain new patterns which, when followed up can lead to knowledge discovery and evolution (KDE) [12].

While KDE is routinely performed by humans, formalising and automating the KDE process is difficult. In Philosophy of Science (PoS), KDE focuses on theories and methods that scientists apply in theory discovery and justification. With prominent theories of scientific discovery like the inductive theory and the hypothetico-deductive (HD) theory of method, philosophers of science have sought to lay out the discovery process in an orderly manner. The inductive

Supported by Hasso Plattner Institute (HPI) for Digital Engineering.

S. Edelkamp et al. (Eds.): KI 2021, LNAI 12873, pp. 241–256, 2021.
https://doi.org/10.1007/978-3-030-87626-5_18

theory focuses on creating and justifying theories by discovering empirical generalizations in the data while in HD, the scientist acquires a hypothesis and aims to test it's predictive success [10]. A more recent abductive theory of method (ATOM) [10, 11] consists of two overarching processes i.e. *phenomenon detection* in which phenomena (unexplained "relatively stable, recurrent, general features that researchers aim to explain in the data") are detected and *theory construction* whereby possible explanations are provided for the detected phenomena. The phenomenon detection process consists of four activities i.e. initial data analysis, exploratory data analysis, close replication and constructive replication which in our work translate to preprocessing, model building, pattern recognition and confirmation. Theory construction encompasses three major activities; theory generation, theory development and theory appraisal.

ATOM provides a more encompassing theory of method and deals with some of the limitations of the HD and inductive methods. It provides a concrete approach for formulating and generating theories and it provides explanations for the obtained empirical generalization. ATOM accommodates both top down and bottom up AI techniques [32] and, while it emanates from the behavioural sciences, it is applicable to a broad array of complex social, physical and sociotechnical systems, especially for KDE in intelligent monitoring applications.

In this paper, we explore and propose a generic architecture for a KDE agent inspired by ATOM. We use an example of a real world data driven sensor application for monitoring and understanding daily electricity consumption behaviour in households across South Africa [29–31] to design and analyse the architecture.

We identify two key actors in the agent's environment i.e. external AI service and the (human) domain expert. The agent uses the AI service for pattern and anomaly detection and relies on the domain expert for knowledge acquisition and theory appraisal. Internally, the agent incorporates a combination of ontologies, rules and Bayesian networks to represent knowledge and generate explanations for unexpected patterns. The architecture shows how different AI techniques can be used to deal with situation detection and analysis, generating explanations and updating the agents beliefs to reflect changes in the physical system.

The rest of the paper is organised as follows: Sect. 2 presents the background and related work. Section 3 presents the design of the architecture. In Sect. 4, we discuss the proposed KDE architecture and present an evaluation of the architecture by demonstrating its applicability in the domestic electricity consumption domain in Sect. 5. We then discuss and conclude in Sect. 6.

2   Background and Related Work

2.1   The BDI Architecture

The BDI architecture is one of the most prominent agent architectures [21, 22]. It views an agent as consisting of three mental attitudes i.e. beliefs, desires and intention. Beliefs consist of the agent's knowledge about its environment, itself and other agents. Desires motivate the agent since they represent its objectives or goals. Intentions represent a subset of desires that the agent has committed to achieving. At run-time, in response to the percepts, the BDI interpreter updates the agent's beliefs and goals and manages intentions [3].

The BDI language is advantageous in agent development because it allows "rapid development, context sensitive and robust behavior, intelligibility and verifiability due to its descriptive and intuitive nature, it facilitates a range of symbolic, stochastic and sub-symbolic AI techniques", formalises the reasoning process in a straightforward way, facilitates "knowledge capture, representation and debugging" and allows the exploitation of available qualitative information, commonsense evidence and psychological theories in the modelling process [1,3]. However, the BDI architecture was originally designed for practical reasoning in real-time planning applications [4]. In its original form, it may not be able to support a KDE agent in more complex data-driven physical systems. The architecture does not provide specific support for processing and detecting patterns from large amounts of data. While it supports mechanisms for deliberation and decision making, generating explanations for non-technical human users is not a primary objective. Supplementing typical BDI agents with machine learning services can deal with pattern recognition. While, at first glance one may be inclined to abstract this out and consider it to be just an implementation or engineering issue, which is internal to the agent's perception and deliberation modules, not explicitly considering this can affect its adoption and usage for implementing real world intelligent monitoring systems.

2.2   Integrating AI into BDI Agents

BDI agents can be enriched by drawing from and incorporating a variety of AI techniques in a number of ways. Bordini et al., [3] discuss the applicability of AI in the sensing, planning and acting phases of BDI agents e.g. in the sensing phase, AI can be used to enrich and update the underlying knowledge representation to handle complex ontologies [17,19] or to work with probabilistic knowledge, beliefs and goals using Bayesian networks [25]. Bordini et al., also present some approaches for integrating AI into the BDI agent architecture i.e. i) AI as a service, an exogenous approach where the agent exploits AI e.g. external image/speech recognition and document analysis. ii) AI embedded into agents, an endogenous approach in which AI components replace or complement the standard elements of the BDI architecture or cycle e.g. the use of Bayesian networks in [7]. iii) hybrid approach in which some AI components are endogenous and others are exogenous. Complementing agents with AI services would leverage complex AI algorithms providing advanced analytical processing, making predictions and supporting knowledge discovery from data [18]. Some architectures are discussed in [18] in which the agent and the AI service can co-exist and co-operate to deliver decision support, one of which (shown in Fig. 1) caught our attention because it can potentially be applied in a KDE agent. In a KDE task environment, different AI algorithms can be applied as part of external AI services to enable the adaptability of the agent by facilitating the understanding of the behavior of data acquired from the operation domain as well as the detection of new patterns in new observations. In [7] on the other hand, an endogenous

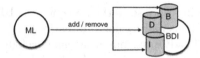

Fig. 1. The AI service (ML component) influences latter agent activities e.g. by adding plans or beliefs that could be synthesised from the agent's operation domain [18].

approach is followed where Bayesian networks are used internally to abstract the BDI mental states and to deliberate about and select the optimal action.

2.3 KDE Systems and Approaches

KDE encompasses pattern detection in observations, situation detection and understanding or explaining their occurrence in order to update or improve the body of knowledge in the respective domain. Patterns, which result from a data mining step [28] are a subset of data behaving the same way [27].

A recent study done to design an agent architecture for novelty detection, characterisation and accommodation in a changing world [20] presents a promising approach when agents encounter sudden changes in their environments. However, it is limited when the agent's role is to detect novel situations in observations with the goal of explaining them. In [24], a domain-specific architecture that combines ML with automated reasoning is applied in taxonomic intelligence i.e. discovering patterns of taxonomic identity and change which involves learning from biodiversity data and reasoning over existing biodiversity knowledge.

Some systems have been designed for KDE e.g. the Robot scientists [14–16] where the aim is to implement laboratory-automated systems with the help of AI techniques to execute cycles of scientific experiments, and the DISK(Automated DIscovery of Scientific Knowledge) system [8,9] that aims at achieving automated hypothesis driven data analysis of science data repositories. Coetzer et al., [5] also developed a domain specific knowledge-based system for discovering ecological interactions in data in which situation detection is performed by combining the observations with relevant available domain knowledge.

Context modelling and situation awareness call for solutions that are semantically designed or incorporate ontologies [26]. Some monitoring systems for sensor based applications have been described for instance in [2] in which air quality monitoring is used as an example application use case. Although in [2] focus is not on KDE but on proactively making decisions and acting on anticipated situations with regard to a continuously monitored property of a feature of interest, we draw ideas from the situation detection layer of this system architecture. In [13] and [26], rule engines i.e. semantic web rule language (SWRL) rules are used. These studies, together with [2] provide approaches for semantic/ontology driven monitoring to generate alerts. The rules are used for situation detection, alerting and transforming continuous variables to qualitative measures. As noted in [6], the main shortcoming of most of the available systems is lack of continuous knowledge base update or knowledge evolution. However, some systems have been designed to overcome this short fall e.g. the ontology driven health monitoring system, Do-Care [6] proposed recently in the medical domain that allows update and refinement of medical knowledge triggered by observations with regard to wearable, nearable and usable devices. This system and others like the ones described in [13] and [18] focus on generating appropriate alerts when wrong, risky or abnormal observations are encountered as opposed to providing potential explanations for unexpected situations.

While there are elements that can be reused in the systems and approaches discussed in this section, an explicit generic architecture for agent-based KDE is absent. We can incorporate the ideas, experiences, lessons learned and the techniques applied in these systems into the design of such an architecture.

3   Design of the KDE Agent Architecture

To inform our design we considered a real world application use case for monitoring electricity consumption behavior in South African households [31]. A simplified summary of the application is given below.

Daily consumption behaviour is highly variable and may differ drastically between households, due to economic volatility, income inequality, geographic and social diversity. Energy planners must understand the electricity consumption behaviour of residential customers in order to predict long term energy demand. The aggregate consumption behaviour, or representative load profiles, of residential customers are standard consumption patterns for dominant groups of households that have common attributes. These representative load profiles consolidate expert knowledge and represent the electricity consumption of typical customer classes. They are an essential tool for demand planning, but are difficult and tedious to construct and do not cater for changes in household behaviour. This is a serious limitation that impacts energy demand planning. Through clustering, the daily electricity consumption behavior and representative daily load profiles are already known [29]. However, the consumption patterns, household profiles and the original clustering are not static and may become obsolete as household characteristics evolve or new groups emerge.

A KDE agent in this environment would interact with an external cluster analyse service and the energy planner. The cluster analysis service provides the current representative load profiles for different types of households and the agent acquires knowledge from the energy planner who serves as the domain expert. The main task of the agent is to maintain and update knowledge about daily consumption behaviour. It monitors individual household consumption on a daily basis, detects and tracks abnormal consumption, i.e. when a household deviates from its expected pattern, and detects new consumption patterns, provides plausible explanations for this, and interacts with the energy planner to updates its knowledge.

The agent architecture is governed by the following design goals/principles.

1. The agent must be able to interpret and analyse incoming observations from the physical system, in this case electricity consumption in a household, via an external AI service
2. The agent must be able to interact with the domain expert, in this case the energy planner, to acquire and align with the domain expert's knowledge of the observed physical systems, and must be able to communicate adequate explanations to the domain expert.
3. The agent must be able to represent and align with the different steps for KDE specified by ATOM.
4. The agent architecture must be generic and support a general class of intelligent monitoring systems for sensor based applications.

We used the mental states specified in the BDI architecture to analyse the application use case and to develop the cognitive loop of the KDE agent. The agent's role is to generate, develop and partly appraise explanations and theories that explain a given pattern and to update its domain knowledge. It has a single goal and intention, i.e. to provide explanations for patterns in incoming observations.

The agent's cognitive loop consists of the following steps; detect the current situation, determine if the detected situation is expected or unexpected, generate plausible explanations for the detected situation, revise beliefs and share explanations and theories with the human experts. On obtaining a pattern, the KDE agent's intention is *achieve(explained ?x)* where *x* is the detected pattern. The agent maintains a set of beliefs which represent its knowledge. It relies on its beliefs to deliberate and generate possible explanations for the observed situations. From these potential explanations, the agent selects the best explanation which is to be followed up further by the human expert.

4   The KDE Agent Architecture

Figure 2 shows the layout of the proposed architecture which applies a hybrid approach where AI is applied both endogenously and exogenously. The architecture is presented as modules connected through data and control flow. It consists of five main distinct and yet dependent modules. These are: The AI service, perception module, deliberation module, the theory construction module and the domain expert module. Details about these modules are discussed below.

4.1   The Exogenous Modules

The exogenous components comprise of two modules; the AI service and the domain expert.

The AI Service: As part of the AI service, bottom up techniques like Machine learning and deep learning can be used to build models from data in the domain

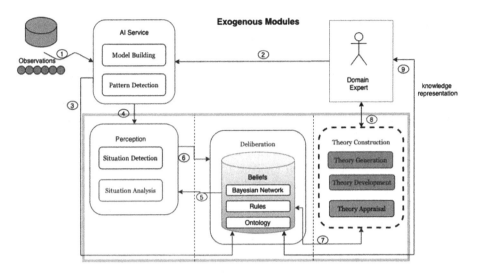

Fig. 2. The KDE abstract agent architecture.

(arrow 1). Clustering techniques, image or speech recognition systems, document analysis capabilities, etc., can be offered as part of the AI service component. The models are used to represent the expected behaviour e.g. the clustering that is used in Sect. 5.1 to represent the household electricity consumption behaviour. The pattern detection (PD) service matches the current behaviour of the observed entity with the expected behaviour and reports when there is any deviation.

The Domain Expert: The domain experts has two overarching roles. They facilitate the bottom up process of model building (arrow 2). They also give input to the top down knowledge representation and reasoning component used to capture the agent's beliefs and known domain theories i.e. Bayesian networks, rules and ontologies (arrow 9) as well as retrieving information from them. While the Bayesian network typically represents causal domain knowledge acquired from the expert it can also be learned or refined from the data (arrow 3).

4.2   The Endogenous Modules

The modules that are endogenous to the agent include the perception, deliberation and theory construction modules.

The Perception Module: The agent receives as its percepts the patterns that result from the pattern detection component of the AI service (arrow 4). The agent has rules i.e. SWRL rules as part of its beliefs that are used to analyse the incoming patterns in order to determine the current situation that the observed pattern represents (arrow 5). The rules are captured using the template: Pattern ⇒ Situation.

As far as the agent is concerned, two different types of patterns may be detected from the observations. These include: expected and unexpected patterns. Expected patterns represent situations that are already defined and explained by current model. Unexpected patterns on the other hand are new to the agent and in some cases to the domain expert. They are unexplained patterns that represent situations that have not been seen previously. The agent then has to carry out situation analysis to establish whether the situation that the pattern is indicative of is expected or unexpected.

Deliberation: The agent attempts to diagnostically generate possible causal explanations (arrow 6) for the detected situations. The assumption is that unlike unexpected situations, expected situations are already correctly explainable by the agent based on its current beliefs/knowledge. The base component of the agent's deliberation process are its beliefs. The agent needs to know the domain variables, their characteristics and their causal interaction in order to be able to generate tentative explanations as to why a particular situation has occurred. In the proposed architecture, beliefs are maintained using ontologies, rules and Bayesian networks. The Bayesian network consists of domain theories captured as causal relationships between domain variables from which explanations about the occurrence of a particular situation are obtained. The ontology is used to integrate aspects of generated explanations or theories. The integration process is dictated by the aspects captured as part of the KDE ontology [32] which is linked to the agent's beliefs. This task entails combining/linking aspects about the patterns, situations and the generated theories including any other required provenance information that come from the discovery process. The KDE ontology captures knowledge in a queryable way which makes it possible for the humans to query and retrieve the KDE information about the generated explanations or theories and their provenance information and further appraise the theories generated by the agent. Parameterised SPARQL queries are used for this aspect in order to query the KDE ontology.

Generating Explanations: Explaining a given situation commences when the Bayesian network is set to capture the the detected situation (Algorithm 1 line 4). An abstract Bayesian network that lays out the the aspects of Algorithm 1 is shown in Fig. 4 appendix 1. Obtaining plausible causal explanations is done through diagnostic reasoning. Causality is leveraged to determine the tentative explanations of a detected situation. Algorithm 1 lays out the procedure of tentative explanation generation from the agent's beliefs in which the intention is to explain the detected situation. Probabilistic information is used by the agent to determine whether a particular explanation is worth further exploration. The assumption made is that if a variable has a causal link to the situation node, then it can tentatively explain the occurrence of the observed situation. All nodes that are parents of the situation node in the Bayesian network are determined and their states that have the highest probabilities are obtained and compared with the predetermined threshold value. The nodes along with the states that present with higher probabilities than the rest of the nodes are added to the possible explanations. (see Algorithm 1 line 5-8).

When probabilities are propagated and the probabilities of the rest of the nodes in the Bayesian network are updated to incorporate the detected situation, states of nodes that have probabilities that are higher than a predetermined probability threshold translate to possible explanations. The possible explanations are further compared in terms of their probabilities for explanatory strength in order to select the best explanation. The theory appraisal task in our architecture is designed to be started by the agent and completed by the human scientist or domain expert. The aspect of theory appraisal that is carried out by the agent entails obtaining the best explanation for the observed situations.

Algorithm 1: Selecting possible explanations

1: options: (B,I,S) $\rightarrow$ *possibleExplanations*
2:        E := null;
3:        X := nodes in the Bayesian Network; /* *the Bayesian network is part of the Beliefs*
4:        Set situation nodes in X to match the situation S
5:        **for each** $x \in Parents(S)$ **do**
6:              **if** max $(P[x = x_i|S = s])$ **then**
7:                    **if** $P >=$ beliefThreshold **then**
8:                          add (x, x_i) to E
9:                    **end-if**
10:              **end-if**
11:        **end-for**
12:        options := E;
13: end-options

Theory Construction: Theory construction consists of three major processes which are theory generation, theory development and theory appraisal which are facilitated by the domain expert. Theories could be constructed for a new pattern or possible patterns. This work mainly focused on explaining encountered patterns with the help of already existing theories.

5   Use Case - Domestic Electricity Consumption

This application use case is based on an existing study which used cluster analysis to determine prominent patterns of daily electricity consumption by different households in South Africa [31]. The daily consumption pattern for a household, h, is reflected by a daily load profile. The load profile, h_i, is a 24 element array of average consumption measurements for each hour in day i. Households are characterised by different socio-economic attributes, e.g. income, years of electrification, ownership of high power appliances and whether there is piped water and other complementary infrastructure. Consumption patterns vary depending on the season, the day of the week and the time of day. For example for a typical week day, households will consume more electricity in winter because of heating, and more electricity in the mornings and evenings, which are peak times when families are at home, meals are being prepared and appliances are used.

Daily consumption behaviour can vary drastically for individual households over time. The dominant daily consumption patterns can become outdated as new groups of households emerge which may not correspond to the current patterns. An example of this is households in rural areas in South Africa, where thatch roof huts with limited appliances have gradually transitioned to brick buildings with modern appliances, resulting in a significant change in electricity consumption. Another issue is that while daily consumption readings are always available for a given period, socio-economic attributes are collected by a once off survey. This data will eventually become outdated as the household changes and evolves and may eventually not align with the observed daily consumption for a household with the attributes on record.

Within this context we consider an individual household h that is being monitored for its daily electricity load consumption.

5.1   Cluster Analysis Service

The cluster analysis service contains the cluster set which represents the prominent daily consumption patterns (daily load profiles) for all households in South Africa. The reader is referred to [31] for details on how such a cluster set can be generated. A cluster represents daily load profiles which are similar with the cluster centroid representing the mean daily load profile for profiles in the cluster. For this household the cluster analysis service can provide the cluster which best represents the consumption for this household based on its socio-economic attributes and daily consumption pattern in a given season and time of day. The pattern detection (PD) service builds a model of the expected usage over time for this household. There are different usage patterns for different seasons (winter, summer) and time of day (morning, evening). This model could be a simple average of previous daily load profiles from historical data for the household or a more complex machine learning model which can predict the load profile for a given season. Given the current load profile, the PD service will match the current daily consumption with the expected consumption and return whether it aligns with the expected consumption.

5.2   Perception

The agent uses its rule set to analyse the current daily consumption pattern. We provide a restricted rule set (example rules are listed below and are presented as SWRL rules in appendix 2) to analyse the consumption, c, on a week day morning between 5am and 8am in summer.

```
day_type(summer_week_day) ∧ time_of_day(morning) ∧ usage(?x>74) ⇒
high_morning_consumption_summer_week_day
```

```
day_type(summer_week_day) ∧ time_of_day(morning) ∧ usage(49<?x<75)
⇒ medium_morning_consumption_summer_week_day
```

```
day_type(summer_week_day) ∧ time_of_day(morning) ∧ usage(?x<50) ⇒
Low_morning_consumption_summer_week_day
```

The agent uses its rule set to analyse the expected morning consumption pattern which it expects to be *medium_morning_consumption_summer_week_day* but the current pattern yields that it is a *high_morning_consumption_summer_week_day*.

5.3   Deliberation to Generate Explanations

The agent then attempts to provide explanations for this new behavior with the help of a causal Bayesian network that is part of the agent's beliefs. Consider a simple example Bayesian network for electricity consumption characteristics in Fig. 3. (The Bayesian network and conditional probability tables (CPTs) do not depict a true setting but it has been simplified to illustrate a concept). The Bayesian network presents characteristics of houses that have the same consumption behaviour. The agent then attempts to explain why h might be exhibiting a high consumption behavior by setting the network, in the situation nodes, to accommodate a high consumption in the morning on a summer weekday. The agent determines all the nodes that have causal links to the situation node i.e. complementary infrastructure e.g. piped water, high consumption appliance ownership and years of electrification. The states of these nodes with higher probabilities are selected i.e. complementary infrastructure e.g. piped water (yes) -52.5%, high consumption appliance ownership (yes) - 73.5% and >=15 years of electrification 42.3%. Assuming the threshold is 50%, complementary infrastructure e.g. piped water (yes) -52.5%, and high consumption appliance ownership (yes) - 73.5% are added to the possible explanations and high consumption appliance ownership is ranked best. The generated explanation and its provenance information are then inserted into and retrieved from the the agent's KDE ontology using SPARQL queries. We argue that the agent's deliberation to generate explanations constitutes a weak form of analogical reasoning as described by Haig [10]. Households with high consumption behavior in the morning on weekdays in summer are households with complementary infrastructure or high consumption appliances. Using analogical reasoning we infer that this household could be one of these households.

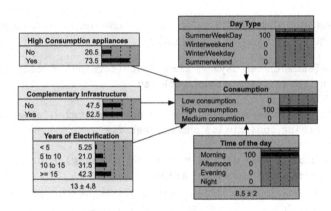

Fig. 3. A sample Bayesian network.

6   Discussion and Conclusion

We have proposed an agent architecture for knowledge discovery and evolution in dynamic and erratic physical sensor systems. We draw from and attempt to formalise the knowledge discovery and evolution process presented in ATOM. We use the BDI architecture as a cognitive model for the agent and hone in on the maintenance and evolution of the agent's beliefs. In this scenario the agent has a single persistent goal to explain its observations in order to evolve and align its beliefs with current observations in the system. Its beliefs must be in a form that can offer explanation and and allow for assessment by a domain expert. At the end of its deliberation process, the agent's goal is to answer the question: "what do I think is the best explanation for the observed percept is". The architecture builds on both the mental states from the BDI and the agent community and the ATOM process of KDE from PoS. We also show how external machine learning services and the domain expert can be incorporated into the agent's deliberation. We believe that an agent's beliefs will comprise of rules, Bayesian networks and ontologies. While many data driven sensor applications have been proposed which use a combination of rules and ontologies, they have not applied these causal theories and reasoning about uncertainty. We show how Bayesian networks can be incorporated into an agent for representing causal theories and applying these theories to identify possible explanations for unexpected situations.

The use case application illustrates certain practical aspects of the architecture for detecting and analysing unexpected observations, finding possible explanations for unexpected situations and establishing how the agent can constantly align its beliefs to changes in the environment.

Exploring new mechanisms for KDE is essential for the next generation of intelligent agents. To our knowledge this is the first attempt to formalise ATOM into an intelligent agent architecture for situation analysis and explanation generation in a physical data driven sensor application. The proposed architecture applies AI techniques for the detection of unexpected situations and generating possible explanations for those situations. The theory construction module requires further exploration. We illustrated a weak form of analogical modeling for theory development as proposed by Haig [10], but will explore richer forms of analogical modeling in future work. We also intend to explore the applicability of the proposed architecture to other use cases to evaluate its generalisability for the broader class of sensor based applications.

Acknowledgements. This work was financially supported by the Hasso Plattner Institute for digital engineering through the HPI Research school at UCT.

A Appendices

A.1 Appendix 1 -An Abstract Bayesian Network

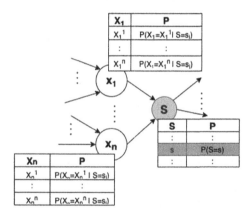

Fig. 4. An abstract Bayesian network.

A.2 Appendix 2 - Sample SWRL Rules

```
Kdeontology:Household(?h) ∧ Kdeontology:has_Consumption(?h, ?c)
∧ Kdeontology:Day_type(Kdeontology:summer_week_day)
∧ Kdeontology:Time_of_day(Kdeontology:morning)
∧ swrlb:greaterThan(?c, 74) → Kdeontology:has_situation(
?h, Kdeontology:high_morning_consumption_summer_week_day)
```

```
Kdeontology:Household(?h) ∧ Kdeontology:has_Consumption(?h, ?c)
∧ Kdeontology:Day_type(Kdeontology:summer_week_day)
∧ Kdeontology:Time_of_day(Kdeontology:morning)
∧ swrlb:greaterThan(?c, 49) ∧ swrlb:lessThan(?c, 75)
→ Kdeontology:has_situation(
?h, Kdeontology:medium_morning_consumption_summer_week_day)
```

```
Kdeontology:Household(?h) ∧ Kdeontology:has_Consumption(?h, ?c)
∧ Kdeontology:Day_type(Kdeontology:summer_week_day)
∧ Kdeontology:Time_of_day(Kdeontology:morning)
∧ swrlb:lessThan(?c, 50) → Kdeontology:has_situation(
?h, Kdeontology:low_morning_consumption_summer_week_day)
```

References

1. Adam, C., Gaudou, B.: BDI agents in social simulations: a survey. Knowl. Eng. Rev. **31**(3), 207–238 (2016)
2. Adeleke, J.A.: A semantic sensor web framework for proactive environmental monitoring and control. Ph.D. thesis, University of KwaZulu-Natal, Durban (ukzn) (2017)
3. Bordini, R.H., El Fallah Seghrouchni, A., Hindriks, K., Logan, B., Ricci, A.: Agent programming in the cognitive era. Auton. Agent. Multi-Agent Syst. **34**(2), 1–31 (2020). https://doi.org/10.1007/s10458-020-09453-y
4. Bratman, M.E., Israel, D.J., Pollack, M.E.: Plans and resource-bounded practical reasoning. Comput. Intell. **4**(3), 349–355 (1988)
5. Coetzer, W., Moodley, D., Gerber, A.: A knowledge-based system for generating interaction networks from ecological data. Data Knowl. Eng. **112**, 55–78 (2017)
6. Elhadj, H.B., Sallabi, F., Henaien, A., Chaari, L., Shuaib, K., Al Thawadi, M.: Docare: a dynamic ontology reasoning based healthcare monitoring system. Future Gener. Comput. Syst. **118**, 417–431 (2021)
7. Fagundes, M.S., Vicari, R.M., Coelho, H.: Deliberation process in a BDI model with Bayesian networks. In: Ghose, A., Governatori, G., Sadananda, R. (eds.) PRIMA 2007. LNCS (LNAI), vol. 5044, pp. 207–218. Springer, Heidelberg (2009). https://doi.org/10.1007/978-3-642-01639-4_18
8. Gil, Y., et al.: Automated hypothesis testing with large scientific data repositories. In: Proceedings of the Fourth Annual Conference on Advances in Cognitive Systems (ACS), vol. 2, p. 4 (2016)
9. Gil, Y., et al.: Towards continuous scientific data analysis and hypothesis evolution. In: AAAI, pp. 4406–4414 (2017)

10. Haig, B.D.: An abductive theory of scientific method. In: Method Matters in Psychology. SAPERE, vol. 45, pp. 35–64. Springer, Cham (2018). https://doi.org/10.1007/978-3-030-01051-5_3

11. Haig, B.D.: The importance of scientific method for psychological science. Psychol. Crime Law **25**(6), 527–541 (2019)

12. Han, J., Kamber, M., Pei, J.: Data mining concepts and techniques third edition. Morgan Kaufmann Ser. Data Manag. Syst. **5**(4), 83–124 (2011)

13. Hristoskova, A., Sakkalis, V., Zacharioudakis, G., Tsiknakis, M., De Turck, F.: Ontology-driven monitoring of patient's vital signs enabling personalized medical detection and alert. Sensors **14**(1), 1598–1628 (2014)

14. King, R.D., Rowland, J., Aubrey, W., Liakata, M., Markham, M., Soldatova, L.N., Whelan, K.E., Clare, A., Young, M., Sparkes, A., et al.: The robot scientist adam. Computer **42**(8), 46–54 (2009)

15. King, R.D., et al.: The automation of science. Science **324**(5923), 85–89 (2009)

16. King, R.D., et al.: Functional genomic hypothesis generation and experimentation by a robot scientist. Nature **427**(6971), 247–252 (2004)

17. Klapiscak, T., Bordini, R.H.: JASDL: a practical programming approach combining agent and semantic web technologies. In: Baldoni, M., Son, T.C., van Riemsdijk, M.B., Winikoff, M. (eds.) DALT 2008. LNCS (LNAI), vol. 5397, pp. 91–110. Springer, Heidelberg (2009). https://doi.org/10.1007/978-3-540-93920-7_7

18. Montagna, S., Mariani, S., Gamberini, E., Ricci, A., Zambonelli, F.: Complementing agents with cognitive services: a case study in healthcare. J. Med. Syst. **44**(10), 1–10 (2020)

19. Moreira, Á.F., Vieira, R., Bordini, R.H., Hübner, J.F.: Agent-oriented programming with underlying ontological reasoning. In: Baldoni, M., Endriss, U., Omicini, A., Torroni, P. (eds.) DALT 2005. LNCS (LNAI), vol. 3904, pp. 155–170. Springer, Heidelberg (2006). https://doi.org/10.1007/11691792_10

20. Muhammad, F., et al.: A novelty-centric agent architecture for changing worlds. In: Proceedings of the 20th International Conference on Autonomous Agents and MultiAgent Systems, pp. 925–933 (2021)

21. Rao, A.S., Georgeff, M.P.: Modeling rational agents within a BDI-architecture. KR **91**, 473–484 (1991)

22. Rao, A.S., Georgeff, M.P., et al.: BDI agents: from theory to practice. In: Icmas, vol. 95, pp. 312–319 (1995)

23. Savaglio, C., Ganzha, M., Paprzycki, M., Bădică, C., Ivanović, M., Fortino, G.: Agent-based internet of things: state-of-the-art and research challenges. Future Gener. Comput. Syst. **102**, 1038–1053 (2020)

24. Sen, A., Sterner, B., Franz, N., Powel, C., Upham, N.: Combining machine learning & reasoning for biodiversity data intelligence. In: Proceedings of the AAAI Conference on Artificial Intelligence, vol. 35, no. 17, pp. 14911–14919 (2021)

25. Silva, D.G., Gluz, J.C.: AgentSpeak (PL): a new programming language for BDI agents with integrated Bayesian network model. In: 2011 International Conference on Information Science and Applications, pp. 1–7. IEEE (2011)

26. Sondes, T., Elhadj, H.B., Chaari, L.: An ontology-based healthcare monitoring system in the internet of things. In: 2019 15th International Wireless Communications & Mobile Computing Conference (IWCMC), pp. 319–324. IEEE (2019)

27. Tiddi, I., d'Aquin, M., Motta, E.: An ontology design pattern to define explanations. In: Proceedings of the 8th International Conference on Knowledge Capture, pp. 1–8 (2015)

28. Tiddi, I., d'Aquin, M., Motta, E.: Dedalo: looking for clusters explanations in a labyrinth of linked data. In: Presutti, V., d'Amato, C., Gandon, F., d'Aquin, M., Staab, S., Tordai, A. (eds.) ESWC 2014. LNCS, vol. 8465, pp. 333–348. Springer, Cham (2014). https://doi.org/10.1007/978-3-319-07443-6_23

29. Toussaint, W.: Evaluation of clustering techniques for generating household energy consumption patterns in a developing country. Master's thesis, Faculty of Science, University of Cape Town (2019)

30. Toussaint, W., Moodley, D.: Comparison of clustering techniques for residential load profiles in South Africa. In: Davel, M.H., Barnard, E. (eds.) Proceedings of the South African Forum for Artificial Intelligence Research Cape Town, South Africa, 4–6 December 2019. CEUR Workshop Proceedings, vol. 2540, pp. 117–132. CEUR-WS.org (2019)

31. Toussaint, W., Moodley, D.: Automating cluster analysis to generate customer archetypes for residential energy consumers in South Africa. arXiv preprint arXiv:2006.07197 (2020)

32. Wanyana, T., Moodley, D., Meyer, T.: An ontology for supporting knowledge discovery and evolution. In: Gerber, A. (ed.) Southern African Conference for Artificial Intelligence Research (SACAIR), pp. 206–221 (2020)

Demystifying Artificial Intelligence for End-Users: Findings from a Participatory Machine Learning Show

Katharina Weitz$^{(\boxtimes)}$ ⓘ, Ruben Schlagowski ⓘ, and Elisabeth André ⓘ

Lab for Human-Centered AI, University of Augsburg, Augsburg, Germany
{katharina.weitz,ruben.schlagowski,elisabeth.andre}@uni-a.de
https://hcai.eu

Abstract. Interactive and collaborative approaches have been successfully used in educational scenarios. For machine learning and AI, however, such approaches typically require a fair amount of technical expertise. In order to reach everyday users of AI technologies, we propose and evaluate a new interactive approach to help end-users gain a better understanding of AI: A participatory machine learning show. During the show, participants were able to collectively gather corpus data for a neural network for keyword recognition, and interactively train and test its accuracy. Furthermore, the network's decisions were explained by using both an established XAI framework (LIME) and a virtual agent. In cooperation with a museum, we ran several prototype shows and interviewed participating and non-participating visitors to gain insights about their attitude towards (X)AI. We could deduce that the virtual agent and the inclusion of XAI visualisations in our edutainment show were generally rated positively by participants, even though the frameworks we used were originally designed for experts. When comparing both groups, we found that participants felt significantly more competent and positive towards technology compared to non-participating visitors. Our findings suggests that the consideration of specific user needs, personal background, and mental models about (X)AI systems should be included in the XAI design for end-users.

Keywords: Explainable AI · Virtual agents · Artificial intelligence · Neural networks · Edutainment

1 Introduction

The results of the survey of the European Commission [2] in 2017 revealed that the attitude people have towards artificial intelligence strongly depends on their level of knowledge and information about these systems. Accordingly, one goal of the research community should be to provide means that help to better educate end-users of AI-based technologies and research methods by which public understanding of AI-systems can be improved. Explainable AI (XAI) refers to

© Springer Nature Switzerland AG 2021
S. Edelkamp et al. (Eds.): KI 2021, LNAI 12873, pp. 257–270, 2021.
https://doi.org/10.1007/978-3-030-87626-5_19

methods that illustrate and make the decisions of AI-systems more understandable. However, authors like Miller et al. [25] point out that XAI approaches focus too much on the needs for AI-experts and do not consider the needs of end-users. Although there are first approaches that introduce X(AI) to end-users in a playful way, these are targeting individuals or small groups [4]. To enable a large group of end-users to understand the abilities and limitations of AI systems, we presented a public interactive machine learning show (ML-show) in the German museum in Munich to over 2200 visitors[1]. Within this show, participants were able to collectively train an artificial neural network for audio keyword recognition after collecting a corpus of audio samples. After about 20 min of training, the audience was able to test how well the keyword classifier performed to gain a better understanding of the system's limited accuracy. After testing the network's performance, participants were shown information, detailing why the system made right or wrong predictions. This information was presented with the help of a the visual XAI framework LIME [28] and a virtual agent, which was previously found to have a potential positive impact on user trust [37]. After the show, participants were asked to fill out a questionnaire about their personal impressions of AI and XAI as well as the virtual agent.

By comparing the questionnaire results of ML-show attendees with baseline data, which was gathered in a separate questionnaire with non-participating museum visitors, we investigated the following research questions:

1. How do end-users perceive a participatory ML-show?
2. How do ML-show attendees differ from non-participants in terms of their attitude towards AI and self-estimated competence regarding AI?
3. How do ML-show attendees differ from non-participants in terms of attitude towards technical systems in general?

In addition to these experiment-related results, our paper presents a novel, participatory approach combining virtual agents with XAI methods to introduce machine learning topics to large user groups.

2   Related Work

2.1   Virtual Agents in Education and Edutainment

The use of animated agents in education scenarios was found to have positive effects on students learning performance in various studies since the 90s. Lester et al. [21] called this phenomenon the **persona effect**, which links the presence of life-like agents with positive effects on student's perception of their learning experience and motivation. This was confirmed by Mulken et al. [34], who found out that certain tests were perceived as less demanding when presented by an agent. They argued that the persona effect can also help to reduce fear that would

---

[1] The presented study in this paper as well as the collected data have been approved by the data protection officer of University of Augsburg.

normally arise when using common educational material. Hammer et al. [8] found similar effects for social robots that were used to foster well-being of elderly people. In their study, elderly people felt more confident when interacting with the robot than with tablet computers and perceived the social robot as less complex. In the study of Jin et al. [16], similar phenomena were observed while using a virtual agent in a computer-aided educational test. During the test, users felt entertained by the virtual agent which led to increased attention and test performance. The observed positive effects during the presence of virtual agents scale with the quality of the agent: The more life-like or realistic the virtual agent appears, the better. As such, the quality of agent features such as human-like voice, gestures, facial expression, eye gaze, and body movement plays an important role [23]. In the edutainment sector, technologies like virtual reality and virtual agents are often used to make communication of knowledge playful and entertaining (e.g., virtual museums [20]). Carolis and Rossano [1] used agents to teach children about healthy nutrition in a enjoyable way. Ming et al. [26] used a virtual reality setting to help participants to learn Mandarin. Here, users interacted with a virtual agent to practice the pronunciation of words.

These examples of the successful integration of virtual agents in education and edutainment settings represent a promising approach that we used in our field study to help end-users to understand the abilities and limitations of AI systems.

2.2 Explainable AI

With the rise of advanced machine learning models such as deep neural networks in a wide application field, the resulting lack of transparency and comprehensibility of an AI's decisions can not only be challenging for engineers and scientists, but also have negative impact on the perceived trustworthiness and user-experience of end-users [12,33]. For this paper we adapt the view of Gilpin et al. [5], who stated that the goal of XAI is the description of a system, its internal states and its decisions, so that this description can be understood by humans. A common approach to shed light on to the decisions of deep neural networks is the highlighting of regions of the input data (e.g., images), that are important for specific decisions, resulting in visual explanations (for the interested reader, we recommend the papers of [14,36]).

Within our user study, we used the LIME framework proposed by Ribeiro et al. [28] to highlight relevant areas within the spectrograms of audio samples that are classified as keywords by a neural network.

2.3 Trust in Technical Systems

One common definition of trust in human-agent interaction sees trust as "the attitude that an agent will help achieve an individual's goals in a situation characterized by uncertainty and vulnerability." [19, p. 51] The approach of Hoff and Bashir [11] distinguishes dispositional, situational, and learned trust. Dispositional trust refers to long-term tendencies based on biological and environmental influences. Situational trust describes external aspects (e.g., the environment) as well as internal aspects (e.g., the mood of the user) in a specific situation. Learned trust refers to the experience a user has already gained, for example with virtual agents. A distinction has also be made between different types of trust, such as distrust and overtrust. Marsh and Dibben [22] present a continuum of trust, where distrust is placed on the negative end, and trust on the positive end of the trust scale. Overtrust refers to unrealistic expectations in the system, which can result in the system being ascribed skills that it does not possess and can end in its misuse [19].

In our participatory ML-show, we focus on situational and perceived trust (not distrust or overtrust), i.e., the trust in an AI system that incorporates a virtual agent for XAI purposes in a public participatory ML-show.

3 Field Study

For six months, visitors of the museum were able to take part in a participatory ML-show. Here, a neural network for audio keyword speech recognition [30] was trained to learn a new keyword live in the show. Simultaneously, a virtual agent named Gloria was displayed on a screen and communicated with the audience via speech output (see right subfigure in Fig. 1).

Fig. 1. *Left*: Stand at the museum, which was used to ask museum visitors about their attitude towards AI and XAI. *Right*: Begin of a public participatory machine learning show visited by non-experts in the museum.

Additionally, during three days, we gathered baseline data using a paper-based questionnaire oriented on the questions used in the Eurobarometer report [2]. We also recorded the affinity of museum visitors for technology using the TA-EG questionnaire [17]. We made sure that we only questioned people who did not visit our participatory ML-show (see left subfigure in Fig. 1).

3.1 Demonstrator Setup

The demonstrator (see Fig. 2) mainly consisted of a **demonstration PC** including a high performance GPU (Nvidea GTX 1060) for improved training performance and a smartphone which was used to record and transmit audio samples for training and prediction of the neural network over WLAN. The demonstration PC was connected to a **beamer** which displayed the virtual agent, the generated spectrograms, and the XAI visualisations generated by the XAI framework. In parallel, the demonstration PC hosted a website providing audio recording and transmission functionalities on a server in the local network. An android app containing a browser window was used on the **smartphone** to access the site when the audience recorded the audio samples. For the recognition of audio keywords we used the neural network architecture proposed by Sainath & Parada [30]. This prediction model uses mel frequency cepstrum coeffiecients (MFCCs) that are calculated from audio spectrograms as input data for multiple convolutional layers for the calculation of abstract features. These features are subsequently passed on to a fully connected layer for the final target class prediction.

The moderator of the show, who was instructed in advance, operated the main application by using a step-by-step structured GUI that enabled him or her to (1) start and stop the training process of the neural network, (2) start prediction for a recorded audio sample, (3) review transmitted audio files, and (4) calculate XAI visualisations after prediction.

The virtual agent Gloria developed by Charamel[2] was integrated into a separate website that was hosted locally and displayed with a browser on the demonstration PC. Communication between the virtual agent and the main application was implemented with WebSockets.

To generate a XAI visualisation for a specific prediction of our classification model, we first used the Felzenszwalb's algorithm for image segmentation [3] to generate so-called superpixels. The LIME framework subsequently determined the most relevant superpixels for the three top predictions and colored them in green (if they contributed positively to a prediction) or red (if they contributed negatively to a prediction). In order to make the resulting XAI visualisations better readable, we used the webMAUS API [18] to highlight areas within the spectograms that contain the phonemes of the actually spoken word (ground truth).

3.2   Study Procedure

The new keyword that was trained to the neural network was freely selected by the audience during a discussion at the start of the show (see Fig. 3 for the study procedure). Afterwards, the visitors recorded a training dataset for the selected word by passing around the smartphone with a connected high quality microphone.

As soon as about 80 audio samples were recorded and transmitted to the demonstration PC, the moderator used pre-programmed software functionalities to label the samples and merge them with a subset of the the speech command dataset provided by Warden [35] (we used data for 11 classes/keywords, 80 samples each) to create the training corpus. Then, the moderator started the training process of the prediction model. To give the participants a feeling of

---

[2] https://vuppetmaster.de/.

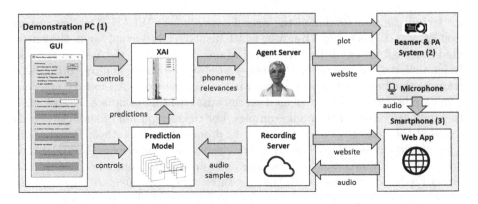

Fig. 2. Demonstrator overview as used in the field study. *Left:* **(1) Demonstration PC**, running the neural network for keyword recognition and calculating the XAI visualisations. *Right:* **(2) Beamer & PA system** were used for agent displaying & sound, the XAI visualisations, and the presentation slides for the show. **(3) Smartphone** and microphone for recording the audio samples.

how good the classifier was after this relatively short amount of time (the typical validation accuracy was about 80%), we decided to not use any pre-trained networks and instead train the network from scratch for each show. While the model was trained, visitors were given a 20-minute lecture on how neural networks for speech recognition work and how the LIME framework can be used to understand the classifiers decisions in this context. As soon as the lecture was finished, the moderator stopped the training. Afterwards, the network could be tested by volunteering participants multiple times by speaking both known and unknown keywords into the microphone. The resulting audio samples were transmitted to the demonstration PC and passed on to the classifier. Together with prediction results, the XAI visualisations generated by the XAI framework LIME were displayed for the audience.

In parallel to the show, the virtual agent Gloria commented on the training, communicated the classifier's prediction results, and commented on the XAI visualisations (e.g., "The most relevant phoneme for the prediction of $< keyword >$ was...").

3.3   Evaluation Method

After the show, participants were asked to complete a questionnaire, either online or on paper. In addition to the collection of demographic information, the following questions were included:

Agent & (X)AI system Evaluation. To evaluate the virtual agent Gloria, we used 5 items on a 7-point Likert scale (e.g., "I liked Gloria") and free-form feedback. We collected participants' feedback about the AI system by using 3 items a 7-point Likert scale (e.g., "I would use the AI system"). To gain insights of the

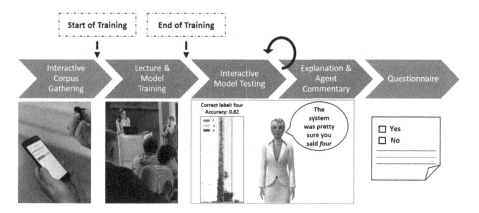

Fig. 3. Procedure during the ML-show: An interactive audio-corpus was collected and used to train a Neural Network during a lecture about Machine Learning. Afterward, the model was tested by the participants. The virtual agent Gloria presented the results and XAI visualisations. At the end of the ML-show, participants had to answer a questionnaire.

perceived helpfulness of the XAI visualisations, we asked 1 item on a 7-point Likert scale (i.e., "Were the explanations sufficient?") and a free-form question about which additional information would be helpful for them to understand the AI system.

Technical Affinity. To measure the technical affinity of participants using the TA-EG questionnaire [17] was queried.

Trust. Subjective trust was assessed with the Trust in Automation (TiA) questionnaire [15].

Attitude Towards AI. At the end of the questionnaire, additional questions about the participant's general knowledge attitude towards AI and XAI were posed (e.g., "How would you rate your knowledge of AI?" and "In general, what is your attitude towards artificial intelligence?").

4   Results

4.1   Information About Participants

ML-show Participants A total of 65 public participatory machine learning shows with an average of 35 participants each were held. A total of 2275 museum visitors took part in the study, of which 51 completed the subsequent questionnaire. Due to missing data in some questionnaires, 47 participants (24 male, 22 female, 1 non-binary) between 13 and 80 years ($M = 42.07$, $SD = 22.6$) were included in the final analyses presented in this paper. The educational background of the participants was mixed and ranged from "no degree" to "university degree". Most participants had no previous knowledge or experience in the use of virtual agents, voice assistants, or audio processing. 88% of the participants stated that they have already heard of the term AI, but only 11% of them rated their AI knowledge as extensive. Most of the participants either had a balanced or a positive view about the impact on AI in the future (see left side of Fig. 4). A majority of the participants saw XAI as an important topic, especially for researchers, companies, and end-users (see right side of Fig. 4). For politicians, participants rated the importance of XAI less compared to the other stakeholders.

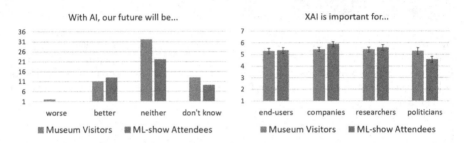

Fig. 4. *Left:* ML-show attendees and non-participating museum visitors answers to the question "What future do you think we will have with AI?". *Right:* Rating of the participants, whether XAI is important for different stakeholders (1=disagree; 7=fully agree). Error bars represent the standard error.

Baseline Participants. 59 museums visitors took part in our field survey which we used as baseline for the comparison with the ML-show participants. We had to remove the answers of one visitor due to too much unanswered questions. Therefore, for the following analyses, answers from 58 museum visitors (29 female, 29 male) between 8 and 66 years ($M = 30.3$, $SD = 16.5$) are considered. The educational background of the participants was mixed and similar distributed as in the ML-shows.

Most of the visitors had heard about AI in the last 12 month (97%), but only 24% of them had heard about XAI. Non-participants saw XAI and the future of AI similar than ML-show attendees (see Fig. 4).

4.2   Results of the ML-show

Agent & (X)AI Rating. Participants gave the virtual agent Gloria a rating of $M = 3.9$ which was slightly above average (7-point Likert scale). The LIME visualisations were rated with $M = 4.15$ slightly higher than the virtual agent. Investigating whether the participants would use such an AI system, the rating was with $M = 3.06$ beyond average (7-point Likert scale). In response to the free-form question about what additional information they would have liked to see in Gloria's explanations, users indicated that they would have liked more details (e.g., "What does Gloria calculate in the training phase?").

Correlations for ML-show Participants. To examine potential connections of the educational background, gender, technical affinity, and age of the participants on questionnaire items like trust in the AI system, virtual agent impression, and the helpfulness of the XAI visualisations, we calculated pearson's product-moment correlations.

We found a significant weak positive linear relationship between perceived trust in the presented AI system and educational background ($r = .47$, $p < .05$), where participants with an higher educational background tend to trust the AI system more. Neither age nor gender had a significant impact on subjective trust in the AI system, as we did not find any significant correlations for these variables. For the impression of the agent as well as the helpfulness of the XAI visualisations, we did not find correlations for age, gender, and educational background of the participants.

4.3 Comparison Between Participating and Non-participating Museum Visitors

We used two one-way MANOVAs to examine if there were any significant differences compared to the non-participating museums visitors (baseline). Holm correction for multiple testing was applied.

Attitudes Towards AI. We conducted a MANOVA to evaluate whether there was a difference between baseline museum visitors and ML-show participants in (1) the perceived knowledge about AI as well as (2) their attitude about the impact of AI on our lives in the future and (3) in their attitude towards AI. We found no significant differences for these three variables, $F(3, 100) = 1.76$, $p = .16$, Pillai's Trace $= 0.51$.

Technical Affinity. To evaluate the TA-EG questionnaire, we looked at the four subscales (excitement, competence, negativity, and positivity) using a one-way MANOVA. The MANOVA showed significant differences between the groups for the TA-EG variables, $F(4, 100) = 28.58$, $p < .001$, Pillai's Trace $= 0.53$. To find out on which subscales of the TA-EG significant differences exist, we then performed an ANOVA that revealed significant differences for the subscales competence $F(1, 103) = 23.15$, $p < .001$, excitement $F(1, 103) = 5.03$, $p < .03$, and positivity $F(1, 103) = 96.15$, $p < .001$.

We then used post-hoc tests to investigate the direction of these differences. For this purpose, we use t-tests or Wilcoxon tests if the requirements for the t-test were not met[3] to evaluate whether there was a difference between baseline museum visitors and ML-show participants in (1) the perceived technical competence as well as (2) their excitement towards technology and (3) their positivity towards technology. Our results (Fig. 5) show:

- **Competence:** Participants of the ML-show ($M = 3.00$, $SD = 0.63$) feel more competent about technology compared to the baseline museum visitors ($M = 2.14$, $SD = 1.08$), $Z = 692$, $p < .001$.
- **Excitement:** Participants of the ML-show ($M = 3.15$, $SD = 0.94$) do not feel more excited compared to the baseline museum visitors ($M = 2.71$, $SD = 1.03$), $t = -2.24$, $p = .05$[4].
- **Positivity:** Participants of the ML-show ($M = 3.62$, $SD = 0.83$) feel more positive towards technology compared to the baseline museum visitors ($M = 2.32$, $SD = 0.52$), $Z = 216$, $p < .001$.

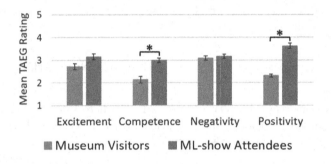

Fig. 5. Mean TA-EG ratings by category for the ML-show participants and for non-participating museum visitors. Subcategories *competence* and *positivity* indicate significant differences between the two groups (*$p < .001$). Error bars represent the standard error.

5   Discussion

We can overall conclude that end-users were receptive towards XAI-visualisations in our ML-show, even though visualisation methods in use were not specifically designed for end-users without any background knowledge in the research fields of AI and XAI. Furthermore, our field study helped us to gain initial insights concerning end-users' views about (X)AI and virtual agents in a participatory ML-show, which we would discuss in the following.

---

[3] The Mann-Whitney U-test is the non-parametric equivalent of the t-test for independent samples and is used when the conditions for a parametric procedure are not met (in our case: homogeneity of variances and a non-normal distribution of the data).

[4] This result was no longer significant due to the alpha error correction.

5.1 Take Users' Attitudes and Experiences into Account

The correlation analysis of our data revealed a connection between the educational background and the perceived trust in our AI system. This result encourages XAI design that fits the user's educational background. As part of our study was a presentation on the basic functioning of neural networks, speech recognition and XAI, better educated participants might have been more receptive to knowledge transfer. Thus, they might have understood the XAI visualisations better which might have resulted in increased trust. Miller [24] argued that explanations for AI systems have to be based on the expectations and needs of humans. Heimerl et al. [10] found out that more XAI information about an emotion recognition system leads not automatically to higher trust in the AI. They concluded that users tend to transfer their own mental models about emotions to the AI. Therefore, having the mental model of users in mind [29] when personalizing XAI for different stakeholders and different AI scenarios is an important step to adjust XAI to the "right amount" for individual users [32].

Here, trust models such as those of Sanders et al. [31] and Hancock et al. [9], which indicate that different components (e.g., agent characteristics, user attributes as well as situation characteristics) have an impact on trust, can be used to examine possible variables that might influence user trust in XAI scenarios.

5.2 Think About Who You Want to Reach with XAI Edutainment

The results of our study show that users who participate in an ML-show differ in aspects of technical affinity from non-participating museum visitors. Due to our study design, which did not contain a pre-study questionnaire, we cannot tell whether the differences occurred due to more technically affine museum visitors being more likely to participate in the ML-show, or whether the observed differences were a result of the ML-show itself. However, there are indications that the interaction with the AI system and the virtual agent in the ML-show could have influenced participants technical affinity. Reich-Stiebert et al. [27] reported in their study similar findings. They stated that positive attitudes towards robots increased among people who had the opportunity to be part of the prototyping process. Even though evidence suggests that virtual agents can have positive effects on user trust in XAI applications [37], it is not quite clear which factors play a role and need to be considered when designing user interfaces. According to Gulz and Haake [7], gender stereotypes is one factor that has a slight influence on the perception of virtual pedagogical agents. Whether the external appearance of a virtual agent (e.g., female or male virtual agent) plays a role in subjective trust for an AI system, or whether they can increase perceived helpfulness of an XAI setting, is still unclear.

5.3   Trust and Distrust Are Important Components in XAI Interaction Design

The ML-show participants had an average trust rating of about 4, which is slightly above average. This positive tendency towards trusting AI systems incorporating XAI and virtual agents has been previously reported by Weitz et al. [37] and demands an ethical perspective on systems that have the potential to increase user trust. In this manner, Gilpin et al. [6] stated that XAI cannot be equated with reliability and responsibility of an AI system. Hoffmann [13] makes similar statements, demanding that distrust and mistrust must also be included in the evaluation of XAI systems. We argue that ethical XAI systems should therefore be able to (1) Encourage user trust if a system performs well, (2) prevent distrust if a system performs badly, and (3) prevent overtrust if a system cannot live up to expectations.

As an average prediction accuracy of about 80% after 20 min of training was far from being perfect, a variety of wrong classifications occurred during the show and resulted in a demystification of AI systems. In fact, it might also have encouraged more distrust into XAI systems for users that were originally trusting AI systems, as they were most likely used to much better prediction models in their everyday lives.

6   Conclusion

We presented a novel public participatory machine learning show where we let visitors of a museum train a neural network together in order to clarify and demystify opportunities and limits of AI systems. During the show, we used a virtual agent and a XAI framework to provide participants with additional information about the decision-making processes of the neural network during a speech recognition task. By examining the results of a post-study questionnaire, we could deduce that the virtual agent and the inclusion of XAI visualisations in our edutainment show were generally rated positively by participants, even though the frameworks we used were originally designed for experts. We also found a correlation between trust in our AI system and the educational background of the participants. Compared to non-participating museum visitors, ML-show participants felt more competent and positive about technology. During the discussion of our results, we pointed out possible causes and limitations of our findings and concluded that consideration of specific user needs, personal background (e.g., education), and mental models is a promising approach for XAI design for end-users.

Acknowledgements. This work was partially funded by the Volkswagen Stiftung in the project AI-FORA (Az. 98 563) and by the German Federal Ministry of Education and Research (BMBF) in the project DIGISTA (grant number 01U01820A). We thank Deutsches Museum Munich, who made it possible for us to conduct the study.

References

1. De Carolis, B., Rossano, V.: A team of presentation agents for edutainment. In: Proceedings of the 8th International Conference on Interaction Design and Children, pp. 150–153. IDC 2009, ACM, New York, NY, USA (2009)
2. European Commission: Special Eurobarometer 460 (2017)
3. Felzenszwalb, P.F., Huttenlocher, D.P.: Efficient graph-based image segmentation. Int. J. Comput. Vis. **59**(2), 167–181 (2004)
4. Fulton, L.B., Lee, J.Y., Wang, Q., Yuan, Z., Hammer, J., Perer, A.: Getting playful with explainable AI: games with a purpose to improve human understanding of AI. In: CHI Conference on Human Factors in Computing Systems, pp. 1–8. CHI EA 2020, Association for Computing Machinery, Honolulu, HI, USA (2020)
5. Gilpin, L.H., Bau, D., Yuan, B.Z., Bajwa, A., Specter, M., Kagal, L.: Explaining explanations: an approach to evaluating interpretability of machine learning (2018)
6. Gilpin, L.H., Testart, C., Fruchter, N., Adebayo, J.: Explaining explanations to society (2019)
7. Haake, M.: Virtual pedagogical agents-beyond the constraints of the computational approach (2006)
8. Hammer, S., Kirchner, K., André, E., Lugrin, B.: Touch or talk? Comparing social robots and tablet pcs for an elderly assistant recommender system. In: Proceedings of the 2017 ACM/IEEE International Conference on Human-Robot Interaction, pp. 129–130. HRI 2017, ACM, New York, NY, USA (2017)
9. Hancock, P.A., Billings, D.R., Schaefer, K.E., Chen, J.Y., De Visser, E.J., Parasuraman, R.: A meta-analysis of factors affecting trust in human-robot interaction. Hum. Factors **53**(5), 517–527 (2011)
10. Heimerl, A., Weitz, K., Baur, T., Andre, E.: Unraveling ml models of emotion with nova: multi-level explainable AI for non-experts. IEEE Transactions on Affective Computing, p. 1 (2020)
11. Hoff, K.A., Bashir, M.: Trust in automation: integrating empirical evidence on factors that influence trust. Hum. Factors **57**(3), 407–434 (2015)
12. Hoffman, J.D., et al.: Human-automation collaboration in dynamic mission planning: a challenge requiring an ecological approach. Proc. Hum. Factors Ergon. Soc. Ann. Meet. **50**(23), 2482–2486 (2006)
13. Hoffman, R.R., Mueller, S.T., Klein, G., Litman, J.: Metrics for explainable AI: challenges and prospects (2018)
14. Huber, T., Weitz, K., André, E., Amir, O.: Local and global explanations of agent behavior: Integrating strategy summaries with saliency maps. CoRR abs/2005.08874 (2020)
15. Jian, J.Y., Bisantz, A.M., Drury, C.G.: Foundations for an empirically determined scale of trust in automated systems. Int. J. Cogn. Ergon. **4**(1), 53–71 (2000)
16. Jin, S.A.A.: The effects of incorporating a virtual agent in a computer-aided test designed for stress management education: the mediating role of enjoyment. Comput. Hum. Behav. **26**(3), 443–451 (2010)
17. Karrer, K., Glaser, C., Clemens, C., Bruder, C.: Technikaffinität erfassen-der fragebogen ta-eg. Der Mensch im Mittelpunkt technischer Systeme **8**, 196–201 (2009)
18. Kisler, T., Reichel, U., Schiel, F.: Multilingual processing of speech via web services. Comput. Speech Lang. **45**, 326–347 (2017)
19. Lee, J.D., See, K.A.: Trust in automation: designing for appropriate reliance. Hum. Factors **46**(1), 50–80 (2004)

20. Lepouras, G., Vassilakis, C.: Virtual museums for all: employing game technology for edutainment. Virtual Real. **8**(2), 96–106 (2004)

21. Lester, J.C., Converse, S.A., Kahler, S.E., Barlow, S.T., Stone, B.A., Bhogal, R.S.: The persona effect: affective impact of animated pedagogical agents. In: Proceedings of the conference on Human factors in computing systems CHI 1997, pp. 359–366. ACM Press, Atlanta, Georgia, United States (1997)

22. Marsh, S., Dibben, M.R.: Trust, untrust, distrust and mistrust – an exploration of the dark(er) side. In: Herrmann, P., Issarny, V., Shiu, S. (eds.) iTrust 2005. LNCS, vol. 3477, pp. 17–33. Springer, Heidelberg (2005). https://doi.org/10.1007/11429760_2

23. Mayer, R.E., DaPra, C.S.: An embodiment effect in computer-based learning with animated pedagogical agents. J. Exp. Psychol. Appl. **18**(3), 239–252 (2012)

24. Miller, T.: Explanation in artificial intelligence: insights from the social sciences. Artif. Intell. **267**, 1–38 (2018)

25. Miller, T., Howe, P., Sonenberg, L.: Explainable AI: beware of inmates running the asylum (2017)

26. Ming, Y., Ruan, Q., Gao, G.: A mandarin edutainment system integrated virtual learning environments. Speech Commun. **55**(1), 71–83 (2013)

27. Reich-Stiebert, N., Eyssel, F., Hohnemann, C.: Involve the user! changing attitudes toward robots by user participation in a robot prototyping process. Comput. Hum. Behav. **91**, 290–296 (2019)

28. Ribeiro, M.T., Singh, S., Guestrin, C.: Why should i trust you? Explaining the predictions of any classifier. In: Proceedings of the 22Nd ACM SIGKDD Int. Conference on Knowledge Discovery and Data Mining, pp. 1135–1144. ACM, New York, NY, USA (2016)

29. Rutjes, H., Willemsen, M., IJsselsteijn, W.: Considerations on explainable ai and users' mental models. In: Where is the Human? Bridging the Gap Between AI and HCI. Association for Computing Machinery Inc, United States (May 2019)

30. Sainath, T.N., Parada, C.: Convolutional neural networks for small-footprint keyword spotting. In: Proceedings of Interspeech, 2015, pp. 1478–1482. ISCA Archive, Dresden, Germany (2015)

31. Sanders, T., Oleson, K.E., Billings, D.R., Chen, J.Y.C., Hancock, P.A.: A model of human-robot trust: theoretical model development. Proc. Hum. Factors Ergon. Soc. Ann. Meet. **55**(1), 1432–1436 (2011)

32. Schneider, J., Handali, J.: Personalized explanation in machine learning: a conceptualization. arXiv preprint arXiv:1901.00770 (2019)

33. Stubbs, K., Hinds, P.J., Wettergreen, D.: Autonomy and common ground in human-robot interaction: a field study. IEEE Intell. Syst. **22**(2), 42–50 (2007)

34. Van Mulken, S., André, E., Müller, J.: The persona effect: how substantial is it? In: Johnson, H., Nigay, L., Roast, C. (eds.) People and computers XIII, pp. 53–66. Springer, London (1998). https://doi.org/10.1007/978-1-4471-3605-7_4

35. Warden, P.: Speech commands: a dataset for limited-vocabulary speech recognition (2018)

36. Weitz, K., Hassan, T., Schmid, U., Garbas, J.U.: Deep-learned faces of pain and emotions: elucidating the differences of facial expressions with the help of explainable AI methods. tm-Technisches Messen **86**(7–8), 404–412 (2019)

37. Weitz, K., Schiller, D., Schlagowski, R., Huber, T., André, E.: "Let me explain!": exploring the potential of virtual agents in explainable AI interaction design. J. Multimodal User Interfaces **15**(2), 87–98 (2021)

Recent Advances in Counting and Sampling Markov Equivalent DAGs

Marcel Wienöbst$^{(\boxtimes)}$, Max Bannach, and Maciej Liśkiewicz

Institute for Theoretical Computer Science, University of Lübeck, Lübeck, Germany
{wienoebst,bannach,liskiewi}@tcs.uni-luebeck.de

Abstract. Counting and sampling directed acyclic graphs (DAGs) from a Markov equivalence class are fundamental tasks in graphical causal analysis. In this paper, we discuss recently proposed polynomial-time algorithms for these tasks. The presented result solves a long-standing open problem in graphical modelling. Experiments show that the proposed algorithms are implementable and effective in practice. Our paper is an extended abstract of the work [24], honored as an AAAI-21 Distinguished Paper at the 35th AAAI Conference on Artificial Intelligence.

Keywords: Graphical models · Causality · Bayesian Networks

1 Introduction

The development of graphical methods marks a key turning point in causal theory since they allow to express and analyse complex causal relationships in a constructive and mathematically sound way. A diagram used as causal graphical model is represented, typically, by a directed acyclic graph (DAG) whose vertices represent random variables of interest and edges express direct causal effects of one variable on another [12,17,20]. They are commonly used in empirical sciences to discover and understand causal effects.

However, in practice, the underlying DAG is usually unknown, since often not only a single DAG explains the observational data. Instead, the statistical properties of the data are maintained by several different DAGs, which constitute a Markov equivalence class (MEC, for short). The DAGs inside a MAC are indistinguishable on the basis of observations alone [11,22,23]. Consequently, it is beneficial to explore model learning and to analyze causal phenomena using MECs directly rather than the DAGs themselves. This approach has led to intensive studies on Markov equivalence classes and resulted in a long and successful track record. Our work contributes to this line of research by providing the first polynomial-time algorithms for *counting* and for *uniform sampling* Markov equivalent DAGs – two important primitives in both theoretical and experimental studies.

Finding the graphical criterion for two DAGs to be Markov equivalent [22] and providing the graph-theoretic characterization of MECs as so-called

© Springer Nature Switzerland AG 2021
S. Edelkamp et al. (Eds.): KI 2021, LNAI 12873, pp. 271–275, 2021.
https://doi.org/10.1007/978-3-030-87626-5_20

CPDAGs [2] mark key turning points in this research direction. In particular, they have enabled the progress of computational methods in this area. Important advantages of the modeling with CPDAGs are demonstrated by algorithms that learn causal structures from observational data [3,4,15,16,20,23]; and that analyze causality based on a given MEC, rather than a single DAG [13,18,25].

A key characteristic of a MEC is its size, i. e., the number of DAGs in the class. It indicates uncertainty of the causal model inferred from observational data and it serves as an indicator for the performance of recovering true causal effects. Moreover, the feasibility of causal inference methods is often highly dependent on the size of the MEC; e. g., to estimate the average causal effects from observational data for a given CPDAG, as proposed in [13], one has to consider all DAGs in the class. Furthermore, computing the size of a Markov equivalence class is commonly used as a subroutine in practical algorithms. For example, when actively designing interventions, in order to identify the underlying true DAG in a given MEC, the size of the Markov equivalence subclass is an important metric to select the best intervention target [6–9,19].

The first algorithmic approaches for counting the number of Markov equivalent DAGs relied on exhaustive search [14,15] based on the graphical characterization from Verma and Pearl [22]. The methods are computationally expensive as the size of a MEC represented by a CPDAG may be superexponential in the number of vertices of the graph. More recently, He et al. [10] proposed a strategy, in which the main idea was to partition the MEC by fixing root variables in any undirected component of the CPDAG. This yields a recursive strategy for counting Markov equivalent DAGs, which forms the basis of several "root-picking" algorithms [5,7,10]. As an alternative approach, recent methods utilize dynamic programming on the clique tree representation of chordal graphs and techniques from intervention design [1,21]. However, the drawback of the existing counting algorithms is that they have exponential worst-case run time.

2   Main Results

The main achievement of our paper [24] is the first polynomial-time algorithm for counting and for sampling Markov equivalent DAGs. The counting algorithm, called *Clique-Picking*, explores the clique tree representation of a chordal graph, but it avoids the use of computationally intractable dynamic programming on the clique tree. Moreover, we show that, using the algorithm in a preprocessing phase, uniform sampling of DAGs in a MEC can be performed in linear time.

Theorem 1 ([24]). *The problem of counting the size of a Markov equivalence class can be solved in polynomial time. The same holds for the problem of sampling a DAG uniformly from a Markov equivalence class.*

The proposed Clique-Picking algorithm is effective, easy to implement, and our experimental results show that it significantly outperforms the state-of-the-art methods. We validate these claims empirically through the experiments presented in Fig. 1.

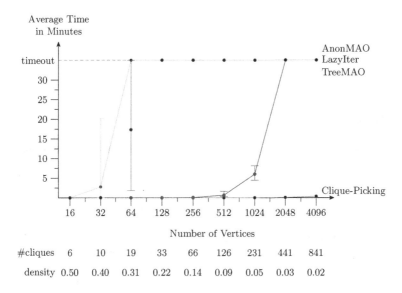

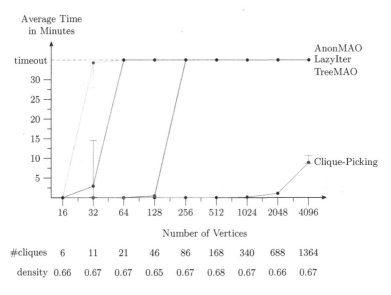

Fig. 1. Experimental results for the solvers Clique-Picking (our paper), AnonMAO [5], TreeMAO [21], and LazyIter [1] on random chordal graphs with $n = 16, 32, \ldots, 4096$ vertices. For the upper plot, we used graphs generated with the subtree intersection method and density parameter $k = \log n$; the lower plot contains the results for random interval graphs. At the bottom, we present the number of maximal cliques as well as the graph density $|E|/\binom{|V|}{2}$.

Acknowledgements. This work was supported by the Deutsche Forschungsgemeinschaft (DFG) grant LI634/4-2.

References

1. AhmadiTeshnizi, A., Salehkaleybar, S., Kiyavash, N.: Lazyiter: a fast algorithm for counting Markov equivalent DAGs and designing experiments. In: Proceedings of the 37th International Conference on Machine Learning, ICML 2020 (2020)
2. Andersson, S.A., Madigan, D., Perlman, M.D.: A characterization of Markov equivalence classes for acyclic digraphs. Ann. Stat. **25**(2), 505–541 (1997)
3. Chickering, D.M.: Learning equivalence classes of Bayesian-network structures. J. Mach. Learn. Res. **2**, 445–498 (2002)
4. Chickering, D.M.: Optimal structure identification with greedy search. J. Mach. Learn. Res. **3**, 507–554 (2002)
5. Ganian, R., Hamm, T., Talvitie, T.: An efficient algorithm for counting Markov equivalent dags. In: Proccedings of the 34th Conference on Artificial Intelligence, AAAI 2020, pp. 10136–10143 (2020)
6. Ghassami, A., Salehkaleybar, S., Kiyavash, N., Bareinboim, E.: Budgeted experiment design for causal structure learning. In: Proceedings of the 35th International Conference on Machine Learning, ICML 2018, pp. 1719–1728 (2018)
7. Ghassami, A., Salehkaleybar, S., Kiyavash, N., Zhang, K.: Counting and sampling from Markovv equivalent dags using clique trees. In: Proceedings of the 33th Conference on Artificial Intelligence, AAAI 2019, pp. 3664–3671 (2019)
8. Hauser, A., Bühlmann, P.: Characterization and greedy learning of interventional Markov equivalence classes of directed acyclic graphs. J. Mach. Learn. Res. **13**, 2409–2464 (2012)
9. He, Y.B., Geng, Z.: Active learning of causal networks with intervention experiments and optimal designs. J. Mach. Learn. Res. **9**(Nov), 2523–2547 (2008)
10. He, Y., Jia, J., Yu, B.: Counting and exploring sizes of Markov equivalence classes of directed acyclic graphs. J. Mach. Learn. Res. **16**(79), 2589–2609 (2015)
11. Heckerman, D., Geiger, D., Chickering, D.M.: Learning Bayesian networks: the combination of knowledge and statistical data. Mach. Learn. **20**(3), 197–243 (1995)
12. Koller, D., Friedman, N.: Probabilistic Graphical Models - Principles and Techniques. MIT Press, Cambridge (2009)
13. Maathuis, M.H., Kalisch, M., Bühlmann, P.: Estimating high-dimensional intervention effects from observational data. Ann. Stat. **37**(6A), 3133–3164 (2009)
14. Madigan, D., Andersson, S.A., Perlman, M.D., Volinsky, C.T.: Bayesian model averaging and model selection for Markov equivalence classes of acyclic digraphs. Commun. Stat. Theory Methods **25**(11), 2493–2519 (1996)
15. Meek, C.: Causal inference and causal explanation with background knowledge. In: Proceedings of the 11th Conference on Uncertainty in Artificial Intelligence, UAI 1995, pp. 403–410 (1995)
16. Meek, C.: Graphical Models: Selecting Causal and Statistical Models. Ph.D. thesis, Carnegie Mellon University (1997)
17. Pearl, J.: Causality. Cambridge University Press, Cambridge (2009)
18. Perković, E., Textor, J., Kalisch, M., Maathuis, M.H.: Complete graphical characterization and construction of adjustment sets in Markov equivalence classes of ancestral graphs. J. Mach. Learn. Res. **18**, 220:1–220:62 (2017)

19. Shanmugam, K., Kocaoglu, M., Dimakis, A.G., Vishwanath, S.: Learning causal graphs with small interventions. In: Processing of the 28th Annual Conference on Neural Information Processing Systems, NIPS 2015, pp. 3195–3203 (2015)
20. Spirtes, P., Glymour, C., Scheines, R.: Causation, Prediction, and Search, Second Edition. MIT Press, Cambridge (2000)
21. Talvitie, T., Koivisto, M.: Counting and sampling Markov equivalent directed acyclic graphs. In: Proceedings of the 33th Conference on Artificial Intelligence, AAAI 2019, pp. 7984–7991 (2019)
22. Verma, T., Pearl, J.: Equivalence and synthesis of causal models. In: Proceedings of the 6th Annual Conference on Uncertainty in Artificial Intelligence, UAI 1990, pp. 255–270 (1990)
23. Verma, T., Pearl, J.: An algorithm for deciding if a set of observed independencies has a causal explanation. In: Proceedings of the 8th Annual Conference on Uncertainty in Artificial Intelligence, UAI 1992, pp. 323–330 (1992)
24. Wienöbst, M., Bannach, M., Liśkiewicz, M.: Polynomial-time algorithms for counting and sampling Markov equivalent dags. In: Proccedings of the 35th Conference on Artificial Intelligence, AAAI 2021 (2021, in press)
25. van der Zander, B., Liśkiewicz, M.: Separators and adjustment sets in Markov equivalent dags. In: Proceedings of the 30th Conference on Artificial Intelligence, AAAI 2016, pp. 3315–3321 (2016)

An Approach to Reduce the Number of Conditional Independence Tests in the PC Algorithm

Marcel Wienöbst[✉] and Maciej Liśkiewicz

Institute for Theoretical Computer Science, University of Lübeck, Lübeck, Germany
{wienoebst,liskiewi}@tcs.uni-luebeck.de

Abstract. The PC algorithm is one of the most prominent constraint-based methods for learning causal structures from observational data. The algorithm relies on conditional independence (CI) tests to infer the structure and its time consumption heavily depends on the number of performed CI tests. We present a modification, called ED-PC, such that – in the oracle model – both ED-PC and the original PC algorithm infer the same structure. However, by using a new idea allowing the detection of a v-structure without explicit knowledge of a separating set, our method reduces the number of needed CI tests significantly. This is made possible by detecting nonadjacencies considerably earlier.

Keywords: Graphical models · Causality · Bayesian networks

1 Introduction

The PC algorithm [12] is a popular and widely used constraint-based method to learn causal structures from observational data. To estimate the skeleton of the structure, the algorithm evaluates a large number of conditional independencies (CIs). The decisions of the algorithm in later stages are based upon those CI tests. Thus, a crucial task, when implementing the algorithm in its generic form, is to provide fast and reliable statistical tests for determining CIs.

However, CI testing is much more difficult than, e.g., unconditional independence estimation [3] and it is still an ongoing research topic [2,5,16,17]. Thus, particularly in the presence of high-order independencies, CI testing remains a challenging task. Many authors have investigated implementations of the generic PC algorithm, assuming specific distribution models. For example, for Gaussian data Kalisch and Bühlmann [7] proposed a method that leads to efficient high-dimensional estimation of sparse causal structures. This method was later extended by Harris and Drton [6] to non-parametric graphical models.

In our work, we make no such assumptions and investigate the basic PC algorithm with oracle access to CI statements. Our goal is to develop a modification of the algorithm, which is able to infer the true causal structure with more efficient use of CI tests. Further research may identify to what extent our method

© Springer Nature Switzerland AG 2021
S. Edelkamp et al. (Eds.): KI 2021, LNAI 12873, pp. 276–288, 2021.
https://doi.org/10.1007/978-3-030-87626-5_21

improves the implementations of the PC algorithm using specific statistical tests for CI estimations.

In this paper, when we refer to the PC algorithm, we mean its basic version proposed by Spirtes and Glymour which is presented in [12] and described in detail, e.g., in Sect. 2.2.1 and 2.3 in [7]. As mentioned above, we consider the common oracle model that assumes the existence of an oracle that the algorithm can use to determine if $(a \perp\!\!\!\perp b \mid Z)$, i.e., if two variables a and b are independent conditioning on variables Z.

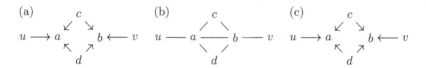

Fig. 1. DAG (a) shows the true structure and graph (b) presents the skeleton computed by the PC algorithm after completing the iteration for CI tests of order 0 and 1. To remove edge $a - b$ the PC needs CI test $(a \perp\!\!\!\perp b \mid c, d)$ of order 2. Graph (c) shows the structure computed by our modified PC algorithm after completing the iteration for CI tests of order 0 i.e. for marginal independencies.

The PC algorithm consists of three phases[1]:

1. Using CI tests of order $l = 0, 1, 2, \ldots$, learn the skeleton and estimate separation sets.
2. Using the separation sets, orient v-structures in the skeleton obtaining a pattern.
3. Orient remaining edges of the pattern with the Meek rules [8] producing the final structure.

For example, for the given CI statements induced by d-separations in the true directed acyclic graph (DAG) presented in Fig. 1(a), we show in Fig. 1(b) the structure learned by the PC algorithm when all the CI tests of order $l = 0$ and $l = 1$ during the first phase have been performed. In the next iteration, with $l = 2$, the algorithm removes the edge $a - b$ after detecting $(a \perp\!\!\!\perp b \mid c, d)$. In the second phase, the pattern is computed, and since no rule in the final phase can be applied, the pattern coincides with the true structure.

We propose a modification of the PC algorithm called ED-PC – Early Deletion PC – that computes the same structure as PC, however, by using a new approach which detects v-structures already during the CI-testing phase. As explained in detail in the following sections, this significantly reduces the order of CI tests necessary to delete edges. For example, applying ED-PC to the same CI statements discussed above for PC, our algorithm computes, in the deletion-orientation phase, the pattern shown in Fig. 1(c) using only tests of order $l = 0$,

---

[1] For exact definitions of the notions used in the algorithm, see Sect. 2.

i.e., tests for marginal independence. This means, in particular, that ED-PC can deduce that a and b have to be nonadjacent *without* finding the separation set $\{c, d\}$ as PC needs to. Through this earlier deletion of edges, ED-PC will reduce the total number of performed CIs tests.

Recently, Talvitie and Parviainen proposed an algorithm with the same objective of reducing the number of needed CI tests in the oracle model [13]. While quite effective on some graphs, it used exceedingly *more* tests than PC on others (often up to a factor 100 or 1000). As we show through an experimental analysis, our algorithm needs less tests than PC in many practical cases while never requiring significantly more tests than PC.

2 Preliminaries

Basic Graphical Concepts. We consider directed and partially directed graphs $G = (V, E)$ with $|V| = n$. In the latter case, a graph has both directed $a \rightarrow b$ and undirected $c - d$ edges. Two nodes a and b are called *adjacent* if there is an edge between them (directed or undirected). The *degree* of a node a is the number of nodes adjacent to a. For an edge $a \rightarrow b$ we call a the *parent* of b and b the *child* of a. A *path* is a sequence $p_0, \ldots, p_t$ of pairwise distinct nodes so that for all i, with $0 \leq i < t$, there is an edge connecting p_i and p_{i+1}. A path from p_0 to p_t is called *causal* if every edge on the path is directed from p_i towards p_{i+1}. A node b is called an *ancestor* of a if there is a causal path from b to a. A node b is called a *descendant* of a if there is a causal path from a to b. We use small letters for nodes and values, and capital letters for sets and random variables. Directed acyclic graphs (DAGs) contain only directed edges and no directed cycles, and partially directed acyclic graphs (PDAGs) may contain both directed and undirected edges but no directed cycles. Every DAG is a PDAG. The *skeleton* of a PDAG G is the undirected graph where every edge in G is substituted by an undirected edge.

Let P be a joint probability distribution over random variables X_i, with $i \in V$, and X, Y and Z stand for any subsets of variables. We use the notation $(X \perp\!\!\!\perp Y \mid Z)_P$ to state that X is independent of Y given Z in P. A distribution P and a DAG $D = (V, E)$ are called *compatible* if D factorizes P as $\prod_{i \in V} P(x_i \mid pa_i)$ over all realizations x_i of X_i and pa_i of variables corresponding to the parents of i in D. It is possible to read CIs over X_i, with $i \in V$, off a compatible DAG through the notion of *d-separation*. Recall, a path π is said to be *d-separated* (or *blocked*) by a set of nodes Z iff[2] (1.) π contains a chain $u \rightarrow v \rightarrow w$ or $u \leftarrow v \leftarrow w$ or a fork $u \leftarrow v \rightarrow v$ such that the middle node v is in Z, or (2.) π contains an inverted fork (or *collider*) $u \rightarrow v \leftarrow w$ such that the middle node v is not in Z and such that no descendant of v is in Z. A set Z is said to d-separate a from b iff Z blocks every path from a to b. We write $(a \perp\!\!\!\perp b \mid Z)_D$ when a and b are d-separated by Z in D. Whenever G and P are compatible, it holds for all $a, b \in V$, and $Z \subseteq V$, that if $(a \perp\!\!\!\perp b \mid Z)_D$ then $(X_a \perp\!\!\!\perp X_b \mid \{X_i : i \in Z\})_P$.

---

[2] We use *iff* as shorthand for "if and only if".

An inverted fork $u \rightarrow v \leftarrow w$ is called a *v-structure* if u and w are not adjacent. A *pattern* of a DAG D is the PDAG which has the same skeleton as D and which has an oriented edge $a \rightarrow b$ *iff* there is a vertex c, which is not adjacent to a, such that $c \rightarrow b$ is an edge in D, too. Essentially, in the pattern of D, the only directed edges are the ones which are part of a v-structure in D.

A special case of PDAGs are the so-called CPDAGs [1] or completed partially directed graphs. They represent Markov equivalence classes. If two DAGs are Markov equivalent, it means that every probability distribution that is compatible with one of the DAGs is also compatible with the other [9]. As shown in [14], two DAGs are Markov equivalent *iff* they have the same skeleton and the same v-structures.

Given a DAG $D = (V, E)$, the class of Markov equivalent graphs to D, denoted as $[D]$, is defined as $[D] = \{D' \mid D'$ is Markov equivalent to $D\}$. The graph representing $[D]$ is called a CPDAG and is denoted as $D^* = (V, E^*)$, with the set of edges defined as follows: $a \rightarrow b$ is in E^* if $a \rightarrow b$ belongs to every $D' \in [D]$ and $a - b$ is in E^* if there exist $D', D'' \in [D]$ so that $a \rightarrow b$ is an edge of D' and $a \leftarrow b$ is an edge of D''. A partially directed graph G is called a CPDAG if $G = D^*$ for some DAG D. Given a partially directed graph G, a DAG D is an extension of G *iff* G and D have the same skeleton and if $a \rightarrow b$ is in G, then $a \rightarrow b$ is in D. An extension is called *consistent* if additionally G and D have the same v-structures. Due to Theorem 3 in [8], we know that when starting with a pattern G of some DAG D and repeatedly executing the following three rules until none of them applies, we obtain a CPDAG D^* representing the Markov equivalent DAGs (that we will call the *Meek rules*):

R1: Orient $j - k$ into $j \rightarrow k$ if there is an arrow $i \rightarrow j$ s.t. i and k are nonadjacent.
R2: Orient $i - j$ into $i \rightarrow j$ if there is a chain $i \rightarrow k \rightarrow j$.
R3: Orient $i - j$ into $i \rightarrow j$ if two chains $i - k \rightarrow j$ and $i - l \rightarrow j$ exist s.t. k and l are nonadjacent.

We note that one obtains the CPDAG D^* by applying the rules not only when starting with the pattern of a DAG D but also, more generally, when the initial graph G is any PDAG whose consistent extensions form a Markov equivalence class $[D]$. We will use this property in the correctness proof of the ED-PC algorithm (Algorithm 1).

CI Statements and Faithful Models. Let V represent the set of variables. An independence model $\mathcal{I}_V$ over a set of variables represented by V is a set of triples of the form $(a \perp\!\!\!\perp b \mid Z)$, where $a, b \in V$ and Z is a subset of V, with $Z \cap \{a, b\} = \emptyset$. The triple $(a \perp\!\!\!\perp b \mid Z)$ encodes that variables X_a and X_b are independent given $X_{z_1}, \ldots, X_{z_k}$, with $Z = \{z_1, \ldots, z_k\}$. We call $\mathcal{I}_V$ a set of conditional independence (CI) statements or CI sets, for short. For a more consistent notation we write $(a \perp\!\!\!\perp b \mid Z)_{\mathcal{I}_V}$ instead of $(a \perp\!\!\!\perp b \mid Z) \in \mathcal{I}_V$, and respectively, $(a \not\perp\!\!\!\perp b \mid Z)_{\mathcal{I}_V}$ for $(a \perp\!\!\!\perp b \mid Z) \notin \mathcal{I}_V$. Additionally, in statements like e.g. $(a \perp\!\!\!\perp b \mid \{c, d\})$, we omit the brackets and write $(a \perp\!\!\!\perp b \mid c, d)$.

For a set $\mathcal{I}_V$ of CI statements, a DAG $D = (V, E)$ is called *faithful* to $\mathcal{I}_V$ if for all nodes a and b and for any $Z \subseteq V$ it is true: $(a \perp\!\!\!\perp b \mid Z)_{\mathcal{I}_V}$ *iff* $(a \perp\!\!\!\perp b \mid Z)_D$.

We denote the set of all faithful DAGs to $\mathcal{I}_V$ by $\mathcal{F}(\mathcal{I}_V)$. Due to [14], we know that, for a given $\mathcal{I}_V$, with $\mathcal{F}(\mathcal{I}_V) \neq \emptyset$, all DAGs faithful to $\mathcal{I}_V$ can be represented as a CPDAG.

Finally, we restate the following well-known technical fact for better readability (for the sake of completeness, a short proof is provided):

Lemma 1. *Given a set of CIs $\mathcal{I}_V$. If we have $(u \perp\!\!\!\perp b \mid Z)_{\mathcal{I}_V}$, $(u \not\perp\!\!\!\perp a \mid Z)_{\mathcal{I}_V}$ and $a \notin Z$, then no DAG faithful to $\mathcal{I}_V$ contains the edge $a \rightarrow b$.*

Proof. Assume, for the sake of contradiction, there is an edge $a \rightarrow b$ in a faithful DAG D. In this DAG, $(u \not\perp\!\!\!\perp a \mid Z)_{\mathcal{I}_V}$ has to hold. This means that there is a path between u and a which is not blocked by Z. But as we have the edge $a \rightarrow b$ in G, there will also be a path between u and b which is not blocked by Z (note that $a \notin Z$). A contradiction.   □

3 Detection of V-Structures in Advance

An obvious way to detect a v-structure $a \rightarrow c \leftarrow b$, used in the PC-algorithm and other causal discovery methods, is as follows: we find a separating set Z, i.e. such that $(a \perp\!\!\!\perp b \mid Z)_{\mathcal{I}_V}$, with $c \notin Z$. Then, if a and c, resp. b and c, remain adjacent after the first phase of the PC algorithm is completed, the v-structure $a \rightarrow c \leftarrow b$ is determined.

The new idea of our algorithm is that we merge the learning of the skeleton and the orientation of the v-structures. We term the graph computed at the end of this phase *extended pattern*. As soon as, in the deletion-orientation phase, a set Z separating two nodes i and j is found, besides removing the edge $i - j$, for all neighbors x of i or of j such that Z separates neither i and x nor x and j, our algorithm orients the edges as $i \rightarrow x$ and $x \leftarrow j$. If $i \rightarrow x \leftarrow j$ constitutes a v-structure in the true DAG, then it will be present in the extended pattern, too. Importantly, our algorithm orients an incident edge between a and b into $a \rightarrow b$ by removing the directed edge $a \leftarrow b$. As a consequence, it can happen that – still during the deletion-orientation phase – the algorithm removes, e.g., the edge $i \rightarrow x$ from the subgraph $i \rightarrow x \leftarrow j$ which means that i and x become nonadjacent. We call such nodes *incompatible* and we will prove that the deletion of such edges leads to the learning of the correct structure. This definition is analogous to the restricted version in [15].

Definition 1. *Let $\mathcal{I}_V$ be a set of CIs. Two nodes a and b are called* incompatible *iff the following holds: there exist $u, v \in V$ and $S, T \subseteq V$ such that $a \notin S$ and $b \notin T$ and*

$$(u \perp\!\!\!\perp b \mid S)_{\mathcal{I}_V} \wedge (u \not\perp\!\!\!\perp a \mid S)_{\mathcal{I}_V} \wedge (a \not\perp\!\!\!\perp b \mid S)_{\mathcal{I}_V} \wedge$$
$$(v \perp\!\!\!\perp a \mid T)_{\mathcal{I}_V} \wedge (v \not\perp\!\!\!\perp b \mid T)_{\mathcal{I}_V} \wedge (b \not\perp\!\!\!\perp a \mid T)_{\mathcal{I}_V}.$$

Corollary 1. *For any set of CIs $\mathcal{I}_V$ and all $a, b \in V$, if the nodes are incompatible, then they are nonadjacent in every DAG faithful to $\mathcal{I}_V$.*

This means that, whenever we encounter the conditions stated in Definition 1, any edge between a and b can be deleted. However, when learning a CPDAG another obstacle has to be overcome. Usually, when removing an edge, we store a separating set Z and this set allows us to detect potential v-structures $a \to c \gets b$ given that $c \notin Z$. When removing an edge due to incompatibility, we do not have access to such a separating set Z. It is the central observation of this paper that the v-structures can still be detected through the additional nodes u and v which are part of the definition of incompatible nodes.

4   The ED-PC Algorithm

The ED-PC algorithm is presented as Algorithm 1. Starting with a complete graph it searches for independencies, which lead to the gradual removal of edges. This is done by iteratively increasing the order l of the considered CIs beginning with order zero. In each iteration, for all currently adjacent nodes i and j, the algorithm goes exhaustively through all candidate separating sets Z of cardinality l (the currently considered order) which can be formed by the neighbors of i. If Z d-separates i and j, i.e. if $(i \perp\!\!\!\perp j \mid Z)_{\mathcal{I}_V}$ holds, the (directed) edges $i \to j$ and $i \gets j$ are removed (that means the deletion of $i - j$). This is done just as in the PC algorithm. The main difference comes next, in lines 10–14.

After detecting $(i \perp\!\!\!\perp j \mid Z)_{\mathcal{I}_V}$ and removing the edge $i - j$, the algorithm immediately tries to orient edges incident to i or to j. We emphasize again that orienting an edge $a - b$ into $a \to b$ actually means removing the edge $a \gets b$. We use the term orientation at times because it is more intuitive, but formally we mean the removal of a directed edge. In the for-loop (lines 1014) the algorithm goes through all nodes x, which are not in Z but are neighbors of i or j, with the aim to orient the edges between i and x and between x and j. For this, it is checked if the conditions stated in Lemma 1 apply.

In case both pairs of nodes are incident by edges $i - x$, resp. $x - j$ and both $(i \not\perp\!\!\!\perp x \mid Z)_{\mathcal{I}_V}$ and $(x \not\perp\!\!\!\perp j \mid Z)_{\mathcal{I}_V}$ hold, this leads to the orientations $i \to x$ and $x \gets j$. Thus, here we proceed similarly to the orientation of the v-structures in the PC algorithm. A major difference, however, is that we do this before knowing the true skeleton. This leads to the crucial distinction between the PC and our algorithm: in case i and x or x and j are incident by a *directed* edge $i \gets x$ or $x \to j$ (since in previous iterations $i \to x$ or $x \gets j$ have been removed in line 12) due to removing $i \gets x$ and $x \to j$ in the current iteration step, nodes i and x, or x and j, become nonadjacent. Thus, executing the ED-PC algorithm, two nodes a and b can become nonadjacent not because a separating set is found, but because the edges $a \to b$ and $a \gets b$ are removed in different iterations of line 12. If this happens, the nodes a and b are incompatible (Definition 1).

At some point, no further separating sets can be formed because l is larger or equal to the number of neighbors of i. In this case, we have learned a structure, that we call the *extended pattern*. Finally, we maximally extend this graph using the Meek rules. Note that, in line 20, we store the extended pattern in G_{ep}. We explicitly need this graph for the proofs of correctness in Sect. 5. In particular,

---

Algorithm 1 The ED-PC Algorithm

Input: vertex set V, access to CI information $\mathcal{I}_V$
Output: PDAG G
1: Let G be the complete undirected graph on V
2: Let $l = 0$
3: **repeat**
4:    **repeat**
5:       Take new adjacent $i, j \in V$ s.t. $|N(i) \setminus \{j\}| \geq l$
6:       **repeat**
7:          Choose new $Z \subseteq N(i)\setminus\{j\}$ with $|Z| = l$
8:          **if** $(i \perp\!\!\!\perp j \mid Z)_{\mathcal{I}_V}$ **then**
9:             Remove $i \rightarrow j$ and $i \leftarrow j$ from G
10:            **for all** $x \notin Z$ s.t. $i \leftarrow x$ or $x \leftarrow j$ is in G **do**
11:               **if** $(i \not\perp\!\!\!\perp x \mid Z)_{\mathcal{I}_V}$ and $(x \not\perp\!\!\!\perp j \mid Z)_{\mathcal{I}_V}$ **then**
12:                  Remove $i \leftarrow x$ and $x \rightarrow j$ from G
13:               **end if**
14:            **end for**
15:         **end if**
16:      **until** no new $Z \subseteq N(i)\setminus\{j\}$, with $|Z| = l$, exists
17:   **until** all pairs of adjacent i and j s.t. $|N(i)\setminus\{j\}| \geq l$ have been selected
18:   Set $l = l + 1$
19: **until** for each adjacent i, j: $|N(i)\setminus\{j\}| < l$
20: For the sake of analysis, let $G_{\mathrm{ep}} = G$
21: **repeat** in G:
22:   R1: Orient $j - k$ into $j \rightarrow k$ whenever there is an arrow $i \rightarrow j$ such that i and k are nonadjacent
23:   R2: Orient $i - j$ into $i \rightarrow j$ whenever there is a chain $i \rightarrow k \rightarrow j$
24:   R3: Orient $i - j$ into $i \rightarrow j$ if two chains $i - k \rightarrow j$ and $i - l \rightarrow j$ exist such that k and l are nonadjacent
25: **until** no further rule can be applied.

---

we show there that G_{ep} has the same skeleton as the true graph D, contains all directed edges of G's pattern, and some other directed edges which are consistent with the edges of the CPDAG representing D.

Before discussing the complexity, we show examples of executions of both algorithms to illustrate the differences between ED-PC and PC. First, we apply the algorithms to the CI statements induced by the true DAG shown in Fig. 1(a). The corresponding executions are illustrated in Fig. 2. To remove an edge between two nodes, the PC algorithm needs an explicit separator of order l between those nodes. In particular, the edge $a - b$ is deleted, when the separator $\{c, d\}$ of order $l = 2$ is found. The ED-PC algorithm removes all edges (in line 9 or line 12) using only CI tests of order $l = 0$. E.g. it removes both directed edges $u \rightarrow c$ and $c \leftarrow u$ in line 9 detecting the (marginal) independence $(u \perp\!\!\!\perp c)_{\mathcal{I}_V}$. The directed edges $a \rightarrow b$ and $a \leftarrow b$ are removed in line 12 in two different iterations of the main repeat-loop. Edge $a \rightarrow b$ is removed when $i = u, j = b, x = a$, and $Z = \emptyset$ is selected, since the conditions: $(u \perp\!\!\!\perp b)_{\mathcal{I}_V}$ (line 8) and $(u \not\perp\!\!\!\perp a)_{\mathcal{I}_V}$ and

$(a \not\perp b)_{\mathcal{I}_V}$ (line 11) are true; Edge $a \leftarrow b$ is removed for $i = a, j = v, x = b$, and $Z = \emptyset$, since we have $(a \perp\!\!\!\perp v)_{\mathcal{I}_V}$, $(a \not\perp b)_{\mathcal{I}_V}$, and $(b \not\perp v)_{\mathcal{I}_V}$.

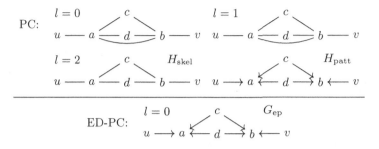

Fig. 2. Examples of executions of the ED-PC and the PC algorithm for the true DAG presented in Fig. 1(a). The upper part shows structures computed by the PC after completing the iteration for $l = 0, 1$, resp. 2, the resulting skeleton H_{skel} and finally the pattern H_{patt}. The ED-PC algorithm finds the extended pattern G_{ep} after completing the iteration for $l = 0$. Both G_{ep} and H_{patt} are the final results of the algorithms since no rule R1-R3 can be applied.

In our second example, we apply the PC and ED-PC to the CIs induced by the following true DAG: $a \leftrightarrow b \leftrightarrows c \leftarrow d$. After completing the main for-loop the ED-PC estimates the extended skeleton G_{ep}: $a \leftrightarrow b \leftrightharpoons c \leftarrow d$. The PC computes the skeleton H_{skel}: $a \frown b \frown c - d$ and next the pattern H_{patt}: $a \frown b \leftrightharpoons c \leftarrow d$. The graph G_{ep} is not identical to the pattern H_{patt} obtained by the PC algorithm, as the edge $a \to b$ is directed even though it is not in a v-structure. This is why we introduced the term extended pattern. After following this example, it is also clear why edges like $a \to b$ can be oriented without being in a v-structure. The reason is that this edge is part of a v-structure $a \to b \leftarrow d$, which only appears intermediately during the execution of the algorithm as the edge $b \leftarrow d$ is later removed. This shows that due to the new ideas in the ED-PC, we are able to direct more edges when constructing the pattern compared to the PC algorithm. We note that the edge $a - b$ is directed $a \to b$ in PC as well. This, however, happens not until the application of the Meek rules.

We complete this section with an analysis of the number of CI tests needed in the ED-PC algorithm. The number is expressed according to n – the size of the vertex set – and the maximum node degree $d_{\max}$ in the underlying DAG. The same worst-case as for the PC algorithm applies. However, in line 11 the ED-PC algorithm employs two additional tests for each neighbor of i or j whenever an edge $i - j$ is deleted in line 9. As only at most n^2 such edges can be removed and there are at most $n - 2$ neighbors, an additional additive term $\mathcal{O}(n^3)$ follows. Asymptotically, the number of CI tests is therefore bounded by $\mathcal{O}(n^{2+d_{\max}} + n^3)$.

While ED-PC does not improve the worst-case number of necessary tests, in many cases, incompatible nodes are found and thus, edges are deleted earlier in comparison to PC leading to a reduced search space (see Sect. 6).

5   Proof of Correctness

Now, we formally prove the correctness of the ED-PC algorithm. We first show that the skeleton of the resulting structure coincides with the skeleton of the true model. Afterwards, we prove that the v-structures are recovered correctly.

Proposition 1. *For all CI statements $\mathcal{I}_V$, with $\mathcal{F}(\mathcal{I}_V) \neq \emptyset$, the PDAG G_{ep} computed by Algorithm 1 (in line 20) has the same skeleton as every DAG D faithful with $\mathcal{I}_V$.*

Proof. The above statement can also be formulated as: The nodes a and b are nonadjacent in PDAG G_{ep} *iff* they are nonadjacent in every faithful DAG D.

First, we show that if an edge is missing from PDAG G_{ep}, it is also missing from D, i.e., whenever during the execution of the algorithm an edge was removed from G, this choice was correct. There are two cases to consider: both directed edges $a \to b$ and $a \leftarrow b$ are removed in line 9 or they are removed in two different iterations of the repeat-loop in line 12. The first case happens only if a set Z was found that separates a and b. But then the nodes a and b cannot be adjacent in any faithful DAG as else a and b would be conditionally dependent given Z. The second case happens if the algorithm selects $i, j = b, x = a$, and Z, with $Z \cap \{a, b, i\} = \emptyset$, such that the following holds: $(i \perp\!\!\!\perp b \mid Z)_{\mathcal{I}_V} \wedge (i \not\perp\!\!\!\perp a \mid Z)_{\mathcal{I}_V} \wedge (a \not\perp\!\!\!\perp b \mid Z)_{\mathcal{I}_V}$ (then the algorithm removes $a \to b$) and if $i = a, j, x = b$, and Z', with $Z' \cap \{a, b, j\} = \emptyset$, are chosen such that we have $(a \perp\!\!\!\perp j \mid Z')_{\mathcal{I}_V} \wedge (a \not\perp\!\!\!\perp b \mid Z')_{\mathcal{I}_V} \wedge (b \not\perp\!\!\!\perp j \mid Z')_{\mathcal{I}_V}$ (in this case $a \leftarrow b$ is removed). This means that a and b are incompatible (see Definition 1) and, from Lemma 1, we can conclude that there cannot be an edge between a and b in any faithful DAG.

Next, we show that if a and b are nonadjacent in a faithful DAG D, they are also nonadjacent in the resulting PDAG G_{ep}. We assume, for the sake of contradiction, that there is an edge between a and b in G_{ep}. Then, there was no set Z found in line 7 which separated a and b. But we exhaustively searched for every subset of the set of neighbors of a (and b) in G_{ep}. This set of neighbors was at all times a superset of the neighbors of a (and b) in D because, as we have seen in the first part of this proof, if a and b are nonadjacent in G_{ep}, they are also nonadjacent in D. But this means that no subset of neighbors of a (or b) separates a and b in D which would mean, by correctness of the PC-Algorithm (see e.g. Lemma 5.1.1 in [12]), that a and b are adjacent in D as well.   □

Proposition 2. *Assume $\mathcal{I}_V$ is a set of CIs, with $\mathcal{F}(\mathcal{I}_V) \neq \emptyset$, and let D be a DAG faithful to $\mathcal{I}_V$. Then for all a, b, c in V it is true: $a \to c \leftarrow b$ is a v-structure in D iff $a \to c \leftarrow b$ is a v-structure in G_{ep} computed by Algorithm 1.*

Proof. First, we show that if there is a certain v-structure in a faithful DAG D, then this v-structure will be in the PDAG G_{ep}. Let the v-structure we consider be $a \rightarrow c \leftarrow b$. We have already seen in Proposition 1 that the edge $a - b$ will be deleted in G_{ep} and a and c, resp. b and c will be adjacent in G_{ep}. It remains to be shown that the edges $a \leftarrow c$ and $c \rightarrow b$ are removed leaving the directed edges $a \rightarrow c$ and $c \leftarrow b$. We consider two cases.

Case 1: The edge $a - b$ was deleted in line 9. Let the chosen separating set by Z. We show that the conditions in the if-statement in line 11, with $x = c$, are met. Because there is the structure $a \rightarrow c \leftarrow b$ in D, it follows that $(a \not\perp c \mid Z)_{\mathcal{I}_V}$ and $(c \not\perp b \mid Z)_{\mathcal{I}_V}$ hold and c is not in Z (note that this holds for every separating set Z). Thus, the edges $a \leftarrow c$ and $c \rightarrow b$ are removed in line 12. Due to the fact that G_{ep} and D have the same skeleton (Proposition 1), the edges $a \rightarrow c \leftarrow b$ will not be removed later.

Case 2: The edges $a \leftarrow b$ and $a \rightarrow b$ were deleted at different iterations in line 12. Thus, similarly as in the proof of Proposition 1, we can conclude that for some i and Z, with $Z \cap \{a, b, i\} = \emptyset$, the following holds: $(i \perp b \mid Z)_{\mathcal{I}_V} \wedge (i \not\perp a \mid Z)_{\mathcal{I}_V} \wedge (a \not\perp b \mid Z)_{\mathcal{I}_V}$ and for some j and Z', with $Z' \cap \{a, b, j\} = \emptyset$, we have $(a \perp j \mid Z')_{\mathcal{I}_V} \wedge (a \not\perp b \mid Z')_{\mathcal{I}_V} \wedge (b \not\perp j \mid Z')_{\mathcal{I}_V}$. Since D is faithful to $\mathcal{I}_V$, the above (in)dependencies hold for D. Moreover, in D there is a v-structure $a \rightarrow c \leftarrow b$. For an illustration, see Fig. 3.

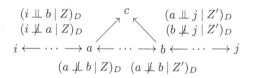

Fig. 3. Case 2 of the proof of Proposition 2. There exists a v-structure $a \rightarrow c \leftarrow b$ in D and sets Z and Z' such that the above (in)dependencies hold. We argue that $(i \not\perp c \mid Z)_D$, $(j \not\perp c \mid Z')_D$, $c \notin Z$ and $c \notin Z'$ hold as well.

Due to the faithfulness of D, further (in)dependencies can be deduced. The independencies $(i \not\perp c \mid Z)_{\mathcal{I}_V}$ and $(j \not\perp c \mid Z')_{\mathcal{I}_V}$ hold as well because of $a \notin Z$ and $b \notin Z'$ and the fact that, with the edges $a \rightarrow c$ and $b \rightarrow c$ in the faithful DAG D, there is neither a collider at node a nor at node b. On the other hand, there is a collider at node c (on the path from i to b as well as from j to a) and therefore $c \notin Z$ and $c \notin Z'$ hold. Combining this with $(c \not\perp b \mid Z)_{\mathcal{I}_V}$ (due to the edge $c \leftarrow b$ in D there cannot be any independence between c and b) and $(i \perp b \mid Z)_{\mathcal{I}_V}$, the edge $c \rightarrow b$ is removed from G_{ep} because the conditions in lines 8 and 11 are satified (with $j = b$ and $x = c$). One can argue analogously that the edge $a \leftarrow c$ is removed. Hence, we also have the v-structure $a \rightarrow c \leftarrow b$ in G_{ep}.

To complete the proof, it remains to show that, if there is a v-structure in the PDAG G_{ep}, this v-structure is also in every faithful DAG. Let the v-structure we consider be $a \rightarrow c \leftarrow b$. From Proposition 1 we know that the edge

$a - b$ is missing in every faithful DAG and edges between a and c as well as between c and b are present in every faithful DAG. We know that when only the edge $a \to c$ (but not $a \leftarrow c$) is in G_{ep} the following holds for some i and Z: $(i \perp\!\!\!\perp a \mid Z)_{\mathcal{I}_V}$, $(i \not\perp\!\!\!\perp c \mid Z)_{\mathcal{I}_V}$, $(a \not\perp\!\!\!\perp c \mid Z)_{\mathcal{I}_V}$, and $c \notin Z$. Due to Lemma 1, we know that no faithful DAG contains the edge $a \leftarrow c$ and accordingly has to contain the edge $a \to c$. The same holds for $c \leftarrow b$. Thus, in every faithful DAG, there will also be the v-structure $a \to c \leftarrow b$.   □

Theorem 1. *For the given CI set $\mathcal{I}_V$ Algorithm 1 computes the CPDAG representing DAGs in $\mathcal{F}(\mathcal{I}_V)$, if $\mathcal{F}(\mathcal{I}_V) \neq \emptyset$.*

Proof. Assume $\mathcal{F}(\mathcal{I}_V) \neq \emptyset$. We have shown in Proposition 1 that the algorithm produces the same skeleton as every faithful DAG. Moreover, due to Proposition 2 the PDAG G_{ep} we obtain in line 20 contains the same v-structures as every faithful DAG and every directed edge $a \to b$ is directed in this manner in every faithful DAG. Then the three rules in lines 22–24 maximally extend this PDAG as shown in [8] to produce the correct CPDAG G.   □

In case $\mathcal{F}(\mathcal{I}_V) = \emptyset$, Algorithm 1 and the PC algorithm can produce different PDAGs. E.g. our algorithm removes an edge in two conflicting v-structures (these are also called ambiguous v-structures [4]), while the PC algorithm, depending on implementation, may keep such edges arbitrarily oriented or mark them as ambiguous.

6   Experimental Analysis

In this section, we empirically validate our main claims that the ED-PC algorithm is able to delete edges earlier than the PC algorithm, which also leads to less CI tests in total. We conduct our tests in the oracle model. Hence, the two algorithms, PC and ED-PC, produce the same causal model, which is the CPDAG representing the Markov equivalence class of the underlying true DAG. This true DAG is known and used for answering CI queries through d-separation tests. We conduct our tests on real life causal structures as well as random ones, which are produced by generating a random graph according to the Erdös-Rényi (ER) model and directing edges by imposing a uniformly chosen topological ordering.

The results of the experiments are shown in Fig. 4. In the upper row, one can see, for the real life structures alarm, water and win95pts [10] as well as random graphs with 60 vertices and expected node degree 4, the ratio of performed CI tests from ED-PC and PC per order. In the bottom row, we show the cumulative number of deleted edges (detected nonadjacencies) up to order l by each of the algorithms as a ratio with the number of all nonadjacencies in the true DAG. As both learn the true skeleton, this ratio converges to one.

For the alarm network, ED-PC actually performs more tests for some orders (the ratio is above 1). As seen in the cumulative plot, this is due to the fact that barely any nonadjacency is detected earlier compared to PC. Hence, only

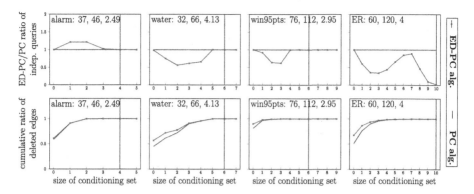

Fig. 4. In the upper row, the ratio of tests per order in ED-PC and PC is displayed; in the bottom row the ratio of detected nonadjacencies up to order l. Three real life networks are considered, as well as the average over 50 random DAGs (ER). Next to the name on the top of each plot, we show the number of vertices, the number of edges, respectively, the average node degree.

the additional effort of ED-PC remains. On many graphs, however, ED-PC is able to detect nonadjacencies earlier. This can be seen for examples water and win95pts, where this leads to significantly fewer tests in particular for orders $l = 2$ and $l = 3$. For the random graphs this behaviour is even more pronounced and ED-PC often needs half as many tests compared to PC.

With increasing order l both algorithms converge to the true skeleton and, hence, the number of performed CI tests is very similar. However, we observed that often, at high-orders, the algorithms search for further independencies even though the true skeleton is already learned. This point, from which on no further independencies are detected, is highlighted with a vertical red line. For practical applications, it seems natural to combine ED-PC with an early termination approach to make the most of its improved nonadjacency detection. Such early termination approaches have been analyzed for PC in the past, e.g., in [11].

7   Conclusions and Outlook

We showed in the oracle model that the ED-PC algorithm is able to remove edges earlier during the course of the algorithm, by extensively utilizing lower-order independencies, while still producing theoretically sound results, i.e., the true CPDAG. This earlier edge removal leads to more efficient learning, meaning the number of performed CI tests is lower than in the PC algorithm as well.

In practice, the CI queries are not answered by an oracle, but have to be tested statistically. For certain distributions, it is known that the analysis from the oracle model holds asymptotically and the correct graph is produced with high probability. However, when dealing with finite samples, some queries will be answered incorrectly and, hence, the algorithm might make incorrect choices. From a practical point of view, it is therefore crucial that the algorithm is robust towards such errors. The ED-PC algorithm relies (even to a larger extent than the PC algorithm) on the correctness of the tests, e. g., an incorrect query answer might lead to a falsely missing edge. For future work, it is therefore an important task to derive such robust versions of constraint-based algorithms and in particular ED-PC.

Acknowledgements. This work was supported by the Deutsche Forschungsgemeinschaft (DFG) grant LI634/4-2.

References

1. Andersson, S.A., Madigan, D., Perlman, M.D.: A characterization of Markov equivalence classes for acyclic digraphs. Ann. Stat. **25**(2), 505–541 (1997)
2. Baba, K., Shibata, R., Sibuya, M.: Partial correlation and conditional correlation as measures of conditional independence. Aust. N. Z. J. Stat. **46**(4), 657–664 (2004)
3. Bergsma, W.P.: Testing conditional independence for continuous random variables. Eurandom (2004)
4. Colombo, D., Maathuis, M.H., Kalisch, M., Richardson, T.S.: Learning high-dimensional directed acyclic graphs with latent and selection variables. Ann. Stat. **40**, 294–321 (2012)
5. Doran, G., Muandet, K., Zhang, K., Schölkopf, B.: A permutation-based kernel conditional independence test. In: UAI, pp. 132–141 (2014)
6. Harris, N., Drton, M.: PC algorithm for nonparanormal graphical models. J. Mach. Learn. Res. **14**(1), 3365–3383 (2013)
7. Kalisch, M., Bühlmann, P.: Estimating high-dimensional directed acyclic graphs with the PC-Algorithm. J. Mach. Learn. Res. **8**, 613–636 (2007)
8. Meek, C.: Causal inference and causal explanation with background knowledge. In: Proceedings of UAI 1995, pp. 403–410. MK Publishers Inc. (1995)
9. Pearl, J.: Causality: Models, Reasoning and Inference, 2nd edn. Cambridge University Press, Cambridge (2009)
10. Scutari, M.: Learning Bayesian networks with the bnlearn R package. J. Stat. Softw. **35**(3), 1–22 (2010)
11. Sondhi, A., Shojaie, A.: The reduced PC-algorithm: improved causal structure learning in large random networks. J. Mach. Learn. Res. **20**(164), 1–31 (2019)
12. Spirtes, P., Glymour, C., Scheines, R.: Causation, Prediction, and Search, 2nd edn. MIT Press, Cambridge (2000)
13. Talvitie, T., Parviainen, P.: Learning Bayesian networks with cops and robbers. In: The 10th International Conference on Probabilistic Graphical Models (2020)
14. Verma, T., Pearl, J.: Equivalence and synthesis of causal models. In: Proceedings of UAI 1990, pp. 255–270. Elsevier (1990)
15. Wienöbst, M., Liśkiewicz, M.: Recovering causal structures from low-order conditional independencies. In: 34th AAAI Conference on Artificial Intelligence (AAAI), pp. 10302–10309 (2020)
16. Zhang, H., Zhou, S., Zhang, K., Guan, J.: Causal discovery using regression-based conditional independence tests. In: Thirty-First AAAI Conference on Artificial Intelligence (2017)
17. Zhang, K., Peters, J., Janzing, D., Schölkopf, B.: Kernel-based conditional independence test and application in causal discovery. In: 27th Conference on Uncertainty in Artificial Intelligence (UAI 2011), pp. 804–813. AUAI Press (2011)

Poster Papers

Unsupervised Anomaly Detection for Financial Auditing with Model-Agnostic Explanations

Sebastian Kiefer[1,2]([✉]) [ID] and Günter Pesch[1]

[1] DATEV eG, Paumgartnerstr. 6-14, 90429 Nürnberg, Germany
{sebastian.kiefer,guenter.pesch}@datev.de
[2] Cognitive Systems, University of Bamberg, Kapuzinerstraße 16,
96047 Bamberg, Germany
sebastian.kiefer@uni-bamberg.de

Abstract. Explainable Artificial Intelligence (AI) has emerged to be a key component for Black-Box Machine Learning (ML) approaches in domains with a high demand for transparency. Besides medical expert systems, which inherently need to be interpretable, transparent, and comprehensible as they deal with life-changing decision tasks, other application domains like financial auditing require trust in ML as well. The European General Data Protection Regulation (GDPR) also applies to such highly regulated areas where an auditor evaluates financial transactions and statements of a business. In this paper we propose an ML architecture that shall help financial auditors by transparently detecting anomalous datapoints in the absence of ground truth. While most of the time Anomaly Detection (AD) is performed in a supervised manner, where model-agnostic explainers can be easily applied, unsupervised AD is hardly comprehensible especially across different algorithms. In this work we investigate how to dissolve this: We describe an integrated architecture for unsupervised AD that identifies outliers at different levels of granularity using an ensemble of independent algorithms. Furthermore, we show how model-agnostic explanations can be generated for such an ensemble using supervised approximation and Local Interpretable Model-Agnostic Explanations (LIME). Additionally, we propose techniques for explanation-post-processing that allow explanations to be selective, receiver-dependent, and easily understandable. In a nutshell, our architecture paves the way for model-agnostic explainability for the task of unsupervised AD. It can further be transferred smoothly to other unsupervised ML problems like clustering problems.

Keywords: Anomaly Detection · Outlier Detection · Unsupervised Learning · Explainable Artificial Intelligence · Human-like explanations

Supported by organization DATEV eG.

S. Edelkamp et al. (Eds.): KI 2021, LNAI 12873, pp. 291–308, 2021.
https://doi.org/10.1007/978-3-030-87626-5_22

1   Introduction

Besides ML research, especially supervised ML is broadly applied to solve data-driven problems in business environments. Many of those "applied" ML domains, whether they are concerned with strongly regulated scenarios like in financial auditing, with decision-critical situations like in self-driving cars, or even with life-changing situations like in tasks of medical diagnosis, require more than purely a high prediction accuracy. Instead, concepts such as transparency and comprehensibility are needed so that humans affected by ML decisions can develop trust into the systems. Especially Black-Box ML classifiers lack the ability to provide an explicit declarative knowledge representation and hide the underlying explanatory structure [15]. To address these shortcomings, two scientific fields have emerged, namely Interpretable Machine Learning (IML) and Explainable Artificial Intelligence (XAI). While IML focuses on creating global and model-intrinsic interpretability by providing intrinsic, ex ante- understanding of the whole ML model's logic, XAI strives for enabling local and model-agnostic interpretability to achieve an ex post- understanding of the models' specific behavior [1]. Combining both results in Comprehensible Artificial Intelligence (cAI), which strives for generating results that are transparent and comprehensible [7]. Those two properties form the basis of trust in AI. Comparatively little attention, in general and in particular from interpretability point of view, has been paid to unsupervised learning approaches. Nevertheless, many data-driven problems in business environments like the one described in the following are hard to tackle with supervised ML, mostly because of missing label annotations that represent the ground truth. The research results, that are presented in the further course of this paper, have been achieved during work for the company DATEV eG. DATEV eG is a software house and IT service provider for tax consultants, auditors and lawyers as well as for their clients. Since the company provides software solutions for automated processes in financial accounting, among other things, quality assurance is of great importance. One possibility to continuously monitor and improve such solutions is the use of AD mechanisms. Therefore, we develop an integrated and explainable AD architecture and demonstrate its functionality prototypical for the domain of financial auditing. As a wide range of customers and companies from different sectors is involved, which all reveal tax and financial singularities, an exhaustive labeling of instances as normal or anomalous is not feasible. Therefore, our approach strives for several objectives. On the one hand, the proposed architecture shall perform efficient AD using unsupervised ML that suggests specific presumably anomalous instances for further inspection. As financial accounting and auditing represent highly regulated processes, the system on the other hand shall provide intuitive and human-like explanations for the ML system's decisions allowing humans to comprehend the system and understand its individual decisions. In such a critical area the ability to explain an AD algorithm might almost be as important as the model's prediction accuracy [3]. By the absence of ground truth and by the usage of different AD algorithms, purposeful feature engineering is complicated (what are good features w.r.t. detection performance and are there differences in feature quality across different algorithms?). Thus, the system shall also be capable of generating more detailed explanations and visualizations for Data Scientists to create predictive features by introspection of the explanations (the feature attributions). Also a restriction to specific AD algorithms like Deep Learning (DL) algorithms (such as Autoencoders) is not desired when lacking class labels (what are outliers and how many outliers are there?). Instead, an ensemble-based architecture shall be harnessed that combines different algorithms and performs the varying AD tasks from different perspectives and in a robust manner while keeping the false positive rate of the system low. As a consequence, the explanation module for such an ensemble cannot be based on global and intrinsic explanations, but rather must comprise a model-agnostic way of generating helpful explanations that describe the AD ensemble's behavior locally. Such model-agnostic explanation generators like LIME [31] or SHapley Additive exPlanations (SHAP) [21] typically are designed for supervised ML approaches, which have access to ground-truth-information. Therefore, we propose to integrate a supervised ML model into our AD architecture that approximates the unsupervised AD ensemble globally. It can then be used as a basis for LIME to generate local and model-agnostic explanations at different levels of granularity.

2   Related Work

Anomaly Analysis aims at identifying datapoints or regions from the data whose characteristics differ from expected values [9]. Those subsets that differ significantly from the remainder of the data are called anomalies and in the following also referred to as outliers interchangeably [23]. As AD is applied to a wide variety of application domains, which all might differ in terms of the nature of the data (be it continuous or discrete data), the type of occurring anomalies (Point Anomalies, Collective Anomalies, or Contextual Anomalies), the availability of data (labeled or unlabeled data), and the evaluation criteria (like Overall Accuracy, Precision, Recall), different AD technologies have been proposed [8,11]. These range from kernel-based over distance-based, clustering-based, density-based, to ensemble-based algorithms [26]. Since a single AD technique usually cannot discover all anomalies in a low dimensional subspace due to data complexity, ensemble-based algorithms have its justification in many application domains [35]. Often, AD approaches are also divided into ML approaches (where DL represents a special case) and statistical approaches, which use stochastic models and the according assumptions of certain data distributions [8]. Approaches from both types can be combined or integrated with visualization techniques (like scatter plot matrix or parallel coordinate plots) and with dimension reduction techniques (like Principal Component Analysis (PCA), Multidimensional Scaling (MDS), or t-stochastic neighbor embedding (t-SNE)) [34].

Recently, the question how AD algorithms can be explained arouses certain interest. On the one hand, there are special explainers for Isolation Forests like an adaptation of the SHAP Tree Explainer [21] and extensions of Kernel SHAP for explaining Autoencoders for AD [3]. On the other hand, there is work using centroids as representation for a cluster of points for cluster-based AD techniques [30], which works well if clusters are compact or isotropic, but malfunctions otherwise. In addition, harnessing PCA or t-SNE enables visualization of identified clusters in two-dimensional space [16,22]. Furthermore, one can use a decision tree per cluster after the clustering process for explaining certain clusters or use approaches like Interpretable Clustering via Optimal Trees (ICOT), where the individual clusters represent the leaves of a decision tree [5]. Another possibility is to apply Deep Taylor Decomposition of a One-Class Support Vector Machine (OCSVM) and to explain the outcomes using support vectors or input features [17]. Summing up, a lot of research either focussed on intrinsic and global explanations for AD algorithms or adapted local and model-agnostic explainers like SHAP to specific AD algorithms like Isolation Forests or Autoencoders. By doing so, the full power of real model-agnostic explainers is often lost. Many times, research on explainability even entirely concentrated on supervised AD approaches. As a consequence, we propose to conduct further research especially on real model-agnostic explanation strategies for unsupervised AD models. Although developed independently from each other, we found work from Morichetta et al. [25] that partially aligns well with ours. In their work the authors propose an architecture for generating model-agnostic explanations for the unsupervised problem of Network Traffic Analysis. Our main idea is to build a supervised ML model that approximates the unsupervised AD ensemble globally and acts as a basis for subsequent model-agnostic local explanation systems like LIME or SHAP. LIME is a method that explains an individual model's prediction by locally approximating the model's decision boundary in the neighborhood of the given instance [31]. It uses a local linear explanation model and can thus be characterized as an additive feature attribution method [21]. For even more expressive explanations it can be combined with Inductive Logic Programming (ILP) in order to generate first-order rules as explanations [29].

3 Explainable Anomaly Detection in the Context of Auditing

An annual audit covers all transactions of a client with all business partners in one year. Due to the huge amount of transactions, the auditor is caught in a dilemma: On the one hand, he is required to conduct the audit very thoroughly. On the other hand, the contract's monetary structure doesn't allow him to run a full examination. Therefore, he restricts the examination on a sample of transactions carefully selected based on his experience. This procedure, however, still creates many blind spots with potential irregularities staying unrevealed. The aim of this paper is to dissolve this dilemma. It provides an integrated approach to detect anomalies in the audit process among the whole amount of transactions. Additionally, it restricts the quantity of anomalies to a feasible size and gives receiver-dependent model-agnostic explanations for the reasons why datapoints were identified as anomalies. Figure 1 gives an overview of the integrated

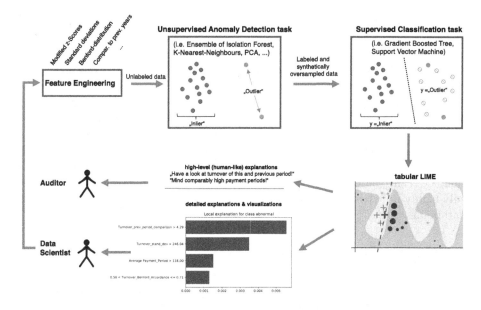

Fig. 1. Architecture of the Anomaly Detection and Explanation process

architecture of our proposed approach. Each step is described in detail in the following subsections.

3.1 Data

This work is based on two different DATEV datasets. The first one is generally used to train aspiring tax advisors during their education at university. Although it consists of artificial data, it provides a good impression exemplary for one client of how the data and the technical issues are made of. The second dataset consists of real client data covering the full bandwidth from small to big clients with many transactions. Table 1 depicts both datasets' characteristics.

Table 1. Characteristics of the used datasets

	University	Real-World
Clients	1	220
Accounts	258	14687
Transactions	6346	998085
Maximum (Transact. per Account)	717	96353
Median (Transact. per Account)	19	22

In general, the used datasets comprise data from one or more clients. A client's bookkeeping is structured in different accounts, which have different intentions. While there are accounts collecting internal transactions only, there are other accounts containing transactions between the client and its business partners. Due to the reason that transactions with business partners are one of the main fields of fraud, our work focuses on accounts with business partners exclusively. In particular, we evaluate accounts that cover sales revenue and incoming goods. Furthermore, we distinguish between ingoing and outgoing accounting entries. As an example, in an incoming goods account an invoice from the business partner represents the ingoing accounting entry, whereas the accounting entry for paying the invoice represents the outgoing one. Both accounting entries build a logical entry couple comprising the whole transaction. Overall, the described datasets are multivariate, unlabeled, and supposedly highly imbalanced with regard to the distribution of normal and anomalous datapoints.

3.2   Feature Engineering

As already mentioned, the smallest unit of consideration in our context is a transaction. It consists of various data fields such as invoice number, date of transaction, discount, amount, currency, tax rate, and a descriptive text. In order to find crucial features for AD, we interviewed several domain experts, who gave us valuable insights. It turned out that it is useful to take two different views when dealing with such data in the context of financial auditing:

Transaction
  Examine one transaction among all other transactions with a business partner. In the following, this view is called *TA*.

Account
  Examine one account among all other accounts. In the following, this view is called *ACC*. As there are no meaningful singular facts for an account, we gain the features from the set of transactions belonging to the account.

Furthermore, AD should be conducted stationary and thus should leave changes over time aside, with a certain feature that compares turnover values to the previous year's values as the only exception. Since the complete feature description is intellectual property of DATEV eG, we are unable to describe each feature in detail. Nevertheless, among others the following features have been engineered during our work for *TA*:

Turnover - Modified Z-Score: Deviation to Median Absolute Deviation (MAD), which is an alternative and more robust measure of dispersion compared to sample variance or standard deviation [18].

Turnover - Smoothness: Smooth turnover values can be a hint for obscure transactions. Therefore, we developed a measure to express the smoothness of turnover.

Tax Rate: In Germany, the general tax rate is 19%. However, for some goods the rate is reduced to 10.7%, 7%, 5.5% or 0%. In the wake of the corona crisis some rates were changed from 19% to 16% and from 7% to 5%.

Payment Period: The period between invoicing and payment.

For *ACC*, the following features are included:

Turnover Standard Deviation: The Standard Deviation of the turnover per account is calculated.

Turnover Maximum Deviation: The maximum of the modified z-scores per account, which internally use the Median Absolute Deviation of the turnover, is calculated.

Turnover - Degree of Smoothness: The share of smooth turnover values is taken as feature for AD.

Turnover - Degree of Accordance with Benford Distribution: Benford's law states that in many sets of numbers the leading digit *1* tends to occur with probability approximately 30%, although the expected probability is 11.1%. It is a common analytical tool when probing financial fraud [4,14].

Turnover - Accordance with Period of Previous Year: This feature describes a value that compares current turnover to previous year's turnover.

Tax Rate: This feature analyzes homogeneity of used tax rates in the account.

Payment Period: A measure that specifies the average payment period per account.

3.3   Ensemble-Based Architecture

Due to the fact that there is no labeled data (i.e., existing anomalies in historical data), we are challenged with an unsupervised task. Moreover, as we suppose that there is a very small share of anomalies, we deal with a very imbalanced dataset. These observations lead us to the question how many anomalies should be detected. A simple answer would be one datapoint per investigation, i.e., one transaction per account. Unfortunately, this approach has several limitations. First, there is not always an anomaly in the account's data. Second, due to the huge number of accounts, there would be detected far more anomalies as an auditor would be able to check. Third, there could be more than one anomaly within an account. As a consequence, a flexible and customizable solution is needed.

There are lots of different AD algorithms available and each of the algorithms has its own strengths and weaknesses. The idea is to use this variety of approaches by connecting different AD algorithms to an ensemble. Ensemble techniques are a proven technology in ML, its advantage is to create a better prediction by linking multiple weak predictions [28]. To achieve this, we constructed an ensemble of nine AD algorithms (see Fig. 2) with the intention that a datapoint is flagged as anomaly only if most of the algorithms (connected by a meta detector) agree with. The hyper-parameter *min_count* usually is set to a value near to the number of different algorithms in the ensemble (in our case, it is set to 8 or 9). Thus, an anomaly is detected only on few accounts, which helps

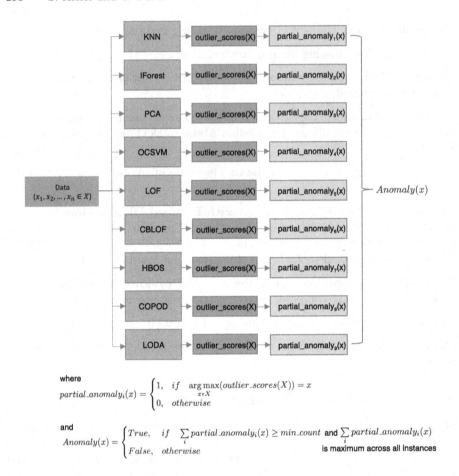

where

$$partial\_anomaly_i(x) = \begin{cases} 1, & if \quad \underset{x \in X}{\arg\max}(outlier\_scores(X)) = x \\ 0, & otherwise \end{cases}$$

and

$$Anomaly(x) = \begin{cases} True, & if \quad \sum_i partial\_anomaly_i(x) \geq min\_count \text{ and } \sum_i partial\_anomaly_i(x) \\ False, & otherwise \qquad\qquad\qquad\quad \text{is maximum across all instances} \end{cases}$$

Fig. 2. Architecture of the Anomaly Detection Ensemble

to restrict the number of identified anomalies in total to a human-manageable size. The remaining partial anomalies give the auditor a good hint where he potentially has to further investigate.

From technical point of view, we use the Python library PyOD. PyOD includes more than 30 cutting-edge AD algorithms that have been used in various academic and commercial projects [36]. Once a detector has been fitted on a dataset, the corresponding outlier scores can be accessed. We construct our ensemble approach by simply iterating through nine preselected AD algorithms. The functionality of the anomaly detector is shown in Algorithm 1 as pseudo-code.

The applied nine algorithms are listed in Table 2 in Appendix A. Those algorithms have been carefully selected according to various criteria as they should be heterogeneous, fast, and stable. Particular attention has been taken on the variety of approaches. While some are proximity-based, others base on a linear

Algorithm 1. Ensemble-based Anomaly Detection

Require: m methods   ▷ user specified; an array of selected AD algorithms to be applied
Require: data ▷ unlabeled data; one object of consideration, either data describing individual accounting transactions or individual accounts
Require: anomalies   ▷ an array of length $len(data)$ initialized with 0
Require: min_count ▷ user specified threshold for anomalies
   for $i \in \{1,2,...,m\}$ **do**
      methods[i].fit(data)
      partial_anomaly $= \arg\max\limits_{x \in data} \; methods[i].outlier\_scores(data)$
      anomalies [partial_anomaly] $+ = 1$
   end for
   anomaly $\leftarrow \{\}$
   if $\max(anomalies) \geq min\_count$ **then**
      anomaly $= \arg\max \; anomalies$
   end if
   return anomaly

---

or probabilistic model. Other promising algorithms haven't been considered as they were either too slow (i.e., Autoencoders) or required specific characteristics of the data like normally distributed data.

3.4 Model-Agnostic and Receiver-Dependent Explanations

AD for financial auditing requires the ability to explain identified outliers. In the following we present a new process of generating receiver-dependent and truly model-agnostic explanations for unsupervised learning. It comprises four steps: Oversampling to account for class imbalances, supervised approximation of the AD ensemble, tabular LIME for explaining the supervised model, and explanation-post-processing to tailor the explanations to the needs of the individual receivers. Each step described in the following is applied to each object of consideration (for views *TA* and *ACC*).

Synthetic Oversampling. Dependent on the choice of the threshold min_count for the AD ensemble (refer to Subsect. 3.3), a certain number of outliers is detected. As usual, the class comprising the anomalies clearly represents the minority class. On average, the AD ensemble identified between 0.007% and 0.17% of all datapoints as anomalous for the view *ACC* and between 0.007% and 0.15% for the view *TA*. For a subsequent approximation via a supervised ML model, which takes the features used by the AD ensemble as well as the decisions of the ensemble (normal or abnormal class) as input, the classes should be balanced at least to some degree. Therefore, we perform a synthetic oversampling harnessing Synthetic Minority Over-sampling Technique (SMOTE) [10]. SMOTE represents an over-sampling approach in which the minority class is oversampled by generating synthetic datapoints rather than oversampling with replacement as proposed earlier. Samples for the minority class are extended by creating new examples along a line that joins the k nearest neighbors of the minority class. Combined with undersampling the majority class, SMOTE is known to significantly improve classification performance in Receiver Operating Characteristic (ROC) space [10]. Therefore, we adopt and extend this procedure as follows: First, we oversample the minority class using Random Oversampling (with a sampling strategy of 0.3) in order to reach a sufficient number of k neighbors for SMOTE. Then, the minority class is oversampled synthetically using SMOTE (with a sampling strategy of 0.5). In the end, we undersample the majority class with a sampling strategy of 0.5. As a result, we receive a class distribution which is approximately evenly distributed.

Supervised Approximation of Anomaly Detector. In the next step, the AD ensemble is approximated globally using supervised ML in order to learn the dependencies between the original input features and the classes *normal* and *anomalous* (as provided by the AD ensemble). Therefore, we experimented with two discriminating classifiers for our supervised approximation task. On the one hand, we tried a Support Vector Machine (SVM) and on the other hand an XGBoost model. The reason for this selection lies in the fact that we initially wanted to avoid extensive oversampling and undersampling and see how effective the supervised algorithms are in approximating the AD ensemble. As a consequence, we looked for classification algorithms that can intrinsically deal with imbalanced data w.r.t. class distribution through hyper-parametrization. Using class-weighted algorithms, the resulting models give classification errors made on the minority class more impact. As the cross-validated macro-averaged F1-score was only around 0.65 due to highly imbalanced data often comprising only one anomaly, we decided to perform over- and undersampling as described above and reached a satisfying F1-score of around 0.9. In the end, we decided to use XGBoost with SMOTE and no train-test-split or cross-validation at all, since our goal is not to make inference on unseen examples, but to globally imitate the AD ensemble using approximation.

Receiver-Dependent Explanations. According to Fig. 1, we provide two different kinds of explanations for all identified anomalies, depending on the characteristics of the receivers (refer to Appendix B for both explanation types). For Data Scientists, detailed and built-in-LIME visualizations are provided as explanations, which show the individual feature attributions (w.r.t. to the supervised approximation of the AD ensemble) to the anomaly-class. We include both categorical as well as continuous features. For the latter, feature importances as well as discretized intervals for the according values are shown. Alternatively, we offer higher-level and more human-like explanations comprising natural-language-elements in order to give auditors hints for further investigation. Such human-friendly explanations shall not only be truthful, general, probable, and consistent with prior believes, but also selective [24]. As a consequence, they do not need to cover the complete list of causes. Instead, one to three causes

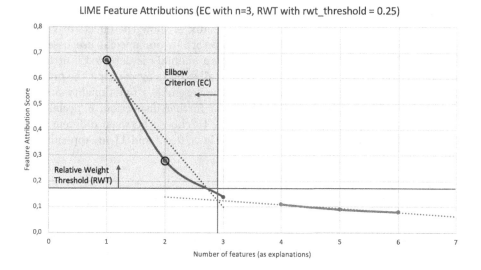

Fig. 3. Selective explanations through explanation-post-processing

should be selected and presented as the explanation. To achieve this, we propose a technique for explanation-post-processing, that comprises two concepts: *Ellbow Criterion* (EC) and *Relative Weight Threshold* (RWT), both depicted in Fig. 3. The EC is found by sorting the absolute feature attributions in descending order and then fitting regression lines through n adjacent points each (depicted in blue and orange in Fig. 3). In a next step, the intersections between all regression lines are calculated and the left-most intersection is taken as EC. Finally, all features lying left of EC are included in the explanation. RWT constitutes a predefined threshold. All features that have a higher relative attribution (compared to the first one, which is the most important one) than the $rwt\_threshold$ are considered relevant. Therefore, all features lying above the RWT are included in the explanation. Combining both EC and RWT results in approximately one to four features as explanation depending on the hyper-parameters (n for EC and $min\_threshold$ for RWT).

Evaluation. As we describe an integrated architecture for unsupervised AD, we are not able to evaluate our approach against any kind of ground truth. Instead, we decided to perform an evaluation by interviewing domain experts and showing them the detected anomalies. We discussed the results with both financial auditors and business experts for the financial domain. All domain experts were supportive of the practical use and especially highlighted three major benefits: First, they considered the ensemble architecture as very effective, as it enables a high variability in the kind of AD algorithms. This statement is also supported by Fig. 6 and 7 in Appendix A. Both figures visualize the correlation between the different algorithms w.r.t. to the identified anomalies. Second, the experts appreciated the possibility to individually and easily specify the granularity of the meta detector and therefore achieve different levels of granularity in the detected anomalies. Figure 4 and 5 in Appendix A show the effects of varying the min_count threshold for the meta detector. In our special use case they decided to choose $min\_count = 8$ such that an anomaly is detected if at least 8 AD algorithms of the ensemble agree. Third, all experts agreed that the provided explanations help a lot in understanding the ensemble's functionality and can provide the auditor with reasonable hints for further inspection. Especially the last point is strengthened by the possibility to choose between different kinds and granularity levels of explanations (see Fig. 8, 9, 10 and 11 in Appendix B).

4   Conclusion and Future Work

A novel proposal for performing efficient and comprehensible unsupervised AD for financial auditing has been worked out. One main merit of the described architecture is the possibility to detect anomalies at different levels of granularity. Worth mentioning is also the fact that all decisions made by the AD ensemble can be comprehended and thus, auditors can develop trust into the system. This is achieved by generating model-agnostic and receiver-dependent explanations despite the lack of class labels. Furthermore, offering different kinds of explanations contributes in two ways. First, Data Scientists might use insights gained from the explanations for constructing purposeful features in an unsupervised setting. This might pave the way for better human involvement in the feature engineering process in the absence of ground truth. Second, persons active in regulatory matters need concise explanations to develop trust in the AD system. Therefore, we developed a technique for explanation-post-processing that consists of an Ellbow Criterion and a Relative Weight Threshold. The combination of both enables the generation of selective explanations that can be easily understood by auditors. Besides all the benefits listed so far, there are also a few prerequisites and limitations of the approach. Although the ensemble-architecture yields many advantages, finding a suitable meta detector often is not straightforward. Furthermore, explaining the ensemble via supervised approximation as intermediate step adds some extra complexity, requires synthetic oversampling, and comes with an additional inductive bias. Lastly, a quantitative evaluation of the whole system is hard to conduct in the absence of ground truth and requires domain experts' input. Summing up, this work leaves some perspectives for further studies. First, adding more types of AD algorithms to the ensemble could improve the AD system. In case of sufficient amount of data, especially DL approaches for AD might add some benefits. Second, optimization of the meta detector, maybe using meta-learning, could be helpful for further adjusting the granularity of the detected anomalies. Finally, building model-agnostic explainers that are directly suitable for unsupervised ML without intermediate supervised approximation might be an interesting research direction.

Acknowledgments. We say many thanks to DATEV eG (Markus Decker, Jörg Schaller, Dr. Thilo Edinger, Gregor Fischer) and the University of Bamberg (Prof. Dr. Ute Schmid, head of Cognitive Systems Group) for professional and organizational support.

A   Anomaly Detection Ensemble

Table 2. Characteristics of the different AD algorithms included in the ensemble

Algorithm	Abbreviation	Principle	References
K Nearest Neighbors	KNN	Proximity-based	[2]
Isolation Forest	IForest	Ensemble-based	[20]
Principal Component Analysis	PCA	Dimension reduction	[33]
One-class Support Vector Machine	OCSVM	Linear model	[32]
Local Outlier Factor	LOF	Proximity-based	[6]
Clustering-Based Local Outlier Factor	CBLOF	Proximity-based	[13]
Histogram-Based Outlier Score	HBOS	Proximity-based	[12]
Copula-Based Outlier Detection	COPOD	Probabilistic model	[19]
Lightweight On-line Detector of Anomalies	LODA	Ensemble-based	[27]

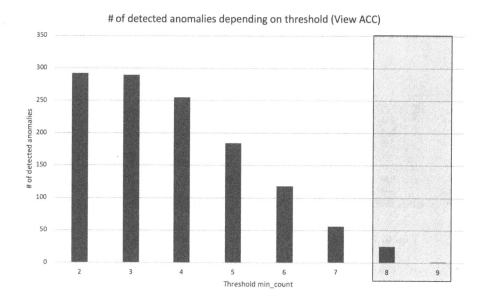

Fig. 4. Number of detected anomalies depending on threshold *min_count* for view *ACC*

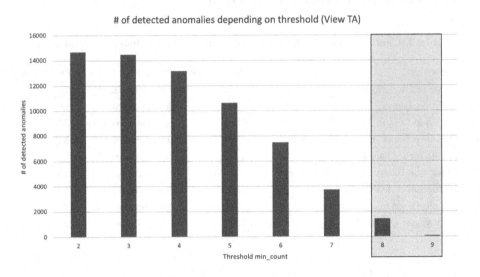

Fig. 5. Number of detected anomalies depending on threshold *min_count* for view *TA*

	KNN	IForest	PCA	OCSVM	LOF	CBLOF	HBOS	COPOD	LODA
KNN	1,00	0,63	0,73	0,85	0,35	0,57	0,34	0,44	0,03
IForest	0,63	1,00	0,58	0,59	0,19	0,39	0,42	0,58	0,07
PCA	0,73	0,58	1,00	0,71	0,31	0,53	0,31	0,42	0,02
OCSVM	0,85	0,59	0,71	1,00	0,32	0,54	0,31	0,40	0,01
LOF	0,35	0,19	0,31	0,32	1,00	0,35	0,14	0,12	0,10
CBLOF	0,57	0,39	0,53	0,54	0,35	1,00	0,19	0,24	0,03
HBOS	0,34	0,42	0,31	0,31	0,14	0,19	1,00	0,47	0,16
COPOD	0,44	0,58	0,42	0,40	0,12	0,24	0,47	1,00	0,12
LODA	0,03	0,07	0,02	0,01	0,10	0,03	0,16	0,12	1,00

Fig. 6. Correlations between different AD methods for view *ACC*

	KNN	IForest	PCA	OCSVM	LOF	CBLOF	HBOS	COPOD	LODA
KNN	1,00	0,73	0,64	0,80	0,35	0,53	0,42	0,60	0,03
IForest	0,73	1,00	0,60	0,74	0,29	0,48	0,47	0,62	0,04
PCA	0,64	0,60	1,00	0,67	0,28	0,49	0,34	0,50	0,01
OCSVM	0,80	0,74	0,67	1,00	0,34	0,55	0,39	0,59	0,01
LOF	0,35	0,29	0,28	0,34	1,00	0,33	0,21	0,22	0,16
CBLOF	0,53	0,48	0,49	0,55	0,33	1,00	0,26	0,36	0,04
HBOS	0,42	0,47	0,34	0,39	0,21	0,26	1,00	0,48	0,14
COPOD	0,60	0,62	0,50	0,59	0,22	0,36	0,48	1,00	0,05
LODA	0,03	0,04	0,01	0,01	0,16	0,04	0,14	0,05	1,00

Fig. 7. Correlations between different AD methods for view *TA*

B   Explanations

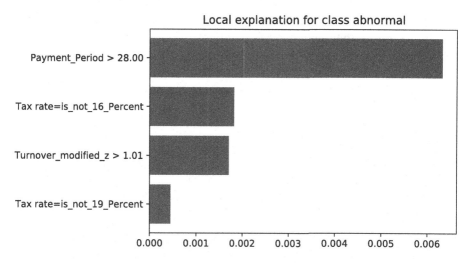

Fig. 8. Detailed explanation for view *TA*

High-level & human-like explanations for view *TA*:
„Mind a comarably long payment period!"
"Have a look at the tax rate, which is neither 16 nor 19 percent!"
"Mind a comparably high turnover!"

Fig. 9. Human-like explanation for view *TA*

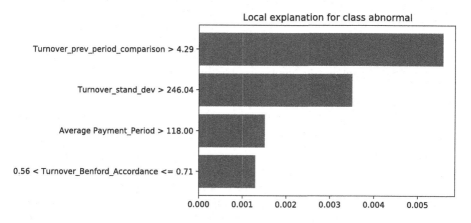

Fig. 10. Detailed explanation for view *ACC*

High-level & human-like explanations for view *ACC*:
„Mind a comparably high turnover compared to previous period!"
"Have a look at the comparably high variation in turnover for this client!"
"Mind a comparably high average payment period!"
„Mind only a partial accordance to Benford distribution w.r.t. turnover!"

Fig. 11. Human-like explanation for view ACC

References

1. Adadi, A., Berrada, M.: Peeking inside the black-box: a survey on explainable artificial intelligence (XAI). IEEE Access **6** (2018). https://doi.org/10.1109/ACCESS.2018.2870052
2. Angiulli, F., Pizzuti, C.: Fast outlier detection in high dimensional spaces. In: Elomaa, T., Mannila, H., Toivonen, H. (eds.) PKDD 2002. LNCS, vol. 2431, pp. 15–27. Springer, Heidelberg (2002). https://doi.org/10.1007/3-540-45681-3_2
3. Antwarg, L., Shapira, B., Rokach, L.: Explaining anomalies detected by autoencoders using shap. arXiv (2019)
4. Benford, F.: The law of anomalous numbers. Proc. Am. Philos. Soc. **78**, 551–572 (1938)
5. Bertsimas, D., Dunn, J.: Optimal classification trees. Mach. Learn. **106**(7), 1039–1082 (2017). https://doi.org/10.1007/s10994-017-5633-9
6. Breuniq, M.M., Kriegel, H.P., Ng, R.T., Sander, J.: LOF: Identifying density-based local outliers. SIGMOD Rec. (ACM Special Interest Group on Management of Data) **29** (2000). https://doi.org/10.1145/335191.335388
7. Bruckert, S., Finzel, B., Schmid, U.: The next generation of medical decision support: a roadmap toward transparent expert companions. Front. Artif. Intell. **3** (2020). https://doi.org/10.3389/frai.2020.507973
8. Böhmer, K., Rinderle-Ma, S.: Anomaly detection in business process runtime behavior – challenges and limitations. arXiv (2017)
9. Chandola, V., Banerjee, A., Kumar, V.: Anomaly detection: a survey. ACM Comput. Surv. **41** (2009). https://doi.org/10.1145/1541880.1541882
10. Chawla, N.V., Bowyer, K.W., Hall, L.O., Kegelmeyer, W.P.: Smote: synthetic minority over-sampling technique. J. Artif. Intell. Res. **16** (2002). https://doi.org/10.1613/jair.953
11. Fahim, M., Sillitti, A.: Anomaly detection, analysis and prediction techniques in IoT environment: a systematic literature review. IEEE Access **7** (2019). https://doi.org/10.1109/ACCESS.2019.2921912
12. Goldstein, M., Dengel, A.: Histogram-based outlier score (hbos): a fast unsupervised anomaly detection algorithm. KI-2012: Poster and Demo Track (2012)
13. He, Z., Xu, X., Deng, S.: Discovering cluster-based local outliers. Pattern Recogn. Lett. **24** (2003). https://doi.org/10.1016/S0167-8655(03)00003-5
14. Henselmann, K., Scherr, E., Ditter, D.: Applying Benford's law to individual financial reports: an empirical investigation on the basis of SEC XBRL filings. Working papers in accounting valuation auditing (2012)
15. Holzinger, A., Biemann, C., Pattichis, C.S., Kell, D.B.: What do we need to build explainable AI systems for the medical domain? arXiv (2017)

16. Jolliffe, I.T.: Principal component analysis, second edition. Encyclopedia of Statistics in Behavioral Science **30** (2002). https://doi.org/10.2307/1270093
17. Kauffmann, J., Müller, K.R., Montavon, G.: Towards explaining anomalies: a deep Taylor decomposition of one-class models. Pattern Recogn. **101** (2020). https://doi.org/10.1016/j.patcog.2020.107198
18. Leys, C., Ley, C., Klein, O., Bernard, P., Licata, L.: Detecting outliers: do not use standard deviation around the mean, use absolute deviation around the median. J. Exp. Soc. Psychol. **49** (2013). https://doi.org/10.1016/j.jesp.2013.03.013
19. Li, Z., Zhao, Y., Botta, N., Ionescu, C., Hu, X.: COPOD: copula-based outlier detection. In: Proceedings - IEEE International Conference on Data Mining, ICDM (2020). https://doi.org/10.1109/ICDM50108.2020.00135
20. Liu, F.T., Ting, K.M., Zhou, Z.H.: Isolation-based anomaly detection. ACM Trans. Knowl. Discov. Data **6** (2012). https://doi.org/10.1145/2133360.2133363
21. Lundberg, S.M., Lee, S.I.: A unified approach to interpreting model predictions. In: Advances in Neural Information Processing Systems (2017)
22. Maaten, L.V.D., Hinton, G.: Visualizing data using t-SNE. J. Mach. Learn. Res. **9**, 2579–2605 (2008)
23. Mehrotra, K.G., Mohan, C.K., Huang, H.: Anomaly Detection Principles and Algorithms. Book (2017)
24. Molnar, C.: Interpretable Machine Learning. A Guide for Making Black Box Models Explainable. Book (2019)
25. Morichetta, A., Casas, P., Mellia, M.: Explain-it: towards explainable AI for unsupervised network traffic analysis. In: Big-DAMA 2019 - Proceedings of the 3rd ACM CoNEXT Workshop on Big Data, Machine Learning and Artificial Intelligence for Data Communication Networks, Part of CoNEXT 2019 (2019). https://doi.org/10.1145/3359992.3366639
26. Munir, M., Chattha, M.A., Dengel, A., Ahmed, S.: A comparative analysis of traditional and deep learning-based anomaly detection methods for streaming data. In: Proceedings - 18th IEEE International Conference on Machine Learning and Applications, ICMLA 2019 (2019). https://doi.org/10.1109/ICMLA.2019.00105
27. Pevný, T.: Loda: lightweight on-line detector of anomalies. Mach. Learn. **102**(2), 275–304 (2015). https://doi.org/10.1007/s10994-015-5521-0
28. Polikar, R.: Ensemble based systems in decision making. IEEE Circuits Syst. Mag. **6** (2006). https://doi.org/10.1109/MCAS.2006.1688199
29. Rabold, J., Schwalbe, G., Schmid, U.: Expressive explanations of DNNs by combining concept analysis with ILP. In: Schmid, U., Klügl, F., Wolter, D. (eds.) KI 2020. LNCS (LNAI), vol. 12325, pp. 148–162. Springer, Cham (2020). https://doi.org/10.1007/978-3-030-58285-2_11
30. Radev, D.R., Jing, H., Styś, M., Tam, D.: Centroid-based summarization of multiple documents. Inf. Process. Manag. **40** (2004). https://doi.org/10.1016/j.ipm.2003.10.006
31. Ribeiro, M.T., Singh, S., Guestrin, C.: "why should i trust you?" explaining the predictions of any classifier. In: Proceedings of the ACM SIGKDD International Conference on Knowledge Discovery and Data Mining (2016). https://doi.org/10.1145/2939672.2939778
32. Schölkopf, B., Platt, J.C., Shawe-Taylor, J., Smola, A.J., Williamson, R.C.: Estimating the support of a high-dimensional distribution. Neural Comput. **13** (2001). https://doi.org/10.1162/089976601750264965
33. Shyu, M.L., Chen, S.C., Sarinnapakorn, K., Chang, L.: A novel anomaly detection scheme based on principal component classifier. In: 3rd IEEE International Conference on Data Mining (2003)

34. Thudumu, S., Branch, P., Jin, J., Singh, J.J.: A comprehensive survey of anomaly detection techniques for high dimensional big data. J. Big Data **7**(1), 1–30 (2020). https://doi.org/10.1186/s40537-020-00320-x
35. Xu, X., Liu, H., Yao, M.: Recent progress of anomaly detection. Hindawi Complex. **2019** (2019). https://doi.org/10.1155/2019/2686378
36. Zhao, Y., Nasrullah, Z., Li, Z.: Pyod: a Python toolbox for scalable outlier detection. J. Mach. Learn. Res. **20**, 1–7 (2019)

A Priori Approximation of Symmetries in Dynamic Probabilistic Relational Models

Nils Finke[1][(✉)] and Marisa Mohr[2]

[1] Oldendorff Carriers GmbH & Co. KG., 23554 Lübeck, Germany
nils.finke@oldendorff.com
[2] inovex GmbH, 22763 Hamburg, Germany
mmohr@inovex.de

Abstract. Lifted inference approaches reduce computational work as inference is performed using representatives for sets of indistinguishable random variables, which allows for tractable inference w.r.t. domain sizes in dynamic probabilistic relational models. Unfortunately, maintaining a lifted representation is challenging in practically relevant application domains, as evidence often breaks symmetries making lifted techniques fall back on their ground counterparts. In existing approaches asymmetric evidence is counteracted by merging similar but distinguishable objects when moving forward in time. While undoing splits a posteriori is reasonable, we propose learning approximate model symmetries a priori to prevent unnecessary splits due to inaccuracy or one-time events. In particular, we propose a multivariate ordinal pattern symbolization approach followed by spectral clustering to determine sets of domain entities behaving approximately the same over time. By using object clusters, we avoid unnecessary splits by keeping entities together that tend to behave the same over time. Understanding symmetrical and asymmetrical entity behavior a priori allows for increasing accuracy in inference by means of *inferred evidence* for unobserved entities to better represent reality. Empirical results show that our approach reduces unnecessary splits, i.e., improves runtimes, while keeping accuracy in inference high.

Keywords: Relational models · Lifting · Ordinal pattern · Symmetry

1 Introduction

To cope with uncertainty and relational information of numerous objects over time, in many real-world applications, dynamic (also called temporal) probabilistic relational models (DPRMs[1]) are employed [6]. We consider an example from logistics, specifically shipping, where the transportation of cargo using vessels (objects) changes over time (temporal) depending on supply and demand (relational). To ensure efficient query answering in DPRMs, objects of the same type and behavior, e.g., vessels transporting the same cargo, are treated together

---

[1] pronounced *deeper models.*

© Springer Nature Switzerland AG 2021
S. Edelkamp et al. (Eds.): KI 2021, LNAI 12873, pp. 309–323, 2021.
https://doi.org/10.1007/978-3-030-87626-5_23

in groups, yielding a sparse representation (*lifting*). Lifted inference approaches use relations in a model, allowing for tractable inference w.r.t. domain sizes [14]. Unfortunately, maintaining a sparse representation to ensure efficient query answering is challenging, as evidence breaks symmetries making lifted techniques fall back to their ground counterparts [11]. To retain a lifted representation the field of approximate inference, i.e., approximating symmetries, has emerged in research. Asymmetric evidence is counteracted by treating similar but distinguishable objects as if they were identical to obtain a lifted solution, while only introducing a small and bounded error in exchange for efficient reasoning.

For static models, Singla et al. [18] propose two algorithms for approximate lifted belief propagation and provide error bounds for them. Venugopal and Gogate [20] determine similarities between domain objects based on evidence to form clusters and project the marginal distribution of one object to all objects of a cluster. As approximate symmetries have an effect on the marginal probability distributions of the models, van den Broeck and Niepert [4] propose an approach that produces improved probability estimates on an approximate model. As all these approaches do not account for temporal behavior, Gehrke et al. [8] propose recreating a new lifted representation by merging groundings, which were introduced over time. Common to all these approaches is that in the first place groundings are allowed and then dealt with afterwards, i.e., by exploiting approximate symmetries within message passing in inference tasks.

While dealing with groundings to recover a lifted representation a posteriori has been studied extensively in research, preventing groundings a priori, i.e., before they even occur, has to the best of our knowledge not been studied yet. In this paper, we investigate how understanding model symmetries a priori can prevent groundings from occurring. Motivated by examples from seaborne transportation, we extend learning a lifted model by finding groups of entities, e.g. vessels transporting the same cargo, that behave approximately the same over time. In particular, we determine entity symmetries through an ordinal pattern symbolization approach followed by spectral clustering. Using these entity clusters, we show how to avoid groundings by keeping similar entities together. In general, as we argue, understanding model symmetries a priori to avoid groundings combines well with existing approaches by merging groundings when objects align again. Furthermore, we introduce the concept of *interconnectivity* and its potential for *inferred evidence*, e.g., evidence observed for one entity also applying to other entities. We conclude with an empirical evaluation and show that our approach significantly reduces groundings, i.e., improves runtime performance while increasing accuracy in inference as the reality is better represented by means of inferred evidence.

2   Preliminaries

We recapitulate DPRMs presented by Gehrke et al. [7], which are based on parametric factor graphs introduced by Poole [16]. We illustrate DPRMs in context of an example from shipping. DPRMs combine relational logic with a factor

Fig. 1. Two-slice parameterized probabilistic model $G_\rightarrow$.

graph, using logical variables (logvars) as parameters for randvars (parameterized randvar, or PRV for short). PRVs compactly represent sets of randvars that are considered indistinguishable without further evidence.

Definition 1 (PRV). *Let $\mathbf{R}$ be a set of randvar names, $\mathbf{L}$ a set of logvar names, Φ a set of factor names, and $\mathbf{D}$ a set of entities. All sets are finite. Each logvar L has a domain $\mathcal{D}(L) \subseteq \mathbf{D}$. A constraint is a tuple $(\mathcal{X}, C_{\mathbf{X}})$ of a sequence of logvars $\mathcal{X} = (X_1, \ldots, X_n)$ and a set $C_{\mathcal{X}} \subseteq \times_{i=1}^{n} \mathcal{D}(X_i)$. A PRV $R(L_1, \ldots, L_n), n \geq 0$ is a construct of a randvar name $R \in \mathbf{R}$ combined with logvars $L_1, \ldots, L_n \in \mathbf{L}$. The term $\mathcal{R}(A)$ denotes the (range) values of a PRV A.*

To represent independent relations, PRVs are linked by parametric factors (parfactors) to compactly encode the full joint distribution of the DPRM.

Definition 2 (Parfactor). *We denote a parfactor g by $\phi(\mathcal{A})_{|C}$ with $\mathcal{A} = (A^1, \ldots, A^n)$ a sequence of PRVs, $\phi : \times_{i=1}^{n} \mathcal{R}(A^i) \mapsto \mathbb{R}^+$ a function with name $\phi \in \Phi$, and C a constraint on the logvars of $\mathcal{A}$. A PRV A or logvar L under constraint C is given by $A_{|C}$ or $L_{|C}$, respectively. The term $gr(P)$ denotes the set of all instances of P. An instance is a grounding of P, substituting the logvars in P with a set of entities from the constraints in P. The term $lv(P)$ refers to logvars in P. A parameterized model PRM G is a set of parfactors $\{g^i\}_{i=1}^{n}$, representing the full joint distribution $P_G = \frac{1}{Z} \prod_{f \in gr(G)} f$, where Z is a normalizing constant.*

Roughly speaking, DPRMs are defined by an initial model and a temporal copy pattern to describe model changes over time.

Definition 3 (DPRM). *A DPRM is a pair of PRMs $(G_0, G_\rightarrow)$ where G_0 is a PRM representing the first time step and $G_\rightarrow$ is a two-slice temporal parameterized model representing $\mathbf{A}_{t-1}$ and $\mathbf{A}_t$ where $\mathbf{A}_\pi$ is a set of PRVs from time slice π. An inter-slice parfactor $\phi(\mathcal{A})_{|C}$ has arguments $\mathcal{A}$ under constraint C containing PRVs from both $\mathbf{A}_{t-1}$ and $\mathbf{A}_t$, encoding transitioning from time step $t-1$ to t. A DPRM $(G_0, G_\rightarrow)$ represents the full joint distribution $P_{(G_0, G_\rightarrow), T}$ by unrolling the DPRM for T time steps, forming a PRM as defined above.*

Figure 1 shows a DPRM illustrating seaborne transportation that is mainly driven by supply $S_t(Z)$ and demand $D_t(Z)$ of commodities across various locations (zones Z). Vessels V move between these zones, captured by $A_t(Z, V)$, representing trade flows: Vessels are in zones with high supply (to load cargo), in zones with high demand (to discharge cargo), and in between while traveling. For transportation, a fee per ton, called freight rate $R_t(Z)$, is charged. In Fig. 1, variable nodes (ellipses) correspond to PRVs, factor nodes (boxes) to parfactors. Parfactors g^S, g^V, and g^D are so called inter-slice parfactors. The submodel to the left and to the right of these inter-slice parfactors are duplicates of each other, with the left referencing time step $t-1$ and the right referencing time step t. Parfactors reference time-indexed PRVs, namely, a boolean PRV $A_t(Z,V)$ and PRVs $S_t(Z)$, $R_t(Z)$, $D_t(Z)$ with range values $\{high, medium, low\}$. Given a DPRM, one can ask queries for probability distributions or the probability of an event given evidence.

Definition 4 (Queries). *Given a DPRM $(G_0, G_\rightarrow)$, a ground PRV Q_t, and evidence $\boldsymbol{E}_{0:t} = \{\{E_{s,i} = e_{s,i}\}_{i=1}^n\}_{s=0}^t$ (set of events for time steps 0 to t), the term $P(Q_\pi \mid \boldsymbol{E}_{0:t})$, $\pi \in \{0, \ldots, T\}$, $t \leq T$, denotes a query w.r.t. $P_{(G_0, G_\rightarrow), T}$.*

In context of the shipping application, an example query for $t = 10$, such as $P(R_{10}(z_1) \mid S_{10}(z_2) = high, S_{10}(z_3) = high)$, contains a set of observations $S_{10}(z_2) = high$ and $S(z_3) = high$ as evidence. Sets of parfactors encode evidence, one parfactor for each subset of evidence that concern one PRV with the same observation.

Definition 5 (Encoding Evidence). *A parfactor $g_e = \phi_e(E(X))_{|C_e}$ encodes evidence for a set of events $\{E(x_i) = o\}_{i=1}^n$ of a PRV $E(X)$. The function ϕ_e maps the value o to 1 and the remaining range values of $E(X)$ to 0. Constraint C_e encodes the observed groundings x_i of $E(X)$, i.e., $C_e = (X, \{x_i\}_{i=1}^n)$.*

Suppose we ask for the probability distribution of supply at a time step $t = 2$ in a certain zone z_1, given that in the previous time step $t = 1$ the supply was high, i.e., $P(S_2(z_1) \mid S_1(z_1) = high$. Then evidence is encoded in parfactors g_1^1 by duplicating the parfactor and using one to encode evidence and one to represent all sets of entities that are still considered indistinguishable. Each parfactor represents a different set of entities bounded by the use of constraints, e.g., limiting the domain for the evidence parfactor to z_1. The parfactor that encodes evidence is adjusted such that all range value combinations in the parfactors distribution ϕ are dropped for $S_1(z_1) \neq high$. During message passing, the splits carry over. Thus, the parfactors g^S and g_1^2 also split into one part for z_1 and another for all other instances. Thus, under evidence a model $G_t = \{g_t^i\}_{i=1}^n$ at time step t, is split w.r.t. its parfactors such that its structure remains

$$G_t = \{g_t^{i,1}, \ldots, g_t^{i,k}\}_{i=1}^n \tag{1}$$

with $k \in \mathbb{N}^+$. Every parfactor g_t^i can have up to $k \in \mathbb{N}^+$ splits $g_t^{i,j} = \phi_t^{i,j}(\mathcal{A}^i)_{|C^{i,j}}$, where $1 \leq j \leq k$ and $\mathcal{A}^i$ is a sequence of the same PRVs but with different constraint $C^{i,j}$ and varying functions $\phi_t^{i,j}$ due to evidence.

3   A Priori Approximation of Symmetries

In relational models evidence leads to splits within the models' symmetric structures, i.e., asymmetric evidence slowly grounds a lifted model over time. In the worst case a model is fully grounded, i.e., a model as defined in Eq. (1) contains

$$k = \prod_{L \in lv(\mathcal{A})} |L| \qquad (2)$$

splits for every parfactor $g_t^i = \phi_t^i(\mathcal{A})_{|C^i}$ such that each object $l \in L$ is in its own parfactor split. We propose learning approximate model symmetries a priori to relieve the model from unnecessary splits due to inaccuracy or one time events. When knowing approximate model symmetries in advance, one can prevent splits through evidence, e.g., if those are only a one time blip. In general, our approach works well with any other approach undoing splits after they occurred when moving forward in time, i.e., in message passing by merging sets of entities when those align again (temporal approximate merging). As we argue, combining both kind of approaches brings together the best of both worlds:

(a) While with *determining approximate model symmetries*, we can use the full amount of historical training data to prevent groundings a priori,
(b) with *temporal approximate merging*, we can merge non-preventable parfactor splits even after they occurred.

Next, we introduce our approach for the a priori determination of model symmetries in DPRMs in two steps. First, we individually encode PRVs behavior by ordinal pattern symbolization. Secondly, we build groups with similar behavior by spectral clustering. Algorithm 1 in the Appendix outlines the corresponding pseudocode combining both steps.

3.1   Encoding Model Behavior by Ordinal Pattern Symbolization

To describe and understand the behavior of entities and to find symmetries between them, historical observations (evidence), encoded in the models PRVs, is used. This means in particular: Every PRV represents multiple entities, e.g., vessels V or zones Z, of the same type. That is, for a PRV $S_t(Z)$, entities z represented by a logvar Z with its domain $\mathcal{D}(Z)$ of size $|\mathcal{D}(Z)|$. For each entity $z_i \in D(Z)$ from this PRV $S_t(Z)$ own observations are made over time, i.e., a time series is generated. Having $|D(Z)|$ entities in Z, we consider $|D(Z)|$ samples of time series in a data matrix

$$\mathcal{X} = ((S_t(z_i))_{i=1}^{|D(Z)|})_{t=1}^T \qquad (3)$$

with observations $S_t(z_i)$ for every $z_i \in D(Z)$ in time $t \in \{1, \ldots, T\}$. Note that a PRV can be parameterized with more than one logvar, but for the sake of simplicity we introduce our approach using PRVs with only one logvar. Symmetry detection for m-logvar PRVs works similar to one-logvar PRVs, with the difference, that in symmetry detection entity pairs, i.e., m-tuples, are used. As an example, for any 2-logvar PRV $P_t(X, Y)$, an entity pair is a 2-tuple (x_1, y_1) with $x_1 \in D(X)$ and $y_1 \in D(Y)$.

To encode the behavior of an entity (or entity pair), we use ordinal pattern symbolization based on the works by Bandt and Pompe [1]. Ordinal patterns encode the up and downs in a time series by the total order between two or

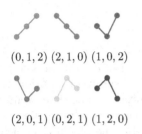

(0, 1, 2) (2, 1, 0) (1, 0, 2)

(2, 0, 1) (0, 2, 1) (1, 2, 0)

(a) All possible ordinal patterns of order $d = 3$.

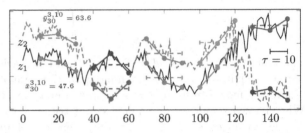

(b) Ordinal pattern determination of order $d = 3$ and delay $\tau = 10$ of a time series concerning two objects z_1 and z_2.

Fig. 2. Ordinal pattern determination. Note, the delay τ refers to the neighbours under consideration within a pattern. The determination of an ordinal pattern is carried out at any time step $t \in [\tau(d-1)+1, T]$. Best viewed in color.

more neighbours and their permutations and therefore give a good abstraction of the overall behavior or the generating process of a time series. Ordinal patterns are formally defined as follows.

Definition 6. *A vector* $(x_1, ..., x_d) \in \mathbb{R}^d$ *has ordinal pattern* $(r_1, ..., r_d) \in \mathbb{N}^d$ *of order* $d \in \mathbb{N}$ *if* $x_{r_1} \geq ... \geq x_{r_d}$ *and* $r_{l-1} > r_l$ *in the case* $x_{r_{l-1}} = x_{r_l}$.

Figure 2a shows all possible ordinal patterns of order $d = 3$ of a vector (x_1, x_2, x_3). For a fixed order d, there are $d!$ different ordinal patterns denoted as $o = 1, ..., d!$. The ordinal approach has notable advantages in applications: (i) The method is conceptually simple, (ii) it is not necessary to have previous knowledge about the data range or type of time series, (iii) the ordinal approach supports robust and fast implementations [10,15], and, (iv) compared to classical symbolization approaches such as the well-known Symbolic Aggregate ApproXimation (SAX) [5] it allows an easier estimation of a good symbolization scheme [9,19].

   To symbolize a time series $(x_1, x_2, ..., x_T) \in \mathbb{R}^T$, each time step $t \in \{d, ..., T\}$ is assigned its ordinal pattern o of order d, as shown in Fig. 2b exemplarily for five time steps in each of two time series. To access overarching trend, delayed behavior is of interest, showing various details of structure of the time series. The time delay $\tau \in \mathbb{N}_{>0}$ is the delay between successive points in the symbol sequences. Finding optimal orders d and delays τ depend on the application and is a challenging problem in research [13]. Practical advice can be found in [17].

   A DPRM, as introduced in Sect. 2, encodes sequential data using its PRVs, e.g., the PRV $S_t(Z)$ encodes supply at time step t in various zones on the globe. Figure 2b shows the time series of two continuous variables, dashed in grey and solid in black, corresponding to observations for the level of supply in two zones z_1 and z_2. Note that for the sake of simplicity we here look at supply over time with its continues range values before its discretization, since DPRMs only support discrete range values. Hereby, the PRVs range values have a total ordering, intuitively, *low* < *medium* < *high*. Note that for example, the PRVs $A_t(Z, V)$

are boolean and thus have no total order. The further procedure can be executed in this case however on the raw data with the disadvantage that no temporal neighborhood relations are included. The figure shows symmetry in the behavior of the time series data for both variables z_1 and z_2. The time series $(x_t)_{t \in T}$ for z_2 follows the time series $(y_t)_{t \in T}$ for z_1 (or vice versa) with varying offset almost the whole time. The only exceptions are the intervals $40 < t < 60$ and $130 < t < 150$, where both curves develop contrary to each other.

Ordinal patterns are well suited to characterize an overall behavior of time series that is independent of the data range. However, the dependence on the data range is often relevant. For example, in Fig. 2b the time series $(x_t)_{t \in T}$ and $(y_t)_{t \in T}$ are similar in terms of their ordinal patterns, but differ when looking at their y intercept. To address this problem, in the next step, entity clustering, we use the arithmetic mean $\overline{x}_t^{d,\tau} = \frac{1}{d} \sum_{k=1}^{d} x_{t-(k-1)\tau}$ of the time series' values corresponding to the ordinal pattern as an additional characteristic or feature of behavior. There are still other features that can be relevant. For simplicity, we only determine ordinal patterns and their means for each PRV of the DPRM, yielding a new data representation

$$\mathcal{S} \in \langle o, m \rangle^{|D(Z)| \times (T - (\tau(d-1))} \tag{4}$$

where $s_{it}\langle o, \cdot \rangle \in \mathcal{S}$ represents the ordinal pattern and $s_{it}\langle \cdot, m \rangle \in \mathcal{S}$ represents the corresponding mean $\overline{x}_t^{d,\tau}$ for an entity $z_i \in D(Z)$ at time step t of a PRV parameterized with the logvar Z. The order d and delay τ are passed in from the outside and might depend on, e.g., the frequency of the data, to capture the overarching behavior of each entity.

3.2   Entity Symmetry Approximation by Spectral Clustering

Lifted models are often used when dealing with large domains, i.e., they represent numerous objects resulting in high dimensional data. When the use of clustering is required to uncover symmetries in behavior, the curse of dimensionality [2] complicates this task. Using spectral clustering became a popular setting for problems involving high dimensional data [3].

Similarity Graph. Spectral clustering is performed on a similarity graph of entities, where each node represents an entity, e.g., for the PRV $S_t(Z)$ entities $z \in \mathcal{D}(Z)$. The edges between the entities of the lifted model represent their similarity, more precisely how closely related two entities of the model are to each other. The new symbolic representation $\mathcal{S}$, containing tuples of ordinals and means, is used to measure *similar behavior* at each time step $t \in \{\tau(d-1) + 1, \ldots, T\}$ individually. As an auxiliary structure, we use a square matrix $\mathcal{W} \in \mathbb{N}^{|D(Z)| \times |D(Z)|}$, where each $w_{ij} \in \mathcal{W}$ describes the similarity between entities z_i and z_j by simple counts of equal behavior over time $t \in T$. The similarity count of equal behavior of two entities z_i and z_j is given by

	z_1	z_2	z_3	...	z_n
z_1	0	9	8	...	7
z_2	9	0	12	...	14
z_3	8	12	0	...	4
...					
z_n	7	14	3	...	0

	z_1	z_2	z_3	...	z_n
z_1	24	-1	-1	...	-1
z_2	-1	35	-1	...	-1
z_3	-1	-1	24	...	-1
...					
z_n	-1	-1	-1	...	25

(a) Auxiliary matrix $\mathcal{W}$ containing counts denoting entity similarity.
(b) Similarity Graph as another representation form of the auxiliary matrix.
(c) Graph Laplacian matrix to project the data onto a lower dimensional space.

Fig. 3. (a) Auxiliary matrix and (b) similarity graph, for the construction of the (c) Laplacian matrix used for dimension reduction.

$$w_{ij} = \sum_{t \leq T} \Big[s_{it}\langle o, \cdot \rangle == s_{jt}\langle o, \cdot \rangle \ \&\& \ |s_{it}\langle \cdot, m \rangle - s_{jt}\langle \cdot, m \rangle| < \delta \Big], \qquad (5)$$

where $[x] = 1$ if x and, 0 otherwise. Simply put, one counts if both time series of z_i and z_j share the same ordinal pattern, and the absolute difference of the two means of the corresponding ordinal pattern is smaller than $\delta > 0$. Once the auxiliary matrix $\mathcal{W}$ is filled, we can derive the similarity graph directly from the auxiliary matrix, since it is just a graphical representation of a matrix as also shown in Figs. 3a and 3b. The counts $w_{ij} \in \mathcal{W}$ corresponds to the weights of the edges in the similarity graph, where zero indicates no similarity between two entities, while the larger the count, the more similar two entities are.

Spectral Clustering. In the worst case, a similarity graph for a PRV $S_t(Z)$ contains $\binom{|D(Z)|}{2}$ fully-connected nodes, where Z is a logvar representing a set of entities whose entity pairs share similar behavior for least one time step. If the dimension of the similarity graph of the potentially large domains of a lifted model becomes too large, classical clustering methods do not achieve good results because in high-dimensional spaces the smallest and largest distances differ only relatively slightly [2]. While the well-known k-means algorithm assumes that the points assigned to a cluster are spherical around the cluster centre and no good clusters are found due to the relatively equal distances, spectral clustering performs a dimension reduction beforehand and is therefore well suited to uncover similar groups or symmetries in a DPRM. The general approach to spectral clustering is to use a standard clustering method such as k-means on k most relevant eigenvectors of a Laplacian matrix, a special representation of the similarity graph $\mathcal{W}$. For undirected graphs, the graph Laplacian matrix is defined as $L = D - A$, where $D \in \mathbb{N}^{|D(Z)| \times |D(Z)|}$ is a degree matrix containing the degree $d_{ij} \in D$ for each node i of the similarity graph, i.e.,

$$d_{ij} = \begin{cases} \sum_{j=1}^{|D(Z)|} w_{ij} & \text{if } i = j, \\ 0 & \text{if } i \neq j, \end{cases} \qquad (6)$$

and A is the adjacency matrix corresponding to the auxiliary matrix $\mathcal{W}$, where $a_{ij} = 1$ if $w_{ij} > 0$, and 0 else. Figure 3c shows the graph Laplacian matrix for the corresponding similarity graph in Fig. 3b. Based on the graph Laplacian matrix L, the first k eigenvectors corresponding to the k smallest eigenvalues of L are calculated. Considering the matrix formed by the first k eigenvectors, the rows are used for clustering by a classical clustering algorithm, such as k-means. The eigenvectors contained in the clusters $C_i^{S_t(Z)}, i = 1, ..., k$ can then be traced back to the entities of an PRV $S_t(Z)$ by indices, and entity symmetry clusters

$$\mathcal{C}(S_t(Z)) = \bigcup_{i=1}^{k} C_i^{S_t(Z)}. \tag{7}$$

are built with each $C_i^{S_t(Z)}$ containing a subset of entities $z \in D(Z)$. As symmetry clustering is done individually for each PRV, $\mathcal{C}$ denotes the set of all entity symmetry clusters for all PRVs. Next, we introduce an approach utilizing symmetry clusters to prevent the model from grounding.

4   Preventing Groundings

Commonly, evidence is set in relational models when moving forward in time while answering queries in inference tasks. Here, based on the entity symmetry approximation described in Sect. 3, we present a procedure for preventing groundings in inference. Algorithm 2 in the Appendix presents the corresponding pseudocode. As entity symmetry approximation also works with other relational formalisms, the procedure can be included in any algorithm before setting evidence that leads to groundings. As the first part of the procedure we address how to avoid model splits, while in the second part we deal with inferred evidence.

4.1   Avoiding Model Splits with Evidence

To avoid model splits, our procedure requires a DPRM, together with a stream of evidence $\mathcal{E}$ and queries $\mathcal{Q}$ as inputs. Furthermore, order d, delay τ, and entity symmetry clusters $\mathcal{C}$ are given as inputs to Algorithm 1. Our procedure contains the following steps.

1. We first loop over all PRVs $P_t(A)$ of the DPRM to initialize for each PRV an auxiliary vector of length $|D(A)|$ that stores the number of times when observed evidence is dismissed due to dissimilar behavior to entities of its symmetry cluster. As follows, when moving forward in time $t = 0, 1, \ldots, T$ evidence $\mathbf{E}_t$ is consumed from an evidence stream $\mathcal{E}$ for that time step t.
2. Since we detect similarity clusters on a PRV level, we consider evidence $\mathbf{E}_t$ on a PRV basis, i.e., we extract evidence from $\mathbf{E}_t$ only concerning one PRV $P(A)$ at the time. We denote evidence at time step t for a PRV $P_t(A)$ from the evidence stream $\mathcal{E}$ as $\mathbf{E}_t^{P(A)}$. Evidence $\mathbf{E}_t^{P_t(A)}$ for a PRV $P_t(A)$ might contain more than one observation, so we additionally cluster $\mathbf{E}_t^{P_t(A)}$ such that we

derive evidence clusters $\mathcal{M}$ and each evidence cluster contains evidence for entities that are in the same symmetry cluster $\mathcal{C}_{P_t(A)} \in \mathcal{C}$.

3. By looping over evidence cluster $\mathcal{M}_i \in \mathcal{M}$, i.e., clusters of evidence containing observations for entities in the same symmetry cluster of a PRV $P(A)$, the observation observed the most $max(x)$ is determined.

4. All other observations x in $\mathcal{M}_i$ for an entity $a_i \in D(A)$, which are different to the observation $max(x)$, are dismissed. Still, observations are only dismissed if they are no longer than a certain time period observed.

5. To ensure this, each dismissed observation is counted in the auxiliary vector created in the initialization phase. Once the count reaches the threshold of $d \cdot \tau / 2$, evidence is no longer dismissed and the entity z_i is outsourced from its entity symmetry cluster into its own parfactor split.

The threshold of $d \cdot \tau / 2$ is set based on the assumption that the symmetry clusters are detected based on windows of length $d \cdot \tau$ throughout the whole time series, i.e., we expect that entities at least over that time horizon align again and therefore discrepancies are allowed at least for half of the window. To allow for different threshold, d and τ can still be overwritten externally. To keep entities of similar behavior together in one parfactor groups, evidence observed for other entities is also applied to those in the same symmetry cluster, introducing the concept of *inferred evidence*.

4.2   Interconnectivity Yielding Inferred Evidence

We introduce *interconnectivity* as the study of relationships that relate to the behavior of an entity or symmetry cluster in context of other entities or symmetry clusters. There are numerous different types of interconnectivity that, if properly understood, can help increase the overall accuracy of the model by making the model more representative of reality. The different forms of interconnectivity all extend to some type of symmetric behavior, e.g.,

(a) *offset symmetry* as entities with similar behavior within different data ranges, e.g., as illustrated in Fig. 2b,

(b) *inverse symmetry* as entities with contrary behavior, e.g., if some variable is increasing for some entities, that the same is decreasing for others, and

(c) *phase-shifted symmetry* as delayed similar behavior, e.g., some entities follow others with a certain delay phase shifted in time.

For example, in Fig. 2b, both curves for entities z_1 and z_2 show similar behavior for almost all times with respect to their ordinal patterns, but not with respect to their y-intercept, which we considered in Sect. 3 by the additional characteristic or feature, i.e., the mean $\overline{x}_t^{d,\tau} = \frac{1}{d} \sum_{k=1}^{d} x_{t-(k-1)\tau}$. Depending on the parameter δ, this may lead to the entities not falling into a cluster together. Nevertheless, interconnectivity exists between the two entities or clusters, so that evidence from one cluster can be inferred for the other cluster.

In the context of our procedure of preventing groundings, not only evidence is dismissed, but evidence can and partly has to be applied to other entities for which observations are not available. More specifically, in our procedure, evidence observed for one entity or cluster is similarly applied to all other entities within another symmetry cluster based on interconnectivity, in the following denoted as *inferred evidence*. In particular, inferred evidence is necessary to prevent the model from being grounded, as, for example, entities in the same parfactor group need to always have the same observations to keep them in a group. That is, evidence for one entity contrary to other evidence for entities in the same cluster, or even no evidence, would cause new splits. The inference of evidence become possible by knowing in advance which entities share the same evidence, and is therefore a direct outcome of the approach described in Sect. 3.

5   Empirical Evaluation

This evaluation of our proposed approach is twofold. We (a) compare runtimes in lifted inferences with and without preventing groundings, using the lifted dynamic junction tree (LDJT) algorithm as query answering algorithm on DPRMs, which was introduced in [7], and (b) compare the models accuracy with and without applying inferred evidence by comparing query answering results. Note, that we do not introduce LDJT here. Details can be found in the original work [7].

To setup a DPRM as shown in Fig. 1, we use historical vessel movements from 2020 based on automatic identification system (AIS) data[2] provided by the Danish Maritime Authority (DMA) for the Baltic Sea. As AIS data provides information about the position of a vessel, including specifications about the vessel itself, the actual supply and demand have to be calculated first. Each AIS signal contains the current geo-position and the total cargo quantity of a vessel. By dividing the Baltic Sea into zones, we derive the total amount of cargo transported between those zones based on the vessel movements and their cargo and thus obtain the data set for this evaluation. We split the data into a training (calendar weeks 1 to 40) and a test data set (remaining weeks). Data and preprocessing can be found on GitHub[3]. All data in the model are fully observable, i.e., the DPRM is derived by counting observations and building a probability distributions for each parfactor by aggregation. Besides, we determine entity symmetry clusters for each PRV of the model based on observation in the training data set. We use the model G_0 with $D(Z) = 367$ and divide all 367 zones into $k = 10$ symmetry groups using the approach described in Sect. 3 with parameters $d = 3$ and $\tau = 1$. To compare runtime and accuracy in inference, we set evidence based on observations in the test data, i.e., we unroll the model for $t = 11$ further time steps. We perform inference by answering prediction queries for $S_{t+\pi}(Z)$ with $\pi \in \{0, \ldots, 11\}$ for each time step t and obtain a marginal distribution for each entity $z \in D(Z)$.

Figure 4 shows the runtime and accuracy to answer queries for each time step. The orange line indicates runtime for answering queries without preventing

---

[2] https://www.dma.dk/SikkerhedTilSoes/Sejladsinformation/AIS/.
[3] https://github.com/FinkeNils/Processed-AIS-Data-Baltic-Sea-2020.

groundings, whilst the blue line indicates runtime with preventing groundings by means of our approach. The red line indicates the Kullback Leibler divergence (KLD) as measure of accuracy between the two approaches. The KLD compares the predicted probability distributions of each entity $z \in D(Z)$ with and without preventing groundings. The average KLD over all entities for each time step, denotes the overall accuracy for a time step. A KLD close to 0 is indicative of similar distributions, thus corresponds to a small error. In particular, Fig. 4 shows that the a priori introduction of symmetry clusters to prevent groundings speeds up inference while introducing only a very small error in inference.

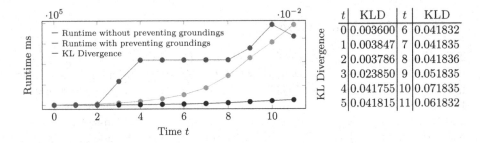

t	KLD	t	KLD
0	0.003600	6	0.041832
1	0.003847	7	0.041835
2	0.003786	8	0.041836
3	0.023850	9	0.051835
4	0.041755	10	0.071835
5	0.041815	11	0.061832

Fig. 4. Runtime [ms] and accuracy with and without preventing groundings.

6   Conclusion and Future Work

Evidence often grounds dynamic probabilistic relational models over time, negating runtime benefits in lifted inference. To maintain a lifted representation, in this paper we propose an approach to detect model symmetries when learning a lifted model, which can be used in inference under evidence to avoid unnecessary splits, e.g., due to one time events. This novel approach uses ordinal pattern symbolization followed by spectral clustering for a priori approximation of model symmetries, preventing model groundings. Moreover, the concept of clusters or entity interconnectivity as a result of understanding model symmetries enables for inferred evidence, i.e., applying evidence, which is observed for one entity, also to other entities. The empirical evaluation shows that by means of our approach unnecessary groundings are reduced, i.e., improving runtime performance, while also keeping the model accuracy through leveraging inferred evidence and therefore representing the reality more realistically. In future work, we use multivariate ordinal patterns introduced by Mohr et al. [12] to incorporate entity clusters based on their partitions in the DPRM, i.e., on their parfactors. We also investigate various forms of interconnectivity between entity symmetry clusters that can help to further increase the accuracy of the model by representing the reality even better.

Appendix

Algorithm 1: Entity Symmetrie Approximation

Input: Model G, Evidence $\mathbf{E}_{0:t}$, Order d, Delay τ, Delta $\delta_{\bar{x}}$

1   **for** *every PRV $P_t(A)$ in G* **do**

2     $\mathcal{X}^{|A| \times T} \leftarrow$ get all evidence from $\mathbf{E}_{0:t}$ concerning $P_t(A)$

3     $\mathcal{S}^{|A| \times (T - \tau(d-1))} \leftarrow$ init an empty symbolic representation matrix

4   **for** *every dimension $i = 1, \ldots, |A|$ of $\mathcal{X}$* **do**

5       $\mathcal{S}_{i\cdot} \leftarrow$ create a time series of tuples with $\langle ordinal, mean \rangle$

6     $\mathcal{W}^{|A| \times |A|} \leftarrow$ auxiliary-matrix initialized with zeros

7   **for** *every time step t of $\mathcal{S}_{\cdot t}$* **do**

8       $w_{ij} \leftarrow$ do similarity counting   // see Equation (5)

9   Create a similarity graph based on $\mathcal{W}$

10   Calculate the graph Laplacian matrix L for dimensionality reduction

11   Perform Spectral Clustering based the eigenvectors of L

Algorithm 2: Preventing Groundings

Input: $(G_0, G_{\rightarrow})$ DPRM, $\mathcal{E}, \mathcal{Q}$ streams, d order, τ delay, $\mathcal{C}$ entity clusters

1   **for** *each PRV $P(A) \in G_t$* **do** // `Initialization`

2    $H_{P(A)} \leftarrow \mathbf{0}_n$ vector with $n = |A|$ to count for contrary behavior

3   **for** *$t = 0, 1, \ldots, T$* **do** // `Query Answering`

4   Get evidence $\mathbf{E}_t$ from evidence stream $\mathcal{E}$

5   **for** *each PRV $P_t(A) \in G_t$* **do**

6       $\mathbf{E}_t^{P_t(A)} \leftarrow$ get evidence concerning the PRV $P(A)$ from E_t

7       $\mathcal{M} \leftarrow$ cluster $\mathbf{E}_t^{P_t(A)}$ by entities using clusters $\mathcal{C}_{P_t(A)} \in \mathcal{C}$

8   **for** *each evidence cluster $\mathcal{M}_i \in \mathcal{M}$* **do**

9         $max(o) \leftarrow$ get most common observation in $\mathcal{M}_i$

10   **for** *observation $P(a_i) = o \in \mathcal{M}_i$* **do** // `dismiss evidence`

11   **if** $o \neq max(o)$ and $H_{P(a_i)} < {}^{d \cdot \tau}/_2$ **then**

12   Dismiss observation o and increase counter

             $H_{P(a_i)} \leftarrow H_{P(a_i)} + 1$

13   **else**

14   Allow Split and reset counter $H_{P(a_i)} \leftarrow 0$

15   **for** *$a_i \in A$ of $\mathcal{X}_{P(A)}$ without observation* **do** // `inferred evidence`

16   Apply $max(o)$ as inferred evidence for a_i

17   Answer queries Q_t from query stream $\mathcal{Q}$

References

1. Bandt, C., Pompe, B.: Permutation entropy: a natural complexity measure for time series. Phys. Rev. Lett. **88**(17) (2002). https://doi.org/10.1103/PhysRevLett.88.174102
2. Bellman, R.: Adaptive Control Processes: A Guided Tour. Princeton legacy library, Princeton University Press (2015). https://books.google.de/books?id=iwbWCgAAQBAJ
3. Bertozzi, A.L., Merkurjev, E.: Chapter 12 - Graph-based optimization approaches for machine learning, uncertainty quantification and networks. In: Kimmel, R., Tai, X.C. (eds.) Processing, Analyzing and Learning of Images, Shapes, and Forms: Part 2, Handbook of Numerical Analysis, vol. 20, pp. 503–531. Elsevier (2019). https://doi.org/10.1016/bs.hna.2019.04.001, https://www.sciencedirect.com/science/article/pii/S157086591930002X
4. Van den Broeck, G., Niepert, M.: Lifted probabilistic inference for asymmetric graphical models. In: Proceedings of the 29th Conference on Artificial Intelligence (AAAI) (2015)
5. Chiu, B., Keogh, E., Lonardi, S.: Probabilistic discovery of time series motifs. In: Proceedings of the Ninth ACM SIGKDD International Conference on Knowledge Discovery and Data Mining. KDD 2003, New York, NY, USA, pp. 493–498 (2003)
6. Finke, N., Gehrke, M., Braun, T., Potten, T., Möller, R.: Investigating matureness of probabilistic graphical models for dry-bulk shipping. In: Jaeger, M., Nielsen, T.D. (eds.) Proceedings of the 10th International Conference on Probabilistic Graphical Models. Proceedings of Machine Learning Research, vol. 138, pp. 197–208. PMLR, 23–25 September 2020
7. Gehrke, M., Braun, T., Möller, R.: Lifted dynamic junction tree algorithm. In: Chapman, P., Endres, D., Pernelle, N. (eds.) ICCS 2018. LNCS (LNAI), vol. 10872, pp. 55–69. Springer, Cham (2018). https://doi.org/10.1007/978-3-319-91379-7_5
8. Gehrke, M., Möller, R., Braun, T.: Taming reasoning in temporal probabilistic relational models. In: Proceedings of the 24th European Conference on Artificial Intelligence (ECAI 2020) (2020). https://doi.org/10.3233/FAIA200395
9. Keller, K., Maksymenko, S., Stolz, I.: Entropy determination based on the ordinal structure of a dynamical system. Discrete Continuous Dyn. Syst. Ser. B **20**(10), 3507–3524 (2015). https://doi.org/10.3934/dcdsb.2015.20.3507
10. Keller, K., Mangold, T., Stolz, I., Werner, J.: Permutation entropy: new ideas and challenges. Entropy **19**(3), 134 (2017). https://doi.org/10.3390/e19030134
11. Kimmig, A., Mihalkova, L., Getoor, L.: Lifted graphical models: a survey. Mach. Learn. **99**(1), 1–45 (2014). https://doi.org/10.1007/s10994-014-5443-2
12. Mohr, M., Wilhelm, F., Hartwig, M., Möller, R., Keller, K.: New approaches in ordinal pattern representations for multivariate time series. In: Proceedings of the 33rd International Florida Artificial Intelligence Research Society Conference (FLAIRS-33), pp. 124–129. AAAI Press (2020)
13. Myers, A., Khasawneh, F.A.: On the automatic parameter selection for permutation entropy. Chaos Interdiscip. Jo. Nonlinear Sci. **30**(3), 033130 (2020). https://doi.org/10.1063/1.5111719, https://aip.scitation.org/doi/10.1063/1.5111719, publisher: American Institute of Physics
14. Niepert, M., Van den Broeck, G.: Tractability through exchangeability: a new perspective on efficient probabilistic inference. In: AAAI-14 Proceedings of the 28th AAAI Conference on Artificial Intelligence, pp. 2467–2475. AAAI Press (2014)

15. Piek, A.B., Stolz, I., Keller, K.: Algorithmics, possibilities and limits of ordinal pattern based entropies. Entropy **21**(6), 547 (2019). https://doi.org/10.3390/e21060547
16. Poole, D.: First-order probabilistic inference. In: Proceedings of the 18th International Joint Conference on Artificial Intelligence, pp. 985–991. IJCAI Organization (2003)
17. Riedl, M., Müller, A., Wessel, N.: Practical considerations of permutation entropy: a tutorial review. Eur. Phys. J. Spec. Top. **222** (2013). https://doi.org/10.1140/epjst/e2013-01862-7
18. Singla, P., Nath, A., Domingos, P.: Approximate lifting techniques for belief propagation. In: Proceedings of the Twenty-Eighth AAAI Conference on Artificial Intelligence, pp. 2497–2504. AAAI 2014. AAAI Press (2014)
19. Stolz, I., Keller, K.: A general symbolic approach to Kolmogorov-Sinai entropy. Entropy **19**(12), 675 (2017). https://doi.org/10.3390/e19120675
20. Venugopal, D., Gogate, V.: Evidence-based clustering for scalable inference in Markov logic. In: Calders, T., Esposito, F., Hüllermeier, E., Meo, R. (eds.) ECML PKDD 2014. LNCS (LNAI), vol. 8726, pp. 258–273. Springer, Heidelberg (2014). https://doi.org/10.1007/978-3-662-44845-8_17

Towards More Explicit Interaction Modelling in Agent-Based Simulation Using Affordance Schemata

Franziska Klügl[1]([⊠]) [iD] and Sabine Timpf[2] [iD]

[1] AASS/NT, Örebro University, Fakultetsgatan 1, 70182 Örebro, Sweden
franziska.klugl@oru.se
[2] Geoinformatics Group, Augsburg University, Alter Postweg 118,
86159 Augsburg, Germany
sabine.timpf@uni-a.de

Abstract. Modelling agent-environment interactions in an agent-based simulation requires careful design choices. Selecting an interaction partner forms an often neglected, but essential element.

In this paper we introduce affordance schemata as an element of agent-based simulation models. We describe how affordances can be generated based on them during a running simulation to capture action potential that an interaction partner offers. We illustrate the introduced concepts with a small proof-of-concept implementation.

Keywords: Agent-based modelling and simulation · Interaction · Affordances

1 Motivation

When building an agent-based model, a critical part is how interactions between agents as well as between agents and other entities in their environment are captured. In this paper, we present the concept of affordance schemata, which we introduce as a mean to explicitly model the selection of interaction partner which is often otherwise hidden in the implementation of the agents' action implementation.

Designing and implementing agent-based simulations is challenging due to its bottom-up nature. A modeller formulates the behaviour of agents situated in their environment; during a simulation run the agents take decisions and change their environment and hereby generate intended aggregate structures and dynamics. All actions and interactions need to be formulated from the participating agents' perspective. For example, in an agent-based simulation model of how humans use park space, the central part of the model contains that the agent enters the park, looks around and decides about to take a seat. In many existing agent-based simulation frameworks, the modeller formulates this behaviour only from the point of view of the agent. In SeSAm [12], this happens in activity graphs, in GAML/GAMA [26] a modeller formulates "reflexes"

© Springer Nature Switzerland AG 2021
S. Edelkamp et al. (Eds.): KI 2021, LNAI 12873, pp. 324–337, 2021.
https://doi.org/10.1007/978-3-030-87626-5_24

as collections of actions, in Mesa[1], the modeller implements a `step` function. There is no additional perspective that supports grouping multiple agent and environmental entities for interactions. Yet, this would be highly relevant for transparently explain why particular structures and overall system behaviour is produced. We believe that affordances and affordance schemata can provide a basis for explicitly formulating the first step creating the connection between two interacting agents.

The idea of affordance forms an attractive means to connect agents and environmental entities in a dynamic way. Conceptually, they are emerging while the agent behaves, e.g. moves around, in its local environment encounters potential interaction partners. Thus, an affordance forms an inherently dynamic relation. We propose affordance schemata as an explicit part of agent-based simulation models from which affordances can be generated during simulation. This work is a full revision of [14], clarifying the concept and streamlining the formalisation, based on experiences gained from a proof of concept implementation.

After a short background on the notion of affordances in the next section, we continue by analysing the process of agent-entity interaction and introduce our specific take on affordances as guidance for interaction modelling. This is followed by introducing the concept of affordance schemata as framework for modelling agent-entity interactions. Section 5 presents a small proof-of-concept implementation of an example, while in Sect. 6 we discuss interaction as a fist-class concept in agent-based modelling. Section 7 places our work into relation of the state-of-art. The paper ends with a short summary and presentation of future work.

2   Affordances in Modelling

The notion of affordance was introduced in ecological psychology by J.J. Gibson [5] about 40 years ago. Gibson defined affordances as action potentials provided by the environment: "The affordances of the environment are what it offers the animal, what it provides or furnishes, whether for good or ill". For example, a bench affords sitting to a human. The potential action of "sitting" depends on properties of the bench in relation to properties of the human, and on the current activity the human is engaged in. Gibson put special emphasis on this reciprocity between animal and environment, insisting that affordances are neither objective nor subjective. Thus, Stoffregen [25] defined affordances as "properties of the animal-environment system [...] that do not inhere in either the environment or the animal". This definition comes close to stating affordances as a concept emerging from the potential interaction between agent and environmental entity. However, it remains unclear how to model this concept with the flexibility inherent in the definition.

In man-machine interaction the most influential work [18] interpreted affordances as cues that tell humans how to use a specific (virtual) object. Modelling the user interface using affordances helped support usability of a specific piece

---

[1] https://mesa.readthedocs.io/en/master/overview.html

of software. This notion relates to "perceived affordances", i.e., the actions the user perceives as being possible based on how an object is presented. A similar point of view can be found in robotics where object affordances enable a robot to reason about what can be done with a perceived object. The usual process hereby is a sequence of classifications: recognising the object, recognise attributes and/or associate affordances with it – the interesting part for robotic research is hereby to learn or determine what recognisable features enable an object to be filled, to be grasped, etc. [6,16].

In agent-based modelling emergence is produced though interaction - but how can we model interaction such that the emerging phenomenon is preserved? Our solution is to model interaction in a reproducible way using a more abstract structure called affordance schema. Affordance schemata allow for the required flexibility in matching agents' capabilities with the properties of environmental objects thus producing a collection of emerging interactions.

3   Agent-Entity Interaction

Current modelling approaches in agent-based simulation focus on modelling agents and entities as well as their behaviour and properties, as those are stable concepts. By contrast, interaction may change with the location of the entity within the environment. It may take very different forms depending on the level of abstraction at which the model is formulated. We aim at creating a framework for modelling interaction that is sufficiently flexible for changing interaction partners, but does not hide this part of overall interactive behaviour within the details of an activity implementation.

Before we can introduce affordances and affordance schemata, first some concepts and assumptions need to be clarified:

3.1   Phases in the Behaviour of an Agent, Agent and Activities

We assume that the agent's behaviour is structured into activities, which we see as explicitly represented combinations of actions (sequences, branches, loops) with a minimum of one action. In this paper, we do not consider the process of determining activities for an agent but take an activity as a given input for the course of the simulation. Therefore, we do not make assumptions about how the agent decides which activity to do next or which cognitive model or reasoning process it follows for generating behaviour. An activity is formulated to produce simulated cohesive behaviour at the individual agent layer. The actions within an activity may also be connected by the idea that each action is executed with the same interaction partner. In the current version of the framework, we assume that only one interaction partner is needed; if not, activities can be split to generate such a situation.

The activity of the agent is explicitly represented, and can be denoted by a label or a symbol that can be used for pointing to this particular activity when fully specifying an affordance. The search for an interaction partner is connected to the activity, not to a single action That means also that the necessity for selecting an interaction is triggered by an activity that the agent wants to carry out. This motivation of the agent for selecting the interaction is important because it defines the need for an interaction partner and also the constraints that limit or guide on the selection. The interaction partner needs to be an "entity", i.e. another agent, an environmental entity or any identifiable spatial element.

The agent has an internal state that can be also used for determining preferences. In case, there are multiple potential interaction partners for the same activity, the agents will need to select one of them. This selection is not random, but influenced by preferences and capabilities based on the agent's current situation and state; of course in relation to some properties of the potential interaction partner.

3.2   The Interaction Perspective

An interaction is initiated by one agent. This agent intentionally scans its (perceivable or remembered) environment for potential interaction partners, be they active agents or passive environmental objects (that are also agents called resources). The interaction partners are selected and a non-trivial activity is performed together or with the passive environmental object.

Intentional interaction starts with the selection of an interaction partner/object to interact with. Thus, it is coupled with agent activity and/or individual goal fulfilment. In the following, we will present our idea of using affordances for formulating the selection of an interaction partner for intentional interaction.

3.3   Affordances as Guidance for Interactions

Our aim is to support agent-based modelling and simulation by introducing the idea of an *affordance schema* that serves as a kind of template for generating an *affordance* during simulation run-time time. An affordance connects a particular type of entity that the agents may perceive with a particular agent activity that realises an interaction with such an entity. Thus an affordance "emerges" in the current situation the agent is in, both in terms of environmental configuration and internal behaviour/motivational state. When we create a model of the agent, the question is how we may enable this emergence, which should not be pre-defined per definition. Our idea is to introduce the notion of an affordance schema that captures information about the circumstances under which the affordance is generated. So, technically an affordance schema can be seen as a kind of template that a modeller can explicitly handle to capture situation-dependent affordances and thus interactions. Therefore, while an affordance itself is a concept at the simulation run-time level, an affordance schema is part of the agent-based model.

4   Affordance Schemata as Framework for Modelling Agent-Entity Interactions

Based on the concept of affordance as a linking element between environmental entity and agent with its activity, we aim at creating a framework for modelling interaction which is sufficiently flexible for changing interaction partners, but does not hide this part of overall interactive behaviour within the details of an activity implementation or selection. We suggest to use affordances specifically in the part of the process that concerns the selection of the entity to interact with. In the following, we first present our specific definition of what an "affordance" means and introduce "affordance schemata" that can represent all information to generate affordances as they emerge.

4.1   Affordance and Affordance Schema

The central concept of our approach to model the decision making about interactions and interaction partners is based on the following formalisation of an *Affordances* as a 4-tuple:

$$\langle a, e, act, p \rangle \tag{1}$$

As in the original concept by Gibson, we conceive an affordance as a particular link between an **agent** a that intends to perform an **activity** act. An activity is hereby seen as a kind of behaviour program consisting of at least one atomic action. This activity cannot be done alone, but needs an interaction partner – like a sitting activity needs something to sit on. This is the third element in the 4-tuple, the **environmental object** e that makes it possible to perform the activity. Thus, an affordance can be seen as a relation between an agent a and an environmental object as interaction partner e with respect to an activity act. The fourth element p cannot be found in other formulations. This represents a preference or priority $p \in [0, 1]$ that allows to compare different, concurrently active affordance relations. For example, when the agent looking for an interaction partner for its intended activity sitting finds multiple benches with different properties. We intentionally widen the perspective on the environmental object using the term interaction partner as we also want to include situations in which the presence of an agent enables activities.

In the original concept, an affordance "emerges" between agent and environmental object. As a consequence, it is a dynamic element that must be generated during a simulation run. It cannot exist independent from a dynamic simulation in which agents move and act on the environment. For explicitly handling the choice of interaction partners in the agents' activity a concept is needed that makes the prerequisites for the generation of affordances explicit.

We suggest to capture these conditions in a structure that we call "affordance schema". An affordance schema expresses which properties an environmental entity needs to possess as well as the overall conditions for the creation of an affordance. We define an affordance schema as a 3-tuple:

$$\langle EType, condition, fpriority \rangle \qquad (2)$$

Every agent possesses a list of affordance schemata $AS_{a,act}$ for each of the activities it has in its activity repertoire $act \in ACT_A$. Each affordance schema combines information about the type of the environmental entity $EType$ with two functions, $condition$ and $fpriority$:

- $EType$ forms a kind of class label for kind of interaction partner the affordance schemata is relevant for. Different schemata for the same activity can concern different types of entities, e.g. benches or walls for an agents who wants to sit down.
- $condition : A \times E \to \{True, False\}$ expresses constraints under which the affordance between an agent $a \in A$ and an entity $e \in E$ can be generated. A is hereby the set of all agents[2] and E the set of all entities who can serve as interaction partner. For reasons of efficiency, E only contains entities of type $EType$[3]
- $fpriority : A \times E \to [0,1]$ maps the combination of agent $a \in A$ and its candidates for interaction partners $e \in E$ to a priority scaled to $[0,1]$. From this function the fourth entry in the affordance 4-tuple is calculated.

Explicitly modelling affordance schemata gives a mean to clearly express, what a suitable interaction partner is for an agent performing a particular activity. Affordance schemata can be formulated by a modeller. The decision about who interacts with whom is not hidden in the operational implementation of the agent activity, but made explicit in the agent-based model. The definition must be accompanied with a clear process of selecting the interaction partner in the agent architecture. In the following, we describe our suggestion for this process.

4.2 Decision Making About Interactions Based on Affordances

The simple generic process with which an agent reasons about interaction and action in an integrated way is sketched in Fig. 1.

Starting point of the generation process for interactive behaviour is that the agent updates its state based on perception and the previous state and determines an activity that it intends to perform. The decision about the activity is not part of the framework and does not need to be fixed on a generic level. One can image a goal-based reasoning in which an activity defines what needs to be done to achieve the goal; or the agent uses some rule-based selection related to a particular perception. This is depending on the particular application. The only assumption is that the activity is explicitly represented as a unit of behaviour. It needs to be identifiable by the agent at this level that the activity needs an interaction partner or not.

---

[2] We assume that all agents use the same affordance-based architecture.

[3] The condition that the entity e is of type $EType$ could actually be part of the condition. Yet, as our goal is to make modelling of interaction partner selection more clear, we decided to separate $EType$ from $condition$.

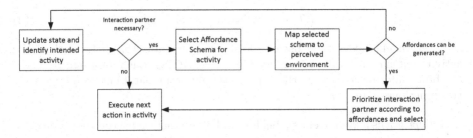

Fig. 1. Processes for overall behaviour generation with explicit interaction partner selection based on affordance schemata and affordances.

If the activity cannot be performed alone, the agent selects the affordance schemata associated with the activity. Technically, the activity can be used to index a set of affordance schemata.

The next step is to map each relevant affordance schemata onto the environment to test possible entities in the environment for their suitability as interaction partners. The function *condition* is used to filter the entities of the given *EType* type as interaction partners. After applying this matching process, the agent has a list of potential interaction partners associated with affordance schemata. For each of the potential interaction partner, the agent generates an affordance including a numeric priority value.

The last step uses these priorities to setup a preference relationship between affordances and as a consequence between potential interaction partners. The agent selects the entity with the highest priority and eventually starts to perform the activity with the entity as interaction partner.

If no affordance for the selected activity can be found, the activity cannot be performed and this is fed back into the state update and activity selection. This process is repeated until the agent actually performs an action. It is important to remember, that this is a process for an agent in a simulation setup; the modeller defines the affordance schemata. If an interaction does not work or results in a dangerous situation for the agent then this should happen as it would happen in the original system.

5   Proof of Concept

5.1   Conceptual Example

To illustrate the definition of this framework, consider the following element in a larger simulation about usage of park space: An agent of the type "Person" may intend an activity of *eating* - e.g. using a park for spending its lunch break. The affordance schema list contains for example the following entries: two for entities of the type "bench", with table (3), and without (4) and a third one for a low wall (5)

$$\langle Bench, \quad \text{clean, free bench with table,}$$
$$\text{the nearer the better, better in shadow}\rangle \qquad (3)$$
$$\langle Bench, \quad \text{clean, free bench without table,}$$
$$\text{the nearer the better, better in shadow}\rangle \qquad (4)$$
$$\langle Wall, \quad \text{clean, free wall patch with right height,}$$
$$\text{the nearer the better, better in shadow}\rangle \qquad (5)$$

These affordance schemata should be defined by the modeller. During a simulation run, a particular agent A enters the park with the activity *eating* in mind. For this activity, the agent needs an interaction partner, in this case an entity to sit on (necessary condition for performing the *eating* activity). Figure 2 shows the example scenario. The agent A enters from the top and observes the situation. A perceives four different benches $B1$, $B2$, $B3$ and $B4$ that are visible from the entrance. It is a sunny, hot day; $B1$ and $B2$ are in the shadow of large trees, $B3$ in full sun. $B2$ and $B4$ have a table; $B4$ is in the sun and dirty. There is also a low wall, which is partially shadowed, slightly dirty and still a little bit wet after the last rain.

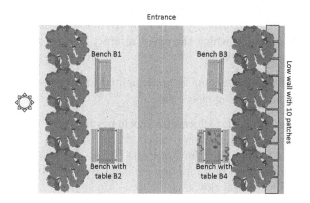

Fig. 2. Example park scenario with different environmental entities that afford "eating" - an activity at which the agents sits down and eats lunch

The schema 3 matches only B2, as cleanliness is not just nice to have, but a required part of the condition. Benches B1 and B3 match schema 4. No schema matches $B4$: it is a bench with a table, so the agent would look deeper into schema 3, but the necessary requirement of cleanness is violated, thus general acceptability is not given. $B1$ matches the affordance schema (4). None of the wall elements is further considered due to being wet. Eventually, the following affordances are generated from mapping the schemata to the environmental situation: $\langle A, B2, eating, 0.75\rangle$, $\langle A, B1, eating, 0.80\rangle$ and $\langle A, B3, eating, 0.5\rangle$.

5.2   Implementation

We implemented and tested the conceptual example above using SeSAm [12] as a platform. SeSAm is a visual programming, fast prototyping platform for developing and running agent-based simulations. The agent behaviour is formulated based on a UML-inspired activity graph. Activities consist of a sequence of actions that link to Java code.

Environmental Model. The environment consists of a continuous map on which discrete environmental entities are placed to form the situation as shown in Fig. 2. Environmental entities hereby have a type (class), such as `GroundTile`, `Tree`, `Bench` or `WallElement`. Those objects have different attributes describing relevant properties, such as which share of the `Bench` is in the shades, etc.

Affordance-Enabled Agent. We define a park-visitor agent class with attributes that describe how important a shadowy environment or walking distance is for an individual agent. The agents also possess basic knowledge structures that contain

- a list of activities that the agent might want to perform in a park, such as {*HaveLunch, SunBath, ...*}. These activities are associated with small behaviour programs in which the agent interacts with a given entity.
- a list of affordance schemata

Hereby, an affordance schema is implemented as a composed data structure that consists of the following elements:

1. Agent class for which the affordance schema is relevant.
2. Name of the associated activity
3. Class of the entity that the affordance establishes a relation during simulation
4. Constraints in the form of a function call that returns a boolean - true, if the entity is suitable, false if not.
5. Priority function that has the agent and the entity as arguments and returns a number

The entry 1) is relevant just because we associate the set of affordance schemata with the overall – in SeSAm explicitly represented – environment. The environment is responsible to generate new agents and thus provide them with an initial list of affordance schemata. Individual priorities are part of the individual agents' state.

Thus, an agent knows about its potential activities and has a number of affordance schemata so that for every interactive activity there is at least one affordance schema in the behaviour definition of the agent. When the agent enters the park, it makes a pre-decision about what it could do in the park. A second step consists of that the agent selects the affordance schema that fits to its intended activity and uses it to generate affordances connecting suitable environmental entities to the activity. If there is no affordance generated, the agent needs to find an alternative activity to do in the park. Affordances Schemata also contain functionality to calculate priorities, etc. So, the activity `SunBath` may be done on a bench, on a wall element or on a `GroundTile` of type meadow. The agent can use the schema definition to generate affordances as well as a ranking of generated affordances. This ranking is then used to decide which is the best available interaction partner.

6 Discussion: Interaction as First-Class Concept

Emergence in agent-based models is produced though interaction. Therefore, it is important to model interactions, especially the selection with whom to interact, in a transparent way. In the approach presented above interactions between agents and environmental entity are not hidden within the implementation details but lifted to the level of modelling and thus made visible and explicit for the modeller.

We use "affordance" as a technical term capturing something that would be not be capture-able otherwise. We do no claim to formalise the psychological, cognitive-science view on how humans actually reason about affordances. Our focus is on helping the modeller understand and think about interactions between agent and environment. Affordance shall make the potential for interaction between an agent and its environment explicit. So, we let the affordance stand per se for a potential interaction independent of how an agent selects its actions during simulation run-time. One can see it as a "shortcut" or abstraction for representing what the agent perceives as relevant for selecting an entity as an interaction partner, without explicitly listing relevant features.

7 Related Work

[14] introduce a first version of these ideas at a rather conceptual level. In that paper the relation to other interaction-based development methodologies for developing agent-based simulation, i.e. IODA and MAIA, are discussed more deeply. When implementing our framework, we noticed that concepts presented in [14] were neither concise enough nor complete. For example, interaction was conceptualised as being with a constellation of environmental objects, yet no mean for capturing such a constellation was provided. However, defining a language for describing what is a suitable set of objects in particular relations to each other and in a particular state, is not easy. One has to compromise between expressiveness and usability of that language. We decided to simplify this into requesting the actual interaction partners' type and a function that filters out those objects which are not suitable at all. In that function all relevant features also of the immediate environment of the potential partner – that means the constellation the entity is in – can be captured. Another aspect that was missing, was the explicit handling of priorities and how to select between different affordances.

Using the concept of affordances as a tool to formulate interactions in agent-based simulation is not new. There have been a number of works that are directly related to the proposed research here. In the following, we describe those works and point to the differences to what we described above.

There are a number of models that aim at reproducing how a human reasons about its environment for achieving more realism. These models are highly motivated by notions from cognitive science. The basic assumption is that the model can achieve a higher degree of structural validity when following hypotheses how humans really think. Examples for those models are [20–22] or [7]. A formalisation focusing on affordances as an emergent property is based on a detailed model of a spatially explicit environment as well as on actions and relations found in that environment [2].

Other works interpret the notion of affordances more freely: Joo et al. [8] propose affordance-based Finite State Automata. They use affordance-effect pairs to structure the transitions between states of a simulated human. Kapadia et al. ([9]) use "affordance fields" for representing the suitability of possible actions in a simulation of pedestrian steering and path-planning behaviour. An affordance is hereby a potential steering action. The affordance field is calculated from a combination of multiple fields filled with different kinds of perception data. The agent selects the action with the best value in the affordance field. A particular interesting approach is suggested by Ksontini et al. ([15]). They use affordances in traffic simulation denoting virtual lanes as an occupy-able space. Agents reason about what behaviour is enabled by the environmental situation. The affordances offered by the environment are explicitly represented by those virtual objects that offer driving on them. [13] labelled environmental entities with "affordances" such as "provides medication" as counterparts of agent needs enabling the agents to flexibly search for interaction partners or destinations.

[27]'s model of individual behaviour in a park uses affordances as a flexible way of connecting agents with resources in the environment. What we describe here can be seen as a generalisation of how the selection of environmental objects for interactions is formulated there. Some examples used here are inspired by this model.

In these approaches, affordances are used more as rules, for representing constraints or for identifying options. They serve as a tool for flexibly connecting an agent to interaction partners. There is no intention to advance research in cognitive science.

Approaches from Agent-based Software Engineering are also relevant for agent-based simulation [23]. Agent architectures form a mean for formulating how agent generate behaviour, so they can also be used in simulation settings. A rather old discussion of classical agent architectures and their relevance for simulation can be found already in [10]. Especially, BDI Architectures have been used in simulations as they allow formulating complex goal-driven behaviour (see [1] for a survey, [24] about integration or [17] for an example). While most BDI agents in simulation are based on PRS-type architectures, an alternative architecture, the IRMA architecture [3], has some similarities with our general approach which could integrate very well. An IRMA agent's behaviour is based on partial plans that the agents commits to and needs to complete, e.g. with an appropriate interaction partner. A so called "opportunity analyser" continuously checks the environment for opportunities to complete the partial plan or to revise what the agent currently attempts to do. The here proposed affordance schemata could be used to support this opportunity analyser component of the overall architecture. During the last years, the so called "Agents & Artifacts" framework and meta-model received a lot of attention [19]. The basic idea is that in an explicitly modelled environment in which the agents in a multi-agent system reside, passive objects as resources can be used to support coordination between agent and decision making of agents. In [4], the authors discuss a wider view on environments for Multi-Agent Systems bridging physical, virtual and simulated environments. The simulated environment hereby is part of the agent-based model, passive objects or resources are part of it, if and only if they play an important role for the simulated agents' behaviour [11].

8 Summary and Future Work

In this research we are aiming at creating a framework for modelling interactions of agents with environmental entities where interactions are treated as first-class concept in the modelling process. That is, we are interested in making it easier for the modeller to change interaction partners without having to re-model activities of agents and structures of environmental entities. This was accomplished by using the notion of affordance from ecological psychology as a concept that lets interactions emerge from agent's activities and properties of environmental entities. Capturing the conditions for this emergence leads to affordance schemata that are the patterns that generate affordances during simulation. In this fashion, affordances add an additional layer of abstraction in models in order to make agents' reasoning about interaction partners explicit and transparent. We provided an example to clarify the notions of affordance, affordance schema, and interaction. In addition we implemented and tested these ideas in SeSAm as a proof of concept. The results of our implementation are highly encouraging.

We are currently exploring the notion of affordance schemata for more geospatial activities and different example scenarios in order to prove the applicability of the schemata. One part of future work is to formally define activities and their actions as well as the needed properties for an activity to be carried out successfully. Another part of future work is to transfer the formulation of affordance schemata to the platform level, so that classes are provided and the modeller just needs to instantiate affordance schemata in order to generate affordances.

References

1. Adam, C., Gaudou, B.: BDI agents in social simulations: a survey. Knowl. Eng. Rev. **31**(3), 207–238 (2016)

2. Afoutni, Z., Courdier, R., Guerrin, F.: A multiagent system to model human action based on the concept of affordance. In: 4th International Conference on Simulation And Modeling Methodologies, Technologies And Applications (SIMULTECH), pp. 644–651 (2014)
3. Bratman, M.E., Israel, D.J., Pollack, M.E.: Plans and resource-bounded practical reasoning. Comput. Intell. **4**(4), 349–355 (1988)
4. Carrascosa, C., Klügl, F., Ricci, A., Boissier, O.: From physical to virtual: widening the perspective on multi-agent environments. In: Weyns, D., Michel, F. (eds.) Agent Environments for Multi-Agent Systems IV: 4th International Workshop, E4MAS 2014–10 Years Later, Paris, France, May 2014, pp. 133–146 (2015)
5. Gibson, J.J.: The Ecological Approach to Visual Perception. Houghton Mifflin, Boston (1979)
6. Heimann, O., Krüger, J.: Affordance based approach to automatic program generation for industrial robots in manufacturing. Procedia CIRP **76**, 133–137 (2018). 7th CIRP Conference on Assembly Technologies and Systems (CATS 2018)
7. Jonietz, D., Timpf, S.: An affordance-based simulation framework for assessing spatial suitability. In: Tenbrink, T., Stell, J., Galton, A., Wood, Z. (eds.) COSIT 2013. LNCS, vol. 8116, pp. 169–184. Springer, Cham (2013). https://doi.org/10. 1007/978-3-319-01790-7_10
8. Joo, J., et al.: Agent-based simulation of affordance-based human behaviors in emergency evacuation. Simul. Model. Pract. Theory **13**, 99–115 (2013)
9. Kapadia, M., Singh, S., Hewlett, W., Faloutsos, P.: Egocentric affordance fields in pedestrian steering. In: Proceedings of the 2009 Symposium on Interactive 3D Graphics and Games (I3D 2009), pp. 215–223. ACM, New York (2009)
10. Klügl, F.: Multiagentensimulation - Konzepte, Anwendungen, Tools. Addision Wesley, Munich (2001)
11. Klügl, F., Fehler, M., Herrler, R.: About the role of the environment in multi-agent simulations. In: Weyns, D., Van Dyke Parunak, H., Michel, F. (eds.) E4MAS 2004. LNCS (LNAI), vol. 3374, pp. 127–149. Springer, Heidelberg (2005). https://doi. org/10.1007/978-3-540-32259-7_7
12. Klügl, F., Herrler, R., Fehler, M.: SeSAm: implementation of agent-based simulation using visual programming. In: Proceedings of the 5th International Joint Conference on Autonomous Agents and Multiagent Systems, pp. 1439–1440. ACM (2006)
13. Klügl, F.: Using the affordance concept for model design in agent-based simulation. Ann. Math. Artif. Intell. **78**(1), 21–44 (2016). https://doi.org/10.1007/s10472-016-9511-0
14. Klügl, F., Timpf, S.: Approaching interactions in agent-based modelling with an affordance perspective. In: Sukthankar, G., Rodriguez-Aguilar, J.A. (eds.) AAMAS 2017. LNCS (LNAI), vol. 10642, pp. 222–238. Springer, Cham (2017). https://doi. org/10.1007/978-3-319-71682-4_14
15. Ksontini, F., Mandiau, R., Guessoum, Z., Espié, S.: Affordance-based agent model for road traffic simulation. Auton. Agents Multi-Agent Syst. **29**(5), 821–849 (2014). https://doi.org/10.1007/s10458-014-9269-x
16. Min, H., Yi, C., Luo, R., Zhu, J., Bi, S.: Affordance research in developmental robotics: a survey. IEEE Trans. Cogn. Dev. Syst. **8**(4), 237–255 (2016)
17. Nilsson, J., Klügl, F.: Human-in-the-loop simulation of a virtual classroom. In: Rovatsos, M., Vouros, G., Julian, V. (eds.) EUMAS/AT -2015. LNCS (LNAI), vol. 9571, pp. 379–394. Springer, Cham (2016). https://doi.org/10.1007/978-3-319-33509-4_30

18. Norman, D.A.: The Design of Everyday Things. Doubleday, New York (1990)
19. Omicini, A., Ricci, A., Viroli, M.: Artifacts in the A&A meta-model for multi-agent systems. Auton. Agent. Multi-Agent Syst. **17**, 432–456 (2008). https://doi.org/10.1007/s10458-008-9053-x
20. Paris, S., Donikian, S.: Activity-driven populace: a cognitive approach to crowd simulation. IEEE Comput. Graphics Appl. **29**(4), 34–43 (2009)
21. Raubal, M.: Ontology and epistemology for agent-based wayfinding simulation. Int. J. Geograph. Inf. Sci. **15**, 653–665 (2001)
22. Raubal, M., Moratz, R.: A functional model for affordance-based agents. In: Rome, E., Hertzberg, J., Dorffner, G. (eds.) Towards Affordance-Based Robot Control. LNCS (LNAI), vol. 4760, pp. 91–105. Springer, Heidelberg (2008). https://doi.org/10.1007/978-3-540-77915-5_7
23. Siebers, P.-O., Klügl, F.: What software engineering has to offer to agent-based social simulation. In: Edmonds, B., Meyer, R. (eds.) Simulating Social Complexity. UCS, pp. 81–117. Springer, Cham (2017). https://doi.org/10.1007/978-3-319-66948-9_6
24. Singh, D., Padgham, L., Logan, B.: Integrating BDI agents with agent-based simulation platforms. Auton. Agent. Multi-Agent Syst. **30**, 1050–1071 (2016). https://doi.org/10.1007/s10458-016-9332-x
25. Stoffregen, T.: Affordances as properties of the animal environment system. Ecol. Psychol. **15**(2), 115–134 (2003)
26. Taillandier, P., et al.: Building, composing and experimenting complex spatial models with the GAMA platform. GeoInformatica **23**(2), 299–322 (2018). https://doi.org/10.1007/s10707-018-00339-6
27. Timpf, S.: Simulating place selection in urban public parks. In: International Workshop on Social Space and Geographic Space, SGS 2007, Melbourne (2007)

Critic Guided Segmentation of Rewarding Objects in First-Person Views

Andrew Melnik[1(✉)], Augustin Harter[1], Christian Limberg[1], Krishan Rana[2], Niko Sünderhauf[2], and Helge Ritter[1]

[1] CITEC, Bielefeld University, Bielefeld, Germany
andrew.melnik.papers@gmail.com, aharter@techfak.uni-bielefeld.de
[2] Centre for Robotics, Queensland University of Technology (QUT), Brisbane, Australia

Abstract. This work discusses a learning approach to mask rewarding objects in images using sparse reward signals from an imitation learning dataset. For that we train an *Hourglass* network using only feedback from a critic model. The *Hourglass* network learns to produce a mask to decrease the critic's score of a high score image and increase the critic's score of a low score image by swapping the masked areas between these two images. We trained the model on an imitation learning dataset from the NeurIPS 2020 MineRL Competition Track, where our model learned to mask rewarding objects in a complex interactive 3D environment with a sparse reward signal. This approach was part of the 1st place winning solution in this competition. Video demonstration and code: https://rebrand.ly/critic-guided-segmentation.

Keywords: Imitation learning · Reinforcement learning · Image segmentation · Reward-centric objects · First person point of view · MineRL · Minecraft

1 Introduction

Training a semantic segmentation network can be a difficult problem in the absence of label information. We propose using sparse reward signals from a Reinforcement Learning (RL) environment to train a semantic segmentation model for masking rewarding objects. Moreover, our approach allows to train the semantic segmentation model completely on an imitation learning dataset without interaction with the environment. This is of interest for a number of use cases. Such technique can contribute to explainable AI [3], symbolic and causal reasoning in the space of detected objects, robotics, or as auxiliary information [7] for an RL setup. Learning the optimal policy in sparse reward environments [4] is an important challenge in Deep Reinforcement Learning (DRL) [1,5,15]. A masking network for rewarding objects can support an actor-critic RL setup

---

A. Melnik and A. Harter—Shared first authorship.

© Springer Nature Switzerland AG 2021
S. Edelkamp et al. (Eds.): KI 2021, LNAI 12873, pp. 338–348, 2021.
https://doi.org/10.1007/978-3-030-87626-5_25

in a way that is intuitive and explainable to a human. Semantic segmentation of rewarding objects can aid transfer learning, better sample efficiency of training, and better performance of a trained agent. In the following we are considering the question how a trained critic model - value network trained on discounted reward values - can guide the direct segmentation of such rewarding objects in a feed forward manner.

To this end we use the critic to select two sets of images characterized by high vs. low expected reward values. Using these two sets of images from an imitation learning dataset we can train a segmentation network for rewarding object regions by applying it to high expected reward images and exchanging the masked region with the low expected reward image. This makes it possible to evaluate how the mask changes the reward value prediction and therefore allows us to train the segmentation network to mask the rewarding objects (Fig. 1, also see Sect. 3 for details).

This work was motivated by the "MineRL NeurIPS 2020 Competition: Sample Efficient Reinforcement Learning in Minecraft" [4] where our AI agent won the 1st place. See Sect. 3 for details on the challenge, goals, and objects that an agent needs to learn in the world of Minecraft. While our approach is formulated in a domain-agnostic way, we evaluate it on first-person views in 3D Minecraft environments from the NeurIPS MineRL 2020 Competition.

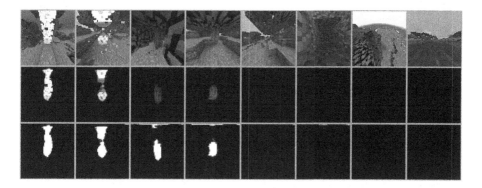

Fig. 1. Segmentation results: The *Hourglass* model learns to segment rewarding objects (tree trunks) without any label information but only from reward signals. In the first four columns, showing high critic-value images, the trained *Hourglass* model detects different instances of rewarding objects (white and brown tree trunks). The model is resistant to generation of false positive masks in low score images (columns 5–8). The first row shows the input images, the second row shows the segments extracted from the input images using the generated masks (not ground truth), and the third row shows the masks generated by the *Hourglass* model. Video demonstration and code: https://rebrand.ly/critic-guided-segmentation (Color figure online)

Phase 1:

-   train a critic network to predict expected reward value of image observations

Phase 2:

-   split the dataset into low and high critic-value images
-   repeat for each high and low critic-value image pair the following two stages:

Stage 1:

-   use the Hourglass model to generate a mask for the high critic-value image

Stage 2:

-   merge high critic-value image with low critic-value image based on the mask from Stage 1
-   reduce the critic's value of the merged image by training the Hourglass model to optimize (with gradients) the merge mask for the pair of high and low critic-value images
-   run a training step of Phase 1 (continue training critic)

Fig. 2. Training pipeline overview. Phase 2 is explained in more detail in Fig. 3.

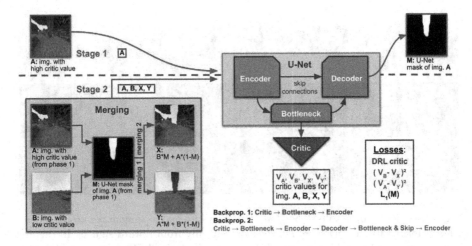

Fig. 3. This figure shows the second phase of our pipeline containing the segmentation training which consists of two stages: Stage 1 (highlighted in red): Image **A** (high critic value) passes through the *Hourglass network*, forming a mask **M**. Stage 2: the mask **M** is used to merge image **A** (high critic value) with image **B** (low critic value) resulting in image **X** (masked parts of **A** replaced with **B**) and image **Y** (masked parts of **A** injected in **B**). Images **A**, **B**, **X**, and **Y** are then passed through the encoder and critic. The losses penalize differences in critic values for image pairs **A**: **Y**, and **B**: **X**. A linear regularization term penalizes mask intensity and prevents collapse to a trivial solution where the mask **M** fills the entire image. Video explanation and code: https://rebrand. ly/critic-guided-segmentation (Color figure online)

2 Methods

Refer to Fig. 2 to see a high level overview of our approach which we will now describe in more detail: We first train a critic model to predict the discounted reward for images and then train an *Hourglass* model [12] to infer a segmentation mask over rewarding objects while continuing to train the critic (Fig. 1). The architecture is based on two sub modules (Fig. 3): A critic network trained to predict discounted reward for a given image, and an *Hourglass* model that produces a segmentation mask for rewarding objects in the image. Such masks, when used to replace parts from high critic score images, lowers the predicted score and, when used to inject these parts into low critic score images, increases the predicted score. To achieve this objective the *Hourglass* model learns to segment the rewarding objects.

We evaluate our approach in the first-person Minecraft environments from the *MineRL 2020 Competition* [4]. The provided imitation learning database consists of data recorded from human players and we use only images and the recorded sparse reward signals from the database to train our model.

2.1 Pipeline

The training is divided into two phases: *Phase 1* contains the initial critic training enabling us to use the critic in *phase 2* to train our segmentation model. *phase two* happens in two stages and is shown in Fig. 3: *Stage 1* is the pass through the segmentation model producing a segmentation mask. We then use this mask in *stage 2* to construct new merged images and pass them through the critic to calculate the gradient with respect to the mask based merging.

Phase 1: Initial Critic Training. We train the critic model to directly predict the time discounted reward value of states which are $64 \times 64 \times 3$ RGB single image observations. We use the time discounted reward from the data set episodes as a supervised training signal together with the mean squared error as loss function. After training converges, we use the critic to split the database into images with high critic values **A** and low critic values **B** for *phase 2*.

Phase 2: Segmentation Training. *Phase 2* is subdivided into two stages and visualized in Fig. 3): In *stage 1* we pass an image through the segmentation model to produce a mask. In *stage 2* we use this mask to swap out pixels in an image pair and pass the resulting merged images through the critic to infer how the mask-based pixel swap changed the original critic value prediction for the image pair. We do this because we don't have explicit ground truth masks segmenting the rewarding objects as a training target. Instead, we pick image pairs such that one (image **A**) has a high critic value and the other (image **B**) a low critic value and use these pairs to formulate a loss which enables learning to segment rewarding objects: The key idea is that reward related parts of images should decrease the critic value when removed and increase the critic value when injected into another image.

Implementation: We implement this idea by first using the segmentation model in *stage 1* to produce a mask M based on the high critic value image A. Next, in *stage 2* we use the mask to swap the highlighted pixels in A and replace them with the corresponding pixels in low critic value image B. This generates a second pair of images: X (image A with masked pixels replaced by content of B) and Y (image B with content substituted by masked pixels from image A). For a "perfect" mask that captures all reward related structures, the critic values between the pairs should be swapped: High in Y since it received all reward related content of A, and low in X since all reward-related content has been replaced by contents from low value image B). The *inject loss* penalizes the squared difference between critic values of A and Y: $L_R = (V_A - V_Y)^2$ And the *replace loss* penalizes the squared difference between critic values of B and X: $L_I = (V_B - V_X)^2$

   To further illustrate this we can consider a bad mask that leaves all essential reward elements in X contributing to a high *replace loss*, since then V_X remains high, while V_B is low; similarly, Y would hardly receive any reward related content from A, keeping V_Y low whereas V_A is high and therefore producing a high *inject loss*.

Regularization: In order to avoid trivial solutions like a full image mask replacing the complete images, we apply a linear regularization to enforce minimal masks: $L_N = |M|$

Continued Critic Training: Training the mask has influence on the encoder weights which are shared across critic and segmentation model and therefore can mess up the critic predictions. A straight forward solution would be to freeze the encoder weights after the initial critic training in *phase 1* is over. This works but we found that we can allow the segmentation model to influence the encoder weights if we also continue to train the critic like in *phase 1* which keeps the encoder functional for reward prediction. This increases performance, see *frozen weights* for comparison in Sect. 3.

Handling False Positives: So far we explained how we pass high critic value images through the segmentation model to produce reward related segmentation masks. But this means that the model would only see high value images and therefore be heavily biased towards producing a mask even for low reward images producing "false positives". Therefore we take low value images for A in half of the time. This means that a batch containing 128 images would contain 32 high value and 32 low value images as A and 64 low value images for B. With this we can keep the above stated losses without producing "bad" gradients since $(V_A - V_Y)^2$ and $(V_B - V_X)^2$ are small because both images have similar (low) critic values already before merging. This allows the gradient from the regularization term that favors sparse masks to drive the segmentation response towards the desired empty mask output when receiving a low critic image as input. Segmentation results for both high and low value images are shown in Fig. 1.

3 Experiments

Data Set: We apply our method on an imitation learning data set from the NeurIPS2020 MineRL Challenge. It is based on Minecraft, a game providing a 3D world where players can interact with the world in first person view. We used the *TreeChop* environment which contains episodes of human players chopping trees and collecting wood: The players can repeatedly use the *attack action* on a tree trunk to destroy it which produces the item *log* which is automatically collected when in proximity. Only upon collection the player receives *reward = 1*, all other images give *reward = 0*. Less then 1% of images get a reward signal, while roughly a third of the images contain views of trees in close proximity and almost all images contain some tree features in sight but possibly further away.

After chopping the base trunk of a tree, players usually stand below the "floating" tree crown to chop the remaining wood in the tree crown. We remove most of this tree crown chopping which makes up roughly 20% of images to focus the reward signal on approaching and chopping the tree trunks. This is automatically done by removing the 35 images after a reward signal. From that we assemble a data set containing 100k images where we clip reward values higher than 1 (when collecting multiple *log items* at once). We then use a factor of 0.98 to discount the reward every time step and use the resulting discounted reward as the training label for that image. This results in a data set with a quite balanced histogram of discounted reward values, meaning that there are roughly equal amounts of images for every reward value in the range from 0 to 1 which stabilized the critic training. Additionally we apply a small data augmentation that shifts the images randomly up to 12 pixels to the right or left which works against the strong bias in the data set that trees are almost always in the middle of the image when receiving a reward signal.

Architecture. We use a convolutional encoder-decoder architecture with skip connections inspired by *Hourglass Networks* which has two outputs: The first output is the critic score estimating the value of images. Its implemented through two additional linear layers after the decoder bottleneck (Fig. 3). The second output is the segmentation mask which is produced by the decoder. Our simple custom-made network has an encoder with 5 convolution layers with 40, 40, 40, 80 and 160 channels respectively and kernel size 3×3. The last layer results in a non-spatial bottleneck (dimensions: $1 \times 1 \times 160$). Each layer is followed by a LeakyReLU and we use max pooling after the first 4 layers. The decoder has a mirrored structure but we switch the pooling layers with up sampling. Its output layer is passed through the Sigmoid function to produce the mask. The critic shares the encoder and after the bottleneck additionally consists of two fully connected layers with 160 units each. Further we use a 50% dropout after the third and fourth encoder layers and after the first fully connected critic layer.

Reward prediction and segmentation demand similar features, so instead of using separate models they both share the encoder: In a first phase the encoder is trained to create a meaningful feature representation of images that makes it possible for the critic to predict the reward. In the second phase the decoder can use skip connections to access the encoder representation, which we found greatly improves mask quality in comparison to a separate critic. See Sect. 4.

Evaluation: To test the performance of our model, we collect a test set containing 18k images from 10 episodes of a player chopping tree trunks. We modified the environment simulator enabling us to extract the ground truth segmentation masks of tree trunks. Such masks where never seen during training. With this we can measure the *Intersection over Union* (IoU) score as a performance metric to evaluate our segmentation model. We report the performance in Table 1 and compare it to a saliency map baseline.

Training Details: We train the critic in *phase 1* on the 100k images for 15 epochs using a batch size of 64 until convergence and use it to split the data set into images with a predicted reward higher than 0.7 (resulting in 20k images) and images with predicted reward lower than 0.3 (resulting in roughly 30k images). This values were obtained through a small hyper parameter grid search with the evaluation dataset. We then use these two subsets to continue our training in *phase 2* for one epoch with a batch size of 128.

4 Results

We report the intersection-over-union (IoU) scores of the segmentation mask achieved when compared to the ground truth data. To better understand how our model works we compare four different model variants with two baseline approaches which we describe in detail below before presenting our final results in Table 1. Further we report the performance when post processing with Conditional Random Fields (CRF) [11,23] which is a common method to improve inaccurate or noisy segmentation masks. We additionally provide some visual segmentation results attained by our approach in Fig. 1 for high and low critic score images. Once again these masks are learned only from a sparse reward signal in the challenging 3D Minecraft environment with differing lighting conditions, tree types and tree colors.

Baseline Full Mask: Full mask covering everything in every image. We report this value for better comparison and interpretation of the other scores. This value can also be interpreted as the percentage of ground truth tree trunk pixels in our test set.

Baseline Saliency Map: Following [21] we compute the Jacobian of the input image with respect to the critic's prediction and weight the Jacobian of each image with the critic's predicted score. We then produce a mask by thresholding each pixels weighted gradient based on a value that is a multiple of the mean pixel gradient values. The exact multiple is determined through a hyperparameter search. This method can act as a baseline for the task, since calculating saliency maps to visualize where a model is "looking" at is common practice and requires no training of an additional model. However, the resulting masks are noisy and do not allow to focus at the area of the rewarding object in the image.

Table 1. *IoU* mean value over 10 training seeds.

Model Variant	IoU
Baseline Full Mask	0.12
Baseline Saliency Map	0.22
Baseline Saliency Map + CRF	0.11
Separate Critic	0.27
No Inject Loss	0.35
Frozen Encoder	0.38
Full Model	0.41
Full Model + CRF	**0.45**

Baseline Saliency Map + CRF: Post processing the saliency maps with CRF. The CRF hyper parameters where obtained through a grid search with the test set. For some images it leads to a improved segmentation but overall the saliency maps are too chaotic and noisy for this method to work properly.

Separate Critic: To test whether our hypothesis is valid that the encoder features learned during critic training are also useful for the segmentation training and therefore motivated the idea of sharing the encoder, we trained a model with a separate encoder for the critic. This means that a separate encoder has to be learned from scratch during segmentation training. The resulting decrease in IoU performance strengthens our hypothesis and favours weight sharing.

No Inject Loss: This model is trained without the *inject loss*, only using the mask to replace parts of high reward images and not injecting them into low reward images. The performance results show a clear decrease of performance emphasizing the usefulness of the inject objective. It seems like only having to decrease the critic value can lead to more degenerate solutions instead of also having to increase the critic value with the same mask.

Frozen Encoder: Here we train the model with frozen encoder weights, since the segmentation gradients will influence the encoder and through that mess up the critic predictions needed for our replace and inject losses. With a frozen encoder the decoder can access the encoder features but not change them to better fit the segmentation task.

Full Model + CRF: The alternative to a frozen encoder is to let the decoder gradients influence the encoder but at the same time continuing to train the critic which prevents the encoder features to become dysfunctional for the critic's reward prediction. This setup results in the best performing variant of our approach without post processing. It combines the inject loss with a shared encoder and continued critic training in phase 2 into our "Full Model".

Full Model: Post processing the model output with CRF. The CRF hyper parameters were obtained through a grid search with the test set. In contrast to the saliency maps, here the CRF improve performance.

5   Discussion

Humans explicitly learn notions of objects. There has been extensive research inspired by psychology and cognitive science [9,10,16] on explicitly learning object-centric and reward-centric representations from pixels [20]. Focusing on the reward quality of objects also adds an interesting perspective on the question of how NN build up their understanding of images. These question have been studied by feature visualization methods [17] and interpretability techniques [18].

Understanding RL Vision is a challenging problem. Hilton et al. [6] proposed to analyze, diagnose and edit deep reinforcement learning models using attribution. Although this technique allows to highlight objects related to positive and negative rewards in 2D environments, it requires human domain knowledge for selection of the right attributions, and it was not shown that this technique will work in more complicated 3D first-person-view environments. To understand how an agent learns and executes a policy a method for generating salience maps was introduced [2]. In this method, a change in the value function was used when sampling a grid of perturbations.

It has been empirically observed that RL from raw pixels is sample-inefficient [8,14]. Learning policies from state-based features is significantly more sample-efficient than learning from pixels. An approach called CURL [22] shows that by extracting high-level features from raw pixels using contrastive learning and then using these features as state in the RL setting results in a superior sample efficiency during training of an RL agent. In contrast, our approach allows learning of explicit masks over rewarding objects. Extracting these segmentation masks which are derived directly from reward can help prepossess the most relevant information from the raw pixel state representation. This is of interest for a number of use cases in explainable AI, symbolic and causal reasoning [13] in the space of detected objects, robotics, as well as in RL setups. Moreover, our approach can learn the segmentation model solely from imitation learning dataset.

DRL has been applied successfully in various domains for training high-performing agents [19]. Our approach could be used as an auxiliary module to train the agent from demonstrations to improve sample efficiency of learning. Our contribution is a novel and an intuitive use of joint training of a critic network and an image segmentation approach to highlight rewarding object segments in reinforcement learning environments. In this contribution we showed that it is possible to train a model to generate high-quality masks depicting rewarding objects in images without explicit label information, but only using feedback from the critic model. Our approach was part of the 1st place winning solution in the "MineRL NeurIPS 2020 Competition: Sample Efficient Reinforcement Learning in Minecraft".

Future work may include further experiments with RL or imitation learning setups extended with our model that provides rewarding-object masks. Identifying a mask or heatmap for negative rewards as well as non-reward entities may be a possible continuation of this work. Self-supervised learning of embedded classification of reward-centric objects can facilitate development of causal and symbolic reasoning models.

References

1. Bach, N., Melnik, A., Schilling, M., Korthals, T., Ritter, H.: Learn to move through a combination of policy gradient algorithms: DDPG, D4PG, and TD3. In: Nicosia, G., et al. (eds.) LOD 2020. LNCS, vol. 12566, pp. 631–644. Springer, Cham (2020). https://doi.org/10.1007/978-3-030-64580-9_52
2. Greydanus, S., Koul, A., Dodge, J., Fern, A.: Visualizing and understanding Atari agents. In: International Conference on Machine Learning, pp. 1792–1801. PMLR (2018)
3. Gunning, D., Aha, D.: Darpa's explainable artificial intelligence (XAI) program. AI Mag. **40**(2), 44–58 (2019)
4. Guss, W.H., et al.: Towards robust and domain agnostic reinforcement learning competitions: MineRL 2020. In: NeurIPS 2020 Competition and Demonstration Track, PMLR, pp. 233–252 (2021). https://proceedings.mlr.press/v133/guss21a
5. Harter, A., Melnik, A., Kumar, G., Agarwal, D., Garg, A., Ritter, H.: Solving physics puzzles by reasoning about paths. In: 1st NeurIPS workshop on Interpretable Inductive Biases and Physically Structured Learning (2020). https://arxiv.org/abs/2011.07357
6. Hilton, J., Cammarata, N., Carter, S., Goh, G., Olah, C.: Understanding RL vision. Distill (2020). https://doi.org/10.23915/distill.00029, https://distill.pub/2020/understanding-rl-vision
7. Jaderberg, M., et al.: Reinforcement learning with unsupervised auxiliary tasks. arXiv preprint arXiv:1611.05397 (2016)
8. Kaiser, L., et al.: Model-based reinforcement learning for Atari. arXiv preprint arXiv:1903.00374 (2019)
9. Konen, K., Korthals, T., Melnik, A., Schilling, M.: Biologically-inspired deep reinforcement learning of modular control for a six-legged robot. In: 2019 IEEE International Conference on Robotics and Automation Workshop on Learning Legged Locomotion Workshop, (ICRA) 2019, Montreal, CA, 20–25 May 2019 (2019)
10. König, P., Melnik, A., Goeke, C., Gert, A.L., König, S.U., Kietzmann, T.C.: Embodied cognition. In: 2018 6th International Conference on Brain-Computer Interface (BCI), pp. 1–4. IEEE (2018)
11. Krähenbühl, P., Koltun, V.: Efficient inference in fully connected CRFs with gaussian edge potentials. CoRR abs/1210.5644 (2012). http://arxiv.org/abs/1210.5644
12. Li, S.: Simple introduction about hourglass-like model. https://medium.com/@sunnerli/simple-introduction-about-hourglass-like-model-11ee7c30138
13. Melnik, A., Bramlage, L., Voss, H., Rossetto, F., Ritter, H.: Combining causal modelling and deep reinforcement learning for autonomous agents in minecraft. In: 4th Workshop on Semantic Policy and Action Representations for Autonomous Robots at IROS 2019 (2019)
14. Melnik, A., Fleer, S., Schilling, M., Ritter, H.: Modularization of end-to-end learning: case study in arcade games. In: 32nd Conference on Neural Information Processing Systems (NeurIPS 2018), Workshop on Causal Learning (2018). https://arxiv.org/pdf/1901.09895.pdf

15. Melnik, A., Lach, L., Plappert, M., Korthals, T., Haschke, R., Ritter, H.: Using tactile sensing to improve the sample efficiency and performance of deep deterministic policy gradients for simulated in-hand manipulation tasks. Front. Robot. AI **8**, 57 (2021). https://doi.org/10.3389/frobt.2021.538773
16. Melnik, A., Schüler, F., Rothkopf, C.A., König, P.: The world as an external memory: the price of saccades in a sensorimotor task. Front. Behav. Neurosci. **12**, 253 (2018). https://doi.org/10.3389/fnbeh.2018.00253
17. Olah, C., Mordvintsev, A., Schubert, L.: Feature visualization. Distill **2**(11), e7 (2017)
18. Olah, C., et al.: The building blocks of interpretability. Distill **3**(3), e10 (2018)
19. Schilling, M., Melnik, A.: An approach to hierarchical deep reinforcement learning for a decentralized walking control architecture. In: Samsonovich, A.V. (ed.) BICA 2018. AISC, vol. 848, pp. 272–282. Springer, Cham (2019). https://doi.org/10.1007/978-3-319-99316-4_36
20. Simonyan, K., Vedaldi, A., Zisserman, A.: Deep inside convolutional networks: visualising image classification models and saliency maps. arXiv preprint arXiv:1312.6034 (2013)
21. Simonyan, K., Vedaldi, A., Zisserman, A.: Deep inside convolutional networks: visualising image classification models and saliency maps (2014)
22. Srinivas, A., Laskin, M., Abbeel, P.: Curl: contrastive unsupervised representations for reinforcement learning. arXiv preprint arXiv:2004.04136 (2020)
23. taigw: Simple CRF python package. https://github.com/HiLab-git/SimpleCRF

Self-supervised Domain Adaptation for Diabetic Retinopathy Grading Using Vessel Image Reconstruction

Duy M. H. Nguyen[1]([✉]), Truong T. N. Mai[2], Ngoc T. T. Than[3], Alexander Prange[1], and Daniel Sonntag[1,4]

[1] German Research Center for Artificial Intelligence (DFKI), Saarland Informatics Campus Saarbrücken, Saarbrücken, Germany
ho_minh_duy.nguyen@dfki.de
[2] Department of Multimedia Engineering, Dongguk University, Seoul, South Korea
[3] Byers Eye Institute, Stanford University, Stanford, USA
[4] Oldenburg University, Oldenburg, Germany

Abstract. This paper investigates the problem of domain adaptation for diabetic retinopathy (DR) grading. We learn invariant target-domain features by defining a novel self-supervised task based on retinal vessel image reconstructions, inspired by medical domain knowledge. Then, a benchmark of current state-of-the-art unsupervised domain adaptation methods on the DR problem is provided. It can be shown that our approach outperforms existing domain adaption strategies. Furthermore, when utilizing entire training data in the target domain, we are able to compete with several state-of-the-art approaches in final classification accuracy just by applying standard network architectures and using image-level labels.

Keywords: Domain adaption · Diabetic retinopathy · Self-supervised learning · Deep learning · Interactive machine learning

1 Introduction

Diabetic retinopathy (DR) is a type of ocular disease that can cause blindness due to damaged blood vessels in the back of the eye. The causes of DR are high blood pressure and high blood sugar concentration, which are very common in modern lifestyles [40]. People with diabetes usually have higher risks of developing DR. In fact, one-third of diabetes patients show the symptoms of diabetic retinopathy according to recent studies [42]. Therefore, early detection of DR is critical to ensure successful treatment. Unfortunately, detecting and grading diabetic retinopathy in practice is a laborious task, and DR is difficult to diagnose at an early stage even for professional ophthalmologists. As a result, developing a precise automatic DR diagnostic device is both necessary and advantageous.

Automated DR diagnosis systems take retinal images (fundus images) and yield DR grades. In the common retinal imaging dataset of DR, the grades of

© Springer Nature Switzerland AG 2021
S. Edelkamp et al. (Eds.): KI 2021, LNAI 12873, pp. 349–361, 2021.
https://doi.org/10.1007/978-3-030-87626-5_26

DR can be categorized into five stages [6]: 0 - no DR, 1 - mild DR, 2 - moderate DR, 3 - severe DR, and 4 - proliferative DR. Specifically, the severity of DR is determined by taking the numbers, sizes, and appearances of lesions into account. For instance, Fig. 1 provides an illustration of five DR grades in the Kaggle DR dataset [12]. As can be seen, the characteristics of DR grades are complex in both structure and texture aspects. Therefore, automated diagnosis systems are required to be capable of extracting meaningful visual features from retinal images for precise DR grading.

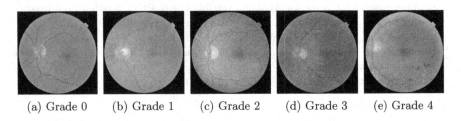

(a) Grade 0   (b) Grade 1   (c) Grade 2   (d) Grade 3   (e) Grade 4

Fig. 1. Illustration of different DR grades.

With the success of deep learning, several CNN-based methods for DR grading of retinal images have been proposed. The paper from 2016 [6] introduces the development and validation of a deep learning algorithm for detection of diabetic retinopathy—with high sensitivity and specificity when compared with manual grading by ophthalmologists for identifying diabetic retinopathy. Jiang et al. [11] also propose an ensemble of conventional deep learning methods to increase the predictive performance of automated DR grading. Lin et al. [14] in other direction introduce a joint model for lesion detection as well as DR identification, in which the DR is inferred from the fusion of original images and lesion information predicted by an attention-based network. Similarly, Zhou et al. in [41] apply a two-step strategy: first produce a multi-lesion mask by using a semantic segmentation component, then the severity of DR is graded by exploiting the lesion mask. Recently, Wu et al. [35] address the problem in a similar way, the classification is performed by employing pixel-level segmentation maps.

While recent works have demonstrated its effectiveness when trained and tested on a single dataset, they often suffer from the domain adaptation problem in practice. In particular, medical images in clinical applications are acquired from devices of different manufactures that vary in many aspects, including imaging modes, image processing algorithms, and hardware components. Therefore, the performance of a trained network from a particular source domain can dramatically decrease when applied to a different target domain. One possible way to overcome this barrier is to collect and label new samples in the target domain, which is necessary for fine-tune trained networks. Nevertheless, this task is laborious and expensive especially with medical images, as the data are limited and labeling requires extreme caution. As a result, it is highly desirable to develop an algorithm that can adapt well in the new domain without additional labeled data for training. Such an approach is known as unsupervised domain adaption.

In this paper, we propose a self-supervised method to reduce domain shift in the fundus images' distribution by learning the invariant feature representations. To this end, feature extraction layers are trained by using both labeled data from the source domain and a self-supervised task on a target domain by defining image reconstruction tasks around retinal vessel positions. Moreover, we also incorporate additional restricted loss functions throughout the training phase to encourage the acquired features to be consistent with the main objective.

At a glance, we make three main contributions. First, we address the domain adaptation problem for DR grading on fundus images using a novel self-supervised approach motivated by medical domain knowledge. Second, we provide a benchmark of current state-of-the-art unsupervised domain adaptation methods on the DR problem. Finally, we show that our approach when using fully training data in the target domain obtains competitive performance just by employing standard network architectures and using image-level labels.

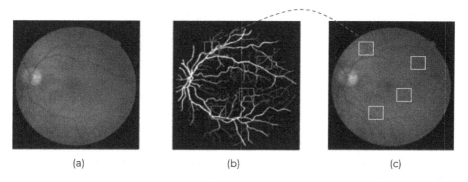

(a)   (b)   (c)

Fig. 2. Illustration of our vessel segmentation reconstruction-based SSL. (a) input image x^t, (b) its vessel segmentation y_v^t, (c) binary masks B^t (inside green rectangles) sampled along edges of y_v^t in (b) (red rectangles). The image regions inside B^t are removed to define $\hat{y}^t$ and asking the encoder-decoder network to reconstruct them given the remaining pixels in $\hat{x}^t$. (Color figure online)

2   Related Work

Over the last decade, research in domain adaption has achieved remarkable results. Tzeng et al. [32] propose a deep domain confusion technique to minimize the maximum mean discrepancy, a non-parametric metric of distribution divergence proposed by Gretton et al. [5], so that the divergence between two distributions is reduced. The algorithm developed by Sun et al. [28] is an extension of their previous work [27], in which CNNs are employed to learn a non-linear transformation for correlation alignment. Recently, Wang et al. [33] have presented a domain adaptation algorithm for screening normal and abnormal retinopathy in optical coherence tomography (OCT) images. The system consists of several complex components guided by the Wasserstein distance [23] to extract invariant representations across different domains.

In other directions, researchers have employed generative adversarial networks (GANs) to learn better invariant features. Tzeng et al. [31] combine discriminative modeling with untied weight sharing and a GAN-based loss to create an adversarial discriminative domain algorithm. Shen et al.'s algorithm [23] extracts domain invariant feature representations by optimizing the feature extractor network, which minimizes the Wasserstein distance trained in an adversarial manner between the source and target domains. In a different way, Long et al. [15] design a conditional domain adversarial network by exploiting two strategies, namely multilinear conditioning, to capture the cross-domain covariance, and entropy conditioning, to ensure the transferability.

Our method in this paper follows the self-supervised learning (SSL) approach [13], which is recently an active research direction due to its effectiveness in learning feature representations. In particular, SSL refers to a representation learning method where a supervised task is defined over unlabelled data to reduce the data labeling cost and leverage the available unlabelled data. Until now, several algorithms based on SSL have been introduced. The method presented by Xu et al. [38] is a generic network with several kinds of learning tasks in SSL that can adapt to various datasets and diverse applications. In medical image analysis, authors in [1] introduce a SSL pretext task based on context restoration, thereby two isolated small regions are selected randomly and swap their positions. A deep network is then trained to recover original orders in input images. Unfortunately, these prior works are mostly designed in the same domain. Recently, Xiao et al. [36] have pioneered to apply the SSL method for domain adaptation problems. Specifically, target-domain-aware features are learned from unlabeled data for image classification through an image rotation-based pretext task trained by a unified encoder for both source and target domains.

Difference w.r.t. Previous Work: Our method follows Xiao et al. [36]; however, we make the following modifications for our setting. First, rather than a rotation task like [36], we study medical domain knowledge to create a novel SSL prediction task, i.e., vessel segmentation reconstruction that has a solid connection to the severity of diabetic retinopathy [6,7]. Second, a two-player procedure is integrated through a discriminate network to ensure mission regions generated in SSL tasks look realistic and consistent with the image context. As a results, our objective function has more constraints on learned features when compared to [36].

3   Method

3.1   Overview

Our proposed method aims at learning invariant features across different domains through encoder layers shared to optimize several relevant tasks. In specific, we define labeled images in the source domain $X_s = \{(x_i^s, y_i^s)\}_{i=0}^{N_s}$ with y_i^s is the corresponding label (DR grades) of image x_i^s and N_s is the total of images. In the target domain, we assume that only a set of unlabeled images denoted by $X_t = \{x_i^t\}_{i=0}^{N_t}$ with N_t samples is available. Our framework, which uses labeled X_s and unlabeled X_t for domain adaptation, consists of four distinct blocks: an encoder network E, a decoder network D, an adversarial discriminator AD, and a main classifier M. These blocks are parameterized by θ_e, θ_d, θ_{ad} and θ_m respectively. For each image $x_i^t \in X_t$, we transform it through the self-supervised learning task based on vessel image reconstruction to define a new set $\hat{X}_t = \{(\hat{x}_i^t, \hat{y}_i^t)\}_{i=1}^{\hat{N}_t}$, which are used to train E and D blocks for predicting removed sub-patch images. To encourage that the reconstructed regions look authentic, the adversarial discriminator AD is integrated through the two-player game learning procedure for distinguishing generated and ground-truth samples. Finally, the block M is built on top of the encoder layer E and acts as the main classification task. We describe below each aforementioned architecture in detail (Fig. 3).

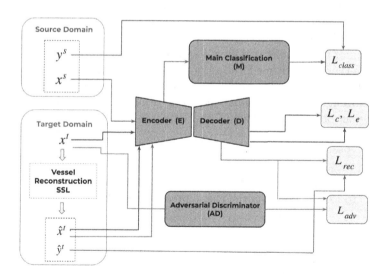

Fig. 3. Overview our proposed unsupervised domain adaption with vessel reconstruction-based self-supervised learning.

3.2   Retinal Vessel Reconstruction-Based SSL

According to medical protocol [6,7], the severity of DR can be predicted by observing the number and size of related lesion appearances and complications. While their positions tend to cluster near vessel positions, we use this attribute to create a new SSL task that forces learnt feature representation to capture such lesions.

Given a sample $x^t \in X_t$, we extract its vessel segmentation image $y_v^t = f(x_i^t)$ with $f(.)$ is a trained deep network (Fig. 2a and 2b). In this work, we use $f(.)$ as a proposed architecture in [29]. Let B^t is a binary mask corresponding to the dropped image region in x^t, with a value of 1 if a pixel was dropped and 0 for input pixels. Unlike related works [1,3], we generate region masks in B^t by randomly sampling sub-patch images along vessel positions in y_v^t as indicated in Fig. 2c. We then define a new pair of samples:

$$\hat{x}^t = (1 - B^t) \odot x^t, \ \hat{y}^t = B^t \odot x^t \tag{1}$$

where $\odot$ is the element-wise product operation.

Reconstruction Loss. We train a context encoder F formed from the encoder E and the decoder D to reconstruct target regions $\hat{y}^t$ given the input $\hat{x}^t$. A normalized $L2$ distance is employed as our reconstruction objective function:

$$L_{rec} = \min_{\theta_e, \theta_d} \mathbb{E}_{x^t \in X^t} ||B^t \odot F(\hat{x}^t) - \hat{y}^t||_2^2 \tag{2}$$

Adversarial Loss. The objective function L_{rec} takes into account the overall construction of the missing region and agreement with its context, but tends to average together the multiple forms in predictions. We thus adapt the adversarial discriminator AD as [21,34] to make the predictions of the context encoder F look real through selecting similar instances from the target distribution. The joint min-max objective function of discriminator AD and generator F is:

$$L_{adv} = \min_{\theta_e, \theta_d} \max_{\theta_{ad}} \mathbb{E}_{x^t \in X^t} [\log(D(x^t) + \log(1 - D(F(\hat{x}^t)))] \tag{3}$$

By jointly optimizing L_{rec} and L_{adv}, we encourage the output of the context encoder F to look realistic on the entire prediction, not just the missing regions as in L_{rec}.

3.3   Relevant Features from SSL

Main Classification Loss. In our framework, the block M takes the feature representation from the encoder E to predict a corresponding label y^t for each image x^t in the target domain. The network M and encoder E are trained with labeled data in the source domain by optimizing the classification problem:

$$L_{class} = \min_{\theta_e, \theta_m} \mathbb{E}_{x^s, y^s \in X^s} [-\log p(y^s|x^s)] \tag{4}$$

where $p(y^s|x^s)$ is a conditional probability distribution of y^s given x^s parameterized by E and M networks.

Constrained Features from SSL. While the SSL task is designed to encourage the encoder E to capture invariant features across different domains and pay attention to vessel positions, there is no guarantee of the compatibility between this SSL task and the main classification target. Inspired from prior works in semi-supervised learning [16,37], we adapt two additional loss constraints on the feature representation generated by the SSL $\hat{x}^t$, the input x^t, and the target label y^t:

$$L_c = \min_{\theta_e,\theta_m} \mathbb{E}_{x^t \in X^t} \mathbb{E}_{\hat{x}^t \in \hat{X}^t} \left[D_{KL}(\hat{p}(y^t|x^t)||p(y^t|\hat{x}^t)) \right] \tag{5}$$

$$L_e = \min_{\theta_e,\theta_m} \mathbb{E}_{x^t \in X^t} \left[-\sum_{y^t} p(y^t|x^t) \log(p(y^t|x^t)) \right] \tag{6}$$

where D_{KL} is the Kullback-Leibler consistency loss [16,37], $\hat{p}(y^t|x^t)$ is a fixed copy of the current $p(y^t|x^t)$ with parameters θ_e, θ_m, it means that $\hat{p}(y^t|x^t)$ is only used for each inference step and the gradient is not propagated through them.

Intuitively, the consistency objective function L_c forces the feature representation in E to be insensitive to data augmentation in defined SSL task while the objective L_e penalizes uncertain predictions, leading to more discriminative representations. However, the equations L_c, L_e require labels y^t in the target domain to optimize, which are assumed to be not available in our unsupervised domain adaption. We address this challenge by integrating pseudo-labels y^t generated by predictions using E and M blocks and updating it progressively after each training step.

Overall Objective Function. In summary, our overall objective function is:

$$L = L_{class} + \lambda_{rec}L_{rec} + \lambda_{adv}L_{adv} + \lambda_c L_c + \lambda_e L_e \tag{7}$$

where $\lambda_{rec}, \lambda_{adv}, \lambda_c, \lambda_e$ are coefficients of corresponding objective functions. Due to the generative adversarial function in L_{adv}, L is the min-max objective problem. We adapt the alternative optimization strategy to first update parameters $\theta_e, \theta_d, \theta_m$, second update θ_{ad} and repeating this process until convergence. In our experiment, we use feature extraction layers from ResNet-50 [8] for both the encoder E, decoder D and adversarial discriminator AD. These layers are shaped in certain architectural constraints as in [22]. For the main classification M, we adapt a simple average pooling followed by a fully connected layer.

4   Experiments and Results

4.1   Evaluation Method

We assess our method, denoted as VesRec-SSL, in two DR grading scenarios: unsupervised domain adaption (UDA) and conventional classification problems. In the first case, all UDA methods are trained using both supervised samples in the source domain and unlabeled samples in the target domain. The performance is then evaluated using the target domain's testing set. In the second case, we train and test in the same domain, i.e., the training set's labeled images are utilized in the training step, and trained networks are measured on the remaining data. For the latter case, our method may be viewed as a pre-training phase [1, 18]; thereby, obtained weights after training VesRec-SSL will be used in the fine-tuning step using partially or completely supervised training samples.

4.2   Dataset and Metrics

We employ two DR-graded retinal image datasets, Kaggle EyePACS [12] and FGADR [42], for training and testing with DR gradings from 0–4 (Fig. 1). We follow the splitting standard in EyePACS with 35126 training images and 53576 testing images. With the FGADR dataset, we can only access 1842 images (SegSet) out of a total of 2842 images at the moment due to data privacy. Because there is no specific train/test on the SegSet, we apply 3-fold cross-validation to compute the final performance. For quantitative metrics, we use classification accuracy and Quadratic Weighted Kappa (Q. W. Kappa) [42].

4.3   Performance of Unsupervised Adaption Methods

In this task, we choose one dataset as the source domain and the other as the target domain. We provide a benchmark of three different methods in literature: Xiao et al.'s Rotation-based SSL [36], Long et al.'s CDAN and CDAN-E [15]. For fairly comparison, we choose ResNet50 as the backbone network for all methods. The quantitative evaluation is shown in Table 1 where "EyePACS $\rightarrow$ FGADR (SegSet)" indicates the source domain is EyePACS the target domain is FGADR restricted on SegSet with 1842 images, and similarly for "FGADR (SegSet) $\rightarrow$ EyePACS". In practice, we found that training baselines directly in our setting is not straightforward due to the imbalance among grading types and the complexity of distinguishing distinct diseases. Therefore, we applied the following training methods:

- First, we only activate the main classification loss using fully supervised samples in the source domain in the initial phase and training until the model converges. Next, auxiliary loss functions will be activated, and the network is continued to train in the latter phase.
- Second, we apply the progressive resizing technique introduced in the fast.ai[1], and the DAWNBench challenge [2] in which the network is trained with smaller images at the beginning, and obtained weights are utilized for training another model with larger images. We use two different resolutions in our setting: 256×256 and 512×512.
- Finally, the optimal learning rate is automatically chosen by the Cyclical Learning method [25] with the SGD optimizer [4], which sets the learning rate to cyclically change between reasonable boundary values.

---

[1] https://course.fast.ai/.

As shown in Table 1, our VesRec-SSL outperforms competitors by a remarkable margin in all settings and metrics. For instance, we achieve 2–3% more for FGADR and 1–3% more for EyePACS, compared to the second competitor CDAN-E. In addition, we can observe that the performance in "FGADR (SegSet) → EyePACS" is lower than that in "EyePACS → FGADR (SegSet)" in most of the cases. We argue this happens due to the number of training instances in the source domain of "FGADR", which is much lower than that of "EyePACS".

Table 1. Performance of unsupervised domain adaption methods.

Method	EyePACS → FGADR (SegSet)		FGADR (SegSet) → EyePACS	
	Acc.	Q.W. Kappa	Acc.	Q.W. Kappa
Rotation-based SSL [36]	0.728	0.672	0.681	0.660
CDAN [15]	0.741	0.685	0.697	0.685
CDAN-E [15]	0.755	0.706	0.702	0.691
VesRec-SSL (Our)	**0.782**	**0.725**	**0.736**	**0.702**

Table 2. Performance of competitor methods on the DR grading prediction. Red, blue, black, and orange represent the top four best results.

Method	EyePACS	
	Acc.	Q.W. Kappa
VGG-16 [24]	0.836	0.820
ResNet-50 [8]	0.846	0.824
Inception v3 [30]	0.840	0.811
DenseNet-121 [10]	0.854	0.835
Lin et al. [14]	0.867	0.857
Zhou et al. [41]	0.895	0.885
Wu et al. [35]	0.886	0.877
VesRec-SSL (ResNet-50) + 0%	0.736	0.702
VesRec-SSL (ResNet-50) + 50%	0.798	0.774
VesRec-SSL (ResNet-50) + 100%	0.864	0.852
VesRec-SSL (DenseNet-121) + 0%	0.744	0.711
VesRec-SSL (DenseNet-121) + 50%	0.815	0.793
VesRec-SSL (DenseNet-121) + 100%	0.871	0.862
VesRec-SSL (ResNet-50 + DenseNet-121) + 100%	**0.891**	**0.879**

4.4 Performance of Baseline Methods on DR Grading Prediction

In this task, we compare our algorithm to the most recent state-of-the-art method reported in [42]. Due to the data privacy on the FGADR dataset, we can only benchmark baselines on the EyePACS dataset. For ablation studies, we also fine-tune our VesRec-SSL with additional 0%, 50%, and 100% labeled data pairs from the target domain. The evaluation results are shown in Table 2. Besides the default backbone with ResNet-50, we consider a variation with DenseNet-121 network for fairly evaluation with two top methods in [35,41]. Moreover, we also utilize feature extraction layers as average pooling of feature maps obtained from ResNet-50 and DenseNet-121 at the last row and train this network with 100% training data.

The results indicate that without labeled data from the target domain, our two settings perform considerably worse than all baselines trained with fully supervised images. However, by progressively increasing the amount of labeled data from 50% to 100%, we can significantly increase performance. For example, the ResNet-50 with 50% data outperforms the 0% case with approximately 6/7% in Acc/Q.W.Kappa. DenseNet-121 follows a similar pattern, improving 7/8% (50% data), and even with 100% training data, our VesRec-SSL can achieve the fourth rank in total. Finally, we observe that utilizing both the ResNet-50 and DenseNet-121 backbones can result in a second-rank overall without modifying the network architecture or adding extra pixel-level segmentation maps for relative lesion characteristics as in [35,41]. In summary, we argue that our method with vessel reconstruction-based SSL has proven effective for domain adaptation under DR grading applications, especially as partial or complete annotations are available.

5 Conclusion

Domain shift is a big obstacle of deep learning-based medical analysis, especially as images are collected by using various devices. In this work, we showed that the unsupervised domain adaption for diabetic retinopathy grading can benefit from our novel self-supervised learning (SSL) based on the medical vessel image reconstruction tasks. Furthermore, when fully integrating annotation data and simply using standard network architectures, our technique achieves comparable performance to cutting-edge benchmarks. In future work, we consider to extend the SSL task to include related lesion appearances such as microaneurysms (MAs), Hard exudates, and Soft exudates [42] to acquire improved invariant feature representation guided by medical domain knowledge. Moreover, making our network's predictions understandable and explainable to clinicians is also a crucial question for further investigation based on our recent medical application projects [17,19,20,26]. We also aim to investigate in the direction of information fusion and explainable AI by incorporating multimodal embeddings with Graph Neural Networks [9,39].

Acknowledgements. This research has been supported by the Ophthalmo-AI project (BMBF, 16SV8639), the Ki-Para-Mi project (BMBF, 01IS19038B), the pAItient project (BMG, 2520DAT0P2), and the Endowed Chair of Applied Artificial Intelligence, Oldenburg University. We would like to thank all student assistants that contributed to the development of the platform, see iml.dfki.de.

References

1. Chen, L., Bentley, P., Mori, K., Misawa, K., Fujiwara, M., Rueckert, D.: Self-supervised learning for medical image analysis using image context restoration. Med. Image Anal. **58**, 101539 (2019)
2. Coleman, C., et al.: DAWNBench: an end-to-end deep learning benchmark and competition. Training **100**(101), 102 (2017)
3. Doersch, C., Gupta, A., Efros, A.A.: Unsupervised visual representation learning by context prediction. In: Proceedings of the IEEE International Conference on Computer Vision, pp. 1422–1430 (2015)
4. Goodfellow, I., Bengio, Y., Courville, A.: Deep Learning. MIT Press, Cambridge (2016)
5. Gretton, A., Borgwardt, K.M., Rasch, M.J., Schölkopf, B., Smola, A.: A kernel two-sample test. J. Mach. Learn. Res. **13**(1), 723–773 (2012)
6. Gulshan, V., et al.: Development and validation of a deep learning algorithm for detection of diabetic retinopathy in retinal fundus photographs. JAMA **316**(22), 2402–2410 (2016)
7. Haneda, S., Yamashita, H.: International clinical diabetic retinopathy disease severity scale. Nihon Rinsho. Jpn. J. Clin. Med. **68**, 228–235 (2010)
8. He, K., Zhang, X., Ren, S., Sun, J.: Deep residual learning for image recognition. In: Proceedings of the IEEE Conference on Computer Vision and Pattern Recognition, pp. 770–778 (2016)
9. Holzinger, A., Malle, B., Saranti, A., Pfeifer, B.: Towards multi-modal causability with graph neural networks enabling information fusion for explainable AI. Inf. Fusion **71**, 28–37 (2021)
10. Huang, G., Liu, Z., Van Der Maaten, L., Weinberger, K.Q.: Densely connected convolutional networks. In: Proceedings of the IEEE Conference on Computer Vision and Pattern Recognition, pp. 4700–4708 (2017)
11. Jiang, H., Yang, K., Gao, M., Zhang, D., Ma, H., Qian, W.: An interpretable ensemble deep learning model for diabetic retinopathy disease classification. In: 2019 41st Annual International Conference of the IEEE Engineering in Medicine and Biology Society (EMBC), pp. 2045–2048. IEEE (2019)
12. Kaggle: Diabetic retinopathy detection (2015). https://www.kaggle.com/c/diabetic-retinopathy-detection/data
13. Kolesnikov, A., Zhai, X., Beyer, L.: Revisiting self-supervised visual representation learning. In: Proceedings of the IEEE/CVF Conference on Computer Vision and Pattern Recognition, pp. 1920–1929 (2019)
14. Lin, Z., et al.: A framework for identifying diabetic retinopathy based on anti-noise detection and attention-based fusion. In: Frangi, A.F., Schnabel, J.A., Davatzikos, C., Alberola-López, C., Fichtinger, G. (eds.) MICCAI 2018. LNCS, vol. 11071, pp. 74–82. Springer, Cham (2018). https://doi.org/10.1007/978-3-030-00934-2_9
15. Long, M., Cao, Z., Wang, J., Jordan, M.I.: Conditional adversarial domain adaptation. In: Advances in Neural Information Processing Systems, pp. 1640–1650 (2018)
16. Miyato, T., Maeda, S.I., Koyama, M., Ishii, S.: Virtual adversarial training: a regularization method for supervised and semi-supervised learning. IEEE Trans. Pattern Anal. Mach. Intell. **41**(8), 1979–1993 (2018)
17. Nguyen, D.M., Nguyen, D.M., Vu, H., Nguyen, B.T., Nunnari, F., Sonntag, D.: An attention mechanism using multiple knowledge sources for COVID-19 detection from CT images. In: The Thirty-Fifth AAAI Conference on Artificial Intelligence (AAAI-2021), Workshop: Trustworthy AI for Healthcare (2021)

18. Nguyen, D.M., et al.: TATL: task agnostic transfer learning for skin attributes detection. arXiv preprint arXiv:2104.01641 (2021)
19. Nguyen, D.M.H., Ezema, A., Nunnari, F., Sonntag, D.: A visually explainable learning system for skin lesion detection using multiscale input with attention U-Net. In: Schmid, U., Klügl, F., Wolter, D. (eds.) KI 2020. LNCS (LNAI), vol. 12325, pp. 313–319. Springer, Cham (2020). https://doi.org/10.1007/978-3-030-58285-2_28
20. Nunnari, F., Sonntag, D.: A software toolbox for deploying deep learning decision support systems with XAI capabilities. In: Companion of the 2021 ACM SIGCHI Symposium on Engineering Interactive Computing Systems, pp. 44–49 (2021)
21. Pathak, D., Krahenbuhl, P., Donahue, J., Darrell, T., Efros, A.A.: Context encoders: feature learning by inpainting. In: Proceedings of the IEEE conference on computer vision and pattern recognition, pp. 2536–2544 (2016)
22. Radford, A., Metz, L., Chintala, S.: Unsupervised representation learning with deep convolutional generative adversarial networks. arXiv preprint arXiv:1511.06434 (2015)
23. Shen, J., Qu, Y., Zhang, W., Yu, Y.: Wasserstein distance guided representation learning for domain adaptation. In: Proceedings of the AAAI Conference on Artificial Intelligence, vol. 32 (2018)
24. Simonyan, K., Zisserman, A.: Very deep convolutional networks for large-scale image recognition. arXiv preprint arXiv:1409.1556 (2014)
25. Smith, L.N.: Cyclical learning rates for training neural networks. In: 2017 IEEE Winter Conference on Applications of Computer Vision (WACV), pp. 464–472. IEEE (2017)
26. Sonntag, D., Nunnari, F., Profitlich, H.J.: The skincare project, an interactive deep learning system for differential diagnosis of malignant skin lesions. Technical report. arXiv preprint arXiv:2005.09448 (2020)
27. Sun, B., Feng, J., Saenko, K.: Return of frustratingly easy domain adaptation. In: Proceedings of the AAAI Conference on Artificial Intelligence, vol. 30 (2016)
28. Sun, B., Saenko, K.: Deep CORAL: correlation alignment for deep domain adaptation. In: Hua, G., Jégou, H. (eds.) ECCV 2016. LNCS, vol. 9915, pp. 443–450. Springer, Cham (2016). https://doi.org/10.1007/978-3-319-49409-8_35
29. Sun, X., Cao, X., Yang, Y., Wang, L., Xu, Y.: Robust retinal vessel segmentation from a data augmentation perspective. arXiv preprint arXiv:2007.15883 (2020)
30. Szegedy, C., Vanhoucke, V., Ioffe, S., Shlens, J., Wojna, Z.: Rethinking the inception architecture for computer vision. In: Proceedings of the IEEE Conference on Computer Vision and Pattern Recognition, pp. 2818–2826 (2016)
31. Tzeng, E., Hoffman, J., Saenko, K., Darrell, T.: Adversarial discriminative domain adaptation. In: Proceedings of the IEEE Conference on Computer Vision and Pattern Recognition, pp. 7167–7176 (2017)
32. Tzeng, E., Hoffman, J., Zhang, N., Saenko, K., Darrell, T.: Deep domain confusion: maximizing for domain invariance. arXiv preprint arXiv:1412.3474 (2014)
33. Wang, J., Chen, Y., Li, W., Kong, W., He, Y., Jiang, C., Shi, G.: Domain adaptation model for retinopathy detection from cross-domain OCT images. In: Medical Imaging with Deep Learning, pp. 795–810. PMLR (2020)
34. Wang, Y., Chen, Y.C., Zhang, X., Sun, J., Jia, J.: Attentive normalization for conditional image generation. In: Proceedings of the IEEE/CVF Conference on Computer Vision and Pattern Recognition, pp. 5094–5103 (2020)
35. Wu, Y.H., et al.: JCS: an explainable COVID-19 diagnosis system by joint classification and segmentation. IEEE Trans. Image Process. **30**, 3113–3126 (2021)

36. Xiao, L., et al.: Self-supervised domain adaptation with consistency training. In: 2020 25th International Conference on Pattern Recognition (ICPR), pp. 6874–6880. IEEE (2021)
37. Xie, Q., Dai, Z., Hovy, E., Luong, T., Le, Q.: Unsupervised data augmentation for consistency training. In: Larochelle, H., Ranzato, M., Hadsell, R., Balcan, M.F., Lin, H. (eds.) Advances in Neural Information Processing Systems, vol. 33, pp. 6256–6268. Curran Associates, Inc. (2020)
38. Xu, J., Xiao, L., López, A.M.: Self-supervised domain adaptation for computer vision tasks. IEEE Access 7, 156694–156706 (2019)
39. Yuan, H., Yu, H., Gui, S., Ji, S.: Explainability in graph neural networks: a taxonomic survey. arXiv preprint arXiv:2012.15445 (2020)
40. Yun, W.L., Acharya, U.R., Venkatesh, Y.V., Chee, C., Min, L.C., Ng, E.Y.K.: Identification of different stages of diabetic retinopathy using retinal optical images. Inf. Sci. 178(1), 106–121 (2008)
41. Zhou, Y., et al.: Collaborative learning of semi-supervised segmentation and classification for medical images. In: Proceedings of the IEEE/CVF Conference on Computer Vision and Pattern Recognition, pp. 2079–2088 (2019)
42. Zhou, Y., Wang, B., Huang, L., Cui, S., Shao, L.: A benchmark for studying diabetic retinopathy: segmentation, grading, and transferability. IEEE Trans. Med. Imaging 40, 818–828 (2020)

BehavE: Behaviour Understanding Through Automated Generation of Situation Models

Teodor Stoev$^{(\boxtimes)}$ and Kristina Yordanova$^{(\boxtimes)}$

Institute of Visual and Analytic Computing, University of Rostock,
Albert-Einstein-Str. 22, 18059 Rostock, Germany
{teodor.stoev,kristina.yordanova}@uni-rostock.de

Abstract. Automated systems for assisting persons to achieve their everyday tasks are gaining popularity, both in the application domains for supporting healthy persons, as well as for assisting people with impairments. The development of such assistive systems is a challenging task associated with a lot of time and effort and often requires the involvement of domain experts. To address this problem, different works have investigated the automated knowledge extraction and model generation for behaviour interpretation and assistance. Existing works, however, usually concentrate on one source of data for the task of automated knowledge generation, which could potentially result in simpler models that are unable to adequately support the person. To address this problem, in this work we present the BehavE methodology, which proposes the extraction of knowledge from different types of sources and its consolidation into a unified semantic model that is used for behaviour interpretation and generation of assistance strategies.

Keywords: Model generation · Automated knowledge extraction · Situation models · Assistive systems · Activity recognition · Behaviour analysis

1 Introduction

The population on Earth is ageing at a rapid pace [1] and finding ways to automatically support the life of elderly people is becoming a priority in many research areas. One way to provide automated solutions in the healthcare domain is to implement personalized *situation-aware (SA)* assistive systems which are able to reason about the person's behaviour and health condition and can provide support where needed in order to prolong an active and healthy life. In such context the assistive system acts as a mediator between the person and the environment by observing the person with the help of sensors, predicting their goals,

This work is part of the BehavE project, funded by the German Research Foundation, grant number YO 226/3-1.

and eventually by providing them with missing information so that a given goal can be completed [8]. Assistive systems comprise two main components (shown in Fig. 1). The first one is the intention recognition component which detects the situation and the behaviour of a person using sensors and the second one is the strategy synthesis component which infers the causes of this behaviour and selects an appropriate intervention, if needed [10]. Despite their different roles, both of them rely on an underlying *situation model (SM)* to operate. SMs are a structured knowledge representation and they provide context information about the situation such as environmental conditions, user profile, activities, goals, possible errors in behaviour, nearby objects and locations of interest for the user, intervention strategies, etc. In this work *semantic models* follow the definition given by Farrell et al. [5] who states that *"A semantic model is a set of machine-interpretable representations used to model an area of knowledge or some part of the world"*. As we want to reason about the behaviour of a person, including goals he or she is pursuing, errors in behaviour and the potential causes of these errors, we model the collected semantic knowledge in terms of Computational Causal Behaviour Models (CCBM), which allow reasoning about the above in a probabilistic manner [9].

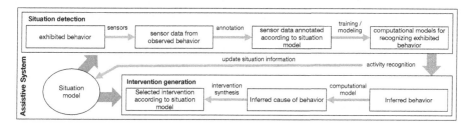

Fig. 1. The general architecture of a situation-aware assistive system (adopted from Yordanova et al. [22]).

The paper is structured as follows. In Sect. 2 we discuss the state of the art on semantic models learning, in Sect. 3 we present our approach to learning situation models from heterogeneous data sources, and in Sect. 4 we discuss the planned experiments and the involved datasets. We conclude the work in Sect. 5 with discussion of the future work.

2   Related Work

There are two ways to create an SM - applying specification-based approaches, or through learning-based methods [17]. The former rely on manually organized expert knowledge and logic rules which make the reasoning about the situation possible. The latter are based on combinations of machine learning techniques applied on sensor and text data [18,19]. The main drawbacks of the manual

SM development are the required time (from several months to several years) and the expert knowledge needed. On the other hand, automated learning-based SMs can be created faster, but they often miss relevant information since the different sources of data used provide different kind of knowledge. Currently, the methods for automatic generation of SMs for behaviour analysis address data heterogeneity (the usage of several information sources) only to a limited extent. For instance, several studies present methods for the generation of planning models from instructional texts [6,11,16,26]. There are also works such as the one of Benotti et al. [2] which propose the usage of unlabelled instructions and agent reactions gathered in a game-like virtual environment for the purpose of plan generation. Yordanova et al. showed that sensor data can be combined with textual descriptions of task execution sequences and general purpose taxonomies in order to create models of human behaviour [19,20]. Apart from textual instructions, a lot of researchers propose methods to predict behaviour by using domain knowledge representation. The main idea is to encode the domain knowledge as an ontology and then use a query language to make implications regarding the observed through sensors behaviour [3,7,13,18,25]. There are also works such as [14] which address the problem of ontology evolution, as well as model adaptation to a person's profile which is relevant for our objective as we also aim to perform situation-specific behaviour analysis and assistance over short to long term time periods. To the best of our knowledge, there are no works which propose a general methodology of creating SMs in an automated way from several data sources and how such models can be adopted to the preferences and the circumstances of a certain person which might change over time.

3   Automatic Generation of Situation Models

3.1   Knowledge Extraction and Consolidation

Existing works have shown that it is possible to automatically generate computational models of human behaviour from textual instructions [19,20]. These models, however, are very general and lack certain steps because these steps are also missing from the source data. To address this problem, we propose combining knowledge from different sources: these are sensor data, textual data, and structured knowledge bases. The combination of the knowledge from several sources will potentially improve the model quality and partially cope with the lack of common sense knowledge in the generated models. Figure 2 illustrates the process of extracting knowledge from heterogeneous sources.

Extracting Knowledge from Textual Data. We consider both instructional and rich texts, such as texts from informal forums or scientific literature. Instructional texts are analysed in order to extract the actions, objects, locations and further context relevant for the given domain. We follow the approach proposed in [20]: we first perform part of speech (POS) tagging and dependencies parsing (DP) in order to identify relevant actions, objects, any properties to the objects,

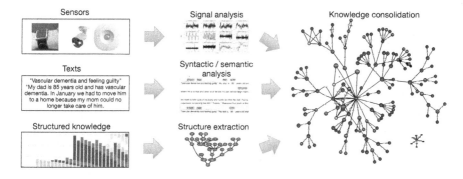

Fig. 2. The process of knowledge extraction and consolidation into a situation model.

and locations where the actions could be executed. We then perform time series analysis on the identified actions to identify candidate causal relations. The collected knowledge is then consolidated into a single situation model where the extracted elements are the nodes and the relations between them are the relations extracted from the DP and the causal relations. As textual instructions consist of sentences with simple structure, we also look into rich texts to extend the domain knowledge. We perform POS-tagging, DP, named entity recognition (NER) and relation extraction (RE) in order to identify elements that could be relevant for our problem domain. The extracted elements are matched with those in the SM with the help of similarity identification methods such as based on language taxonomy e.g. using WordNet [12] or language models such as Bidirectional Encoder Representations from Transformers (BERT) [4]. The same is performed for the identified relations, in that manner extending the initial SM.

Extracting Knowledge from Sensor and Visual Data. Sensor data usually captures the behaviour of a person over a period of time. This type of data contains information both about certain classes of activities and the behaviour change over time. In our work we are interested in different types of sensor data such as accelerometer data, data from environmental sensors, and data from sensors detecting the manipulation of objects (e.g. RFID, accelerometer). For data that have been annotated, we match the annotated elements to those in the SM generated from textual sources with the help of approaches for detecting similarities as discussed above. Any new elements are added to the model. We perform time series analysis to identify any correlations that could indicate relations between different elements and we add them to the SM. For data that are not annotated, we use transfer learning in order to extract relevant knowledge. For example, we use pretrained object recognition models on visual data to identify objects of interest. These objects are then mapped to the ones already identified in our SM and to the corresponding activities.

Extracting Knowledge from Structured Knowledge Bases. One problem that persists in approaches for automated generation of semantic models is the lack of common sense knowledge that we would encode in a manually developed model [20]. To address this problem, some works have proposed the usage of ontologies or taxonomies in order to extend or disambiguate the extracted knowledge [18,20]. We adopt this idea by integrating knowledge both from general language taxonomies such as WordNet and domain specific knowledge encoded in ontologies (e.g. ontologies for supporting patients with dementia [24]). Concepts from the ontology are mapped to the elements in the SM in the same manner as already described through similarity detection approaches. Any new relations identified from the knowledge bases are added to the SM.

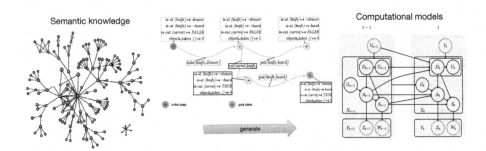

Fig. 3. Generation of computational model for behaviour analysis from the consolidated knowledge.

3.2   Generation of Computational Causal Behaviour Models

The knowledge from the SM is encoded in the form of Computational Causal Behaviour Models that allow reasoning about one's behaviour given new observations. Figure 3 illustrates this process. First, the semantic knowledge encoded in the SM is represented as precondition-effect rules in a PDDL-like[1] notation. Each rule represents an action from a given domain and the corresponding conditions that have to hold in order for the action to be executable, as well as the way it changes the world when executed (see Fig. 4). These rules, together with a definition of the initial and goal states are used to generate a state space graph that represents all states and actions that lead from the initial to the goal states. Dynamic Bayesian Networks are then used to reason about the person's behaviour in the presence of new observations [9]. Finally, to adapt the generated model to the specific behaviour of a person or to long-term changes in behaviour, new sensor data are used. The model is automatically optimised by adding information in the same manner as described in the section above while obsolete behaviour is removed from the model when no longer observed.

---

[1] Planning Domain Definition Language.

4   Planned Experiments

In order to evaluate our approach we plan to build SMs for the domain of patients with dementia. In terms of sensor data, we plan to use the Kitchen Task Assessment (KTA) dataset [23]. The KTA problem measures to what extent a person with a cognitive impairment is able to perform kitchen tasks without additional assistance. The dataset contains normal and simulated erroneous runs of cooking tasks. The errors in behaviour follow the definitions described in [15]. The dataset consists of sensor data (object sensors and a full body motion capture suite), as well as video data. It also contains semantic annotations following the labelling approach in [21]. Finally, it contains textual instructions in the form of scripts describing the experiments' execution. Another candidate dataset for our experiments is the youcook2 dataset [27]. It contains 2000 instructional cooking videos and their corresponding natural language texts. These texts can be used for the creation of a semantic model for cooking tasks and the knowledge from the resulted model can be consolidated with the knowledge from the KTA dataset described above. Furthermore, we plan to use data from informal texts to enrich our models. Currently we are experimenting with the automated extraction of ontologies from internet forums, where caregivers describe common problems with dementia patients. For that purpose we have created a dataset consisting of 775 questions and 5567 answers. Finally, we will use both the general purpose language taxonomy WordNet, as well as domain specific ontologies describing the behaviour of patients with dementia [24] to enrich our models.

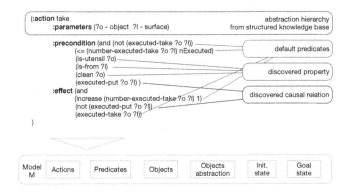

Fig. 4. Precondition-effect rule generated from the SM and the elements of the CCBM model: description of the actions in terms of preconditions and effects, a list of the predicates used in the action definition, a list of objects, object hierarchy for abstracting the rules, and initial and goal states, based on which the state space graph is expanded.

5   Conclusion and Future Work

In this work we presented the BehavE methodology that aims to automatically generate models for behaviour analysis and assistance from heterogeneous data sources. In the future we plan to conduct experiments from the domain of patients with dementia and their caregivers in order to evaluate our approach in a challenging and complex real world domain.

References

1. Beard, J.R., et al.: The world report on ageing and health: a policy framework for healthy ageing. Lancet **387**(10033), 2145–2154 (2016)
2. Benotti, L., Lau, T., Villalba, M.: Interpreting natural language instructions using language, vision, and behavior. ACM Trans. Interact. Intell. Syst. (TiiS) **4**(3), 1–22 (2014)
3. Culmone, R., Giuliodori, P., Quadrini, M.: Human activity recognition using a semantic ontology-based framework. Int. J. Adv. Intell. Syst. **8**(2), 159–168 (2015)
4. Devlin, J., Chang, M.W., Lee, K., Toutanova, K.: BERT: pre-training of deep bidirectional transformers for language understanding. arXiv preprint arXiv:1810.04805 (2018)
5. Farrell, J., Lausen, H.: Semantic annotations for WSDL and XML schema. IEEE Internet Comput. **11**(6), 60–67 (2007). W3C recommendation 28
6. Goldwasser, D., Roth, D.: Learning from natural instructions. Mach. Learn. **94**(2), 205–232 (2014)
7. Hooda, D., Rani, R.: Ontology driven human activity recognition in heterogeneous sensor measurements. J. Ambient. Intell. Humaniz. Comput. **11**(12), 5947–5960 (2020). https://doi.org/10.1007/s12652-020-01835-0
8. Kirste, T.: A reference model for situation-aware assistance. In: Proceedings of Mensch & Computer, Bad Honneff, Germany (2001)
9. Krüger, F., Nyolt, M., Yordanova, K., Hein, A., Kirste, T.: Computational state space models for activity and intention recognition. A feasibility study. PLoS ONE **9**(11), e109381 (2014). https://doi.org/10.1371/journal.pone.0109381
10. Krüger, F., Yordanova, K., Burghardt, C., Kirste, T.: Towards creating assistive software by employing human behavior models. J. Ambient Intell. Smart Environ. **4**(3), 209–226 (2012)
11. Lindsay, A., Read, J., Ferreira, J., Hayton, T., Porteous, J., Gregory, P.: Framer: planning models from natural language action descriptions. In: 27th International Conference on Automated Planning and Scheduling (2017)
12. Miller, G.A.: WordNet: a lexical database for English. Commun. ACM **38**(11), 39–41 (1995)
13. Okeyo, G., Chen, L., Wang, H., Sterritt, R.: Ontology-based learning framework for activity assistance in an adaptive smart home. In: Chen, L., Nugent, C., Biswas, J., Hoey, J. (eds.) Activity Recognition in Pervasive Intelligent Environments. Atlantis Ambient and Pervasive Intelligence, vol. 4, pp. 237–263. Springer, Heidelberg (2011). https://doi.org/10.2991/978-94-91216-05-3_11
14. Safyan, M., Qayyum, Z.U., Sarwar, S., Iqbal, M., Castro, R.G., Al-Dulaimi, A.: Ontology evolution for personalised and adaptive activity recognition. IET Wirel. Sensor Syst. **9**(4), 193–200 (2019)
15. Serna, A., Pigot, H., Rialle, V.: Modeling the progression of Alzheimer's disease for cognitive assistance in smart homes. User Model. User-Adap. Inter. **17**(4), 415–438 (2007)
16. Sil, A., Yates, A.: Extracting strips representations of actions and events. In: Proceedings of the International Conference Recent Advances in Natural Language Processing, vol. 2011, pp. 1–8 (2011)

17. Ye, J., Dobson, S., McKeever, S.: Situation identification techniques in pervasive computing: a review. Pervasive Mob. Comput. **8**(1), 36–66 (2012)
18. Ye, J., Stevenson, G., Dobson, S.: USMART: an unsupervised semantic mining activity recognition technique. ACM Trans. Interact. Intell. Syst. **4**(4), 1–27 (2014). https://doi.org/10.1145/2662870
19. Yordanova, K.: From textual instructions to sensor-based recognition of user behaviour. In: Companion Publication of the 21st International Conference on Intelligent User Interfaces, pp. 67–73 (2016)
20. Yordanova, K.: Extracting planning operators from instructional texts for behaviour interpretation. In: Trollmann, F., Turhan, A.-Y. (eds.) KI 2018. LNCS (LNAI), vol. 11117, pp. 215–228. Springer, Cham (2018). https://doi.org/10.1007/978-3-030-00111-7_19
21. Yordanova, K.: Towards automated generation of semantic annotation for activity recognition problems. In: 2020 IEEE International Conference on Pervasive Computing and Communications Workshops (PerCom Workshops), pp. 1–6 (2020). https://doi.org/10.1109/PerComWorkshops48775.2020.9156147
22. Yordanova, K., Bader, S., Heine, C., Teipel, S., Kirste, T.: Towards a situation model for assessing challenging behaviour of people with dementia. In: Proceedings of the 3rd International Workshop on Sensor-Based Activity Recognition and Interaction, pp. 1–6 (2016)
23. Yordanova, K., Hein, A., Kirste, T.: Kitchen task assessment dataset for measuring errors due to cognitive impairments. In: 2020 IEEE International Conference on Pervasive Computing and Communications Workshops (PerCom Workshops), pp. 1–6. IEEE (2020)
24. Yordanova, K.Y.: Ontologies to support patients with dementia. In: Wolkenhauer, O. (ed.) Systems Medicine, pp. 396–405. Academic Press, Oxford (2021). https://doi.org/10.1016/B978-0-12-801238-3.11473-4. http://www.sciencedirect.com/science/article/pii/B9780128012383114734
25. Zhang, S., McCullagh, P., Nugent, C., Zheng, H.: An ontology-based context-aware approach for behaviour analysis. In: Chen, L., Nugent, C., Biswas, J., Hoey, J. (eds.) Activity Recognition in Pervasive Intelligent Environments. Atlantis Ambient and Pervasive Intelligence, vol. 4, pp. 127–148. Springer, Heidelberg (2011). https://doi.org/10.2991/978-94-91216-05-3_6
26. Zhang, Z., Webster, P., Uren, V., Varga, A., Fabio, C.: Automatically extracting procedural knowledge from instructional texts using natural language processing. In: 8th International Conference on Language Resources and Evaluation, pp. 520–527 (2012)
27. Zhou, L., Xu, C., Corso, J.J.: Towards automatic learning of procedures from web instructional videos. In: Thirty-Second AAAI Conference on Artificial Intelligence (2018)

Correction to: Explanation as a Process: User-Centric Construction of Multi-level and Multi-modal Explanations

Bettina Finzel, David E. Tafler, Stephan Scheele, and Ute Schmid

Correction to:
Chapter "Explanation as a Process: User-Centric Construction of Multi-level and Multi-modal Explanations" in: S. Edelkamp et al. (Eds.): _KI 2021: Advances in Artificial Intelligence_, LNAI 12873, https://doi.org/10.1007/978-3-030-87626-5_7

The original version of this chapter was inadvertently published with a misspelling in the explanatory dialogue of Fig. 5. It has been updated as follows:

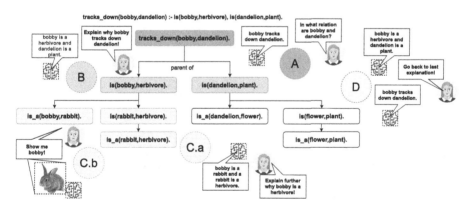

Fig. 5. An explanatory tree for `tracks_down(bobby,dandelion)`, that can be queried by the user to get a _local_ explanation why Bobby tracks down dandelion (steps A and B). A dialogue is realized by different _drill-down_ questions, either to get more detailed verbal explanations or visual explanations (steps C.a and C.b)). Furthermore, the user can return to the last explanation (step D).

The updated version of this chapter can be found at
https://doi.org/10.1007/978-3-030-87626-5_7

© Springer Nature Switzerland AG 2021
S. Edelkamp et al. (Eds.): KI 2021, LNAI 12873, p. C1, 2021.
https://doi.org/10.1007/978-3-030-87626-5_28

Author Index

Printed in the United States
by Baker & Taylor Publisher Services